MW00992842

INTO DUST
AND FIRE

INTO DUST
AND FIRE

FIVE YOUNG AMERICANS WHO WENT FIRST
TO FIGHT THE NAZI ARMY

Rachel S. Cox

NAL
CALIBER

NAL CALIBER
Published by New American Library, a division of
Penguin Group (USA) Inc., 375 Hudson Street,
New York, New York 10014, USA
Penguin Group (Canada), 90 Eglinton Avenue East, Suite 700, Toronto,
Ontario M4P 2Y3, Canada (a division of Pearson Penguin Canada Inc.)
Penguin Books Ltd., 80 Strand, London WC2R 0RL, England
Penguin Ireland, 25 St. Stephen's Green, Dublin 2,
Ireland (a division of Penguin Books Ltd.)
Penguin Group (Australia), 250 Camberwell Road, Camberwell, Victoria 3124,
Australia (a division of Pearson Australia Group Pty. Ltd.)
Penguin Books India Pvt. Ltd., 11 Community Centre, Panchsheel Park,
New Delhi - 110 017, India
Penguin Group (NZ), 67 Apollo Drive, Rosedale, Auckland 0632,
New Zealand (a division of Pearson New Zealand Ltd.)
Penguin Books (South Africa) (Pty.) Ltd., 24 Sturdee Avenue,
Rosebank, Johannesburg 2196, South Africa

Penguin Books Ltd., Registered Offices:
80 Strand, London WC2R 0RL, England

First published by NAL Caliber, an imprint of New American Library,
a division of Penguin Group (USA) Inc.

ISBN 978-0-451-23475-9

Set in Berkeley Oldstyle Std
Designed by Ginger Legato

Printed in the United States of America

PUBLISHER'S NOTE
While the author has made every effort to provide accurate telephone numbers and Internet addresses at
the time of publication, neither the publisher nor the author assumes any responsibility for errors, or for
changes that occur after publication. Further, publisher does not have any control over and does not
assume any responsibility for author or third-party Web sites or their content.

ALWAYS LEARNING   PEARSON

Book Club Edition

For my father, Max Cox, who planted the writing seed, and for my husband, Glenn Berger, the rainmaker

"You may be certain that we shall prove ourselves ready to suffer and sacrifice to the utmost for the Cause, and that we glory in being its champions. The rest we leave with confidence to you and to your people, being sure that ways and means will be found which future generations on both sides of the Atlantic will approve and admire."

—Winston Churchill, letter to Franklin Roosevelt upon his election
to a third term as president, November 1940

"If you have never yourself had the experience of feeling that you are yoked to the great steam engine of history, then allow me to inform you that the conviction is a very intoxicating one."

—Christopher Hitchens, *Hitch-22*

CONTENTS

Author's Note   xiii

Prologue   1

PART 1: Celebrity Soldiers

1. Decision   7

2. Convoy   30

3. Riflemen   54

4. Officers   87

PART 2: Around the Cape of Good Hope

5. Interlude *Doña Aurora*   119

6. Lost in the Honeycomb   139

7. Interlude *Duchess of Atholl*   157

PART 3: Desert Rats

8. Into the Blue   171

9. El Alamein   196

10. Recovery   219

11. Spring   240

12. Home   275

Acknowledgments   301

Sources   307

Notes   313

Index   329

MAPS

1. Journey to Battle, July 10, 1941—April 28, 1943   6

2. Battle of El Alamein, October 23—30, 1942   198

3. Battle of Mareth, March 20—27, 1943   242

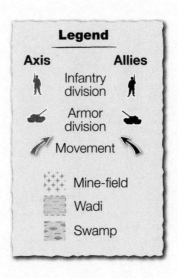

AUTHOR'S NOTE

When I was growing up in New York City in the 1950s and 1960s, strangers occasionally approached my father on the subway and asked him flattering questions, such as "Are you Paul Newman?" He had the arresting blue eyes and strong, regular features of the actor, but was taller, rangier. Thus, "You look like the Marlboro Man. Have you ever been in commercials?" His were the iconic sort of good looks that used to be called "all-American." His four brothers and two sisters had them too.

But their all-American aura extended beyond looks. They belonged to a distinguished American family of a kind the world has now acknowledged bore little resemblance in reality to America at large, in the same way that movie stars were not representative of actual humans. Or perhaps they were, if we remember that Michael Douglas would bear a quite different surname if his father, another fair-haired boy with strong bone structure, hadn't changed his own name from Issur Danielovitch to Kirk Douglas.

Illusion or no, within my father's family circle when I was young, we breathed the air of American righteousness, and America was us. No one pretended the American government was always right. Indeed, as the Vietnam War unfurled its bloody battle flags across our television screens, blind allegiance became more and more suspect. But we believed that the foundations were sound. The government went astray when it lost track of its principles. And these principles were exemplified in our family stories.

Consider my great-great-great-great-grandfather Roger Sherman, also known as "the great compromiser," who saved the Constitutional Convention by proposing a bicameral legislature with one house apportioned according to state populations, the other fixed in size, and the only American to sign all four of the country's founding documents. Or his son-in-law Jeremiah Evarts, who led the Christian crusade to stop Indian resettlement and fought against the terrible Indian Removal Act of 1830 until the day he died. His son, the lawyer William M. Evarts, successfully defended President Andrew Johnson when he was impeached, represented Lincoln's Republican Party as counsel for Rutherford B. Hayes in the disputed election of 1876, and went on to become secretary of state and then senator of New York.

My favorite was a story of principled heroism and the Civil War. At his Princeton commencement in 1863, my great-grandfather Rowland Cox, a Pennsylvania Quaker, listened to the college president as he contended that all loyal sons of Princeton would go forth and fight for the noble Confederate cause. Afterward, Great-grandfather Cox, as my grandmother told it, went back to his room, packed his bags, and that very night, before leaving, pushed a note under the college president's door. "To hell with you," it said, "I'm off to join the Union Army."

Their accomplishments seemed to promise, even require, great things from the rest of us, though admittedly from boys more than girls, and to a surprising degree experience bore out expectation. Of my father's four brothers, the oldest, Archibald, would gain national, even global renown as the Watergate special prosecutor, an icon of moral rectitude, of old-time Yankee honesty and independence. The youngest, Rowland, an Episcopal minister, became headmaster of the high-minded Massachusetts prep school Groton when it was still considered more elite than elitist.

But the aura of American exceptionalism always shone most forcefully from the brother who, by the fifties, when I was born, was already gone for good and so could only and evermore be what we supposed him to be. A portrait in pastels—he looked confoundingly like my father—hung over my grandmother's desk at her comfortable Federal-era house in Windsor, Vermont. His prep school medals—*ob egregiam diligentiam atque virtutem*: "for outstanding diligence and virtue" . . . Best Boy!—decorated a dining room side table. And near Grandma's bed hung a photograph, a head shot in rich, taupey hues, that seemed to embody the very essence of heroism. There, Uncle Robbie gazes forward eternally in semi-profile, a handsome blond in the flat tin helmet of a British Tommy, the leather chin strap accentuating his firm, sharp jawline, the curve of the brim suggesting, it occurs to me now, a halo. Matted below the photo is a small rectangle of type, which I have learned contains the words of his cenotaph, the bronze memorial plaque that still hangs near the altar of the family church in Windsor. They were written by my grandmother's brother Max Perkins, fabled editor of Hemingway and Fitzgerald and Wolfe. Awash in grief, he nevertheless crafted a brief, elegant tribute that evokes the sacrifice of every soldier who volunteers himself to war.

ROBERT HILL COX II

Lieutenant in the King's Royal Rifle Corps, killed in the Battle of Tunisia April 19, 1943, who, at the age of twenty-two, convinced that his own country should share in the great war for human freedom, joined the British Army in July 1941 and so gave to that cause all of America he could command.

With a few additions, all that I knew of the story was contained in that paragraph. While my missing uncle cast a strong and mysterious after-glow, my grandmother spoke of him rarely. I picked up a few things. She adored him. He was a paragon. Foreseeing the Nazi menace, he had been among the first Americans to fight. There had been a group of them; one, a Dartmouth man from Connecticut named Chuck Bolté, still dropped in from time to time to see my grandmother, decked out for her benefit in a handsome green British officer's tunic and cap. As a child, I was fascinated by the knowledge that under his crisply creased trousers Lieutenant Bolté had only one real leg. But just as it clearly would have been rude to ask about the gory details, I knew that in that traditional Yankee household nothing more would be said.

It would take decades, my father's death, and growing confidence in myself as a journalist to get back to that story. What exactly *was* it? I had long since recognized my relatives' actual imperfections, one of them a frustrating reticence about any question touching on sex or death, ill health, or bad behavior. Was Uncle Robbie really as heroic as he looked? Was he really the first to fight? Why did he go, this attractive young man with the future before him and plenty of good connections and priceless credentials to ease the way? With two sons of my own, I struggled with the terrible depth of my grandmother's loss, but also recognized the male affinity, even relish, for combat. How could she have let him go? Who went with him, and what became of them? How did he die? Was the sacrifice worth it? Chuck Bolté had come back. He named his son after my uncle. He had an artificial leg, but he lived. My uncle died. Why the difference?

PROLOGUE

El Alamein, Egypt
October 29, 1942

B olté's toes were cold.[1] It was strange, even humorous, if you could focus long enough to think about it—to be worried by cold toes in a place that had so effectively refined and deepened his understanding of *hot*. When the troopship *Duchess of Atholl* had turned north, two months ago, and entered the Red Sea, the heat had closed around them like a sweaty palm—four thousand of His Majesty's soldiers packed into a space designed for eight hundred, so that at night the intrepid ones arranged themselves like spokes on a wheel, heads by the stairwells, hoping to catch a breath of air as yet unpoisoned by their own male stink.[2] The riflemen coped in their usual way. Creatures of damp and dusk and shade, Englishmen and never more self-consciously nor proudly so, they joked in that sarcastic, self-effacing way that Bolté and his American compatriots had at first found so disarming. "Get closer to the fire," they enjoined gleefully. "Nice cool day, Joe, ought to be hot pretty soon." They relished the irony inherent in the otherwise disheartening fact that the cold shower water was at long last nice and warm.[3]

After disembarking in Suez and through the weeks of waiting and preparation that followed, Bolté felt the dry, dusty heat of the Egyptian

1

desert bore in at every pore. Surprisingly, it even invaded up through the soles of his feet, something that never happened at home in New England no matter how oppressive the weather. But oh, how it sharpened the joy of an afternoon plunge in the Med,[4] his comrades whooping and diving beside him in the spangled surf—a soldier's reward after days filled with marching and training, poor food, and tedium, to mention only the most clichéd of a soldier's challenges and deprivations. Who could have imagined such contrasts of feeling existed, back when he had been simply a Dartmouth man, his worries as insubstantial, it now seemed, as air— essay deadlines, honor societies, whether his latest piece for *The Dartmouth* would run on page one or page two?

Then had come the heat of battle—a jolt as intense and electric and uncontrolled as he had learned to imagine it, and far more so. He had been scorched very badly; that much was clear. Not literally—if he were going to die, it would be from the flesh wound in his leg, not burns—but nevertheless, effectively. For three days now in the Casualty Clearing Station just behind the Alamein lines, the kind, patient Kiwi doctor had been waiting, hoping, for blood circulation to return to his right lower leg. The piece of metal that had harmed him—a fragment of 88mm high-explosive antitank shell—was remarkably small, considering how effectively it had demolished the big artery in his thigh—so small that he would lose track of it when, a few days later, it would work its way out of the shambles.[5]

From the cold in his toes and the numb ache that seemed to creep toward his heart, Bolté guessed that circulation was not returning, and he later would contend that he was glad to see them all go—foot, ankle, and calf in addition to toes—on account of the trouble they'd given him,[6] the "guillotine amputation" a tactical maneuver to stop gangrene's advance. Shortly thereafter, an ambulance carried him to a British military hospital in Cairo, where he joined a big ward full of other soldiers also damaged by metal of many and various deadly forms, as well as by flame.

They led a nightmare life there—"in death's dream kingdom"; T. S. Eliot's line rang over and over in Bolté's head.[7] "Hollow Men" indeed. The restless, damaged soldiers lay in rows, narrow iron beds like life rafts, all adrift on the same dark morphine sea, each exhausted man, maimed man, moaning or mumbling man struggling in his delirium to ride the sudden, heaving swells of time and chance and physical pain and make sense of what had happened to strand him there. Bolté found himself again and again returned to the company of the cockney rifleman Nobby Clark as he had looked in the hellish light of a brewed-up tank that burned all night in the minefields of Kidney Ridge, Nobby's leg sheared off clean above the knee by the shell that had penetrated the back of No. 1 section's three-tonner. A few nights later a stranger mounted two machine guns on Bolté's bed and ordered him to advance around the ward tank-hunting. This shook him so that in the morning he told the doctor about it. "Everybody has it that way at first," the doctor said, then handed over the first of the antinightmare pills.[8]

When the nightmares stopped, Bolté thought hard about the chain of events that had brought him there. As the days progressed, his sense of time unhinged by morphine, the effort to remember became his weapon of choice against the inhuman weight of pain that lived in what remained of his leg and, despite the guillotine, moved up.[9]

PART 1

Celebrity Soldiers

Gentlemen, songsters, off on a spree
Doomed from here to eternity.
Lord have mercy on such as we,
Baa! Baa! Baa!

—from "The Whiffenpoof Song"
by Meade Minnegerode as derived from Rudyard Kipling

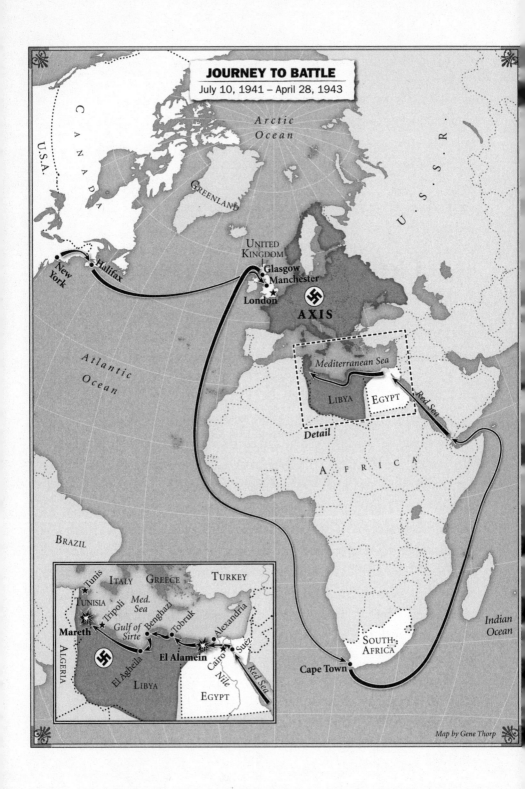

JOURNEY TO BATTLE

July 10, 1941 – April 28, 1943

Arctic Ocean

CANADA

U.S.A.

GREENLAND

U.S.S.R.

New York

Halifax

UNITED KINGDOM

Glasgow

Manchester

London

AXIS

Atlantic Ocean

Mediterranean Sea

LIBYA

EGYPT

Red Sea

Detail

AFRICA

BRAZIL

ITALY GREECE

TURKEY

Tunis

TUNISIA

Tripoli

Med. Sea

Benghazi

Tobruk

Alexandria

Mareth

Gulf of Sirte

ALGERIA

El Agheila

LIBYA

El Alamein

Cairo

Nile

Suez

Red Sea

EGYPT

SOUTH AFRICA

Indian Ocean

Cape Town

CHAPTER 1

Decision

Hanover, Concord, and Manchester, New Hampshire
April 24–May 31, 1941

> Now we have waited long enough. . . . The world we know
> is breaking up around us, and we try to maintain business as
> usual . . . the loudest voices are those crying peace, peace;
> when there is no peace. . . . Having waited long, sir, we now
> ask you to override these voices: to override the personal dis-
> taste for death and armies held by every one of us: and to make
> us our best selves by waging war.
>
> —Charles G. Bolté, "Letter to the President of the
> United States," *The Dartmouth*, April 24, 1941

In the light of six decades' hindsight and the glow of tenderness for fathers, uncles, and grandfathers, veterans now aged or dead, America's entry into World War II sometimes appears to have been all but providential. As the heroes of the story, weren't we bound to ride in to the rescue of the civilized world?

In the spring and summer of 1941, however, the question of whether and how to join the War in Europe—finally decided for us by the German declaration of war on December 11, 1941—was deeply fraught, highly divisive, and resistant to simple labeling. As the list of Nazi conquests lengthened and Britain grew ever more beleaguered and isolated, the argument

for belligerent engagement appeared ever more compelling—to its propo-
nents. To the many who, for any number of reasons, resisted the prospect
of American blood once again being spilled to resolve squabbles abroad,
popular support for in-kind aid to Britain—for sending supplies and weaponry and providing naval escorts for their delivery—reinforced a determination that assistance must end there.

The arguments played out with particular ferocity among the young
men most at risk of dying for them, as the political and ideological struggles that divided America in 1941 roiled the customarily placid atmosphere at America's leading colleges and universities. At Dartmouth
College in Hanover, New Hampshire, where the stolid, white-brick school
buildings lining the village green before a picture-perfect steeple still
seem to embody the ideal type of high-minded New England liberal arts
education, the conflict came to a head at the end of April.

On Thursday, April 24, the front page of *The Dartmouth*, the student-
run daily and self-proclaimed "Oldest College Newspaper in America,"
carried two electrifying items. One reported on the war in Greece: With
British and Greek defenders on the run, the Nazi *Wehrmacht* stood on the
brink of adding yet another trophy to its growing string of subject nations. Beginning with Poland, advancing into Denmark and Norway, the
Netherlands and Belgium, bagging the great prize of France, then over-
running Yugoslavia, the Germans now had violated the very birthplace
of democracy. At the top left of the page ran a more unusual piece, hard
to pigeonhole at first by its headline—"To the President"—but fiercely
pointed in its rhetoric. It was a lengthy, powerful, and inflammatory call
to arms.

Only the day before, isolationists had commanded the campus stage.
On Wednesday the Student Committee Against War (SCAW) had spon-
sored Peace Day demonstrations, the lead-up to a fiery evening address
by the isolationist New Hampshire senator Charles W. Tobey, who famously opposed allowing American naval vessels to protect aid ship-
ments to Britain. A counterpetition circulated that day by the local
Student Defenders of Democracy nevertheless garnered more than three

hundred student and faculty signatures urging Congress "to take any measures necessary to defeat the Axis powers."[1] That night, the Defenders' questioning of Senator Tobey turned aggressive, his replies sarcastic. The address had devolved into bitter, heated discord.

Now *The Dartmouth* had printed a letter addressed to President Roosevelt from one of the college's most high-profile seniors, Charles G. Bolté, and while not writing an actual editorial, had endorsed it as "the best current expression of *The Dartmouth*'s editorial opinion."[2] Bolté enjoyed a reputation as an able and prolific writer, though some called him glib, and the letter—plainspoken, incantatory, even Whitmanesque—channeled all the fervent certainty that had evolved in him over the last year as he moved away from ardent peace advocacy to a desperate conviction that America and all she stood for faced extinction if she failed to fight, and soon. He had pulled out all the stops:

> Now we have waited long enough. We have seen the Greeks go down and we have heard the words of a Greek: "On October 28 Roosevelt pledged America's complete aid to Greece, but not a single cartridge has yet arrived from the United States." Greece held on no longer.
>
> Now we have waited long enough. We hear that Greece has fallen and on the same radio broadcast we hear that the United States is sending Britain some ships—"small ships, 20 torpedo boats." It is travesty in the midst of tragedy. . . .
>
> Now we have waited long enough. We have seen the United States move slowly toward war, through conscription, industrial defense mobilization and the lease-lend act: we have known that it moved too slowly.
>
> We have not produced enough guns, tanks, airplanes, bombs.
>
> We have not supplied the ships. . . .
>
> We have not supplied the men. . . .
>
> Now we ask you to order complete industrial mobilization of this country on wartime lines. . . .

Now we ask you to authorize the sending of supplies across the seas in American ships, convoyed by the American navy.

Now we ask you to send American pilots, mechanics, sailors and soldiers to fight wherever they are needed.

Contrasting a dark vision of a world "breaking up around us" and doomed to a future under the fascist boot against a bright, heroic alternative wherein Americans do what they must to "save the last best hope on earth . . . of staying free and bringing freedom," "Now, having waited long enough," Bolté asked Roosevelt "to make us our best selves by waging war."

It was a gutsy move, to address the president of the United States with such hortatory certainty, but Bolté, a tall, dark, and handsome young man whose wide forehead and dimpled chin evoked comparisons to the youthful Orson Welles, whose name was frequently coupled with the word "brilliant," and whose opinions were repeated by the likes of the poet Robert Frost, had never lacked confidence. His nimble mind and exceptional drive had earned a certain fame among the faculty and won him the honor of spending his last year at Dartmouth as a senior fellow, one of seven who could study as they chose with the goal of producing a long senior paper, which the college would publish in an annual book. His essay on *Moby-Dick* cast Captain Ahab as a symbol of American individualism hunting down the monstrous evil of fascism.

His simultaneous courtship of the dark-haired Wellesley sophomore Mary Brooks Elwell had been prosecuted with similar determination and confidence. Spotting her at a party, he immediately judged her "the most beautiful and vital girl I'd ever seen."[3] Undeterred by her initial demurrals, he continued the pursuit until, six months later, she agreed to a secret engagement.

But Bolté's outspoken confidence also inspired rivals and detractors. Two days after publication of "Letter to the President," one classmate threw down the gauntlet in a letter to Bolté containing a personal challenge: "Meet me Saturday morning by the Hanover post office and we'll hitchhike to Manchester and enlist." Two days later, on Monday the twenty-eighth, the letter appeared, with Bolté's response, in the "Vox Populi" section of *The Dartmouth*. "I have always thought you an extremely clever person," goaded Bolté's friend Arnold W. Bartlett. "I still do. You can write glibly for peace in one instance and write just as glibly for war in another. . . . I accuse you of being a carbon copy of a big moment."[4]

By then the appointed day had passed, and Bolté explained. "Your line has been that I ratted on my conviction by refusing to accept your challenge." But Bartlett, he said, had proposed a small gesture when he himself was talking about large ones. "I wasn't figuring on Bolté or Bartlett; I was figuring on the nation. The letter was bigger than me." He closed with a suggestion that the two of them spend their last weeks of college spreading the argument for national mobilization and urging on the president and the Congress. Then, in June, "if we're still not in the war, you come with me when I go to Montreal to sign up for the Royal Canadian Air Force."

Meanwhile, Dartmouth's two leading debaters had issued their own challenge, to "meet Bolté and any partner he chose on a public platform." Consequently, the night of Tuesday, April 29, saw the largest room in Dartmouth Hall packed with undergraduates, faculty, and townspeople eager to watch Bolté and his second defend the premise "Resolved: That the United States should immediately enter the war on the side of Great Britain." A lively question-and-answer period lasted past midnight.[5]

The next morning, *The Dartmouth* again scathingly asserted its position, dismissing the isolationists' insistence on recognizing the "facts" of the argument as naive and outmoded, since so many supposed facts—the impregnability of the Low Countries, the advantage that defense always has over offense, the impossibility that Stalin would ever let Hitler march into the Balkans—already had proved fallacious. The conflict boiled on for days on the pages of "Vox Pop" in long, troubled, satirical, thoughtful, outraged, or, in one case, shockingly anti-Semitic letters. (The writer declared publication of Bolté's opinion to be "either a publicity stunt or inspired by Jew members of your board."[6]) Meanwhile, Bolté's "Letter to the President" was reprinted in part or in whole in the *New York Herald Tri-*

bune, the *Des Moines Register,* and the *Boston Herald.* On May 8, New Jersey senator William H. Smathers (a Democrat) read it into the Congressional Record. Dartmouth College itself, proud of the model of persuasive rhetoric crafted by one of its most promising students[7] (and led by an avowed interventionist, President Ernest Martin Hopkins), reprinted the letter as a booklet, which the alumni office, where Bolté was undergraduate editor of the Dartmouth alumni magazine, mailed out.

The threat of war cast a long shadow over college classes of 1941. At Harvard, the annual spring dance organized by the final clubs was called "The Lost Generation," not "The Greatest Generation."[8] It was hard to focus on your studies when you thought you might be drafted, and the draft greatly complicated planning for life after graduation. Some took the bull by the horns and, asserting what control they could, enlisted in the marines or the air force or the navy. A few, perhaps inspired by the American flyboys who had helped save Britain from the Luftwaffe in the Battle of Britain, or, even earlier, more idealistically, and less successfully, the International Brigade in the Spanish Civil War, sought out more direct routes to the battlefield. American Field Service volunteers would man ambulances and aid stations. The Canadian military accepted some Americans, but the prospects for action there were murky. A very few, Charles Bolté among them, found their way into the only military service that seemed certain to see action soon—the British army.

On the day Harvard senior Rob Cox decided to go to war, he did the thing most likely to make that Saturday, May 31, seem like every other last day of May since boyhood. He returned to his prep school alma mater. In 1941, Anniversary at St. Paul's School was a celebration akin to homecoming at other schools, but with straw boaters and gravitas. Set amid rolling farmland near Concord, New Hampshire, the cluster of red-brick buildings and grassy playing fields populated by some four hundred boys aged eleven to eighteen and their schoolmasters formed the intellectually rich, architecturally Spartan archetype of the New England boarding school, an idealistic amalgamation of monastery, fraternity, and orphanage where Christian charity intermingled with athletic rivalry, a classical education was maintained as a necessary stepping-stone to gentlemanly distinction, and noblesse oblige was cultivated as the beneficent counterweight to economic entitlement.

The school that prided itself on molding the characters of America's leading families' male heirs had a way of imprinting its own history and its spiritual mission nearly everywhere. The founder's initials, G. S., had been forged into the weather vane and the long iron door hinges of the old chapel that stood at the school's heart. In the oak paneling of the Upper School dining room were incised the names of every graduate back to the first class, of 1858, whose seven members included the founder's elder son, George Brune Shattuck. Even the school power plant added in the 1930s displayed beneath its eaves a quotation from the Book of Common Prayer: "O Ye Fire and Heat, Bless Ye the Lord."

On Saturday, May 31, 1941, Rob Cox drove up from Harvard with a friend, the pretty, brown-haired Boston debutante Lee Thacher, to enjoy Anniversary celebrations. He had a lot on his mind. Safe to say, on that springtime Saturday—typically for New England a tantalizing mixture of soft blue sky behind a scudding scrim of cloud, warming sun, and rising dampness—no question weighed more heavily on the collective American mind than that of if, when, and how American soldiers would take up arms against the Nazis and their Axis allies, and Cox had been wrestling with his own personal version of that multifaceted conundrum for some time now. In just nineteen days he would graduate from college. Twelve days earlier, German paratroopers had fallen on Crete—an astonishing feat of military enterprise that only increased the frightening aura of nearly superhuman ingenuity and skill that Hitler's war machine radiated. Their rout of British forces now raised the specter of Nazi control of the Suez Canal and the indispensable Middle Eastern oil fields beyond.

Throughout New England, yesterday's Memorial Day events had resonated with foreboding. "Memorial Day Keynote Is National Security," the *Boston Globe* headlined. Amid holiday crowds, American soldiers in new uniforms stood as reminders of the gathering storm. "Never has Memorial Day been observed in an atmosphere deeper fraught with sober, brooding reflection," Dorothy Wayman wrote in her front-page story.[9] Newspapers nationwide reported the return from London, recently devastated by its most ferocious bombing yet, of John Gilbert Winant, who two months earlier had replaced Joseph Kennedy as the American ambassador to the Court of St. James's. The diplomatic pouch under his arm suggested dramatic developments, even if his landing at LaGuardia by Pan Am flying boat produced nothing more newsworthy than a tip of his gray fedora, a friendly word to a familiar photographer, and the spontaneous utterance, as newsreel cameras rolled, "This is worse than a bombing."[10]

In his fireside radio chat the previous Tuesday night, May 27, President Roosevelt, alarmingly, had proclaimed an "unlimited national emergency," thereby assuming broad military and civilian powers that, by law, could be exercised only when the president believed war to be imminent. Just forty miles north of Concord, a Laconia, New Hampshire, defense contractor posted guards at the plant for fear of sabotage.[11]

Last October, for the first time since the Great War ended in 1918, American men aged twenty-one to thirty-six had registered for the draft, as required by the Selective Training and Service Act passed by nearly two votes to one in September. Born on April 13, 1919, Rob too had done his duty. The agents at the draft board in New York, where his mother lived in an apartment on East 72nd Street, had given him a registration number. The order in which the numbers would be called to service was determined by national lottery. On October 29, 1940, amid much media hoopla, a blindfolded Secretary of War Henry Stimson drew the first number from a giant fishbowl that had been used for the same purpose in World War I. When all 7,836 numbers had been drawn,[12] Rob's number was unsettlingly close to the top of the list.

At intervals all that winter and early spring, Rob had telephoned his mother in New York and asked her to go around to the draft board and check when his number would come up. Now he felt sure that fateful event was, at best, just weeks away. As Harvard commencement approached, he had cast about for a more promising and interesting alternative to being drafted into an army that might never go to war. He was well aware of the prejudices and assumptions of friends and classmates—that one would go as an officer was taken for granted, whether navy, air force, or marines was debatable, but usually decided in line with family traditions.

One day that spring when Rob called home, he amended his usual request. "Cambridge calling," the operator told Mamma, and then Rob came on. "Would you go around to the draft board, because I am thinking of joining a British regiment and to go over with some volunteers."

"I was pretty startled when he told me this," Fanny Cox later remembered. But she recognized the plan as a gesture of American support, or of the boys who would volunteer, at least. She herself had been busy with a charitable organization called Bundles for Britain, one of several efforts of the women in her circle to aid British civilians displaced and injured by the Blitz.

"Well, you think this over like a man, not like a boy," she told her son. "Then, whatever you decide is all right with me."

At St. Paul's, things British had long been admired and emulated. The curriculum was heavy with classics, British history, and British literature. Lunch was called "tuck," snack time "tiffin." Teachers were "masters," grades were "forms," as in English "public" schools such as Eton and Harrow. The rector, Dr. Drury, even insisted that cows be driven every morning from the school barn to a meadow below his office because he had been taken with just such a tableau on a visit to Eton.[13]

This year, reunion weekend had begun Friday night with a special demonstration for Britain. As dusk descended over the New Hampshire hills, a brass band organized just for the occasion led a parade to the playing fields, where the assembled company of students, masters, and alumni sang "Hail Britannia," then were stirred further by an address by sixth-form president Douglas W. Franchot, who declared unreserved sympathy and support for the British struggle in defense of freedom, and eager willingness to embrace the new sense of purpose offered by the prospect of war. A British-born master delivered an equally heartfelt thank-you for funds collected at the school—the equivalent of about $25,000 in 2011 dollars—to be given to alumnus and former master in history John Gilbert Winant, who in his capacity as American ambassador to the Court of St. James's would apply the gift as he thought best. After a vigorous rendition of "Battle Hymn of the Republic," the ceremonies ended with fireworks.

When Cox arrived on Saturday, the mood was more customarily genial. Old friends shook hands warmly. "Whitey" Cox was a favorite, in many ways the embodiment of all that St. Paul's held dear. He was handsome in a fair-haired, square-jawed way (though his left ear flared out a bit more than his right); tall, at nearly six-foot-three; and very athletic. His slap shot was remembered as a thing of grace and power. On the first line of the freshman hockey team at Harvard, he had garnered mention in *The Crimson* for scoring two goals at Boston Garden in the team's 7–0 victory over Andover, their sixth consecutive win. On the Harvard varsity, junior year brought him the Angier trophy, a silver box with his name engraved on the lid, "awarded annually to the player showing the greatest improvement during the year 1939–40."

In the sixth form at St. Paul's, he was an editor of the literary magazine *Horae Scholasticae*. His stories and poems published there have an old-fashioned, Latinate ring today, possibly the reflection of a curriculum weighted heavily toward classics. But they still resonate with youthful high seriousness, lyrical ardor, love, valor, and a romantic view of death. Even his mother's brother, Uncle Max Perkins, editor of the era's new American greats Wolfe, Fitzgerald, and Hemingway, spoke of Rob's promise as a writer.

At a time and place where the ideal of the scholar athlete was a very serious matter, Rob Cox was it. At St. Paul's graduation in 1937 he was awarded the highest possible honor—the School Medal *Ob egregiam diligentiam atque virtutem MCMXXXVII*—for outstanding diligence and virtue. He was Best Boy. "That was quite a thing," observed one close friend and classmate seven decades later. At a school that considered its student body to be the best American society could boast, "It meant you were chosen as the best of your generation."[14]

Cox had accepted the prize with characteristic self-effacement. Modesty was a virtue, too, without which such an award would be unthinkable. He had gained the respect of peers and masters for his kindheartedness, unfailing fairness, and a certain principled simplicity that set him slightly apart from most of his highly privileged classmates. During third form, at fourteen, his essay "Greatness" won the Thanksgiving Prize. Starting from the question, "Is it true that a broken heart is better than loneliness?" he proceeded to argue that hardship is indeed the key to living life "to its fullest possibility, and that is greatness." In a sort of coda that suggested precocious self-awareness about the lives most of his peers could at that point look forward to, the last paragraph acknowledged the difficulty of achieving greatness. "For we have been brought up to believe that if we are good we will be happy. We have listened to a hedonistic philosophy for so long that we will never be able to face the fact that virtue is not always pleasant. . . . Instead we shall live a comfortable life, give a little money to charity, and adopt a philosophy of life that excuses us from real ambition. If only we had the courage to dream and suffer for our dreams, we could all develop the powers within us."

Rob's own experience of hardship was delineated and defined by the event that had upended his family eleven years earlier: the loss of his father. His father and mother had met each other while next-door neighbors in the quiet railroad suburb Plainfield, New Jersey; eighteen years younger than her husband, Frances Perkins Cox had known Archie virtually all her life. Fanny Cox's people were Boston Brahmins—the descendants of wealthy tea merchants and sea captains, patrons of Harvard, founders of the Boston Museum of Fine Arts. Like her kin, she still served tea every afternoon, and like many of them she was no longer wealthy. Archie was, like his father before him, a successful patent attorney in New York, and while he lived, their seven children enjoyed a comfortable, well-ordered existence in a big house not far from where their parents grew up. There were poetry readings after supper every Sunday, and the cook and the maids and the nanny would hover on the fringes of the living room to listen when the growing family—Rob had an older brother and two older sisters, then three younger brothers—gathered for morning and evening prayers.

Then his father, at fifty-six, had grown tired and thin and then ill, and when Rob was ten and utterly ignorant of the gravity of the illness, his father died of lung cancer. Soon after, the servants were let go. One night the children found their mother, who had never learned to cook, sprawled on the kitchen floor among cookbooks and recipes, weeping. Before long, the big, comfortable house with the tennis court and a wild acre out back that Father, a quoter of Kipling, had teasingly called the Jungle would be put on the market, and Fanny found a walk-up apartment in New York. Whether or not her sons knew of the special tuition arrangements she made with the rector, Dr. Drury, to keep them at St. Paul's is unknown.

In September 1931, still numb from his father's death just seven months earlier, Rob, like his older brother, Archie, and their father, Archie, before him, like his grandfather and three uncles, four great-uncles and countless cousins, was left at St. Paul's to get settled in one of the three-sided, bead-board cubicles that flanked the long corridor of the barnlike Lower School dormitory. There was a narrow bed, a dresser, a bookshelf, a towel rack, his trunk . . . his new home. With just a curtain door, he slept at night cocooned by the small noises of his classmates—a cough, a scratch, a whimper. With time, he got to know these boys better than his own brothers and sisters. Well, why not? From age twelve to eighteen he lived most of his life in their company. Apart from the Christmas holidays, visits home were rare. He ate with them, studied with them, roughhoused and joked with them, marched into chapel with them seven days a week and twice on Sundays, listened as the resonant voice of Dr. Drury made the high-vaulted, ornate choir feel cavelike and intimate, his invocations and exhortations washing over them as a group.

Rob became accustomed to taking long walks on the school grounds with or without his classmates, striding around the Lower School pond—said to be the place where the game of ice hockey first took hold in America—past the stone shrine erected by an alumnus where the path entered thick woods, a little house on a pedestal sheltering a crucifix and entreating passersby with Ecclesiastes, "Remember now thy Creator in the days of thy Youth," then along a path to the northwest through the woods to the top of Jerry Hill, where the farms and forests of New Hampshire spread out at his feet, to the west the distant billows of the Green Mountains fading into the Adirondacks, to the northeast the rugged ramparts of New Hampshire's Whites, with the town of Concord clearly visible to the east, the Merrimack River, its banks crowded with vast redbrick mills spouting smoke, winding off southeast toward the sea. He learned to love the ever-changing landscape, looked back at the school, its buildings tucked cozy and villagelike into the Turkey River Valley, its paired spires, belfry and smokestack, barely visible above the trees, and found he loved it in an encompassing way that stretched from individual schoolmates out into all the world, seen and unseen, around them.

In the fifth form (junior year) Rob wrote a story called "Shadows of the Clouds," about a ten-year-old boy whose father has died, leaving his mother remote and unresponsive. The boy remembers happier times: how his father would comfort him when he was hurt—"Be brave and it will stop hurting at any moment"—how the three of them had climbed together to a hilltop, where his father read a poem that captured the boy's sense of longing: "Come out, pull out on the old trail / The trail that is always new." Later, back in his cheerless home, the boy indulges an impulse to do something forbidden: He builds a fire in the fireplace, just as his father used to do. As he works, he hears a sob. "It was so like him," his mother cries, and as they weep together, the wound of his father's death begins to heal. He knows "that all would be as it used to be and that next June, when the sun was warm, they would walk up 'the Hill' together and, sitting on the summit, would watch the shadows of the clouds drifting slowly across the valley."

Strolling now beneath the fountaining elms of the chapel lawn, Cox greeted old classmates, like himself back for the day from Harvard, Yale, or Princeton, possibly Dartmouth or West Point. For all the day's reassuring familiarity, they too had war on their minds, and talk turned to whether and when to enlist. Already, some of his classmates were gone. Tony Duke, who had argued the Nazi threat ever since a terrifying, accidental encounter with some soldiers in Austria in 1934, had enlisted in the navy in 1939.[15] Rob's St. Paul's friend and Harvard roommate Chris Herter had left for the U.S. Army. Paul Moore Jr., one of Rob's two close school friends whose conversion experiences at St. Paul's would lead to religious vocations (Moore eventually becoming Episcopal bishop of New York), had signed up for the marines. But here was Cox's St. Paul's roommate "Baldy" McLane, ready as always to join in conversation. (Despite a tall, slim physique and distinguished aquiline profile, Charles McLane could not escape being teased for his high forehead.) Cox was considering, he told Baldy, a British regiment—he'd heard about it at his club—the very one that held up the Nazi army at Calais, setting the stage for the evacuation at Dunkirk, that heroic and moving rescue of the British Expeditionary Force by every kind of vessel from destroyer to pleasure launch. As McLane would explain decades later, "Everyone was looking for something."

The day, which had begun cool and breezy, grew warmer. As the sun climbed behind thin clouds, the crowd increased. Boys and masters, their sweethearts and friends, jostled into line along Dunbarton Street to applaud the alumni parade, processions being, in a community knit together by ecclesiastical ritual, a familiar form of celebration. The Halcyon banner splashed red between spring-green elms, where it hung across the school street as it had every year since the late, legendary master Willard Scudder, for decades president of the Halcyon boat club, first hung it outside his rooms in the Middle School. Across the street, girls and women tripped across the lawns, took the men's arms. This fact alone had transformed the atmosphere, lent it unfamiliar lightness and fizz. And only two weeks off, the bittersweet rites of Last Night, then graduation, awaited the sixth formers, with summer vacations beckoning hopefully just beyond.

Grouped by class, the old men marched first, then the merely mature, ranks swelling as the year displayed on the placards they carried grew more recent, all of them regardless of age seeming to have been cut from the same wholesome cloth, all upright of carriage and fair of face, all cheerfully at ease in their navy blazers, white button-down shirts, rep ties, and gray flannels, or white flannels and white shoes, school blazers with pocket crests and white piping, many of them sporting straw boaters or fedoras.

After the parade, celebrations took a still more quintessentially Pauly turn. Even the old boys had an athletic contest to take part in. The Alumni Dash, a footrace of one hundred yards or so, had two chief requirements: You needed to be a good sport, for there was generally much confusion about the locations and timing of start and finish, and you needed to wear a hat for the entirety.[16] As his reward, the behatted winner would enjoy the enduring honor of having his name inscribed on a handsome silver cup.

The schoolboys themselves did what they had done every school-day afternoon rain or shine since the ice went out on Long Pond two months earlier: They rowed, only this time with added urgency and zest. It was Anniversary. It was Race Day—the two were one and the same. The old boys were watching, and many an old boy was a student's father or grandfather or uncle. The masters who had served as surrogate, bachelor fathers to the boys at school looked sporty and festive in their boat club blazers—navy for Shattuck, crimson for Halcyon. They overflowed with old stories, prodded the boys with new challenges. Good-natured chaffing abounded.

It was a fine spring day in New England, this May thirty-first, the land smelling of grass and pine needles, the pond of fresh mud. Along the shore the bright, budding leaves of the hardwoods winked and shimmered, tender as a girl's ear. The tall pines mottled the hillside dark and light. After the short drive to the pond, the women, in coats and hats and sturdy shoes, the men in their blazers and boaters, wandered beneath the pines seeking conversation and comfortable vantage points for the races.

At two big, shingled boathouses at one end of Long Pond, the boys had divided themselves by rowing club, teams to which, since the first Race Day in 1871, they were assigned at admission, usually in line with family tradition—Shattuck, named for the school founder, or Halcyon, for the ancient Greek bird believed in legend to bring calm to its breeding grounds, but with time simply an adjective synonymous with youth, peace, and happiness: halcyon days.

The boys wore tan knitted briefs with padded bottoms and a stripe at each cuff in their team color, blue or crimson. As Cox watched from the bank, one after another crew of eight brought a long, sliver-shaped cedar shell out of the boathouse, lifted, overturned it, and carried it overhead to the dock. The boys' legs looked reedlike and pale, walking the narrow craft in unison to dock's edge, where in one smooth, well-practiced maneuver, they pressed it up, flipped it over, and set it down on the lapping lake water. Each club put up eight boats organized by skill level, and before long a flotilla of eight-headed craft, long oars bristling, crowded the lakefront, forming an archaic, strangely moving tableau reminiscent of some preindustrial time when the phrase "manpower" had real force—ancient Greece, perhaps, in the days of the trireme.

Rob himself was never a great rower—football and hockey were his sports—but with his rangy build he'd pulled his weight. The Coxes were Shattuck—he himself third seat, second crew—and as he watched the shells gain speed off the start he couldn't help but feel a sympathetic tension in lats and biceps, a rhythmic tensing of calves. The long oars, moving precisely in sync, swept back, swept forward at a hastening pace. He'd always relished being part of a team.

As the afternoon wore on, the rowing improved in speed and grace until the climactic contest when the first boats, rowed by the most skilled and powerful boys, pulled up to the start. The gun barked. The shells surged forward, slowly gaining momentum, each rower lost in collective rhythm, each vessel assuming its own larger life, like a beating heart or a well-machined piston. The coxswain, hunched under his windbreaker in the stern, strained toward the oarsmen, shouting through his little megaphone—"Stroke . . . stroke . . . stroke . . . stroke . . . stroke . . . stroke . . . stroke . . . stroke . . . stroke"—as the eight bare-chested young men pulled away and away from him. The white-painted deck of the committee boat flared at the finish line. One bow crossed—crimson blades—the winner was Halcyon! Sighs met cheers. Oh, but it's all in good fun, well fought, good contest.

Congratulations tendered, hands clasped and shaken firmly, the crowd, awash in bonhomie, dispersed back toward the center of campus. Before long the winning crew would reappear, resplendent in crimson and white, would clamber into the Halcyon barge and, singing, oars in the air, ride back to campus in glory. (Barges were large, low wagons drawn by teams of horses; the origin of the term, reminiscent of royal outings on the Thames or the Nile, is obscure.) When they climbed down at the school flagpole, cheers and applause would buoy them. Their red-bladed oars would lean on their grips against the flagpole, while the stroke oar, knotted onto the halyard, would be raised with the club banner toward the sky.

Rob had made plans to join Baldy McLane for dinner at Three Acres, the hilltop apple orchard outside Manchester, New Hampshire. There the McLanes had relocated a tumbledown seventeenth-century barn to create a setting for their holiday gatherings, which entailed Scottish country dancing and kilts. Baldy's grandfather had emigrated from the Isle of Skye in the mid-nineteenth century, then made his fortune manufacturing the metal banks of small, locking mailboxes that to this day line the walls of rural post offices throughout America.

Charles's mother, Ibbis (Elizabeth Bancroft McLane), had discovered the barn in far northern New Hampshire, bought it, had it moved, added a massive stone fireplace at one end, repaired the diamond-shaped panes of leaded glass and the wooden shake roof, and equipped it with iron candelabra and a huge central chandelier—no electricity, thank you, just candlelight. The problem of falling wax distracting the guests below had been solved when she located a Jewish religious supply house in New York that sold dripless candles. She bought them by the crateful.

For tonight, Ibbis had organized cocktails and a simple supper for family and friends—Baldy's father, "Judge" McLane; his older brothers, Malcolm and Jock, and their families, as well as the Evartses and the Howards, family friends whom Rob also knew well. He had spent two summers with the Howards tutoring their children, a common summer job for well-educated young men at that time and a helpful supplement to the family coffers. The Evartses were cousins through Fanny Cox's grandfather, William M. Evarts, who in addition to his many successes in public life had sired twelve children and established an expansive family compound in Windsor, Vermont, where his large extended family would summer together for decades.

In the mellow light in the ancient room, now comfortably furnished with chairs and sofas and rugs, the turmoil in Europe seemed far away indeed. As usual, there were parlor games after supper. For charades, Baldy was teamed with Rob's puckish thirteen-year-old cousin, Carol Evarts, who climbed onto the back of a settee and mimed the sinking of the *Lusitania* with such fervor that the seat toppled over backward, she with it. Charles McLane would remember the incident all his life. It proved to be his first encounter with his wife.

At the time, however, McLane was enamored with a young woman of more suitable age and, under the circumstances, more unusual background. Teru Osato was a Japanese-American student at Bennington and roommate of the daughter of Sidney Cox, one of Baldy's English professors. Teru would play a pivotal part in the running discussion that Cox and McLane pursued off and on all that night about their futures—military and otherwise.

Charles McLane was one of Rob Cox's closest friends. They had been counterparts and rivals in debating at St. Paul's, fellow editors at the *Ho-rae* and the yearbook, and they shared New England roots and a deep affection for the countryside. Charles had wanted to attend Harvard, as nearly 40 percent of his St. Paul's class would do, but his father had persuaded him that he would find more success in a smaller college where he wouldn't have to compete with socially prominent Bostonians and New Yorkers. Like his father, Charles went to Dartmouth. There he'd become captain of the ski team and a mainstay of the drama club, his campus achievements recognized at the end of junior year with a "tap," the notice of his election to Casque and Gauntlet, the prestigious residential secret society, where he shared a study with Charles Bolté, known to his friends as Chuck. But McLane and Cox had continued to ski together in Vermont and New Hampshire, and every spring they sought out the last snow at the headwall of Tuckerman Ravine on Mount Washington. At 6,288 feet, Washington is New England's tallest peak, and Tuckerman's, a snow catcher that furrows the north face like a ragged scar, posed a hair-raising, irresistible challenge. The ascent required hours of trudging, skis strapped to their backs, up a slope so steep that an arm extended at shoulder height touched the snow face. The descent rushed dizzily by in a few thrilling, perilous minutes. In both cases, the price of a fall was an uncontrollable, immeasurable, and possibly mortal tumble, nothing to stop you but the boulders at the snowfield's hem.

Rob hoped to persuade Baldy to enlist in the King's Royal Rifles and go to England with him. They discussed the possibility in detail. Cox's draft number was nearing the top of the list. Alternative plans were more or less nonexistent. He knew one other probable volunteer, a fellow Harvard student, Heyward Cutting, but he was only a sophomore and a member of the Porcellian Club, not Rob's club, the A.D. In those days, a Harvard man's final club formed the focus of his social life. Rob rented a room down the street in a row of boardinghouses known affectionately as the "rat houses," and he generally slept there, but the club was the convivial place, the place to eat and, especially, drink in comfort and privacy with others of your ilk.

That night, Rob emphasized to Baldy the advantages of enlisting as a British officer over waiting to be drafted as an American GI. He talked about the heritage and the character of the King's Royal Rifle Corps, also known as the 60th Rifles, whose colonel in chief was King George VI himself. Unlike any other military unit they might join, this one was at that moment actively engaged in North Africa with the 7th Armoured Division—the fabled Desert Rats—as they struggled to drive out the quick and deadly panzers of the Afrika Korps led by Erwin Rommel, the Desert Fox.

Rob could have talked about the KRRC's inspiring American roots: how Rogers' Rangers, the band of New Hampshire irregulars celebrated by Kenneth Roberts in *Northwest Passage,* had contributed their expertise as guerrilla warriors during the French and Indian War, when the regiment first formed up in the American colonies. It was a twist that gave enlistment now a gratifyingly patriotic historical resonance, even if they would be serving a foreign power. In 1756, after a disastrous battle near Fort Duquesne hammered home the need for local knowledge and improvisational tactics, a British act of Parliament had allowed American colonists to serve as British soldiers. The 60th Royal American Regiment, as it then was called, won its first battle honors for the capture of Louisburg, on Cape Breton Island, in 1758. The American presence had, of course, ended with the Revolution. Now the British military had reasserted the connection in order to bring in at least a few Americans to fight the Axis. Since the Battle of Britain, a growing number of American fliers had joined the Royal Air Force. But the KRRC volunteers would be the first American men to fight with the British on the ground.

That spring and the previous winter Rob had hashed over the issues with his elder brother, Archie, the effective male head of the family. He too had attended St. Paul's and Harvard, but his temperament was less ebullient than Rob's. Whereas Rob, easygoing and witty, had enjoyed the glossy conviviality of deb parties on the North Shore or in town and was a skilled participant, if not a true believer, in the Boston and New York social scenes, Archie had worked doggedly at his studies, sights trained squarely on law school; it suited his careful, abstract habit of thought. What they shared was a devotion to doing what was right—however each of them defined it. Archie graduated from Harvard Law School and went to work at the Boston law firm Ropes and Gray. One evening, talking together in the house Archie shared with his new wife, Phyllis, in the Boston suburbs, Archie and Rob had identified four reasons why Rob wanted to go: "Nothing better to do; adventure; curiosity; and belief." According to Archie, only the last one was valid, but Rob wasn't so sure.[17]

He talked to Baldy about the urgency of rescuing the high culture of Europe. On a school-organized trip abroad the summer after prep school graduation, it had captured Rob's imagination. "He was fascinated by Vienna," Charles McLane would remember, "the music and the culture. He was even sentimental about all that." McLane acknowledged the attraction of joining a British regiment burnished by the same old-world glow. "It was very, very chic, very elegant."

But Charles's draft number was less imminent than Rob's. He had summer plans—painting with well-known artist and Dartmouth professor Paul Sample in Colorado—and, as he put it, an "urge to push forward" with them. He felt that military discipline might drive him mad, but if it proved unavoidable, he wanted to enlist in the ski troops.[18] And there was Teru. Over and above his romantic feelings, he had a sense that as hostilities intensified in Asia, she might in some way need his protection.

Rob had a sweetheart, too. Kit Motley had caught his eye at one of the dances that spring and before long became the lodestar of his social and emotional universe. A graduate of St. Timothy's boarding school for girls and a resident of Boston's Back Bay, Kit had made her debut the previous winter at the Somerset Club, then passed her nineteenth year in the usual way for Boston girls of her background—visiting with friends, preparing for parties, and going to parties. "Coming out" to society was a full-time occupation.

A petite young woman with tiny feet and slim, elegant fingers, Kit had big brown eyes, which looked out beneath dark, wavy bangs with an open, inquiring expression—curious and sympathetic and filled with something like fun, or mischief. At the next dance, she and Rob discovered their shared interest in poetry, which was serious. "We talked all night," Kit would remember much later. "He knew a *lot,* all sort of A. E. Housman. I think he kissed me good night that night. I don't think he'd had another girl before."

Kit, by contrast, had spent time enough with another Harvard man to be—in the way that attraction, in a culture where chastity was assumed before marriage, could morph very quickly into a commitment for life—"sort of engaged." But that didn't stop her from falling for Rob. "We had a passionate affair," she said seventy years later, though it is perfectly clear that the passion was circumscribed by the chaste mores of their time and class. For Rob, the situation was complicated. He knew Kit was "taken"; she had told him so herself. Her intended, William Emmet—a wealthy scion of the Standard Oil Pratt family[19]—had been only a year behind him at St. Paul's. They moved in the same circles. Word got around. But so powerful was the attraction, so profound the sympathy between them, that Rob still couldn't help believing that he and Kit might be the real thing. She had continued to see him, after all, driving Willy Emmet wild in the process. They had picnicked by a stream before a concert at Tanglewood. She had stayed for one revelatory weekend with the family in Windsor.

By ten p.m., when the party at Three Acres broke up, it was agreed: While McLane would not join Cox and Cutting in the 60th Rifles, three or four of his Dartmouth friends, he felt certain, would go—Bolté, of course, who had publicly committed himself to enlisting one way or another as soon as he graduated, but also McLane's closest friend, "brilliant," "utterly special" Jack Brister, who like Cox was a talented, idealistic writer, but unlike Cox was already deeply committed to making writing his profession; and Bill Durkee, an economics major from California, an internationalist, a sailor, and like Bolté and McLane a member of Casque and Gauntlet. Bill Durkee was the second William Porter Durkee to attend Dartmouth, and with every intention of following in his father's successful footsteps, he majored in economics as an entrée to law school. His father, a vice president with Shell Oil Company, had moved, as he moved up, from Chicago to California. There, Bill was elected student body president and graduated second in his class from the Menlo School for Boys, a boarding school where the main building resembled a limestone miniature of the porticoed and colonnaded Newport mansions of the robber barons back east.

Excited, McLane raced through the dark back to Hanover and the stolid brick honor society house beside the village green. Locating Bolté and Durk took a matter of minutes; the members all slept in rows of beds under the eaves, in a chilly, open attic they called "the wind tunnel."[20] No sooner had they comprehended the news than they rushed off to find Brister and his roommate, Tom Littlefield, who shared an apartment on Main Street.

More discussion and debate among the Dartmouth friends would follow. Within weeks, their applications to the 60th Rifles would be received and approved. Tom Littlefield, who wanted to go too, was rejected on account of a bum shoulder. But that night, May 31, 1941, the die was cast. Cox, Cutting, Brister, Durkee, and Bolté would offer themselves to become British soldiers, officer candidates in the King's Royal Rifle Corps. In less than six weeks they would ship out for England. Other Harvard and Dartmouth men would follow; eighteen Americans in all joined the 60th Rifles, and some seventeen months later the U.S. Army itself finally would enter the fray. But these five young men went first, and in war timing truly is everything.

Before going to sleep that night, Charles McLane, as was his habit, wrote in his diary. Sixty-five years later, in the small, book-lined rooms where he lived alone at a Hanover, New Hampshire, retirement village, he showed me the entry. It seemed to have surprised him. "Fear was not a viable thought or emotion during those days," he mused.

Cox, he had written in 1941, "has started me thinking. He wants me to go with him. The idea is very attractive—it is clean, no waiting, exciting—but I am dubious of the chance of coming back."

CHAPTER 2

Convoy

New York, New York, to Manchester, England
July 10–August 1, 1941

> *Wish me luck as you wave me goodbye*
> *Cheerio, here I go on my way*
> *Wish me luck as you wave me goodbye*
> *Not a tear, but a cheer, make it gay*
> *Give me a smile I can keep all the while*
> *In my heart while I'm away*
> *Till we meet once again, you and I*
> *Wish me luck as you wave me goodbye. . . .*
>
> —Gracie Fields's "Goodbye Song,"
> transcribed in Rob Cox's diary

How do you stage a good-bye party when no one knows when the welcome home will be? The possibility that a welcome home would never come was, as Charles McLane might have said, "not a viable thought." The weather cooperated, setting a cheerful tone. A fresh northwest breeze the day before[1] had scrubbed New York City's multifarious face until it shone in the sun. On Thursday, July 10, 1941, Chuck Bolté, Jack Brister, and Bill Durkee gathered with their closest friends and relations for a last American meal at Chris Cella's, a onetime speakeasy on East 45th Street frequented by journalists, artists, and left-leaning political types, who now came for the steak.

Bolté's father had organized the event as a stag luncheon, thereby neatly sidestepping the question of whether or not Bolté's stepmother should join them. Bolté's mother had lost a seven-year battle with ovarian cancer in 1934, when Chuck was fourteen.[2] Not much later, his father (known to many as the handsomest man in Greenwich, Connecticut)[3] had married a recently divorced neighbor, but the blending of households had not gone entirely smoothly.

Jack Brister's best friend, Tom Littlefield, had generously agreed to escort Bolté's younger sister, Linda, a freshman at Wellesley, to eat elsewhere.[4] The arrangement displeased her. Linda had always admired and appreciated her big brother, not to mention loved him. "He was a hero to me," she would say, decades later. He had brought her the toys she needed before she could walk, had pulled her out of a swollen stream that threatened to sweep her away when she was a girl, and once, during a trip with their parents to Florida, his quick confidence had saved them from being left behind at a rail siding. The train had stopped, and the two climbed down for some fresh air. Then the train started moving. Chuck sprang into action, clambering onto a baggage wagon to leap onto the accelerating railcar. He found a conductor and convinced him the train had to be stopped. Linda's relief as she watched the train slow down, then reverse had been huge.[5] When Jack Brister showed up for the farewell meal, supposed to be men only, with his girlfriend in tow, it was nearly more than Linda could bear.

Linda Bolté had thought about falling in love with Brister herself for a while—not for his looks, though they were quite acceptable; he had thick, bristly hair and a firm, strong build, was nearly six feet tall, and had an infectious grin. But his personality was almost irresistible. Jack's friends valued him above all for his ebullient generosity, his human sympathy, his inventiveness, his humor. Driving back to Dartmouth from one weekend road trip, he had entertained himself and everyone else in the car by improvising a comic epic in rhymed couplets that lasted all the way from Wellesley to Hanover.

It wasn't what you might have expected. Brister grew up in the small mill town of Ambler, Pennsylvania, a stop on the Reading Railroad about twenty miles from Philadelphia. The town's dominant features were an asbestos factory and a convent, the surrounding farmland not yet having been divided up for commuters. Jack was the youngest of eight; his mother had died of a hemorrhage within days of his birth. Growing up, he competed companionably with his two older brothers and was doted on by his five older sisters. Simply by reason of numbers, the Brister clan enjoyed a certain prominence in town; for a long time at the local schools there seemed to be a Brister in every grade. Jack's grandfather had founded the Ambler bank in the nineteenth century. His father, iconoclastic and outspoken Frederick Brister, was a company doctor for the Reading Railroad, but he welcomed townspeople needing medical attention to the Brister home day and night, whether or not they could pay for it. The town policeman indulged Jack's sisters' delight in galloping the family's big draft horse bareback down Ambler's dirt main street. Jack and his brothers sneaked cigarettes on the roof of their sprawling, somewhat tumbledown Victorian house right next door to their grandfather's. Jack threw himself into all he did: the local scout troop, then activities at the high school, where he played football, basketball, and tennis, ran track, and swam, was active with the drama club, edited the school paper, played in the band for four years, and excelled academically.

When Jack followed his brothers to Dartmouth, his imagination, which had flowered amid the security and freedom of Ambler, began to draw admiring attention. He earned a reputation as a writer of light verse, stories, and plays. Senior year he won an award from *Story* magazine that included a promise to consider seriously any future submissions. In the Dartmouth Drama Club's 1940 festival of new plays, his entry, a droll one-act about three convicts on the lam and the self-sacrifice of one that allows the rest to reach home, won not only an honorable mention but also praise from Pulitzer prize–winning playwright Robert Sherwood, who took Jack aside afterward and told him, "You stick with this."

That same year Jack was part of the crowd that launched a new campus magazine that eschewed the tweedy, old-school-tie tenor of other Dartmouth publications. Taking *LIFE* as its model, *The Pictorial* was over-size, glossy, and sophisticated. Each issue featured a glamorous cover girl (usually one of the editors' girlfriends), daring graphics, and a story by Jack. In the spring of 1941, the commencement issue also included an editorial explaining the staff's position on the war in Europe, which had evolved rapidly during that tumultuous spring. Its tone was characteristic of Jack's writing—vexed, paradoxical, and more nuanced than Bolté's polemical approach.

> Four months ago we wrote a bitter satire on war. We wrote it because war offends our most deeply rooted and our most sincere emotions.
>
> We hate the misunderstanding and conceit which makes [*sic*] people fight one another, maliciously. . . . The fighting of one human against another is bad and wasteful. . . . This should be realized along with the knowledge that the destruction may still at times be necessary. . . .
>
> We have continually said we were not a Conscientious Objector. Somehow that title seemed to dignify our position too much, like quoting the scriptures in an argument.
>
> Now we realize that we do conscientiously object to war. But we realize too that America must fight Hitler. . . .
>
> We're ready. Ready to fight. Ready to destroy. Ready, if necessary, to be destroyed.[6]

The previous summer, between junior and senior years, Brister and Bolté and Tom Littlefield had decided to hitchhike cross-country together. Bolté and Littlefield covered eight thousand miles in eight weeks, Bolté traveling from the front door of the family house in Greenwich—he'd refused the offer of a ride to the highway[7]—to the West Coast and back on just $200, and proud to get home with thirty-five cents still in his pocket. But Brister had to be left along the way. When the friends stopped for several days of paying work at Chuck's cousin's farm in Indiana, mucking out a ditch in temperatures above a hundred degrees, Jack had gotten sunstroke. That he had to stay behind had seemed the worst possible luck, until Chuck and Tom started calling him "the original good-luck kid."[8] The attractive ranch woman who nursed him, a Wellesley graduate named Betty Turner, fell in love, and he with her, and they enjoyed a happy love affair that summer that would endure, despite Brister's father's misgivings, right up until the moment of good-bye.

Seeing the grandeur and scope of America for the first time that summer catalyzed the Dartmouth seniors' change of heart about the war. In the autumn, Bolté wrote a letter about it to Robert Sherwood, who by 1940 was a speechwriter for FDR and a spokesman for the citizens' group Committee to Defend America by Aiding the Allies. Bolté had met him when the playwright visited Dartmouth in 1940 to accept an honorary degree and met with *The Dartmouth*'s editorial board to discuss America's role in the war in Europe.

"I saw *some* country," Bolté told Sherwood. "I am more of an American after the inventory." It had left him eager to see more. "I have to go back and get deeper into the broad rivers, the high, shining mountains, the treeless, burned-off grasslands, the upland meadows, the thousand cities and hundred million people I saw and nodded to."[9]

"It was our first view of the whole country," Bolté would remember much later, "and we returned profoundly moved by its majesty and diversity."[10] He judged America to be up to a fight. "I will say that the land is big enough and rich enough to absorb the backfire of a war if it must come, and the people strong enough and sure enough to fight it," he told Sherwood. While Bolté at that point still opposed intervention in the European war, he saw abundant reasons for defending his country "to the death if it became necessary."[11]

The following spring, when Bolté's "Letter to the President" appeared in *The Dartmouth,* Sherwood sent him a telegram of praise from the White House and was instrumental in getting the letter published in the *New*

York Herald Tribune the next day. It was Bolté's father's fifty-third birthday, and he too sent his son a telegram: "Best birthday present I ever had."[12]

The festive mood of the Dartmouth men's farewell had suffered somewhat when it developed that Bolté's paperwork was not entirely in order. That morning, Colonel Rex Benson, the British assistant military attaché at the embassy in Washington, had met all five of the American volunteers, including the Harvard men, Rob Cox and Heyward Cutting, at the St. Regis Hotel for a somewhat official send-off. Over drinks, Benson had assured them that passports were unnecessary, but birth certificates would be required. Bolté's was missing. Fortunately, though raised in Greenwich, he had been born in New York, and Linda and Tom Littlefield set off on an emergency trip to City Hall to get a copy.

That mission accomplished, the group walked after lunch three bustling blocks south to Grand Central to catch the train for Boston, whence they would travel that night to Nova Scotia and there embark for England, their status legitimized by an official-looking paper signed by Benson and embellished with a big red seal, urging "all those to whom these presents come" to expedite passage of the five young men "on His Majesty's Service."[13] There would be jokes about serving the sovereign whose yoke their forebears had fought and bled and died to escape. Littlefield and Fred Brister would ride along as far as Halifax. Bolté's father, saying his good-byes at the track at Grand Central, bestowed on the excited young men a last piece of fatherly advice: "Keep your bowels open and your mouth shut."[14]

"Well, there goes good-bye to what I've known," Heyward Cutting mused nervously some eight hours later as the night train from Boston to Halifax groaned out of North Station. Sitting beside him on the scratchy velveteen seat of the Boston & Maine, Rob Cox was unhappily aware that Cutting— fair-haired, slim, impeccably dressed, and unfailingly, sometimes maddeningly, polite—would be his project for some time to come. At nineteen, he was only a sophomore at Harvard and in these circumstances had only the one connection with Cox; he would doubtless rely on him.

Cutting was something of an odd duck, anyway. Sprung from the New York City epicenter of the mannered, gilded world of Edith Wharton and Henry James, he enjoyed a level of privilege that Cox had encountered before among his classmates and, if he was honest, sometimes envied. Of the five compatriots, Cutting alone enjoyed the ease, and peculiar insecurities, that came along with real, serious money. His female relations had married counts and princes and donated priceless *objets* to the Metropolitan Museum of Art. When his male relatives got into scrapes, they wound up as morality tales in the New York papers. His father, also Heyward, had been a man of elegant profile, with sleek black hair and a neat, dashing mustache, who occupied himself with the management of his inherited estate, big game hunting, partygoing, and other sports. When he married Heyward's mother, they honeymooned in China as part of a 1921 expedition to the Gobi Desert organized by the Museum of Natural History. There, his mother, herself a crack shot, bagged one of the few specimens ever taken of the Himalayan black deer.

When Heyward Junior was only three, the marriage ended in a tragic accident. As Heyward Senior motored home in his convertible one spring night after a party on Long Island for the crown prince of Sweden, a tire blew, the car overturned, and the handsome new father was pinned beneath it. His wife and the three children—Heyward had two younger sisters—returned as fast as they could by ship from a springtime visit to Europe. The obituaries credited Heyward Senior with contributing significantly to the introduction of the motorcar to Mongolia.[15]

While he lived, Heyward Senior had said that he wanted his son to graduate from Eton, the most prestigious of English "public" schools, and from Harvard, among the most prestigious of American universities. Perhaps for this reason, and doubtless because she felt less lonely and more at home among the British hunting and shooting set, Heyward's mother raised her children among the aristocracy in the English countryside.

Afternoons at Eton, like all the boys preparing to protect and defend the British Empire, Heyward had practiced military exercises in uniform. After the Blitz began in September 1940, the family had returned to America and settled in the wealthy New York suburb of Far Hills, New Jersey. Heyward had entered Harvard, but he never felt entirely comfortable there. His talents as an artist and ornithologist found little traction, and during sophomore year he took a leave of absence. He must have felt keenly England's wartime peril, Cox thought, and looked forward to rejoining his friends in their hour of need.

"I don't believe the war will be over for eight years," Cutting said, which rattled Cox. Cutting being nearly an Englishman, he might know something.

"Three years," Cox countered, then leaned his head out the window for some fresh air and privacy. He preferred to relive the last couple of hours in Boston at the Ritz Bar with Kit. She'd been late, and he'd thought he might explode with impatience as train time approached unrelentingly. But her brown eyes peering up at him beneath soft, brown bangs soon revived the usual sweet bliss of their companionship, and a couple of champagne cocktails in the mirrored comfort of every Harvard club man's favorite watering place had turned them, strangely, carefree and serious, both at once. Even now, he felt pleasantly effervescent.

Cox let his mind wander back farther still to Kit's June visit to the family place in Windsor. She had fit in wonderfully. The dreadful topic of his rival, Willy Emmet, had come up, but his existence had seemed spectral against the vividness of their connection. They had walked through the hilly pine forest behind the house, a primeval spot that the family called Paradise, and it had seemed so. During poetry reading after supper Sunday night, she recited "The Barrel-Organ" by Alfred Noyes—"Go down to Kew in lilac-time (it isn't far from London!) / And you shall wander hand in hand with love in summer's wonderland." Now, testing his longing as Boston's unlovely rail right of way streamed past, he thought, "I don't really feel as if I had left her."[16]

The train rattled on for hours and hours along the eastern seaboard, through the North Shore towns where Cox had spent so much time socializing during the last two years, past Maine's rocky, ragged coast, into the Dominion of Canada. There, a friendly American in Canadian uniform asked them, "Are you Yanks?" and, well, yes, they supposed they were. Cox liked the word's romantic ring, but it also signaled a change of status. They had crossed the border from their own country, contentiously at peace, into the war-torn British Empire—still, here, quite peaceably at war.

The long, narrow harbor at Halifax, among Canada's busiest ice-free ports, was a vital staging ground for one of the most crucial, and the longest-running, of World War II battles—the six-year struggle to "organize, protect, and manage the movement of war materials and shipping" that Winston Churchill dubbed the Battle of the Atlantic.[17] In peacetime, the British had imported an estimated total of fifty to sixty million tons of material per year[18]—about 50 percent of their food and almost all raw materials.[19] With the islands of Great Britain now isolated by the Axis— Hitler's surprise invasion of the Soviet Union on June 22 had gained the British a new ally and relief from the Blitz, but no significant immediate aid—maintaining uninterrupted sea passage for supplies and war material was as crucial a challenge in its way as RAF resistance of Luftwaffe attacks had been in the Battle of Britain the summer before.

Halifax was the chief assembly port for the convoys—orderly groups of merchant vessels escorted by warships—that were the method of choice for maintaining the beleaguered British islands' lifeline. Since the war began in September 1939, 138 such flotillas had left Halifax—about seven per month, on average, though the number and tonnage of the ships varied over time. Lately, a group of forty to sixty ships had been leaving Halifax every five or six days. It was an immense organizational challenge in harbor and an unprecedented feat of seamanship—keeping dozens of ships of widely varied size and class and category,[20] each with its own peculiarities of speed and steerage, age and function, of hull shape and maintenance needs, steaming steadily forward in formation for two weeks, through five time zones, in all weather, and across some twenty-five hundred miles of the heaving, capricious North Atlantic.[21] A ship that could not hold its station, correcting speed and course constantly to maintain its place in column—one thousand yards from the ships to left and right, five hundred yards from those fore and aft[22]—was likely to be left behind to take her chances alone against the U-boats and the Luftwaffe.

It was dangerous business indeed. Nearly as soon as war was declared, the Nazi U-boat had signaled its ability to pick off ships even when they traveled in convoy. A U-boat carried twelve or fourteen torpedoes, each capable of traveling three miles in just under two minutes.[23] The "wolf-pack" tactics devised by Admiral Karl Dönitz, commander of the U-boat fleet, and introduced in September 1940, made them even more lethally effective.[24] Between October 16 and 20, 1940, one U-boat wolf-pack attack had sunk thirty-two ships in a single convoy, with no German losses. Between September 1939 and July 1941, Nazi U-boats sank 848 British, Allied, and neutral merchantmen, totaling 4,058,909 tons, at the cost of just forty-three of their number.[25] In March 1941 convoys en route to British ports were losing about 10 percent of their ships.[26] Air attacks and mines compounded the danger just as the merchant ships at last approached land. June 1941 had seen the second-highest monthly total of sinkings of the war, sixty-eight. (Sixty-nine had been sunk in February.[27]) The Nazi assault on the sea trade was working. Total imports to Britain fell from fifty-five million tons in 1939 to thirty million tons in 1941.[28] The advent of summer weather meant smoother sailing for the convoy ships on the North Atlantic, but also easier hunting for the wolf packs.[29]

The Yanks' convoy, when it formed up in Halifax, comprised sixty merchant ships of the Allied nations: forty-two British, nine Norwegian, five Dutch, two Belgian, and one each from Sweden and Greece.[30] In the tankers were tens of thousands of gallons of oil and gas of various kinds, and one, the 8,882-ton *Athelprincess,* was filled with molasses. The freighters carried raw industrial and agricultural materials—benzene, pig iron, scrap iron, iron ore, steel, lumber, phosphates—or foodstuffs: flour, rice, wheat, and beans, as well as three shiploads of sugar. The ships ranged in size from the 2,588-ton phosphate carrier *Prinses Maria-Pia,* a Belgian freighter, to the massive British *Largs Bay,* a 14,182-ton freighter that in addition to a refrigerated general cargo carried 473 tons of mail and 513 passengers. The vessels ranged in age from the newest, the British *Empire Foam,* built in 1941 and carrying 7,047 tons of grain, to the British *Empire Redshank,* built in 1919 and carrying 6,615 tons of scrap iron and steel.[31] One among them, the big, new British oil tanker *San Demetrio,* already had endured the sort of near-death experience that engendered heroic seafaring survival stories in the newspapers and newsreels. In early November 1940, as part of another convoy out of Halifax, she had taken fire from the huge Nazi battle cruiser *Admiral Scheer* and been abandoned, in flames. Two days later, one life boat of survivors rediscovered the hulk, reclaimed her from fire and water, and, after a week at sea guided by little more than instinct and guts, made landfall at Ireland.[32] Seven months later, *San Demetrio* was back in service, part of a life-or-death effort from which no available ship could be spared.

The factotum who met the five Americans when they arrived in Halifax late Friday night brought disappointing news. Their ship wouldn't sail until Monday at the soonest. The next day when the Yanks sought him out, the news was the same: no news. They settled restlessly into their rooms at the Carlton hotel, a stolid brick building dating to the 1750s that stood a few blocks from the waterfront. Cutting's nervous impatience seemed ever more understandable.[33] As they waited, Cox took stock of his new companions, noting in his journal, "All good company. Inquiring minds, good senses of humor. Bolté leader of conversation."[34]

Under cool, cloudy skies, the streets of the orderly old Canadian seaport were busy with soldiers in the uniforms of many nations. The Americans bought the local newspapers and remarked on their slant. "The Canadian papers talk about the eventual victory, different from American papers which talk about 'if Hitler wins,'"[35] Cox noted. After lunch, he found some funny postcards bearing a caricature of Winston Churchill, plump and pink cheeked, a cigar clamped between upturned lips, but his face scowling. Written across his shirtfront beneath his bow tie was the message, "Keep Smiling." Rob sent one off as a birthday card to his youngest brother, Rowland, addressing him, in one of their running jokes, "Dear Ronald." "Look at the funny man on the other side," he wrote. "He's quite a fellow."

They went to the movies. They climbed Citadel Hill behind their hotel to see the spectacular view of harbor and countryside and visit Fort George, which since the eighteenth century had protected the British colony from first the French and later the Americans. They appreciated the irony. They bought some bootlegged whiskey and drank it. After dinner and more walking, they headed back to the hotel. Talk moved from their shared, growing impatience—"Why did we have to come so soon if we can't sail?" they griped—to the girls they'd left behind. Bolté's seriousness about Mary impressed Cox: "actually as real and probably as real in hopes as with me," he recorded. He showed the others Kit's picture, "mostly because we must be good friends and close to each other, more because I am proud of her until things change anyway . . . Please God don't let her change." Talk led to poker, poker to midnight, and so to bed. Cox had learned his first lesson as a soldier. "I want action as much as anything," he wrote, "but I guess 90 percent of war is waiting."[36]

The next day brought more of the same. Sleep until noon, drink beginning at four. Diversion arrived in the form of a kilted and drunken Canadian soldier who bemoaned his own lack of action, because Canada was sending so few men overseas. He "considered Roosevelt as does all Canada the hope of the world," Cox noted.[37] That evening a call came: embarkation likely tomorrow. "Hope so," Cox told his diary. "Waiting is rather hell. I want action and knowledge."[38]

Monday, July 14, brought the Yanks' first encounter with the British officer class. The admiral of a British naval ship in harbor had a brother who was an officer of the 60th Rifles. Eager to meet the new recruits, he invited them aboard. Their reception, while polite in the extreme, was also somewhat troublesome. Cox couldn't stop himself from thinking about the British author P. G. Wodehouse, whose novels about the British valet Jeeves lampooned, if sympathetically, the feckless lives of Britain's perpetually boyish, incomparably comic upper class, their peculiar slang and their many mysterious assumptions. This made Cox feel ungenerous. The conversation, while genial, kept veering onto topics with little meaning for the Yanks—jokes about the naval tailor protecting his bills from being bombed and about some sort of uniform, perhaps a "mess jacket," which wouldn't cover the oldish officers where they needed it most, "i.e., across la derriere."[39]

That evening, the Americans at last boarded their own ship, the 3,489-ton *Sicilian Prince,* a nineteen-year-old British vessel formerly a part of the Prince Line's Mediterranean service and, at 364 feet long, the second-smallest in the convoy. It felt good to have accomplished the next step of their journey, even if they plainly wouldn't sail for some time more.[40] After supper the five new friends pulled chairs on deck, propped their feet on the rail, and sat smoking cigars, lazily observing the harbor and throwing out the occasional joke about convoy sinkings to keep up their spirits.

It was very peaceful. Night fell. The lights of the ship winked on. Overhead, searchlights played. When a plane buzzed into view, the searchlights converged in a geometrical pattern that followed the plane across the sky. After that, the Yanks went inside to play craps.

On Wednesday, July 16, the convoy at last got under way. All that morning, *Sicilian Prince* had buzzed with anticipation as other vessels waiting in harbor moved out one by one toward the sea. The Yanks played bridge for most of the day. At about nine p.m., Cox's fears about his history of motion sickness were realized and he lost his supper.

The next morning, with the other passengers, they made the acquaintance of the ship's machine guns, which would be important in case of aerial attack. "Jesus Christ!" said René, the small, childlike Frenchman who was traveling from Syria all the way around the world to join the Free French in England. With the Mediterranean all but shut down by German U-boats, there was no other way to travel, and with all the conquered governments of Europe now surviving only in exile, London had become the capital of Norway, Denmark, Belgium, the Netherlands, Poland, Czechoslovakia, and Greece, as well as headquarters for de Gaulle's Free French. As the Yanks concentrated on their first lessons in weaponry, the sailors argued and insulted one another in the background. "Quite colorful," Cox noted. Jimmy McRae, the naval gunner, was a blond tough, an unpolished gentleman.

In the afternoon came lifeboat drills: assembly points, loading regimens, lowering maneuvers. One of the crew wore a derby hat with a faded paper rose in the band, or perhaps it was a poppy.

"Son of a gun. Oh, boy," René said—two more of his pet English phrases. To the Yanks, he appeared at once admirable and pathetic.

A Lithuanian sailor with a broad, flat face and a genial grin—though sixty-one, he was still the strongest man on board—reassured them, "Don't get your wind up worrying about submarines."

They would be at sea, they were told, for seventeen days. For diversion, there was the ship's crew, the ocean, and the cards and the dice. There were smokes, tea, and sometimes books: Galsworthy's *Forsyte Saga* made the rounds, along with detective novels. Gaming went on day and night: Russian bank, bridge, poker, craps. Cox had to discipline himself not to fall into debt. Senior year at Harvard, when at last he'd been admitted into the entitled, carefree atmosphere of the A.D., his father's club, he'd gotten carried away, and it had shamed him mightily to ask his mother for unbudgeted funds to pay his debts.

Sometimes the other passengers joined in. Gordon Pope was also American, an unattractive blond with pale blue eyes and a seedy mustache, the sort who said that things "were really very comical." There was the Frenchman, René, whom they liked; an inscrutable nineteen-year-old Scotsman named John; and Dave Bryson, a "very intelligent, quite interesting Englishman" in Cox's view, "but a little tiring."

When Cox thought about it, seventeen days seemed a long time to be on a boat.[41] He noticed that Cutting whistled too much.

Thoughts of Kit recurred and recurred again. "Please, God," Cox told his diary, "may I forget Kitten until this is over and then have us both just as we were before I left. That is impossible. Since it is, I hope we stay the same."[42]

Fog had closed in when they pulled out of Halifax harbor. Only now and then, when it lifted, did another ship come into view, until the fog, settling down again like a great velvety curtain, once more enclosed them. Foghorns lowed, loud nearby, softer at a distance. They felt the ship roll. Brister said, "Suppose the crew and all the other ships in the convoy were ghosts."[43]

The second night out, they heard shouting. A searchlight crazily cut the gray mist as the first mate, a man like a big, shaggy dog, shouted into his radio, "This is ninety-one," identifying their position in the convoy.[44] The searchlight shone from a ship that had lost position. Afterward, in the hazy blackness, they could see the red tip of the first mate's cigarette on the bridge. Later, stars emerged above them, but all around still was fog.

Brister combed his hair before settling into his bunk for the night. He said, "You never can tell who you'll meet in your dreams."[45]

Sometimes crew members wandered into the card room. The chief engineer, a thin, ungainly man, lingered in the doorway and surveyed them like a vulture. "You could have made it if you shinned the diamond," he gloated to the man who had failed to play trump and gone down one. The chief steward, a man confident in his modernity, played twenty-one with an attitude: "I know this game; I know gambling; I'll stand on sixteen because I know you'll go broke."

The Yanks talked frequently among themselves about the many flaws of Gordon Pope. He was going to England with an unscrupulous plan: He would take a double salary, one from the government and one from his company. He was completely self-centered and fundamentally small. His face already was beginning to sag. His cheeks drooped. He was patronizing and pompous. "When Gordon says 'Ah' the way he says it, he might just as well be saying 'I see what you are trying to express, it does throw interesting new information on the subject. However, the crux of the situation is what I have stated before and although I do not wish to disparage your taking an interest in the problem, nevertheless,'" Cox wrote in his diary. His "ah" killed all desire to talk to him. And he was a poor sport at craps.

René, the little Frenchman, agreed. "I don't like him. I like the way you fellows play. You have 'scourage."

René rapidly became the Yanks' favorite person on board. His fervent malapropisms amused them. When he told the story of an encounter he had enjoyed at Coney Island, his habit of confusing pronouns, "he" for "she," made it a challenge to catch the gist. "'Scraps!" he exulted, rolling a seven. "Jesus Christ!" "Some of a bitch!" And every noun was a plural. Sometimes he bet one bucks.

Bolté was considering the problem of homesickness, and he would discuss it at length, pro and con.[46] Would it be better, if you could, to spend one day a week in the U.S., or would that just make you miss what you did miss even more? Cox found the notion undesirable.

Cutting, at last, had relaxed. After supper one night, the five "mates," as they now were known, played follow-the-leader all over the boat, for the exercise.

Dave Bryson, it emerged, was rude and offensive, a man who would borrow your last pair of pants, as Cox put it. But he could talk, and he had theories on music. By the windup Victrola in the dining room were records of popular songs, along with some odd Hungarian melodies. There was Gracie Fields, the music hall queen, singing the sad-cheerful, famous "Good-bye Song." There were others that blended longing and insouciance: "Beer Barrel Polka," "I Wonder Who's Kissing Her Now," "Missouri Waltz," "The Great Waltz," "I Found a Million-Dollar Baby," "She Had to Go and Lose It at the Astor," "Smoke Gets in Your Eyes," "When You've Got a Little Springtime in Your Heart."

"Good to hear a little music. Eases the tension," said the wireless operator. The first mate leaned on his hands on the red cloth of the dining room table and asked to hear "She Had to Go and Lose It at the Astor," then stood listening with a grin on his face.

The Yanks drank their tea and talked about buying suits and flying home on the Pan Am Clipper—afterward.

It was Dave's theory that war, by reducing everyone to the lowest common denominator, produced real folk music.

Three days out, on the morning of July 19, the weather cleared, and as the fog lifted, one by one the distant ships of the convoy became visible, sixty in all, spanning the horizon. The Yanks watched the other ships through binoculars as one might spy on one's neighbors: a sailor hung up his washing; a captain stood on the bridge. Now and then the heliographs flashed messages. A new group of ships was joining the convoy from Sydney harbor, Cape Breton. Through the glasses they appeared as wisps of smoke on the heaving, watery edge of the world, then grew bigger. They mooed to the convoy and the convoy ships mooed back. With the sun out, there was an almost holiday feeling, all the other ships in view.

That night, just before sunset, the light on the water shone very bright, dancing and dazzling like white gold. After dark, the phosphorescence below and stars above were brighter and more numerous than the Yanks had ever seen before.

When the fog returned, the mood on board darkened, too. Any argument or friction flared quickly, then abruptly was dropped, for peace. Or there was nothing to talk about. "What are you going to do today, Chief?" the

first mate asked the chief engineer over lunch. What could he say? More of
the same.

There were no napkins at lunch. The Yanks asked for some.

"You don't need napkins, for Christ's sake," Bryson snapped, his tone,
in his annoying and superior way, disgusted. "Use a handkerchief."

On the night of July 21, the ships of the convoy, moving along at eight
knots, altered course "twenty to starboard," twenty degrees to the east.
The order was communicated with horizontal red lights and four long
blasts from the commodore's ship, in the van. Within half an hour, in
dense fog, two collisions occurred, one of them between two British tankers filled with gasoline, *San Ambrosio* and the storied *San Demetrio,* but
they produced no significant damage.

On July 22, the fog lifted for good, though clouds remained. Sun,
breaking through now and then, turned the rough, whitecapped sea gray-
black and gold. It was very cold now. Cox guessed they must be near
Greenland.

He had a talk with Fred, the wireless operator, who had survived a
torpedoing, about how wet and cold it was in an open life boat and just
what they got to eat—three biscuits, one teaspoonful of condensed milk,
and half a cup of water per day. Fred had been returning to Halifax—
boats going home didn't get convoyed—and midway between Ireland and
Newfoundland the torpedo struck. It was nighttime, of course, and he
was wearing pajamas and an overcoat, but he gave the coat to the cabin
boy, who had been caught naked. In the lifeboat it was rough and very
cold, every able body rowing or bailing all the time for five days. At last,
a Norwegian vessel picked them up. One survivor, a man of fifty, pulled
himself up the ladder and over the ship's rail, then collapsed. Ten minutes
later, he was dead from exposure.

It was an unstated rule of the Yanks that no one left the gaming table
when he was ahead. If you were tired and beginning to long for your
bunk, this could be an annoyance. They worked hard, if unobtrusively, to

keep winnings even. Sometimes it was necessary to change stakes to correct an imbalance. Twice they rolled craps for $100 a game, so as to bring Durkee, the most ardent and focused gamesman, back into line. Still, there was joy in winning. When René won a big pot at poker, he bared his right forearm, pounded it with his left fist, and leaped up, exclaiming, "Free French, that's me! Oh, boy! Let's go!"

When you did get to bed and lay in your bunk and listened, even just for a minute, the hurried roar of the waves sounded like a powerhouse dam in the distance or maybe a mountain stream after a rain. Cox dreamed of black water tumbling downward through leafy tunnels of green. He woke with a cigarette taste stale in his mouth and went outside to let the cold mist wash the sleep from his face.

"Bless you, Kitten," he thought. "What are you doing now?"

When they entered the danger zone south of Iceland, vigilance intensified, and tension on board thickened. The captain, vice commodore of the convoy, was a Scotsman with a broad red face, blue eyes, and a pointed chin. In his stateroom he kept a photo of two shaggy white Sealyham terriers—a family man, the Yanks felt certain. He inspired trust. Smile lines appeared to have been carved into his face almost to dimples by confidence, because he knew his business.

But the sailors disliked both the captain and the first mate, because they worked them too hard. Once the captain had ordered them below to clean out the hold in the middle of the danger zone, sending them down into the ship's bowels just when anything might happen. The first mate couldn't even operate a derrick.

Once when Cox went down to the pantry for hot water, he overheard John Sparks, the assistant steward, sending the cabin boy to the galley. The cabin boy was young and baby faced, with a thin mustache that merely advertised his desire to look older. "And don't be hanging around for as bloody long as you usually are. Up and down quick now," Sparks barked. He, too, was young, but cultivated and, ordinarily, quiet. He had plans to be an architect before the war started and still hoped to be, afterward. He seemed completely out of place.

They had emergency drill and machine gun drill—"the tracer bullets look like the stars you see when you knock your head," Cox noted—and the Yanks began standing watches, keeping the lookout for Luftwaffe or U-boats.[47] Cox watched the sky and the water. "The sea is many colored and many shaped," he wrote. "It is white, silver, grey gold, ruddy, blue, purple and black. I like it best when it is grey wrinkled and looks like a fruit skin swelling slowly."[48] He spotted a life raft lost from a sunken ship. Three biscuits, one teaspoonful of condensed milk, and half a cup of water a day, he remembered.

One night when they went on deck after supper, there was a rainbow. The northern sky was blue with big dirty clouds, but in the southeast it was dark, and first there was the column of the rainbow almost straight ahead, very bright; then it began to grow, and in time the whole arch painted the sky, one end in the water between *Sicilian Prince* and her neighbor, about half a mile away. "Wouldn't it be fun," Brister said, "to climb up one side and slide down the other—on your belly?"

Thoughts ran forward as Britain grew nearer, and thoughts ran backward. The Yanks hungered for news. Had Hitler's Russian campaign succeeded? What about DiMaggio's hitting streak? When they left New York, the Yankee Clipper had earned a base hit in every game since May 15. They discovered that DiMaggio's importance had increased right in step with their distance from home.[49]

A sailor on board, an Irishman, was seen wearing ice skates. Cox understood: He carried them with him because he liked to skate better than anything, and sometimes when he was thinking of home he put them on to get their tight-laced feeling around firm ankles.

One day at cards, René was dealing. "Look, boy," he said. "When we get to England, yes, when we get to England an' are all in different—how you say eet—in different serrveece—sometimes you think of René and remember heem, yes?"

One night a loud, low boom roared up from the rear of the convoy and *Sicilian Prince* shuddered deeply. Seven times. Seven depth charges loosed. They couldn't know why: a U-boat sighting, a sonar blip, a tip over ship's radio, simple fear? The destroyers ahead of them hurried toward the rear, carving a green wake frothed with white as they curved across the *Prince*'s bow.

Then, after fourteen days at sea, it emerged from the horizon like a long-neglected desire. Land! The low silhouette of the Scottish Hebrides had power enough to change the atmosphere entirely. The third mate began playing his Victrola nonstop. Everyone breathed easier.

The next day, they listened to the radio for the first time since boarding. All along the broad Eastern Front from Baltic to Black Sea, the Nazi war machine continued to advance into Soviet territory. Casualty numbers on both sides were already into the hundreds of thousands, but Stalin held out. DiMaggio went unmentioned.

Cox had a chat with the assistant steward that revealed a new facet of the myriad agonies the Blitz had engendered. On one recent journey from Halifax the *Prince* had reached Liverpool successfully, only to be held up there for ten days before continuing on to Manchester, the final destination. No one could go ashore. It was the time of the worst bombings, and all the crew were worried sick about their families. They knew letters awaited them, but no one in Manchester ever thought to send them down. On board it had grown so tense that no one spoke.

The assistant steward had other complaints, as well: He got only six days off a year, less than anyone else aboard. But the thought of mail so long and needlessly denied struck home with Cox. All letters were handled carelessly anyway, he was told. Sometimes they sat pigeonholed in the post office for months.

"The islands are green, tan, gray," Cox wrote in his journal. "You have a definite sense of steaming down a channel home, with the long line of the convoy strung out behind you and the sea blue-green, [a] destroyer in front or cutting up along the starboard rail. It's a proud sight with the Irish coast on the right and clouds hanging low over its low silhouette."

As the convoy steamed south, ships peeled off for destinations in Ireland or Scotland or Wales. Others headed for London or Avonmouth or Hull. After lunch on August 1, *Sicilian Prince* nudged into the oily waters of Liverpool Harbor. England's largest west coast seaport had taken a pounding by the Luftwaffe, and here and there twisted superstructures of sunken ships broke the surface. Ashore, many buildings were gutted. The Americans watched soberly with their Free French comrade as the broken city edged by, their first look at war damage. Uncowed, René encouraged them. "We must now take triple courage to beat the son of a beach."

After a brief wait at anchor, *Sicilian Prince* took its place in the line of ships moving through the Manchester Ship Canal. Here it was quiet. Flowers of gold and pink, small willows, and green fields lined the banks under a soft, pale sky. On board whiskey was passed around in celebration. When the *Prince* had tied up for the night at Runcorn, the Yanks raced ashore to find a pub before closing time. The beer was strangely thin and bitter, but most welcome. They identified a human type previously unknown to them—"the international drunk." Too much liquor made people everywhere, it seemed, act much the same, just in different accents.

Next morning, as the ship plowed on to Manchester, only occasional machine gun emplacements sandbagged along the banks hinted at war.

Awaiting the Yanks when they disembarked was a tall, thin-faced man in a green uniform. Lieutenant Ritchie welcomed them graciously and inquired about their journey. He had come up from the rifle barracks at Winchester and would accompany them back there next day. Meanwhile, they would visit a recruiting office to "regularize their status."

The question of how the American recruits would deal with the problem of national allegiance had never been formally addressed. In its determination to keep the United States out of war, the American government had enacted a series of regulations that, among other things, made it illegal to join a warring power's military service, travel on a belligerent ship, or use a U.S. passport to go to a foreign country to enlist. Anyone caught would be subject to a $10,000 fine, several years' imprisonment, and loss of their American citizenship.[50] But by March 1941, the U.S. government had announced it would not prosecute Americans who enlisted in British or Canadian forces, even though doing so remained illegal.[51] Prior to volunteering, the Yanks had received assurances that they would retain their American citizenship and, with it, the capability of transferring to the American military if and when American forces finally entered the fray. At the St. Regis on July 10, Rex Benson had warned them not to take the usual British oath of allegiance, since they then would lose their American citizenship.

Yet when Lieutenant Ritchie hurried them into the recruiting office and the officer there, Bible in hand, lined them up to pledge the oath of loyalty to the king, no one objected. Hazy in any case about exactly what was being asked of them, the five American volunteers were simply too intimidated to decline.

Back in the States, as Americans continued to debate their role in the growing global conflict, President Roosevelt pursued his policy of "all aid short of war." On August 12 a bill to renew the Selective Service Act squeaked through the House of Representatives by only a margin of one.

In Windsor, Vermont; Balboa Island, California; Ambler, Pennsylvania; Greenwich, Connecticut; and Far Hills, New Jersey, telegrams arrived for the Yanks' parents, origin Washington, D.C. "BOYS ARRIVED SAFE

ENGLAND" Rex Benson reported from the British embassy. Their boys had been lucky. Only later would they learn that they also had benefited from one of the great intelligence breakthroughs of the war. In the spring of 1941, British cryptographers had succeeded in breaking the Enigma code by which the German command communicated with its U-boats. Losses at sea fell for about nine months thereafter, until the Germans modified the code.[52]

Enjoying a leisurely summer in Windsor, Fanny Cox took immeasurable joy from a cablegram that arrived from England: "BEST OF HEALTH AND SPIRITS AND LOVE, ROB COX."

None of the parents was aware that the five young Americans who were now British soldiers also had become, for the moment at least, sworn lieges of His Majesty the king, George VI.

CHAPTER 3

Riflemen

Bushfield Camp, Winchester, England
August 4–November 20, 1941

> There is the confined space known over the world (at war)
> as the barrack room. Eighteen to twenty men usually live in
> one. Spend a large part of their leisure in one. There isn't much
> privacy, there isn't much room to think even, and hardly room
> to breathe. It can be the loneliest place or the liveliest.
>
> —Jack Brister[1]

In 1938 American actor Robert Taylor, the matinee idol with a dazzling widow's peak, starred in a bit of cinematic froth called *A Yank at Oxford* made by the British arm of Metro-Goldwyn-Mayer. With Maureen O'Sullivan and Vivien Leigh playing Taylor's English love interests, the plot turns on the rivalry that develops between glad-handing, slang-spouting American Lee Sheridan—who was before his Oxford scholarship the star athlete at Lakedale State College somewhere in the mythically friendly and unpretentious Midwest and is, in the words of the *New York Times*,[2] "as cerebral as a well-worn Indianclub"—and the class-bound British hypocrite Paul Beaumont and his gang of snobbish, effete, and duplicitous university chums. Most of the humor in the romantic comedy springs from culture clash, and the film remains a useful window onto the stereotypes through which Americans and Britons were apt to view one another in an age before global travel and television made foreign countries seem less alien, or at the very least diversified our misconceptions.

In addition to being boorish and dull, Lee Sheridan is cocky, loud, and clownish. More seriously still, he is rapaciously competitive—gloating in victory, ignorant of defeat—and intemperate, ready at the slightest provocation to "show those Beefeaters what's what," often as not with his fists. The Oxonians are, by contrast, pompous and judgmental, absentminded and maudlin—"Nothing of any real significance has happened since the fall of the Roman Empire," Sheridan's tutor says with a sigh—or, in the case of his white-haired "scout" (a student's personal porter-valet, much like the "batmen" assigned to British military officers), possessed of Dickensian stores of sentimental kindness and crafty wisdom. The film laughs at the Brits' funny accents and vocabulary, their overly formal clothing, undersized railway cars, and sniffy standoffishness, and finds them cowardly unless operating in a pack. The plot, baroque and simplistic at once, turns ultimately on the two sides' learning to appreciate each other's meaningful virtues. In the American, these are forthrightness, loyalty, honesty, and egalitarianism. But the Brits have a thing or two to teach Sheridan as well—about modesty and good sportsmanship in particular—and the central conflict is resolved not with a fistfight, but with a handshake.

The movie's conceit proved successful enough that Mickey Rooney soon was signed to star in a sequel, *A Yank at Eton*, but by the time shooting started, Great Britain's fortunes had vastly changed. As England suffered the ravages of the Blitz and confronted the possibility of a German invasion, the film had to be shot entirely in the United States (as was Laurel and Hardy's 1940 variation on the theme, *A Chump at Oxford*). The 1942 film once again, and doubtless more poignantly, emphasized the notion that despite differences of culture, custom, and language, Yanks and limeys common values that made them brothers under the skin.

The American volunteers in the King's Royal Rifle Corps were perhaps more knowledgeable than many about British history and culture by virtue of their educations and their travels—Cox and Durkee had been to England on summer trips organized by their high schools—but they were no less enthralled by the movies, and no less proud of democratic America's openness and individualism. They would have ample opportunity to test all these assumptions, as would the Britons they trained with beginning on August 4, 1941.

Lieutenant Ritchie, a former stockbroker now administering the KRRC training camp, seemed very civilized and unmilitary as he showed them to a comfortable Manchester hotel for the night. The next morning, he escorted them by train to London and took them to lunch at the Ritz. "Slightly chilly atmosphere," Cox noted in his diary. The hotel restaurant was all but deserted. The Yanks were seated "on little chairs at a little table instead of taking the Ritz Barish chairs in a corner," and the old-fashioneds seemed diminished without the usual orange slices and maraschino cherries.

At Waterloo station, the five compatriots boarded a train for Winchester, about sixty miles away. As the train chugged southwest out of the grim, damaged city, the countryside gradually opened around them: broad, sloping fields and orderly hedgerows, manor houses and gardens, little clustered villages of red and yellow brick, all looking neatly manicured and timeless. Eight months of brutal bombardment by the Luftwaffe had not diminished the full green flush of high summer in England.

The town of Winchester spread in picturesque array around the Norman tower of Winchester Cathedral on the Hampshire downs about fifteen miles north of Southampton and the English Channel. Like so many English places, it was, and remains, a palimpsest, revealing the effects of war and rebellion, fire and pestilence, the waxing and waning fortunes of church and state as they intertwined with the steady, necessary push to work and eat and love and raise children of the ordinary English all the way back to the days of Saxon king Alfred the Great, who fought off the Vikings and established the capital of Wessex there in 901 A.D. William, the Norman conqueror, made Winchester his seat in 1066, and the castle he built was home to the kings until 1302, when it was heavily damaged by fire. On a wall of the Great Hall that survives has hung for six centuries a huge, thick wooden disk known as King Arthur's Round Table, which shaped the belief that King Arthur himself once ruled there. In recent years, historians have come clean about the table's actual age; it was made in the thirteenth century, about seven hundred years after Arthur would have died, if he in fact ever lived. But the Yanks bought the story that they had arrived at the home of King Arthur and his knights of the round table. It tickled them to think that they would learn to be soldiers in the very place where the notion of fighting for king and country gained much of its heroic luster, the very homeland of the chivalric tradition.

Just south of the Great Hall and west of the cathedral, alongside the train tracks, stood the Rifle Depot, a gated complex of pilastered brick buildings designed in the gracious neoclassical style of Chrisopher Wren and ranged around an open parade ground not unlike the quads that Cox and Cutting knew at Harvard, though vastly larger. Since 1858 the depot had been home base and training ground for the King's Royal Rifles and its sister regiment, the Rifle Brigade. From here the regiment also known as the 60th Rifles had set out for Afghanistan, South Africa, Egypt, Sudan, India, Burma, and Palestine to help prevent the sun from setting on the British Empire.

The outbreak of World War II had so increased the number of recruits to the regiment that training now took place at a "hutted camp," a complex of shedlike wooden buildings, Nissen huts, shooting ranges, and playing fields set around a rectangular parade ground on a hilltop two miles south of Winchester. Here the five Americans clambered out of a truck from the depot and lugged their new gear—uniforms, gas masks, and countless other strange accoutrements—into their barrack, a long, plain building with dark wood siding, a peaked roof of corrugated metal, and three tall windows in each side. Indoors, eighteen narrow iron beds projected evenly from the walls, with blankets and pillows placed at alternating ends so that adjacent sleepers would align head to foot. Their commanding sergeant greeted them. Sergeant Fawcett was "a tough cockney from London's East End," in Jack Brister's words,[3] and a man they would soon come to admire.

The sergeant led them around the parade ground to the mess hall. Over a simple supper, he explained what lay ahead. As to schedules, the timing of their arrival put them somewhat betwixt and between. They were two weeks behind the last batch of recruits to arrive[4] and two weeks ahead of the next group of prospective officers. Consequently, they would spend a week or so as a squad unto themselves while the sergeant endeavored to teach them in one week what the other recruits were learning in three. Then they could join up with a regular squad. After five weeks, total, of recruit training, they would prepare to become lance corporals in the "cadre," the school for NCOs (noncommissioned officers). If all went well as lance corporals, they would be recommended for commissions and graduate to OCTU, the Officer Cadet Training Unit.

Settling into bed that night, windows blacked out by rectangles of plywood and scratchy blankets unmediated by sheets, the five Americans agreed that the road ahead was far longer than anyone had anticipated. They wouldn't see officer's "pips" before March at the soonest. "Christ, if I'd known it was seven months, I would have joined the Air Force."[5]

Eagerness to get on with things would gnaw at them continually, but the Yanks' impatience soon was overpowered by a wave of mental and physical exhaustion. While British military authorities did a great deal to enable the Americans to serve—bending procedures to allow them to join, then dedicating a single, well-seasoned instructor to bring them up to speed—they would not coddle them. Nothing so impressed the Yanks about their new life at Bushfield as the brute physical challenge that confronted them.

"From the liberal college to the Territorial Army! There is a jump!"

Jack Brister wrote in his first letter home. "Every emphasis is changed—drill, sameness, the greatest smartness is in uniformity—this is the way you make armies of mobs."

The ancient martial choreography of drill proved the most agonizing challenge. It required precision, physical self-control, and mental quickness, along with a tolerance of repetition for which nothing in their experience had prepared them. The regimental pace of 140 to 160 steps per minute was one of the "battle honours" that distinguished the King's Royal Rifle Corps from other regiments, which marched at 116 to 120 steps per minute. It translated into a rushed, unnatural thirty-inch gait. "I get knots in both thighs and hardly have time to lift my feet off the ground," Bolté wrote home.[6] Cox, whose long legs and arms now seemed to be a sort of curse, often found himself alone, marching ahead of the others; he concentrated on curbing his stride. "Cox looks funnier [than] any of us," Brister commented. "He's so big, so long, he can't move all of him forward with one movement; certain portions of him have to move before the others; he's a study in the syncopated jerks."[7]

Bolté described the scene one evening to his father. "This is the quiet hour, just after tea, but three of the boys are practicing . . . on the barrack floor, with a friendly corporal saying, 'By the quick march, hate, height, hate, height no NO you're all out of step!' We've been drilling two days, and our heads are full of 'quick march, left turn, hold your arms down, bend your wrists, Gor blimey you look like a — guardsman, get in step you bloody —' . . . Old Brister just jerks to a stop and nearly falls over backwards, with Durk roaring. So the corporal marches Durk into a stove. What a comedy."[8]

It was funny, but also discouraging. "I feel like a ten-year-old at a charity camp," Cox wrote home. "Sometimes I have my doubts if I'll ever make a good soldier. . . . I'm a stooge in a pair of overalls which are big enough for two. . . . Right now I feel less like a soldier than before I got me a uniform, but maybe that's because I have an idea of what you ought to learn now whereas before I had an idea that anyone would be a good soldier merely by enlisting. Maybe I'll come home with a cockney accent."[9]

And not only their feet needed disciplining. Rifle drill, too, involved complex manipulations. The Lee-Enfield rifle of the British infantry weighed about the same as a robust newborn (approximately 8.8 pounds) and measured nearly four feet long, with a fifteen-pound trigger pull and a protruding bolt that raised a nasty welt if you lost track of it and hit yourself during the process of presenting arms, for instance.

"The gun-handling itself is fast and tricky," Bolté reported. Here again, the routines often had historical import. The men of the 60th Rifles carried their rifles "at the trail," which meant parallel to the ground and pointing forward, the right hand grasping the weapon near the base of the barrel, the shoulder strap dangling in a neat arc below; never was the rifle to be carried in the more conventional slope arms position, rifle butt in hand and barrel resting on shoulder. Instead, the Riflemen used the march-at-ease, a battle honor won for storming the gates of Delhi, which was essentially just the reverse. It required the rifle to be raised from the trail to the left shoulder, where it rested with the butt on the shoulder and the muzzle pointing downward and forward. "We nearly knock each other's brains out," Bolté wrote.[10]

The Yanks learned to load, aim, and shoot the rifles, how to prepare for the Lee-Enfield's weighty recoil so as not to cut an eye (or miss the target) and how to clean them with the little can of oil and the pull-through cord stored in a compartment in the rifle butt. They learned how to load a Bren gun—the standard-issue light machine gun—in six seconds[11] and how to disassemble, then reassemble it. They learned how to do all this with their gas masks on. They learned how to do it blindfolded. They began to savor "the efficient, determined feeling when you fire the Bren gun."[12]

Then came bayonets, which for reasons dating to the first quarter of the nineteenth century the riflemen called swords. They affixed the seven-inch blade to the end of the Enfield's muzzle and used them in man-to-man combat against a sack of straw, bellowing at the top of their lungs as they skewered the target, then hammered it with the rifle butt. "Handling the guns and thinking in terms of enemy is rather clean sport,"

Brister wrote his father, "none of his blood and innards on you, none of yours on his, but from the bayonet drill we had yesterday I see how it can be very messy and personal."[13]

In his "Diary and Military Study Book," Brister recorded the detailed series of orders and responses used to make a soldier turn, halt, salute, come into line, salute at pay table—no action was too small to be assigned a command. In the margins he jotted down some of Sergeant Fawcett's running commentary: "On the word of command." "Everything smart." "You're fucking right." "Fuck their luck." "I 'eard a cunt singing down by the NAAFI—sounded like a cat pissing into a tin plate. I don't know fuck-all about sharps and flats."[14]

But Brister soon abandoned his academic approach. "It's no good writing down. You've got to have it come as natural as pissing—open flies, pull out cock, piss, close flies—all the small things in Drill, Rifle Drill, Rifle Handling."

The logic of the method, he decided, was marvelous. "They get you concentrating completely on the stuff by making you shout out and do it as you shout it. Sergeant Fawcett: 'Only a lunatic says one thing and then does something else while he says it.' Christ you can learn anything by concentrating this way on it—and in a short time too."[15]

Cox was less sanguine. After the first exhausting week he remembered in his record book the "Please God make me a soldier feeling when you think you'll never learn the drill." After a letter from Kit arrived, he added another prayer: "Please God make her wait."[16]

Slowly, they learned to adapt to routine—from laying out just so all the parts of their kit, boots to gas mask and steel helmet, on their smartly made beds for inspection each morning to lining up for roll call each night. They accepted the drudgery of polishing their boots to a high shine—spit and polish, it turned out, were literally the best method—of scrubbing web belts and anklets until they looked like new, of cleaning and recleaning the barrack room in a regimen quaintly termed "interior economy." They grew accustomed to the unfamiliar food, simple and starchy—boiled potatoes, meat pies, and puddings, no fresh milk or butter or coffee and the rare fresh green, one egg a week if they were lucky, with bacon and sausage that Durk described evocatively as being "like eating a bag of saw dust"[17]—to the absence of sheets and hot water and toilet paper, to the slimy feel of the dishes they washed in greasy warm water with lumps of food in it.[18] Or they had grown too tired to mind.

They learned to cultivate the available forms of relaxation—informal soccer games (football, to the British), trips after supper to the NAAFI (Navy, Army, and Air Force Institutes, which sold refreshments and personal supplies) or, when the days grew less arduous, into town for some food or a movie, parties with other recruits or the officers, and dinner invitations from well-to-do local families, which to the Yanks' amusement and, before long, gratitude usually included the offer of a bath as well. But the best relief of all, typically, was comic.

"Lots of laughs," Brister wrote his old friend Tom Littlefield on August 21. "Bolts and the rest of us hopping around in the gym during the P.T. (Physical Training) period. The funny paraphernalia, uniforms with gaiters that look like ski outfits, the way we flop behind our rifles when the sergeant says 'load.' The comical little clown-martinets they have for corporals to demonstrate all this stuff to us!"

But while training was as rough as for any recruit, the Yanks enjoyed some extraordinary perquisites. After all, they were celebrities, or at least curiosities, and their presence carried enormous symbolic weight. They were the Americans who had come at last to fight shoulder-to-shoulder with the British, even if their country itself still hung back. "About the camp we are those Americans," Brister wrote. "Everyone points us out and when they get a chance other recruits quiz us about America, the land of opportunity, the home of the brave and the free."[19]

The Yanks were lounging in the barrack after lunch on Saturday, August 9, the first week of training behind them now, arms stiff and sore from typhoid and tetanus shots, Achilles tendons aflame where the stiff boots cut their ankles, when a sergeant arrived and delivered an invitation military style, which is to say an order: "All right, be in your best suits by four thirty, wash behind your ears, and report to the detachment office. You're going to tea at the Deanery. Oh, yes—the American ambassador wants to see you."[20]

The young men were surprised and excited. Their friend Charles McLane had told them a lot about Gil Winant. After teaching history at St. Paul's, he had settled in Concord, New Hampshire, where he won election to the state legislature, then to three terms as governor. Although a Republican, Winant had embraced Roosevelt's sweeping program of governmental assistance during tough times, and the president had appointed him to head the three-man Social Security board following the program's enactment in August 1935. In 1939, he had become director of the International Labor Organization in Geneva, where McLane had worked one summer as tutor to the three Winant children.

Among the English, Ambassador Winant was loved and revered, and not just because he came as such a relief after his predecessor, Joseph Kennedy, returned to America in January 1941 predicting England's defeat and arguing against the Lend-Lease Act. Walking the London streets after a bombing raid or visiting other stricken cities, Winant emanated a kindly concern and a certain reassuring confidence that endeared him to all he met. A man of strong moral and spiritual convictions, he believed entirely in the rightness of the British cause, even as he hewed to FDR's public policy of pursuing "all aid short of war." He did all he could to counter stereotypes and build mutual understanding between Britons and Americans. In the last war, he too had volunteered, paying his own way to France to join the fledgling U.S. flying corps, and he admired the five young Ivy Leaguers who had placed their lives on the line with their convictions. "It takes great moral courage to join a foreign fighting force in another country, even though you believe in the cause for which that country is fighting," he later wrote.[21] He doubtless also felt at least somewhat responsible for them, since it was his collaboration with his friend Anthony Eden, the British foreign secretary and a former KRRC officer, that had facilitated the special arrangements allowing the Americans to serve.

Escorted by Lieutenant Ritchie, the young men arrived punctually at the Cathedral Deanery. They congratulated themselves: Army life had improved their habits. They crossed a peaceful, shady courtyard to a sturdy old stone house, the massive gray tower of the cathedral rising behind it, passed through a dark hallway and then out again onto a dazzling green lawn, in the distance a lawn-tennis court and coming toward them the ambassador himself, tall and a bit gawky, just as advertised, and clearly very glad to see them. The dean in his medieval black frock coat and gaiters looked archaic and fussy beside him. "Winant is as impressive as they make 'em," Bolté wrote home. "Shaggy, jutting eyebrows, black unruly hair, black suit, firm handshake, amazingly like Lincoln in looks, speech, and manner . . . terribly shy, terribly sincere, wonderfully interested in us."

When the Dartmouth men relayed to Winant personal messages from the McLanes, the ambassador became still more cordial and insisted that they visit him in London. In his hesitating way, he talked intensely and intimately, even sharing the painful family news of his daughter Connie's recent elopement to Brazil. There would be no tea—it was closely rationed, and the dean hadn't enough—and the encounter lasted only about ten minutes, but it left a deep impression on all the Yanks. As the dean led Winant away, the ambassador stopped, then returned. "Isn't there anything I can get for you in London?" he asked, seeming genuinely disappointed he couldn't be of more help. "A toothbrush or anything?"[22]

Cox left the Deanery, he wrote later, with "kind of a soulful feeling," remembering Connie's words to her father in the telegram that announced her elopement: "'Trust me. I love you.'"[23]

The next day, Sunday, brought another engagement for tea at the Deanery, this time with Sergeant Fawcett. For all his earthy brusqueness, the Americans had already become firm fans of their drillmaster and mentor. Among themselves they called him Mother Fawcett, because he looked after them so well.

"He is quite a man," Brister told his father, "very likable. He is the backbone. . . . The Empire is weak, but when men like the sergeant stand when they play God Save the King, she is by no means ready to fall."

After being bombed out of four different houses in London, Sergeant Fawcett, his wife, and his two little boys, aged four and two, had been given a home at the Deanery. Mrs. Fawcett was a shy, worn, motherly woman with a timid smile. As she and her husband showed the Americans around the dean's garden, their two little boys demonstrated their grasp of the drill on the lawn.

"A couple of suds really they are," Sergeant Fawcett said, though he regretted their penchant for swearing. When the dean first asked the two-year-old, "How are you?" the toddler had answered, "Fucking well."

"Blimey," said Fawcett, "he disgraces me, the little fucker. But I wouldn't bash 'im for swearing; he might get worse habits."

This time, the Yanks enjoyed an ample tea, which left them feeling vaguely embarrassed. "You can never tell if it was half the week's rations or not."[24]

The next weekend brought a first forty-eight-hour leave in London. It was raining, but on Friday afternoon the Yanks were marched, regardless, three miles to Winchester train station. When they reached the city, Bolté, Brister, and Durkee reconnoitered with Bolté's cousin Lieutenant Colonel Charles Lawrence Bolté, who was in England as head of a small group of American army observers.

Bolté described the meeting to his father: "L. and his fellow Colonels greeted us as if we were the seven lost tribes of Israel (which we felt like) and wined, dined, slept, and bathed us for two days and nights. They all had double rooms [at the Dorchester Hotel] so we moved in, one Rifleman to a Colonel; we had hot baths for the first time in several weeks; we dirtied up towels, had breakfast in our rooms, drank G. Washington instant coffee (the only good coffee we've had since we left), went to Simpson's for direly-rationed roast beef (but delicious), drank Scotch, slept late and between sheets, and especially enjoyed the good plain American talk, common sense, and the sight of Americans drinking in a smoky hotel room."[25]

Brister described the experience differently. "Ate too much at the Dorchester, the Piccadilly, Simpson's, Chung Lung Fung's, and all around. Drank too much too, but had enough sense to stop. The Colonels didn't. They swill it. Bolté in [the] lead as usual."[26]

As the Dartmouth boys regaled the American colonels with their new experiences, it dawned on them for the first time that they might have sacrificed their American citizenship. The oath they had taken in the Manchester recruiting office not only would prevent them from ever transferring to the American military. "We're now subjects of the King!" Brister, alarmed, recorded in his diary.

Colonel Bolté agreed to look into the matter. Chuck got back the attestation papers in Winchester and relayed them to his cousin. Colonel Bolté took them to the British War Office, which returned them to Manchester. When the papers arrived back at Winchester, the oath had been crossed out and across it in green ink was scrawled, "Oath not taken," along with the signature of the very officer who had pledged them on the Bible. Before long, the commanding officer at Winchester called the five Americans into his office and told them solemnly, if good-humoredly, "I'll have to ask you to behave like gentlemen, because you haven't promised to obey any orders from anyone."

At camp, in town, or in the city, the Yanks drank in an atmosphere of British invincibility. "As far as the world situation goes, all the sergeants told us that we'd be invading 'him' soon," Cox told his family after the first week at Bushfield. "I'm sure if you knew how these people felt . . . you would realize England couldn't lose. They all pray that 'Gerry' will invade so that they can make up for the way London has been treated. . . . They are proud enough to think that as long as America keeps sending the guns, they don't need more men, and they would rather have guns than men." Cox himself expected that both guns and men would be required, and everyone the Yanks met in town, once they'd recovered from the surprise of hearing American accents from the mouths of British soldiers, was thrilled they'd come.[27]

"The people in England are incredible," Bolté raved. "With barrage balloons over their heads and great piles of rubble around them, they grin and go to the pubs and curse Gerry with the conviction of people who know they'll win."[28]

In London, the citizenry's determination strengthened the Yanks' faith in the Allies' eventual triumph, but the young Americans were unprepared for the level of destruction they found there. "You must imagine downtown New York . . . to the Wall Street area just flattened," Bolté told his father, "bricks and rubble in great heaps, and the office-buildings on lower Broadway gutted out with fire. Then up through the 20's and 30's there are burnt-out blocks, and around Times Square a theater or two on every street caved in, and brownstone fronts gone in the 50's, showing pictures and mirrors still hanging on walls."

"Meanwhile everyone is cheerful," he went on. "Piccadilly Circus packed with people like Times Square Saturday night, officers and soldiers of France, Netherlands, Poland, Canada, all over (your arm drops off from saluting), theaters and movies running, concerts, and complete confidence." It had been more than a month since the last air raid. The Russians were holding out against the German onslaught. The RAF and, increasingly, American bombers were punishing the Germans at home with growing regularity. The British people were feeling optimistic, and so was Bolté. "I don't think they can be licked," he wrote.

Durkee, characteristically, had a more measured response to wartime London. "It was very strange to walk in a big city and not see the neon lights," he wrote his family. "After a while you are accustomed to it, and one is able to make his way about quite effectively. The only real danger is from cars; the headlights are very dim and their driving on the wrong side makes them doubly dangerous for us."

Meanwhile, Cox and Cutting enjoyed the luxuries of a hotel room, good food, drink, music, and seeing a play on their own. Yet despite these pleasures, or perhaps because of them, Cox suffered. "Terrific yearning," he recorded, "wondering if a woman would kill it. But missing Kit too much."[29]

The split between the Harvard and the Dartmouth men on their trip to London reflected their relations generally at that point and for some time to come. Cutting, who spoke with an English upper-class accent, had a mannered reserve the Dartmouth boys found off-putting. He still rankled at the memory of Durkee calling him "playboy of the Western World" on shipboard,[30] but he was not shy about preferring the refinements. Cox was comfortable with, though not proud of, the kind of "snob talk" he had encountered at St. Paul's and mastered at Harvard as he worked his way into the A.D. club, and he appreciated Cutting's steady supply of the minor luxuries, such as Band-Aids, chocolate, and soap. And, truth be told, Cox liked the finer things, too. One summer evening on an overnight hike in the Green Mountains of Vermont, he had surprised and amused his younger brother Max when, at suppertime, he pulled from his rucksack a pair of white flannel trousers. Even if it was cooked over a campfire, Rob would dress for dinner.

On Thursday, August 14, back at Bushfield, Cutting had invited Cox alone to a cocktail party "with a lot of captains and things," Cutting's old friends, followed by dinner "at Winchester's best hotel with a bottle of wine and a cigar and liqueurs," none of which could be easily or inexpensively had during wartime.

"It was most pleasant," Cox reported to his mother. "The situation amongst the five of us is fairly funny. Bolté, Brister, and Durkee (the Dartmouth boys) are very anti-social . . . and they don't really think much of Cutting because of his having been at Eton and because he is kind of aloof, has lots of friends in England, etc. I'm sort of referee, I guess, and vacillate between the two sides, which is quite good fun. None of this is at all real, just sort of an atmosphere. But looking over the officers we were drinking with last night, I think it is good to remember which fork to use and that you shouldn't drink port with your soup as Durkee did the other night. That, however, is in the distant future."[31]

That Cox may have overestimated his importance to the American quintet is suggested by Brister's comment to his father while describing their sergeant: "a swell guy. A natural gentleman. Rough and tough and dirty but a gentleman, far more so in many ways than the 'Cox' we brought over with us."[32]

Still, the five young men remained united by their common American identity. Regaled with hospitality, they found it to be the one thing they could offer in return. Enjoying dinners in the cathedral close with a family important in the English-Speaking Union, they nevertheless "made pigs of ourselves, [and] acted over-American to amuse them," Cox wrote.[33]

"Everyone continues to be wonderful to us," Brister reported to his father on September 8. "We in turn try to reply from our limited hospitality with tales of the [American] promised land."

They placed bets on how many straight games DiMaggio hit. Cox implored his mother in his second letter home please to get the answer from his brothers and not forget to send it. They started a basketball team, even though three of the Yanks had never played before, to show the Brits how it was done. "They've never seen basketball as it ought to be played," Bolté wrote home. "Our one-handed shots amaze them, our teamwork and speed, well, they just get fagged out watching us." Chuck took particular pride in the Yanks' licking of "the gym teachers" (PT instructors to the locals): "Guess who was Frank Merriwell? Bolté! For the first time a BB star, I tied the score in the last minute with a swish from the floor and sank the winning basket 30 seconds later."

By mid-September, in the small circle of troops around Bushfield, the Yanks were becoming fairly famous, or so Cox boasted. One night after returning from a party they entertained everyone in the barrack with "a genuine Indian war dance," improvised on the spot. It went over so well that they frequently were requested to repeat the performance.

One English soldier pointed out a habit they had never before been aware of. "Everyone thinks we're quite mad because we always insist that whatever we're doing is by far the best thing to be doing," Cox wrote home. "For instance, if we spend the evening sleeping or reading we build

it up in our conversation into the only way to spend an evening." At bayonet drill they counted themselves the best yellers in the army by far.[34]

Upon returning from London, with two weeks of drill and gun handling
under their belts, the Yanks were judged ready to join other trainees in a
regular squad. It gave a huge boost to their confidence.

"You didn't raise your son to be a soldier," Cox wrote home on August
15, "but I guess he'll gradually become one. Things are going better now."
They had covered in ten days what the others had learned in three and a
half weeks. They had reached the point where they caught on more
quickly, or so it seemed at the moment. They also had learned that everything went in ups and downs.

"Two weeks ago the food was lousy," Brister told his friend Tom Littlefield. "Now it's good—the same food, though."[35]

Their new instructor, Sergeant Holmes, was a tallish, well-set man
with a beaked face like a hawk, except when he relaxed in laughter, which
was often, and a boyish look entered his smile. "Knows himself perfectly,"
Cox thought.[36]

Holmes used a method of instruction entirely different from that of
kind Sergeant Fawcett, though they shared a common vernacular. "He
'cunts, and fucks, and dears, and dog's dinners' his boys into learning,"
wrote Brister. "He plays a game of teaching with no holds barred. He ca-
joles, threatens, beats, and laughs his boys into learning the stuff. Nothing sacred—he shreds them down—if the squad needs it. He instills
pride—squad pride in their drill, their shooting, their cleaning—It's
'fuck-all' or everything with him. The big thing is his natural humor—he
pulls laughs . . . out of every lesson—he is merciless this way. . . . The best
are those that develop between the master and the stooge—'dearie,' 'cun-
tie,' 'prick!' can all be the same man."[37]

One day, while Sergeant Holmes explained the workings of the Bren
gun, a spring flew from Rifleman Webster's breech block and disappeared
across the room. Sergeant Holmes made a horrified face and shouted at
Rifleman McNamara, "Tell Webster what he is."

"He's all right," McNamara answered sheepishly.

"He's not," corrected Holmes, turning to Webster. "I'll tell you what you are. You're a cunt, aren't you?"

"Only to some people," Webster joked.

"If you were in a trench and you let that spring fly into the mud and you didn't have another, what would you be?" Holmes challenged.

"I'd be fucked," Webster said. In his cockney accent, it sounded like "fooked."

"All right then, you're a cunt, see. If you're fucked, you're a cunt."[38]

The barrack, which the Yanks had had to themselves for the first two weeks, now was filled with English recruits, and the Americans began to take stock of their comrades. Brister found amusement watching "Duke," a tough car thief from London's East End who aspired to be dapper and important and a leader, pursue a friendship with Cutting. Their accents, looks, and backgrounds were entirely dissimilar, yet they enjoyed an affinity. All the Yanks liked Rifleman McNamara, who had played the stooge to the sergeant, finding him "sound, sincere, and helping handish."

Then there was "Chubber," whom everyone judged to be pathetic. He was older than the rest, in his thirties at least, and soft, the opposite of all they were striving for. "Anytime we're to do anything a bit strenuous (bayonet, drill, march)," Brister wrote, "the Sarge looks at old Chub. 'Fuck off, out of it,' he says."[39] When the squad went out for some "square bashing," practicing drill on the parade ground, Chubber followed behind, picking up any fallen caps and watching. Changing clothes for PT, the younger men kidded him and grabbed for his teats, while he tried to smile, defenseless, weak and fat like a baby. The assisting lance corporal, Hooper, liked to call him in for discipline and bully him. "There are some cruel things in the army," noted Cox. "Sort of sadistic."[40]

Before long, a new crop of officer candidates had moved into camp, too, apparently all fresh out of boarding school, younger than the Americans except Cutting by a few years, and considerably younger than many of the other recruits. They arrived with some experience of military organization and terminology, familiar with drill, and accustomed to shooting and caring for guns, not only through military training at school but also from years of hunting birds and game. These young gentlemen would be the Americans' fellow officers, and the Yanks observed them closely. "The OCTU boys came in the other day," Brister recorded. "Awfully young. It's interesting to watch them change—language, carriage, outlook."[41]

Brister, as an aspiring writer, found the novelty and variety of his new companions thrilling. "All the people in the world! All characters are possible. A writer may be granted some sort of license to create characters, but he'll never outdo nature," he wrote.[42] "One thing war brings out, your imagination can leap and jump about and yet not go the limit of all the absurd, dramatic, or comical situations people get themselves into. The papers are full of plot twists."[43]

After four weeks, Sergeant Holmes took aside the Yanks—he called them his "five lease and lend pennies," in reference to the Lend-Lease Act by which America was supplying material assistance to Britain—and read them part of his report to Captain Baring, their company commander. The Americans had "arrived late but worked hard to catch up to the rest of the squad, and have succeeded in passing many of the other men. The drill has been difficult for them, as they lack snap and tend to walk carelessly—perhaps an American habit? . . . [But] they have caught on quickly, worked well with the other members of the squad, and have very strong senses of humor.

"Good, huh?" he asked when he'd finished.[44] He would recommend them for promotion to lance corporal. In a week they each would be assigned to a squad of new recruits to help instruct them.

Recruit training climaxed in four lectures on poison gas: choking, nose, blister, and tear. For anyone even slightly acquainted with World War I, the subject held considerable interest. "Blister gas vapor: not felt at first—eyes go in 24 hours. Phosgene—lethal." Sergeant Holmes summarized, "A good lungful and your luck's fucked."[45] Everyone in Winchester had carried a gas mask since the start of the Blitz for fear that the Luftwaffe would drop poison gas from the sky. "This is a pretty serious affair,"

Bolté wrote home, "and you never go to sleep at these lectures. . . . We listen as if it were a matter of life and death."[46]

On Friday, September 5, the Yanks finished recruit training. In a final shooting competition with the other squads in their company, Brister, "who couldn't hit his hat a week ago," won a green hat for highest score at both rifle and combined rifle and Bren gun. It validated, in Bolté's view, Brister's belief that he could do anything he set his mind to.[47] He had a special kind of inertia, Brister did, slow to get going—at drill and Bren-gun time trials he was comically slow—but once in motion, irresistible. His shooting scores, Sergeant Holmes said, were the best he could recall for a recruit. Bolté, who finished behind both Brister and Cutting, was quietly furious. "The big shaft to Bolty is that I used his rifle," Brister gloated.[48]

They had finished recruit training in record time, and their squad won all the drill and shooting competitions. "The 'Yanks' are standing out," Brister wrote home proudly.[49] Sergeant Holmes said, "If it wasn't for the Yanks, we'd've got fuck-all."[50]

A constant in the days at Bushfield was a nagging concern about the mail, which was slow and unpredictable. A letter from home could take a month to arrive, or never come at all. Nearly every letter the Yanks wrote home included a discussion of how many letters had been received, how many mailed, and what news the earlier missives had covered. Sending letters to and from America was unusual for the Army Post Office, and they didn't always handle it successfully. When letters were delayed or failed to arrive, the young men grew anxious, even homesick. "I guess you really don't begin to appreciate friends and family and sweethearts and hometowns and colleges until you get away from them," Brister wrote to his father. "It's a damn good thing they have American movies over here—I saw some shots of the Rockies last night that almost melted me down to a sentimental blob of nothing. I think of you all, wish you good luck with all your saner ventures, and will greatly rejoice when I see you again."[51]

Because of the time lag, the Yanks' thoughts often ran in three temporal dimensions at once. There was their immediate experience, of course, but when a letter arrived from the States, it cast them back at least a month, while in writing, they imagined where the recipient would be six weeks forward. As the days began to grow shorter and cooler in England, Cox was vicariously enjoying high-summer softball games and picnics in Vermont. Even Bolté, habitually enthusiastic, grew rueful when reporting to his father his successful completion of recruit training and imagining the trees turning colors at home in New England, as they would be when his letter arrived. "Do have people write, and tell me things like what they eat and how the trees look. When this war's done, I'm coming home and live in America forever, eat chocolate and jam and honey, smoke Camels, read the new books and tell tall stories about the gay old days in the King's Royal Rifles."[52]

A happy man was one who had just received a letter from the States, unless it brought news of the sort that hit Cox in early September. Excited to find a letter from Kit, he ripped it open. Then the first line knocked the wind out of him: "Engaged or not, I can't help writing you." It was the only reference in an otherwise chatty, blithe letter to just about the worst occurrence Cox, at that point, could imagine. The girl he loved and longed for had agreed to marry someone else—Willy Emmet, he could only assume. A previous letter explaining the situation apparently had been written but had never arrived. Cox only could guess what exactly Kit's feelings were, why she'd made the decision, how she still felt about him. With the time lag, he thought, she might be married already, or her engagement might not yet be announced. "It's awfully hard to cope with all these things when you're two thousand miles away and don't even get all your mail," he told his mother when he wrote her the news.

Cox found it hard to be angry at Kit, or to blame her. As he wrote home, "She and Willy Emmet have been a big combination for a couple of years and were half engaged before the boat races, and even if that weren't so, I wouldn't wish anyone the job of sitting pining on the ocean's edge, because I found it rather hell myself."

What ate at Cox was the question of whether or not Kit would have chosen to marry Emmet if he himself had not left for England. It was a responsibility, and a loss, he was not prepared to handle. "I hope and pray she would have," he wrote, and yet he couldn't help doubting it. He couldn't accept that Kit had been lying to him; that flew in the face of everything he felt and believed. There had been something awfully big in the air the week or so before he'd left, and the last letter he'd received gave no hint that her feelings were changing. Cox was thrown into a black depression, and he hated it. His feelings for Kit hadn't changed. He confided in Cutting, knowing him to be discreet as a wall, and against all reason, in a few days, began to feel more positive. He simply enjoyed again a general sense that things would work out. "Maybe it's my saving feeling," he told his journal, "as if the first depression had lasted, I don't think I could go on."[53]

"It's certainly pretty complicated for any life and much too complicated for my present one," he wrote his mother, "so I am trying to forget about the whole thing. She is rather wonderful though. One good thing is that I have one less reason to want the war to come to a speedy end now. So much for that."[54]

To mark the completion of recruit training, the whole of Bushfield Camp joined in a ceremonial parade. The riflemen called it "the fainting parade," because some among them inevitably passed out from strain and heat. It infuriated Brister, who recorded the event succinctly: "The company commandant's brass, nerve, and rudeness in keeping nearly one thousand men waiting on their feet in [the] sun. His final arrival. The inspection. The fainting. In one parade five passed out like lights. After that parade, Captain Baring said to his company, after complimenting them on their marching, 'I wish to remind you that there will be more trying ordeals in this war from which you will be unable to fall out.'" Brister took a measure of satisfaction from the colonel commandant's evident discomfiture when he acknowledged Jack's achievement in rifle shot. Never one to obsess over the details of his appearance, Jack had prepared for parade even more haphazardly than usual. "I went on it never so ill dressed," he recorded, "funny-looking pants, gaiters backwards, safety-catch off, everything." While complimenting Brister, Jack wrote, the colonel "visibly shook."[55]

The Yanks said good-bye to the men of their squad who now would move on to training battalions from which soldiers were drafted to the front. On September 9 they began NCO cadre, where, as Brister explained to his father, "they teach how to attain that commanding voice and attitude, they teach how to teach everything we've learned to date."[56] Now it was their turn to shout at the recruits, "Swing your bloody arms," "Put some smartness into it," "Wake up your ideas," and other encouragements they'd picked up along the way.[57]

After nearly two months total of training, on September 26 the Yanks received their lance corporal stripes. As the lowest-ranking noncommissioned officers, they would supervise their barrack and assist with instructing the recruits. Two days later Cox wrote home: "Well, I have taken the first step up in my climb towards Commander-in-Chief of the British Expeditionary Force. I've discarded my overalls and wear a green sidecap and carry a little black stick with a silver knob on the end, which is much more fun than swinging a rifle around on drill."

"Now we get a small taste of the other end of the stick," said Brister.[58] The new role agreed with them. "I am more alive in front of a squad than shuffling in its ranks," Bolté wrote. "While on drill I run about checking, shouting the time, and being obnoxious. The squad is half OCTU, nice boys who grin amiably, and half cockney, good guys who grin toothlessly. They all address me with marked respect, a phenomenon to which I am not yet accustomed, and call me 'corporal.' Well, Napoleon and Hitler were corporals. I go into the dining hall without standing in line, [but still] have to serve out food."[59]

Pay rose a bit—a quid each instead of fifteen bob. A week of living within pay meant not smoking or drinking, writing only two letters because of postage costs, and getting several invitations out to dinner.[60]

Perhaps more precious was a new portion of free time, when the squads were at PT or lectures. Bolté dived into the letters of T. E. Lawrence, the British archaeologist-adventurer who fought with the Arabs during World War I to gain them independence from the Turks. Chuck's days gained yet another dimension—one his own life, the other Lawrence's. "Mine pleasant and monotonous," Bolté reported, "his suffering and deranged."

The American lance corporals lived in a larger barrack now with twenty-three lively others, toughs to toffs. It would be a happy phase for the Yanks. "In the barrack room, it is pleasant gags, constant funny complaining and cursing at the sergeants," Cox wrote. "Singing, [and] one poor joke after another. A certain amount of real filth. But mostly laughs."[61]

The weather was pleasant and sunny during the days; mail was beginning to arrive more regularly, and food parcels, too, which were shared around the barrack. "We're in the rhythm. We qualify as old soldiers, are sought out for advice, and feel confident," Bolté wrote home.[62]

Reveille at six thirty had become routine, "healthy and a habit now," Jack wrote.[63] They awoke each morning at the bottom of a sea of fog. It dampened their clothes, utensils, weapons—"but our spirits, never," Jack said. Lights-out came at ten fifteen. As the men settled into their beds, a few planes might mumble by overhead, but if the warning siren didn't sound, they knew the planes to be RAF and found the sound almost comforting. Even when the siren sounded, it was usually ignored. The recruits would ask, "Who's blackout tonight?" meaning, Who is supposed to turn out the lights at the main switch and take down the blackout boards? Lights-out!

As the blackouts came down, the moon streamed into the barrack room. Four kittens born recently under Bolté's bed squeaked a little, and twenty-eight men settled down for the night. It wasn't really home, but it was homelike.

In their free time, the Yanks learned to play "rugger," the "English idea of football," as Brister saw it,[64] in which you passed the ball only backward on your way to the goal, and Jack began boxing lessons "from a very capable instructor (if his merit is in any way indicated by the cuts on my face)," a fellow officer candidate named Tony Van Bergen, affectionately known as "Van Bollocks." Brister hoped to return home able to stand up to his eldest brother, Bill, and he considered it useful preparation for the battlefield: "Like thinking when shells are bursting all around you."[65] He appreciated Van Bergen's willingness to teach him patiently when he could easily have beaten Jack to a pulp. "The modesty his boxing prowess has given him is typical of that English reserve which holds itself aloof and superior or, as in his case, plays the meek and mildly foolish scapegoat." But behind the mild-mannered exterior dwelled a calculating ruthlessness. "It's hard to get over the feeling you shouldn't hit a guy when he's on the way down," Jack reported, "but you must, that's what you're waiting for, that's your chance. Whenever the guard drops 'get im in!'"[66]

The lordly airs of the English public school boys sometimes irritated the Americans. "It's hard to get used to these boys who have been 'to the Manor born'—the ruling class and educated to it," Jack Brister told his father. "The American and the British (Democratic) ideologies are far apart. It's going to be our problem, somewhat, to find the vital differences and the means for reconciling them."[67]

Brister had been waiting more or less impatiently for a letter from his girl back home, whom he referred to by her last name, Turner. When it finally arrived on October 9, he was joyous. But by then, at a dance one night, another young woman had caught his eye. Maureen Robins was an Irish brunette born in India who worked at a nearby naval tracking station, HMS Flowerdown. She wore the neat white blouse and navy blue suit and tie of the Women's Royal Naval Service, WRNS; such women were called wrens. She was wren Robins.

That Maureen was a serious reader had felt to Jack like a relief. She liked good books, even poetry. She talked the kind of talk he liked. She too came from a big family, of eight, and she knew how to ski. There was an attraction.

"Pretty? Yes, I'd say so. Yes, quite." Jack considered the prospects in his diary. "A fine Irish brunette with character and strength in her face and body." He saw only one hitch. "She seems a bit of the party girl. She's been around. I don't know how much, how far, how often." But the attraction was definite. "We'll see, we'll see."[68]

On Monday, October 13, the five American British soldiers took another step up the ladder. In OCTU cadre, they went back to school. Two daily lectures would cover "interior economy," or how to organize a barrack; map reading and assessing terrain; tactics; message writing; ranging weapons; memorizing directions; observation; selecting lines of approach; reconnaissance. It was exciting finally to be learning about being soldiers, instead of training them, but the change brought some regret, especially to Cox, who had been in his element instructing recruits. He had worried, as was his habit, about how well it would go. All of his group were much older than he, over thirty-five, and one of them, a White Russian, had served in the czar's Imperial Guard at the age of twelve and had traveled the world. But Cox had stores of native sympathy and good humor to compensate for his youth. "I managed to get quite a few laughs and work out of my section," he wrote home. "I would especially get laughs when I said 'gather around, my children, and I'll give you a lecture on gas.'" He found a particular commonality with the Russian, Tchiechoff, on a long march one day when Cox was limping after a rugby injury. They stopped for a rest together.

"Ever have a mint julep?" Cox asked.

"Don't be evil and try and make me unhappy," the Russian answered. "Ah, yes, a mint julep in New Orleans." Then he continued, "But what I like best is an old-fashioned." For the rest of the rest, they were silent, mouths watering.

The weekend before they moved up to OCTU cadre, the five Yanks took leave together in London. Friday night their hotel, the Regent Palace on Piccadilly, was a madhouse, the lobby and bar crammed with Polish officers, Czech soldiers, fliers from all over, Dutch sailors, and more. It was "like the League of Nations," Durk told his family. He found it very strange to hear so many languages spoken at once. "Four months ago I would have hardly imagined myself with such surroundings,"[69] Durk wrote home.

When the Yanks encountered a group from the Eagle Squadron, the famous American unit of the Royal Air Force, "You would have thought it was old home week," Cox wrote, "and America the size of Switzerland, whereas actually, as one of them said, 'You could put England five times inside of my state (Texas) and still have room for cactus and some drinking space.'"[70] Durkee savored the rare treat of remembering California with a pilot from Hollywood. They met other Americans, too—some in Canadian uniforms, one who ferried bombers across the Atlantic, and a couple who had come over as radio operators. Afterward, a couple of English RAF boys, one of whom had spent two months in Connecticut, invited the five to go along to a bottle club; since everything public closed at eleven p.m., you had to know a member to keep drinking. Bolté assumed his normal place in the lead, and the jolly evening ended somewhat ignominiously when he "fountained," to use Brister's word, all over one of the friendly pilots.

It got better. On Saturday they telephoned Ambassador Winant, hopeful of seeing him but concerned about interrupting his work; a delegation had just returned from Russia. They were told he was anxious to see them and before long found themselves, hardly trusting their senses, settling into the comfortable leather couch and chairs across from the old-fashioned desk in his office. "The minute we walked in we were at ease," Durkee wrote home, "because he is so sincere and easy to talk to. He seemed very happy to see us and I am sure that he enjoyed being able to talk to someone who knew his old friends, it seemed to enable him to relax." It was intoxicating for the young men to hear, in addition to news of family and friends, the latest on the war situation from a man so near the very top. When Winant asked them, as they were preparing to leave, if they would lunch with him on Sunday, they were over the moon.

The next day they arrived for drinks at the ambassador's apartment. He served them sherry and a wonderful cigar in the drawing room and presented them each with a carton of Lucky Strikes, apologizing, to their amazement, that he couldn't offer more. They looked over his library, which reflected his political interests, with a complete set of the works of Edmund Burke and an extensive collection on Abraham Lincoln. He showed them the gifts he had received on a recent trip to Scotland—a silver casket from the city of Edinburgh, roughly equivalent to an American "key to the city," and a handmade, limited-edition history of the university there—"one of the most beautiful books I've ever seen," Durk judged.[71]

They made quite a sight, they decided later: five young Americans in the uniforms of British lance corporals entering Claridge's—"about the best hotel in London," Durk explained to his parents—around the imposing, black-suited figure of one of the most important men in the world at that moment. "When we walked into the dining room, everyone looked up," Durkee remembered, "and you could hear the buzzing around the room."

Although shy by nature, Gil Winant possessed the gift of engaging a listener so that he or she felt, as they talked, like the most important, if not the only person on earth. For two hours, speaking sometimes so quietly that he was hard to hear, the ambassador held the young Americans spellbound. They enjoyed anecdotes about his experiences in World War I, learned how he got started in politics, and discussed the current world situation, along with his hopes and fears for the future, when, he asserted, young men like themselves would need to connect more with the people and get ahead through merit rather than by wealth and connections. They left feeling a bit dazed, but prepared to a man, on returning home, to work for his election as president. "He is a democrat in the best tradition of the word," Durkee raved. "His opinions follow no party line; he will hold fast to his opinions regardless of the consequences and best of all, in the tradition of Lincoln, his faith and strength are to be found in the common people."[72]

The visit emboldened Bolté, who rarely lacked boldness anyway, to ask the ambassador for a favor. Ever since he had left the States, his girl, Mary, had been hunting for a way to join him. Now she had identified some prospects, working for the British War Relief Society or other American organizations in England. What she needed was a passport and ocean passage, and Chuck hoped that Winant could help her obtain the former, at least.

His pitch to the ambassador was characteristically effusive. "She's very serious about coming here to see what it's all about, and to help wherever she can. She's a pretty mature twenty, and combines beauty, charm, honesty, and intelligence in an unusual degree."

Chuck asserted that romance had little to do with her desire to serve, though he confessed to his own bias. "I have a terrific desire to leave a root behind me when I go out East in the spring," he explained. "Hell, I'd even like to leave an heir. But I'd also like to feel I was leaving you, or someone, a very good worker, and this girl has it."[73]

While in London, the Yanks discovered an article about themselves in the *Times*. A couple of weeks earlier, the two KRRC colonel commandants, Sir Hereward Wake and Sir John Davidson, had taken them sightseeing in London. After visiting the House of Commons and Westminster Cathedral, they had tea at the *Times* with the publisher, Colonel Astor, and were fascinated to learn how the paper was published during air raids. Apparently, the article was one result. It proved to be the start of a disconcerting flurry of publicity. "The Ministry of Information has gone mad," Durkee wrote home.[74] Five journalists and photographers arrived at Bushfield to interview them and take pictures. Within days a photographer was documenting every aspect of their daily lives with the intention of producing a photo essay entitled "A Yank at OCTU."

The young Americans protested. "We don't want this type of thing and we thought we made it clear before we agreed to come," Durkee wrote his parents. "It is said that even the Prime Minister is much interested in us."[75]

Cox found the intrusion infuriating. Forced to leap trenches brandishing a bayonet and drill a squad to no actual purpose, he fought an urge to smash the cameras. "I didn't come over here to be a puppet show," he fumed. With Cutting acting as squad sergeant and himself as corporal, he imagined that the men they marched back and forth, forth and back must hate them. Afterward, he retreated to the barrack and sulked, sure that the whole arrangement that had brought them to England was unfair, that no one took them seriously or cared whether they did well or poorly, and that they had always been intended as symbols, and symbols only.[76]

The Yanks were again on display on Saturday, November 1, when Anthony Eden, the foreign secretary who won the Military Cross with the 60th Rifles in World War I, arrived with his friend Gil Winant to review the troops. The occasion was tremendous. The regimental band, resplendent in full dress uniforms for the first time since the war started, performed Sousa marches, "Stars and Stripes Forever," and "The Star-Spangled Banner," while the American ambassador took the salute during the march past.

"Mr. Winant and Mr. Eden put in a splendid appearance," Bolté reported, "while we stood straighter than we ever stood before."[77] As newsreel cameras whirred, the five American lance corporals instructed their squads in lesson eighteen: rifle. "The rapid fire is used only in case of emergency" was second nature now. The great men walked around trailed by reporters and photographers. The BBC recorded an interview with Durk and Bolté.

Over drinks afterward in the officers' mess, the Yanks met Anthony Eden, who seemed just as boyish and charming as Winant had described him. Sir John Davidson said he had good reports of them, which was gratifying, and told them that they would spend only four months at OCTU, instead of the usual five, and then go straight east to the North African battlefields, or for that matter wherever they wanted. Cox was mollified. At some level, he supposed, the arrangement was still somewhat unfair. Why just because they were Americans should they move through the system faster than anyone else? But the plan suited him; the point, after all, was to fight the Germans. "From now on they can take all the pictures they like," he thought, "as long as they stick to the present idea."[78]

The Yanks' work at Bushfield was essentially done. There would be a few more lectures after they returned from a ten-day leave, but they were beginning an interlude of relative ease and even glamour. Brister visited Cliveden, the great estate of Colonel Waldorf Astor and his American-born wife, Nancy Langhorne, purchased by William Waldorf Astor from the Duke of Westminster in 1893 as the New York hotelier remade himself into the richest of British peers. Cliveden had recently weathered a rough period when it was rumored to be a center for German sympathizers, but it remained renowned as a social gathering place for influential politicians and artists from Winston Churchill to Charlie Chaplin.[79]

Brister had launched a last-ditch campaign to advance his stagnating writing career. But if his diary is a true indication, what impressed him most about the visit to the vast and elegant country house was what he picked up about the war. "The Germans are moving through the Crimea . . . in the anticipation of a chance at the Caucasus—the heart of the Russian oil supply. There's great talk about a new kind of discipline in the enemy's army. A camaraderie, everyone saluting, men respecting no one, or no thing excepting their officers and their commands. Out of this comes a wanton lust for killing—just for practice."

The next day, Brister returned to London for dinner with David Astor, publisher of the *Observer*. At the Travelers Club he met E. M. Forster and Arthur Koestler. A meeting with the editor of the magazines *Picture Post* and *World Review* produced a request for a two-thousand-word article on recruit training at Winchester, to be followed up with a report on the OCTU.

Jack also met up with the wren Maureen. Any misgivings about the bookish Irishwoman had by now evaporated. "*Maureen* a bright—shining bright—angel of a dream that you never could really dream (it's so natural). She's a sensitive, kindly, pretty, lovely girl. Her perception rivals Turner's and rises above it in sheer enjoyment. She's keen on the world she finds herself in. She is a great lover—in the fine sense of the word. She's the Irish I like. She saves a soldier's day. 'A thing of beauty' ah, it makes a joy in your heart."[80]

When Jack emerged without assignments from a meeting at the offices of *Horizon* magazine, Maureen was there to meet him, and as they walked away, he felt thankful indeed for how she filled the emptiness.

Cox and Bolté traveled by ship and train to neutral Ireland, where food and drink were plentiful and the streets were lit up at night. Staying in previously unimaginable luxury at the country estate of Lady and Lord Dickie Adare in county Limerick, they "shot miscellaneous birds, rode one morning, went to the races, went to a dance, went on a snipe shoot, and relaxed."[81] An American by birth, Lady Adare had sent her three small children off to the States two years earlier. Arriving back at Bushfield, Cox was reminded poignantly and confusingly of the world he'd left behind there, his waiting mail filled with autumn invitations to alumni dinners after various games at school and college.

As November passed, the days in England grew short and cold. "To hear about the California sunshine breaks my heart," Durkee wrote home. "The [English] climate as I have mentioned before is very damp and when the wind blows, it penetrates to the bone." When reveille sounded each morning in pitch dark, he struggled to haul himself from the warm covers. Winter clothing was issued. The long underwear and gloves helped, but not, in Durk's view, enough.

"Our camp is perched atop a hill," he went on, "so that the wind sweeps and cuts around us. . . . It is so bad sometimes that marching is almost impossible; you can't march against it, and with it you are nothing but a human sail."

The change put Jack Brister in mind of winter in New Hampshire, and though it was rain that fell on Britain, not snow, he remembered a Dartmouth drinking song:[82]

Fill the pipe. Pass the bowl
With a skoll, with skoll.
For the north wind is howling in the doorways
And the Great White Cold walks abroad.

He never could abandon entirely his vigilant self-criticism, but Brister himself was in a state of near euphoria. "Turner's long letter today," he wrote on November 11, "and a sweet one from Mrs. Littlefield [his friend Tom's mother]. How come I deserve such good friends—or do I?

"There are some beautiful words to express all thoughts," he mused on. "Words that are close to experience and which force a greater sensitivity, a greater perception to (and of) the experience. Like this rainy day: if I find words for the sound of the rain and note [the] way it falls, the puddles it forms, then I forget its immediate disagreeableness."[83]

The last few days at Bushfield passed in a round of sociability—dinner with Captain Baring, tea with the colonel, farewell visits to their local English friends. In the last exams, four of the Yanks finished in the top ten—Cutting second, Bolté eighth, Durkee ninth, and Cox tenth. On the last night before heading off to OCTU, Cox passed up a squad "binge" in favor of drinks and dinner with Tchiechoff, his Russian friend. "In some ways it was the pleasantest evening in some time. He was in the squad I had as a lance-corporal and said that I had been very successful at that job, from the men's point of view anyway, and he wasn't just being flattering."[84]

CHAPTER 4

Officers

Officer Cadet Training Unit, Perham Down, and other training camps
near Salisbury, England
November 20, 1941–June 18, 1942

> For three days now I have been Cadet instead of Rifleman
> or Corporal and have the great distinction of wearing a white
> band around my hat to show that I am training to be an officer.
> We are referred to as gentlemen now. There is hot water all the
> time and we don't have to wash our dishes after meals. Such
> things assume major importance at times. . . . The next four
> months look to be quite hard mental work and very interesting.
>
> —Rob Cox[1]

With their resemblance to collapsing walk-in storage sheds, it is easy to imagine that the first military tanks were conceived by their British inventors as "land ships," simply because of their ungainliness. Winston Churchill, when he was First Lord of the Admiralty, was instrumental in initiating the process that led eventually to their deployment. In settling on a code name to protect the secrecy of the new armored attack vehicle, the story goes, the supervising committee at first called them "mobile water tanks." The shorter term "water containers" was considered but soon rejected. What self-respecting Englishman would want to be associated with the WC

Committee? Whether this version of events is merely amusing or actually apocryphal, by 1916 a new machine with the power to transform the nature of land warfare—combining mobility and protection with fire-power, much like a warship—had entered the world.

As the Great War devolved into gory stalemate, the tank was promoted as the weapon that, by its imperviousness to machine gun fire and its ability to breach barbed wire and other defensive works, would swing back the balance of power in favor of the attacker. Indeed, the new, twenty-eight-ton traveling armored fortress offered unprecedented levels of protection and potential for destruction. It could bridge trenches, crush abutments, smash through walls.

It also was huge. The Mark I, the first tank to be used in battle, was a steel-clad leviathan, colossal and slow. At thirty-two feet long and nearly fourteen feet wide, it occupied as much ground as a modest-size town house. The tank's forward lean—its lopsided, rhomboid shape—gave the caterpillar tracks an effective "climbing face," but in an arrangement that seems impractical at best in retrospect, the tracks ran all the way around the four faces of the tank itself—front, top, back, and bottom. Elevated at the front of the vehicle, the tracks could pull the huge armored box of its body over a five-foot-high parapet. It was long enough to cross an eight-foot-wide trench as it carried its eight-man crew and four to eight guns—machine guns and light artillery pieces—right through enemy lines.

But the Mark I's speed of four miles per hour (six kilometers per hour), which matched the pace of the marching infantry with whom they advanced, and its size made the tanks vulnerable to direct hits by artillery and mortar shells and to being overrun by infantry and attacked with grenades. In one of history's myriad ironies, German military planners initially rejected the new device as too vulnerable to concentrated fire to be of much use. Instead, they developed antitank weapons. Before long there were "K bullets" capable of piercing the Mark I's side armor, and when the next generation of tank was produced with thicker armor, a larger purpose-made antitank rifle and more explosive grenades called *Geballte Ladung* ("Bunched Charge") were produced. The arms race has endured since the first rock was thrown and the victim ran off to find a bigger rock.

The Mark I made its battlefield debut at Flers on the Somme on September 15, 1916. Results were mixed. Of forty-nine tanks shipped to the area, only eighteen actually took part in the battle, and the heavy machines became mired in the wallowlike terrain. But enough succeeded in penetrating the line to inspire British commander Field Marshal Douglas Haig (a horse cavalryman) to place an order for one thousand more. On July 28, 1917, a separate British Tank Corps was established.

By the fall of 1917, the Mark IV tank had introduced several significant improvements. While maintaining the rhomboid shape of the Mark I, the new model was more reliable, better armored, and more maneuverable. Opinions still varied as to its value, but Lieutenant Colonel John Fuller, the chief of staff of the Tank Corps, successfully argued its usefulness in drier field conditions, and at dawn on November 20, 1917, 476 tanks joined six infantry divisions and one thousand additional guns to assault German lines before Cambrai, a French crossroad town near the Belgian border.[2] Fourteen squadrons of the Royal Flying Corps stood by—an early attempt at a multiforce, unified attack of the sort the Germans would master in the next war.

Within a day, British troops advanced an unprecedented six kilometers toward Cambrai, eight thousand prisoners and one hundred guns were captured, and the trenches of the Hindenburg Line were pierced for the first time. Back in Britain, church bells pealed in celebration. The British army, however, could not exploit the breakthrough. Reserves to follow up their successes were lacking, while the Germans brought forward division after division. Within a week they had reversed virtually all British gains. The cost: about fifty thousand German soldiers, about forty-five thousand British.

"The English attack at Cambrai for the first time revealed the possibilities of a great surprise attack with tanks," German army chief of staff Paul von Hindenburg reflected afterward. "The physical effects of fire from machine-guns and light ordnance with which the steel Colossus was

provided were far less destructive than the moral effect of its compara-
tive invulnerability. The infantryman felt that he could do practically
nothing against its armoured sides. As soon as the machine broke through
our trench-lines, the defender felt himself threatened in the rear and left
his post."[3]

The German commander's words were a prescient summary of the
effect that German blitzkrieg tactics had on their opponents in the first
two years of World War II. The British apparently grasped the tank's
power as a weapon of penetration and entrapment, but they struggled to
master the kind of coordinated all-arms, mobile assault that the Germans
had been practicing for years.

That in 1941 the officer training unit of the King's Royal Rifle Corps
shared quarters with the Tank Corps's OCTU was evidence of the effort
by British military strategists and trainers to improve all-arms cooperation. When the Yanks arrived at Busigny Barracks, a hutted camp
built in 1938 in Brimstone Bottom,[4] Perham Down, at the edge of Salisbury Plain about ten miles from Andover, they found the soldiers there
enjoying a special dinner to commemorate the Battle of Cambrai, one of
the Tank Corps's battle honors. To the new arrivals, it had an *Alice in
Wonderland* quality, as by tradition on this occasion officers and sergeants served dinner to cadets. But they appreciated it. November 20 was
Thanksgiving Day in the U.S., and the relative bounty of the meal and the
luxury of beer eased the pain of remembering what they were missing
back home.

Later that evening came another, more poignant surprise. After dinner, huddled around a radio in the Armoured Corps barracks, the young
Americans strained to hear every word of a fluctuating wireless signal
that had traveled via Manchester, New Hampshire, and Boston all the way
from Dartmouth College.[5] The broadcast was part of a series produced by
American interventionists to transmit "messages from New England
towns to their namesakes in 'Old England.'" It began with a salute to
cadets of the naval academy in Dartmouth, England, but within moments,
to the Dartmouth College graduates' astonishment, their old professor

Joseph McDaniel was addressing them: "to those sons of Dartmouth, New Hampshire, who are now serving with His Majesty's forces, we send a Wah-Hoo-Wah and wishes for the best of luck."[6]

The Dartmouth Glee Club tugged at their heartstrings, another professor spoke of the college's long-standing ties with the town in England where in the eighteenth century much of the seed money for the college was raised, and then followed the familiar, well-remembered voices of their friends: Jerry Tallmer, Bolté's successor as associate editor of *The Dartmouth,* who passed along the latest campus news—that the first snow had fallen, that their friend Tom Braden had also volunteered for the 60th Rifles and soon would be joining them in England, that Charlie McLane was with the ski troops in Washington state ("Too bad," Cox quipped, "I'd hoped he'd arrive with some smokes"[7]), that, in a nod to the Harvard men, "we had a very good football team until one afternoon last month when a well-bred gentleman named Endicott Peabody III of Harvard took our line apart with his bare hands and strewed the remnants from Cambridge to Brookline"—and another Dartmouth friend who addressed them by name. "If you were here, Chuck, you'd find *The Dartmouth* office as incoherent and exciting as ever. . . . By-Jack [as he called Brister] you'd find life just as easy-going and yet full, your friends just as talkative . . . and Durk, you'd find the Corner [site of the Casque and Gauntlet] just as noisy and just as much fun.

"There is some difference though," he went on. "We don't argue any more whether this is our war. For a majority of people now think it is our war, and most think it inevitable that we'll get in. . . . And while we can't meet you in Hanover this year, we'll hope to see you all in Berlin year after next." When President Hopkins himself signed off "almost with tearful affection" and a line from their alma mater—"The still North remembers them, the hill-winds know their name"—the Dartmouth men in the group were left, as Rob Cox put it, "a little moist around the eye."[8]

———

"Yes, it's the freshman year all over again for us," Jack Brister wrote in his diary the next day. The Yanks' new situation at OCTU offered a number of significant improvements over camp life at Winchester. Bolté listed enthusiastically the "many swell pleasures" for his father: "There is hot water nearly always, even for shaving in the morning; lights in the wash-room; all the toilet seats are whole, and there is usually toilet paper (un-heard of at Bushfield), the food is much better, we don't have to parade for meals, we can read the paper at breakfast, there are no plates to wash; the barracks have *central heating* and we don't have to scrub them every Fri-day; there is a cadets' reading room with a fair military library and good tables to write on. . . . We get leave from Saturday noon till Sunday mid-night, with good trains up to town, except when we're on duty."[9]

But the change shook the five Americans' confidence nevertheless, especially Brister's. Jack could be judgmental about his friends—his dia-ries are salted liberally with criticisms and complaints—but he was harder still on himself. "My acclimating ability doesn't seem as functional as it should," he berated himself on his first day as an officer cadet. "I am the most reticent of the 'Yanks.' Why is this? It may have something to do with a muddled mood I get in—spend an awful amount of time trying to find something to worry about. Shear it off—you've only got so much energy per day, boy! You're rationed, look to it. There's no use making your own hurdles."

The new program was both more practical and more theoretical than the Yanks' work at Bushfield. They had a particular role to learn now. They would train as officers for the motorized infantry, which, in theory at least, worked hand in glove with the Armoured Corps. They would prac-tice the very support and coordination functions that had been problem-atic for the British army since Cambrai. That true cooperation still remained some ways off was suggested by a much-discussed social rift at the camp, which was said to divide the Armoured Corps cadets, a number of whom had worked their way up through the ranks, from the Rifle Corps candidates, nearly all effectively preselected on the basis of educa-tion and pedigree.

The schedule included plenty of review—tests of elementary training on Bren gun and rifle, and drill again, and before long there was a ceremonial parade, which as always required seemingly endless polishing and standing in the cold.[10] But they moved forward with map reading, tactics, "and various other advanced 'and highly censorable' topics," Bolté reported home proudly. They began to be given more responsibility. Each week one cadet was chosen as officer of the week and another as sergeant of the week, and they had to take full charge of their platoon. Bolté felt they had attained a whole new level when they were given two instructional pamphlets marked, "This information must not fall into Enemy Hands."[11]

The pamphlet covering training and employment of a motor battalion was stamped, "Provisional," on the cover, an indication of the tentative quality of the Yanks' instruction. "Apparently we are in a position where initiative and resourcefulness are essential," Bolté enthused, "and where our role constantly changes: wonderful, the thing is so new it can't be concreted or stultified because the brass hats don't know exactly what they want us for." One day they would storm a strongpoint or defend a river line, the next night patrol an armored division's harbor, or resting place. Bolté was thrilled. "Every man in the battalion has to know every weapon, driving, tactics; every section has to be able to work on its own; every subaltern is a Stonewall Jackson. And the armored divisions can't do anything without us."

That the reality in practice did not always match up with theory and training was suggested by two lieutenants Bolté met. "We have the most interesting time because we may be called upon to do anything at all," one told him. "It's always a shambles," the other said.

The cadets listened attentively when veteran officers discussed their battlefield experiences, and they followed closely the situation in North Africa. In late November the 8th Army under General Claude Auchinleck launched Operation Crusader to relieve the besieged British garrison at the vital Libyan port of Tobruk, and the offensive was going well. "Good news—they have really carried forward a modern panzer advance with air and naval cooperation," Brister recorded in his diary on November 22. "No need for propaganda war. Just a hell of a lot of inter-forces liaison. This will look good at home. AT LAST THE BRITISH MOVE the headlines will shout."

The Yanks looked ahead to applying their new skills in action. December 4 brought two lectures about confronting the Germans. Some information was practical: "In meeting tanks aim for weak points: joints, loopholes, and periscopes. Put tank out of action first then deal with infantry." Some was psychological. "Be ready for anything," the sergeant warned. Appreciate the German's strength as a soldier due to his great faith in his führer. "He will try any and every method of beating you, however unorthodox. . . . Remember he is ruthless. He would shoot you, your wife, your child had he the chance. He is your enemy. If you show him mercy, he counts you weak. You must hate your enemy if you love your friend."

Brister considered his capacity for ruthlessness in light of his recent, enthralling encounter with Robert Graves's novel of ancient Roman intrigue and militarism *I, Claudius*. He could be ruthless toward the evil Caligula, he judged. He confessed to feeling ruthless in PT when "a horrible little boy" named Miller was thrown to the mat. He recorded a pledge: "The German shall be unorthodox! So shall I. My men shall have the advantage of my time, my energy, my imagination, my blood."

On December 10, 1941, Rob Cox sat down to write a letter home. Recent events had apparently changed everything, and he was eager to discuss them, even if only in writing and without any chance of immediate reply.

"Well, I certainly would like to be home for about a week just at this minute and see what America is like when she declares war," he began. "As far as I can gather, everyone is running around like chickens with their heads cut off with air raid alarms, etc. It sounds pretty funny in the papers, but I suppose they make the most of it. Maybe I had better come home so I can see what an air raid is like. The only things I've ever heard since I've been over here are the 'all clear' signals."

On Sunday evening, December 7, as the Yanks walked in the dark back to their barrack from the reading room, another cadet came racing up to them. He was very excited, almost breathless, and he didn't wait for them to ask what he wanted. It spilled out: Japan had attacked Hawaii and the Philippines! The five Americans were shocked. They had been following the progress of U.S. relations with Japan, which had been extremely tense for some time, but when it came, the blow was an utter surprise, as it was to the English. "Actually, when I heard about Japan, I was a little sick," Rob wrote home. "Although in the long run I guess it's a good thing and although I've been hoping America would get into the war, when the actual moment came, I didn't feel very happy because you wouldn't want to wish war on anyone."

President Roosevelt's speech to Congress on December 8, famously describing the seventh as "a date which will live in infamy," was broadcast at the barracks, and even the president seemed to have been taken by surprise. The American lance corporals struggled to keep their minds on their work. They were beginning the serious business of learning "mechanization" and needed to focus on clutch plates, brakes, and axles. But whenever possible they sat by the radio listening with nervous excitement.

"'I told you so' is at best a sterile phrase," Durk wrote his family on December 9, "but the situation America now finds herself in must convince those who would bury their heads that the world, and most of all America, can't tolerate nations who would destroy the efforts of a thousand years. Honesty, liberty, justice, and the inherent worth of every individual; these qualities of living nourished by the blood and spirit of countless men must not perish before the onslaught of the gangster nations.

"As tragic as it is for the loss of life, Japan's actions must once and for all convince the American public of the utter futility of dealing in any way with nations so motivated. It will . . . unite the American people in unanimous action, a thing England has been hoping and praying for, as have those in the U.S. who have long foreseen the dangers of disunity."[12]

On the night of December 11, the Yanks returned to their barrack room with still more exciting news. Germany had declared war on the United States, and Italy followed suit. It was the event they all, British and American alike, had been hoping and waiting for. Now they were in it together. America, too, was at war with the Axis. "You should have heard the uproar," Durk wrote home. "It was a great day."

But balancing excitement was concern about how things might change at home. The Yanks had lived in a country at war for some time. "I hope the American public is alive to the difficult task in front of them," Durkee wrote. "The long-run considerations are all in our favor, but the short-run factors are heavy against us." Cox worried about his younger brothers, Max and Louis, who would certainly be drafted, and about friends caught unawares in the Far East. "It would be nice if wars could still be fought by professional armies, wouldn't it?" Rob wrote. "I imagine that more and more life [over there] will get more like it is for everyone over here. Not even uncomfortable, but always under pressure, if you see what I mean."

With his family living on the California coast, Durkee worried most of all. The radio carried news of air raids and even sightings of Japanese planes along the Pacific coast. Would the family move inland? Would his father be called up by the navy? How would the war affect his business? "I will be anxiously awaiting news," he wrote home. "It seems strange to be doing this, the picture is reversed. I am wondering and worrying about you instead of the other way around."

For the Dartmouth men who had been so involved in the arguments between isolationists and interventionists at college, war came as a vindication of their opinions, not only about Nazi Germany but about the proper character of government as well. "In basic essentials, disregarding balance of power considerations, this war is as it always has been a conflict of ideas and at last we are to support the tradition that is the backbone of any civilized nation. Especially the younger generation, of which we are members, must rediscover a faith in truth, liberty, and in a democratic way of life. President Hopkins has been talking in such a vein for some years, his despair being the disappearance of what he calls 'the

Upright Man.'" The Yanks felt they had rediscovered him in the form of Ambassador Gil Winant. They hoped, as Durkee put it, that as England "recovered at the edge of too late," so had America.

Rob Cox regarded the inevitable changes in life at home less abstractly, and more wistfully. "The old wheel of frivolity will stop for good now I guess, and by the wheel of frivolity, I mean all kinds of pleasant things," he wrote home. "Still, I was just as angry at America before as I am sorry now and actually it might be the salvation of the country."

Cox had been reading the gospel according to John, which he accepted from a Bible society member making the rounds at camp one day, and he already had been reevaluating his hedonistic approach to life. The passage from John most often cited in war is the famous line, "Greater love has no man than this, that he lay down his life for his friends." But Rob was taken by the verse that read, "I am the true vine, and my father is the husbandman. Every branch in me that does not bear fruit He takes away." As Rob interpreted it, the idea was, "You didn't choose me, I choose you, so you don't have much to say about what you want to do." "'Pears as though according to John, we aren't meant to do so much relaxing," he wrote home.

A few days later, a letter arrived from Rob's old friend McNamara, his cockney squad mate at Bushfield. Along with Christmas and New Year's wishes from "Your pal forever," Mac offered condolences, and then encouragement: "I am very sorry to hear of the way those little yellow bastards have attacked America, but I think, as no doubt you do, that the Yanks can look after them, and I hope it is not long before your country delivers back some harder blows than they gave you. I noticed it was in the typical Hitler style, but I think they will end in the same style as Hitler will, don't you? It must have upset you, hearing such bad news from home, but keep smiling, Bob, we'll have them in the end. . . . I am proud to be in the same regiment as you 'Yanks' at a time when our two countries are allies."[13]

But while the dramatic events at Pearl Harbor altered profoundly the calculus of the war in general, the officers in training remained focused on mastering the immediate specifics they needed to become leaders in the motorized infantry: bearings plain, split-bush, radial ball, radial roller, single and double thrust, double purpose, and tapered roller; lubrication and maintenance. Gears single helical, double helical; spur-toothed bevil, spiral bevil; gear ratio; lubrication; maintenance. The mechanical training was a challenge for Cox. "There is something about a piece of mechanism and me that don't get on. I appreciate that the inside of a car is miraculous and fascinating. But me and a carburetor are like poles of a magnet. We simply repel each other. I look at a thing and my first impulse is to quickly look away and I have to force myself to examine it."[14] Brister sharpened his attention by reminding himself of the larger purpose: ". . . when the machine means Death to the enemy and Life to yourself, it's not too difficult to maintain interest."[15]

The regularity of the days allowed Brister time to attempt the promised article on recruit training, but he failed to progress beyond a few notes. Bolté and Durkee passed time daydreaming about food. "Chu-chu and Durkle forever feed their stomachs through their imaginations and spoken words," Brister noted. "Oh, a great bellyful of words they devote each day to this strange pastime. Is it because they eat three times a day? So do I! And day breaks, the clouds move, people follow this strange war dance—every day! Still their bellies. Why? I begin to feel the deficiency lies only in me."

The lordly young graduates of English public schools who populated the OCTU barracks often irritated the Yanks, but some were becoming friends. At Christmastime, Cox went home with Tony Van Bergen, who was spending the holiday with his father, a businessman, and his brother Vivian, who was an RAF officer.

Tony had revealed his qualms about bringing home friends on account of his father's icy demeanor and sharp judgments, but the time passed pleasantly with movies and meals in London interspersed with country life—walking with shotguns through fields and woods, and reading. Cox began T. E. Lawrence's *Seven Pillars of Wisdom*. At breakfast Christmas morning Mr. Van Bergen passed out gift envelopes, and Cox was surprised to be handed one marked, "For Bob—a very Happy Christmas good luck and may God keep you safe." Inside was a crisp pound note, which seemed just right and quite moving, given Mr. Van Bergen's reputation for crustiness. That evening brought a gigantic turkey and champagne, and they drank to the health of the eldest Van Bergen son, just landed in Palestine.

Talk focused on the contribution of the upper classes to the war effort. "Although there have been very few casualties in this war, there have been a great many among the public school fellows," Cox reported. "All sorts of people came up in conversation with Vivian and Tony and they mentioned a great many friends and acquaintances who were dead. As my friend Corporal Lewis of Bushfield soundly remarked in the corporals' club one day when someone was talking about the upper classes, 'No matter what you say about them, they've given more to this war than anyone and more quickly and gladly. They don't wait to be asked like we do.'"

Cox learned about Boxing Day, a British national holiday, by tradition the day after Christmas, when the aristocracy would give gifts to their servants. He left with a pleasant feeling of having passed inspection. Even though Mr. Van Bergen had disapproved highly when he heard that Americans were getting commissions in the British army, "His parting words were to be sure and come back and if the others are anything like you, you can bring them. . . . Like most people he's pretty soft at heart."[16]

Back from Christmas leave, Cox discovered that he was, like it or not, a soldier. When reveille sounded, he was shaving before he'd even decided to get up. On New Year's Eve, the Yanks' platoon crept into the next-door barrack room and enjoyed a practice long favored at the Casque and Gauntlet, back at Dartmouth—overturning all the beds "just for something to do." At midnight they lustily sang "Auld Lang Syne" until someone said, "Shut up, there are the pipes," and sure enough they could hear the distant droning of the Scottish regiment's bagpipes. When the music ended, the men marched out into the moonlit square and performed sentry drill, 160 paces a minute, dressed in pajamas. Their old nemesis now was as natural as breathing, and a source of great pride.

In the cold, dark days of January, thoughts turned to home. The driving part of driving and maintenance was far more fun than the maintenance, and almost nothing was more fun than careening over the English countryside on motorcycles. But the days were short and the nights were chilly and long and the patriotism that America's entry into the war had inspired was at times simply the flip side of homesickness. Durkee's mother mailed him a sweater and his favorite Mexican foods to try to cheer him up: green olives and chilis and tamales created quite a stir in the barracks, but he remained inconsolable. It was in fact one of the coldest winters in years. "We have seldom been warm or completely dry," he wrote home in January.[17] And in March: "You really can't imagine another climate in the world as uncomfortably cold as this."

Jack and Maureen saw each other ever more often, and the visits mattered to them more and more, but the comfort and the flights of imagination Maureen excited in Jack also could turn him sour and sad, by comparison with the daily grind. At times, bumping along frosty roads in an army truck on a freezing morning, he simply ceased to believe that he was there, stamping his feet over and over to try to get the blood flowing. He imagined that his friends at home—the ones he so valued for their insight and their honesty, the ones he had cultivated so loyally and taken so long to make—were waiting for him just around the next corner. In these daydreams he was no longer adrift and freezing somewhere on an island of forty-five million strangers. But then he remembered: The friends were three thousand miles away.

Then on Thursday, January 22, there came an invigorating reminder of home. Snow! The Dartmouth boys and Cox ran yelling up and down the barrack room in a frenzy of recollection. "Woodstock. Four inches fresh snow over a six-inch base. Snowing. 29 degrees. Bertram, 6 a.m." They spouted ski reports from the *Boston Herald*. The next morning when they headed out in their trucks, the countryside looked beautiful, every tree limb delicately edged with white.[18]

Meanwhile, as the dreary English winter dragged on, war news degenerated. The advance in North Africa turned to rout. On January 21 Rommel, attacking in Libya, drove the British 8th Army back to a line little more than a hundred miles from the Egyptian frontier. The loss of Singapore to the Japanese in early February affected the British as a national disaster. The shaky military situation caused uncertainty about when the Yanks would be commissioned and where they would go thereafter. Talk of retraining, or longer training, reflected the broader struggles of government and military to master new tactics, strengthen command, and identify leaders capable of countering the *panzer-armee*'s mortally effective way with tanks. But while the precise timing of the Yanks' next move remained uncertain, a visit to Busigny Barracks by Sir John Davidson at the end of January brought the news they had hoped for: After receiving the King's Commission in April, they would join the 1st and 2nd battalions of the King's Royal Rifle Corps with the 8th Army in North Africa. "Eight months from now I might be retaking Benghazi," Rob told his mother brightly. "I don't see how things can help but get better and better from now on because for sure, they've reached the lowest possible ebb."[19]

About that, Cox was mistaken. In the year since Rommel had arrived in North Africa, the fortunes of war had ebbed and flowed in mammoth, furious waves of men, machinery, and blood, favoring first the Axis, then the Allies, then again the Axis. In the summer of 1941, after the British 8th Army's two failed attempts to relieve the besieged port city of Tobruk, Prime Minister Churchill had appointed a new Middle East commander, replacing General Archibald Wavell with General Claude Auchinleck. In November, the 8th Army was briefly resurgent, as the *panzer-armee,* its supply lines overstretched and troops exhausted, made a tactical retreat west across Libya's Cyrenaica peninsula to Agedabia to await reinforcements. But the fierce Axis counteroffensive launched in January had by February 1942 driven the British back once more to the Gazala-Bir Hacheim line just west of Tobruk. They would remain on the defensive through the English winter and into the spring. Rommel's attempt to break through the Gazala line at the end of May would offer, in some historical interpretations, the Allies' best chance for a killing counter-blow, but the British would squander the opportunity, setting the stage for Rommel's next advance toward Cairo and the Suez.

The resolution of uncertainty about future plans conspired with a satis-factory end of driving and maintenance training to put Cox in great good spirits, despite occasional longings for "black ice and powder snow and the blades and the boards." The next course of study, wireless, re-quired the Yanks to learn Morse code, no simple matter. But it also al-lowed them to apply their new skill "cruising about—wirelessing each other," and Cox was happiest when he was moving.[20] Even discontent about the weather, which had caused chronic colds and discomfort for all, could be rendered lightheartedly. "I wish it were spring," he wrote home in early February. "I think the English do part of their seasons very badly. They don't know that fine word 'the Fall' because the Fall isn't worth no-ticing and their winter is the bottom."

One night, some of the men in the barrack pulled out a Bible to learn what it predicted by opening it randomly and reading a passage aloud. The fellow called McKenzie read out, "'I will go into the land of Egypt and the trumpets shall blow and the sound of the battle will cease,'" in Cox's view "an appropriate one and not bad news at all." His passage, he re-ported home, was more cryptic: "all about vengeance and destruction, but I couldn't quite figure out if I was supposed to be the avenger or the avenged. Taking it literally, I was the avenger, but it seemed a bit pre-sumptuous to identify the I of God with myself, and I didn't want to identify myself with the avenged, so I let it pass. My motto as I believe I wrote [to] you is Lord Adare's famous quotation about shooting birds: 'We will get some guns and pursue them in a motor car.'

"It's all the most delightful game of cowboys and Indians imaginable,"

Cox exulted, "and the brilliant feats of arms accomplished would hearten the most gloomy. . . . Most of the time is spent in practicing giving and receiving orders and using the correct terms. We sit with maps in front of us and pretend we are part of a brilliant plan of attack and order each other all over the map. If things get dull you invent some enemy to suddenly attack you, and if you are feeling in a heroic mood, shortly announce you have destroyed them."[21]

But even when the cadets forgot the exercises' ultimate purpose, the games were freighted for them, as they were in fact being carefully watched and judged by their superior officers. "I've just had one of the best weekends and worst Mondays since I've been over here," Cox wrote home at the end of March.[22] The best weekend comprised the simple pleasures of two days in London with Cutting and another fellow officer, seeing the new movies, eating well, sitting in comfortable chairs and drinking and talking. "I guess the Army makes you appreciate these things more," Cox mused, "since in my jaded youth I never felt so excited about such an evening since it was my nightly (far too often) fare."

On Monday, short on sleep, he learned with alarm that he had been designated the commander in that day's wireless "scheme." In these training exercises, one group of cadets would attempt to drive from a location at the top of a map to a location at the bottom, while those in another group—the enemy—tried to stop them. To put an opponent's car out of action, one needed to get one car in front and one car in back of him, at which point he was "dead." "So you scoot around the roads finding the enemy and radio a car to come down behind him just like they do in the films," Rob explained.

All of which would have been fairly simple if not for the necessity of using military jargon and passing messages along the correct chain of command. It helped if your nerves were steady and you were feeling alert, which on that particular morning Rob was not. "Your nerves must be in a good state," he explained. "Otherwise, just as you think everything is going all right a harsh voice breaks out in your earphones and it's an officer saying that you've done something wrong and you suddenly realize that all the officers and sergeants in the British Army are listening in to you and writing down comments in their little books."

On this day in March, everything seemed to be fine—no harsh voices so far in the earphones and Cox's group of trucks traveling unmolested along the many tiny roads of England toward their destination at the bottom of the map—when Cox realized suddenly that he had been so busy directing everyone else and marking their positions and enemy positions on the map that he had lost track of just where he himself was. In the telling, he made light of the problem, along with all the many things that the cadets had been taught about finding their way in the countryside.

"Well, that's all right, you say. You know the general area you're in, you know there's a road coming in from the left, all you have to do is find out which direction you're facing and you can find the place on the map. [But] you don't know the direction because you have to sit in the back of the truck so that you can barely see out and while you've been jotting down the other data, you have wound about and in and out with no chance to see. But wait, all you have to do is set your watch at Greenwich time, point the hour hand at the sun, bisect the angle between 12 o'clock and the sun and you know where south is. Fool, the sun never shines in England so that it never has to set on the Empire. Moss, however, grows on the leeward side of trees, so all you need [to] know is where there's a tree with moss and which way the wind usually blows—that never works anyway. Aha! Observe the flight of geese: they go north unless they are white, in which case they hover over Dunkirk. I know, the Big Dipper! All we have to do is wait until night, then wait three months more and we'll get a starry night and find the North Star. And all the time, 'Hullo, Flotsam, over.' And you quickly have to think of some brilliant place to send Flotsam when what you really want to say is, 'Hullo, Mike, where the hell am I?'"

Excepting the day when he'd had dirt on his sword, or bayonet, at inspection, it was Cox's first real mistake since arriving at OCTU. All in all, in the end, it did not go too badly, but he couldn't help thinking that the best job of all was to command just one's own truck. You didn't have to keep track of so much, and when you got bored, you could radio the "company commander" that you were proceeding to such-and-such a place and all the officers listening in got out their pencils and wrote down "initiative" and you looked like a leader. "Ah well," he concluded, "we shall see what we shall see."

As the situation in North Africa continued to deteriorate, the Yanks learned to shoot revolvers. They completed a nine-mile route march "in fighting order," equipped with rifles and Bren guns, in two hours and fifteen minutes.[23] They saw a motor platoon at war strength mounting trucks and moving off in twelve seconds and spent an afternoon in Bren gun races, positioning and loading and changing barrels as fast as they could. They maintained a running Anglo-American rivalry with their comrades, Durkee ultimately proclaiming that whatever the exchequer had paid for their passage was little enough in return for the Yanks' great contribution to international cooperation. They refined their theories of the historical continuum. "This war," Bolté wrote Mary, "won or lost, means the death of the laissez-faire individual. But not the end of the individual, who is always everything, the world within himself, and the only thing that can ever make the world."[24] Durkee developed similar theories in a long letter to his economics professor at Dartmouth.

In a lighter vein, everyone got a laugh out of the plight of another American recently arrived at Bushfield, Deering Danielson, Yale '35, who made the mistake of informing his family about the absence of toilet paper. Concerned, and not without resources, they promptly dispatched six thousand sheets of Scott tissue; then, fearing that the packet might be lost at sea, they asked some merchants to send a package, too—another seven thousand en route. Somehow an order was duplicated, all the boats arrived, and Danielson became the slightly baffled possessor of no less than nineteen thousand sheets, all arrived in two days, leaving him chagrined at the sight of the postman and short on room in his locker for anything else. Yet the toilet paper kept coming. The situation climaxed when, along with six thousand new sheets, a letter arrived from the customs saying they had confiscated thirteen pounds of it.[25] He shared the wealth as best he could, and it was much appreciated by friends and barrack mates, as was the punch line: Each toilet-paper packet was inscribed with these words: "The Consumption of Paper Is the Measure of a Nation's Culture."[26]

With April and the arrival of fine weather, the training program became exhaustingly and pleasantly active. Outdoors all day every day, and sometimes overnight, the cadets practiced attacks, ran and walked and crawled for miles. Driving cross-country, they took up defensive positions. They crossed the Avon River in boats and took up new defensive positions, "harbored" for the night and camouflaged vehicles, slept for three hours, then drove some more and dug in all morning.[27] Back at camp, tailors arrived to take measurements for the new officers' uniforms, and on April 17 they received the King's Commission. They all felt proud when Durkee won the golden baton as best cadet in their unit, and all were rewarded with fourteen days' commission leave.

At about the same time that Brister was rediscovering in *I, Claudius* the delights and transports of a really good book—"It's refreshing to have something to go overboard for, again!" he wrote in his journal—he was falling hard for the Irish wren Maureen Robins. They arranged to meet on Sunday, December 7. He invented nicknames for her—Maurob, Sparrow—and before long learned the intimate Irish endearment Mavourneen. He recorded an encounter that later would inspire a poem: "Saw Maurob in Andover. Wandered around, found a haystack, a setting sun, some kids' playing noises, later a church, and sometimes ourselves."

With weekends free and considerable chunks of leave at his disposal, Brister pursued the relationship avidly. Throughout the remaining months in England, they would meet regularly and write each other often. When they read, they jotted reactions and observations in the book margins; then they sent each other their books.

Jack had found a home away from home with the owners of a comfortable British country house called Heckfield. He headed there to begin leave on Friday, April 17. "Heckfield is overrun with spring and flowers," he noted in his new military service yearbook, which Cutting gave him some time after receiving it for Christmas from his grandmother. It was a small book, about the size of a passport, with a given space for each day. "Sun on the terrace with Jean's typewriter," he noted on the nineteenth. On Monday, Maureen met him and they went to London for two days of shopping, errands, movies, and supper at the Café Royal, the glittery French Regent Street nightspot favored by Oscar Wilde, George Bernard Shaw, and Winston Churchill.[28] Jack took Maureen to meet Ambassador Winant, whose apartment next door to the embassy on Grosvenor Square had become a regular stopping place in London for all the Yanks. Winant called them his "five musketeers." Sometimes the great man himself would wander in and tell stories of his travels or discuss the world situation. Frequently, he was too absorbed by his frantic work schedule, and they would pass the time with his housekeeper, Orol Mears, a quiet Englishwoman who had followed Winant from New Hampshire to Geneva to London. Brister often recorded her observations, as if making a study of Winant. "Miss Mears says: 'He stands in queues sometimes seven hours getting across the borders. There's no need for it, but he feels he's no better, he's one of the common people.'"

The other side of conjugal joy with Maureen was the feeling of emptiness without her. When Maureen left London to return to work, Brister was miserable. "Eire left. I'm lonely, tired and lonely," he moaned on Wednesday. Thursday was worse: "I'm more lonely. Eire, why did you leave?" Saturday she returned, along with her mother and brother. "They are fine people," Brister noted—from him, high praise.

When the course at Perham Down ended, the Yanks for the first time were divided into two groups and sent off to separate training battalions on the Salisbury Plain. Life here was in many ways like life at Perham Down. Field exercises were similar: They camped out, shot guns, navigated, and drove. But this time they were leaders. Each newly minted second lieutenant was assigned a platoon of thirty-some riflemen to command. "Hell of a lot of fun," Brister noted. "Awful lot to learn."

The focus of their exercises was the organization of the forward body, whose purpose was twofold: to make contact with the enemy, giving the main body time to select the ground it wished to fight on, and to gain complete information about the opposition for the armored regiment that followed behind.

There were the usual routine chores: truck maintenance, car maintenance, equipment and weapons cleaning and repair, vehicle inspection. May 15 and 16 entailed an extra measure of polishing and preparation: Winston Churchill was coming to visit. The KRRC men rode on the backs of the British training tanks, Covenanters. Brister found the show absurd, but "the P.M. was pleased—at our completely untactical attack."

The three days of division exercises that followed were refreshing, as the subalterns led their platoons overland to the south. "The boys enjoyed the change, the air, the country," Brister noted. "A chance to do for themselves. And I enjoyed it too, sleeping in turf under great trees whispering to me." At Thetford, Brister's men waded across the river and took the high ground right up forward, with Chuck's unit beside them. That night they bivouacked in a farmer's sheds. When Jack's driver ran over one of the farmer's petrol tins, spilling a precious one and one-half gallons, Jack took the law into his own hands and gave him some of his own. When they reached camp the next evening, two letters were waiting—one from Maureen and another, confusingly, from Betty Turner, his girl back home. "She's still a swell girl, damn it!" Jack thought, and the next day he wrote back to both of them.

One morning at camp, Cox came face-to-face with the British class system in the person of his old pal Mac, who had written to him after Pearl Harbor. At breakfast time, there he was, handing Rob his bowl of porridge. Mac was now a batman, essentially the personal servant of an officer in another company. "I spoke to him afterwards," Cox wrote home, "and it was all rather embarrassing because both the English and military feudal laws came into play, and it was 'sir' and 'McNamara' instead of Bob and Mac. I must break all the rules and in the secrecy of my room have a beer with him, because I can't stand the present situation. In fact I very much miss . . . being on equal terms with all those fascinating creatures. I find I really hate telling people to do this and that, and yet I do think I should be an officer and don't think I shall be a bad one eventually. In the field I like giving orders."[29]

By June, the Yanks were preparing for North Africa. The last month in England included two weeks of embarkation leave, and it passed in a gay round of visiting, lunches, and cocktails, dinners and dances, shopping and preparations, concerts, restaurants, and, in Brister's case, love. Jack and Maureen visited the Winants. They went to Heckfield together and dined with friends in Winchester. They stayed at the Park Lane in London and went to the movies, went shopping, went to dinner, went to bed.

Cox, in London, liked to wander down to the Eagle Club, originally the headquarters of American RAF pilots, but now, as more and more American military arrived in England, a clubhouse for other American soldiers as well. There was good coffee to be had, and he would sit from ten to twelve thirty sipping and talking. Conversation was easily begun; everyone was curious to know why a British officer was lounging in a room reserved for Americans. "There were lots of fascinating people and it was fun to be yourself and not Mr. Cox, Sir," he wrote home.

One morning Rob found himself surrounded by a crowd of men wearing the uniforms not only of America, but also of Canada, Britain, France, and Holland—all of them, of all ranks, American. They decided the only thing to do was to start an International Brigade, like the heroic band that had fought Franco and his fascist allies in the Spanish Civil War. Other times, when he talked with men who, like him, had served in England before America herself joined the war, he indulged in reminiscing about the "good old days," when the club offered limitless free cigarettes, the hamburgers weren't all eaten even before they were cooked, and a man could always find a seat at the counter. One RAF Texan wanted to go out with a volunteer group to Burma; he felt things in England now were getting too well organized and missed the feeling that this was his own personal war. "Funny, isn't it?" Rob asked his mother rhetorically. "It's a sort of vanity, I guess. But with the best of them it's a sort of pioneer spirit too. Because there are no boundaries and no frontiers to what you believe in (whatever it is). Nobody would say they are fighting for democracy. (I mean none of my pro-war Americans.) They'd just say what I say to them, 'I was a sucker.' I don't know if they ever stop and think what it's all about—I don't very often—and you can't say it, because it's not an idea, it's an act. I mean we're not fighting for democracy, we are democracy because we are fighting or training to fight. A lot of these people are transferring now [to the American army] and that is only natural. But it's fun to talk to the ones who won't transfer and grumble about how little we get paid compared to the American Army."[30]

Leave climaxed for all the Yanks with a farewell dinner arranged for them in a private room at Claridge's by Ambassador Winant and Foreign Secretary Eden. The young Americans felt greatly honored, of course, and enjoyed the luxurious setting and mouthwatering food, but when Eden and Winant themselves arrived for the coffee and brandy, they nearly burst. Only Jack sensed the ambassador's underlying unhappiness—"Oh, he was low," Jack noted[31]—as he struggled with the lingering effects of a cold.

The next day, Brister met his Mavourneen at Paddington Station and they traveled together to Stratford-upon-Avon for four days at the Bancroft, a pleasant small hotel in town with a pretty garden out back. In perfect weather they enjoyed the delights of Shakespeare's birthplace. They took in *Hamlet, King Lear,* and *A Midsummer Night's Dream.* Brister thought Puck a delightful batman. They swam naked among swans in the Avon, and the sun dried and warmed them in a cushioned punt. Their hotel room was large and airy, street noises wafting in making it feel close and remote at once. Maureen, it emerged, knew how to shave a man with a straight razor, and mornings she did the honors, while Jack lay in bed, trusting her.

It wasn't entirely possible to forget there was a war on. Mrs. Bancroft chatted with them as they lingered over a late breakfast in her sunny garden: "Everyone's a son or two, or a daughter in something," she said. But when the time came to catch the morning train back to London, getting up early felt strange. Jack, the writer recording his experiences, sounded as foolishly besotted as any satisfied man new to love. "Soft, sweet, listless happiness; yet as vital as pain—demanding and wanting to be demanded. Love contains the secret—the poet's secret."

Then began a period of waiting. The Yanks, like all the others preparing to ship out to the front, had purchased their tropical kit—khaki shirts and long, baggy shorts the color of the desert. (The word itself, "khaki," came from the Hindi word for dust.) They had loaded up with writing paper and books to pass the time en route. Brister invested in an atlas of the world and a Spanish dictionary. Cox found a large blank book bound in tooled black leather, the perfect journal for a sea voyage. On June 8 they moved on to Tidworth, where they were to camp under canvas "for an indefinite period," with more military exercises to keep them sharp. Then, a week later, they were transplanted to Transit Camp, Liverpool. There were movies, poker, and the occasional drinking binge. Brister and Durkee kept Bolté company on the night of June 7 as he booted and slobbered into Durk's brand-new canvas bucket.

It was a time for reflection and summing up. "I am fed to the eyes with inspections and demonstrations," Bolté wrote to his father. "I wonder about how I'll be under fire, but here comes my chance to learn. Of course, I care if I die, but it's not nearly so important as it was a year ago. . . . Beneath almost ceaseless levity and laughter I feel oppressively the foolishness of most of man's effort and the vanity of most of what we call life. . . . If they get me (I would not cause you pain, but let's face it), you must know that I had no reservations—regrets, of course, for I had more of the good things of life than most people, and still have—but at least no reservations, and no question but what I am doing the only thing left for me to do."

On June 17 Cox wrote home in a thoughtful mood. He could see now why people became fond of England. He had a store of pleasant memories—the bend of a river in Yorkshire where *his* platoon lay for three hours defending against nothing at all and feeling extremely peaceful in the morning sun; road bends and hedgerows and chalk pits and even Salisbury Plain on a hot day as they drove across it in Bren carriers, wanting to get back and have tea and yet not wanting to, because it had been a good day when all had done well and everyone was pleased with everyone.

But when he remembered where he had been a year ago, in Vermont, England still paled by comparison. "Needless to say, I would be most happy to be at Windsor now. It was very wonderful last year. Quite objectively, I shall never forget those couple of days when Miss Motley was up there. Because it was like seeing everything for the first time. Not exactly that but as if you had always known it was as it was, but had never really seen it, and then suddenly you did see it and that was exciting—to find it true. It is rather a wonderful place, you know. There isn't any sham there. One feels there particularly 'rooty,' as if, if one tried to be anyone but oneself, one would be most unhappy whereas sometimes in some places one is inclined to 'feign' a little."

Cox vacillated between embracing the high-flown—explaining life as the pursuit of noble precepts like dignity, tolerance, understanding, humanity, honesty, courage—and playing the fool a bit, for pleasure. "What I think is true I don't quite know," he wrote. "Still . . . I am constantly more sure of it." The best lines in Shakespeare, to his mind, were Marc Antony's last words: "I am dying, Egypt, dying—give me some wine and let me speak a little." "A man after my own heart," Cox wrote, "even in his most extreme moment he wanted to get a little tight and talkative."

Then he told his mother the best story he had heard in some time, which concerned two men riding a double-decker bus. They were very different types of men, one satisfied to go about his business unquestioning, one who gave some thought to what life was all about. Neither had ever been on a bus before. "But one of them," as Rob put it, "stumbled on a symbol of all [of] us."

The story went like this. "Since they had never ridden a bus before, they decided that one would ride on top of the double decker and one on the bottom. Then by comparing experiences they would know all about bus riding. When the ride was over, the one from the top of the bus said to his friend, 'What was it like with you?' 'Oh very satisfactory. A little crowded but quite capable. A very sound way to travel. How was it with you?' 'With me,' said the other, 'it was lovely—absolutely lovely. Big broad seats, a cool spring breeze through the windows, and through the windows, too, a view of the trees and the people and the houses.' He paused. 'Dangerous as hell though. There wasn't any driver.'"

"Looks like we're stuck here," Brister wrote in his yearbook on June 22, so he escaped once more to meet Maureen in London. On the morning of June 25 she came up by train from Winchester to wake him. They didn't see daylight until five, when they went out for fish and chips and a movie and coffee at the Café Royal before returning to their room.

On Saturday the twenty-sixth, it was over. Or perhaps not. Brister recorded their parting in his yearbook. "Breakfast at 10:00 and then we said goodbye—Mavourneen and I. She is a wonderful person. There aren't many like her—there aren't any! I'll be back, Maureen!" He stopped on Grosvenor Square to say good-bye to Gil Winant and his family, too.

Cox spent his last forty-eight-hour leave in London visiting a new British friend, a fellow officer who was a gifted musician. Micky Heming had studied at the Sorbonne in Paris and at the Royal Academy of Music and had won a coveted position as student assistant to the renowned conductor John Barbirolli. But when war broke out, he gave it up to enlist in the Artists Rifles, just as his father, a successful opera singer, had done twenty-five years before. He was commissioned to the KRRC in July 1940.[32]

Percy Alfred Heming, Micky's father, was a large, gregarious bass baritone, Micky's mother similarly warm and robust, and the informal, theatrical atmosphere in their flat on Abbey Road near Regent's Park charmed and excited Cox. "People are constantly rushing in and out to sing this or that in preparation for this or that broadcast or performance," he wrote home, and "between times, Micky is playing a Beethoven Symphony on the Victrola and accompanying it with the piano. Mr. Heming is dressing to go out and accompanying the dressing with operatic arias and Mrs. is washing clothes in the kitchen sink."[33]

In two days, Rob and Micky took in a musical comedy, the amusing new Ginger Rogers film *Roxie Hart*, and a ballet version of *Hamlet*. "Down in the theater section getting tickets, one ran constantly into this producer, that conductor, such and such a stage manager, etc., and nipped in and out of pubs with each one in turn," Cox said. The boisterous street life called to mind Ben Jonson, Shakespeare, the Elizabethans—"all peculiarly English and ancient."[34]

Not mentioned in letters home were the gloom and apprehension that recent military events had cast over England. Rommel's eastward strike from the Gazala line launched at the end of May had by June 11 forced the British into precipitate retreat. On June 21, the "much-bludgeoned" port city of Tobruk, a strategically vital Libyan harbor not far from the Egyptian frontier, fell in a day and with it some thirty-two thousand men and immense stores of petrol, food, and vehicles.[35] Eighty percent of the transport with which Rommel would continue his pursuit of the 8th Army consisted of captured British vehicles.[36]

The blow followed hard on the heels of other alarming setbacks. The Axis had achieved total superiority in the central Mediterranean, and the crucial island of Malta hung on by a thread. In Russia the *Wehrmacht*'s advances toward Stalingrad and the Caucasus continued to raise the specter of an assault from the north on Middle Eastern oil fields. In the Pacific, Allied troops had endured a succession of disasters, and the English had watched as one by one the jewels of empire were snatched away—Malaya, then Singapore, then Rangoon, then on May 20 the whole of Burma. The fall of Tobruk was "felt by Great Britain as a national disaster second only to the loss of Singapore," according to the historian James Holland. Churchill later judged it worse than a defeat, a disgrace.[37]

Rommel's boast upon capturing Tobruk and being promoted to field marshal—"I am going to Suez"—sounded all too plausible.[38] Since the end of May, the 8th Army had lost more than 50 percent of its fighting force.[39] In little more than one month Rommel would drive back British Commonwealth troops nearly three hundred miles[40] to pause just sixty miles from Alexandria. As evacuating civilians spread panic east to Cairo, on June 25 Churchill faced a motion of no-confidence in the House of Commons.

On June 28 General Auchinleck prepared contingency plans for withdrawal of troops to Alexandria, Cairo, and the Canal Zone. On the twenty-ninth the port of Mersa Matruh fell. The tattered and dispirited soldiers of the 8th Army hastened to dig in along a forty-mile line stretching from a tiny desert railway depot near the sea, called El Alamein, south to an impassable landscape of cliff and salt marsh known as the Qattara Depression. Here, its flanks protected to north and south, the vital Suez and Middle Eastern oil fields at its back, the 8th Army of the British Empire prepared its last stand.

That same day the Yanks' wait in England ended. Officers were wanted to fill vacant accommodations in a convoy. The wee hours of morning saw them hustled onto a train, and they arrived in Glasgow, Scotland, in time for breakfast. The next morning at about eleven, they boarded the ship that would take them toward North Africa.

Back in Windsor, Vermont, the hillsides of Paradise were in full leaf, and dairy farmers trucked fresh milk to the train station each dawn. Fanny Cox and her Evarts family relations had settled into a new summer routine, gathering every evening around the console radio in her sitting room to try to make sense of what war news reached them. In the morning, after a short walk down Main Street, she peered into her post office box, hoping for word from Robbie. One day in July she found a thick envelope postmarked Washington, D.C. Enclosed with a cordial note from British military attaché Rex Benson was a letter from his brother-in-law Sir Hereward Wake, colonel commandant of the 60th Rifles, reporting to Benson on the progress of the American officers:

> I wonder if you could find time to let the parents of the first five American fellows . . . know that they have sailed for the Middle East? . . . My Peter [Wake's son, also a second lieutenant] went with them. . . .
>
> These lads will all make first-class Officers, every one of them. They are exceptional—in a class by themselves. . . .
>
> We are most grateful to you and to Mr. Kenneth Howard especially for having done so much to get these Americans to join the Regiment in this war. It has, of course, far greater significance than a merely Regimental one, and is sure to have repercussions now and in the future that can only be good for all concerned . . .
>
> That our American Officers will be worthy of the Regiment is a foregone conclusion and certainty. We do our best here behind the battle to help the Regiment to live up to the highest traditions of the British Army, of the British Empire, and of the United States of America where the Regiment was born nearly two hundred years ago.
>
> At the moment of writing, three of our battalions, if not four, which include our sons and nephews, are in the thick of the fray in Egypt where the battle on which so much depends still hangs in the balance.

PART 2

Around the Cape of Good Hope

When I would muse in boyhood
The wild green woods among
And nurse resolves and fancies
Because the world was young
It was not foes to conquer,
Nor sweethearts to be kind
But it was friends to die for
That I would seek and find.

—A. E. Housman

CHAPTER 5

Interlude *Doña Aurora*

Glasgow, Scotland, to Cape Town, South Africa
June 29–July 27, 1942

> *Bless 'em all, Bless 'em all*
> *The long and the short and the tall*
> *Bless all the sergeants and W.O.1s*
> *Bless all the corporals and their blasted sons,*
> *For we're saying good-bye to them all*
> *As back to their billets they crawl.*
> *You'll get no promotion*
> *This side of the ocean*
> *So cheer up my lads, Bless 'em all.*
>
> —Popular soldiers' song, in waltz time, that Cox wrote down
> after hearing it sung from the bus tops by riflemen
> returning to camp from the pubs[1]

"**M**ostly in my mind hangs the question of what we are sailing towards," Rob Cox wrote in his careful vertical hand on the blue-lined pages of a big, black leather-bound record book that he had bought himself for this journey. The five Americans had been at sea now for a week. Their ship, the freighter *Doña Aurora*, at 439 feet, was a bit larger than *Sicilian Prince* and considerably newer, with two decks, and quite comfortable. The only other passengers were eleven officers of the 60th, which made for a congenial atmosphere, and the fact that it was an American vessel—although the captain and nearly all the crew were Philippine—meant that the food, once Cox got over seasickness, was wonderfully familiar and plentiful.

This convoy, OS.33, comprised forty-one merchant vessels, most of them bound for Freetown, Sierra Leone;[2] Ten of them, including the *Doña*, were stocked with "dangerous cargo"—ammunition and explosives. A cheerful and profane group from the American navy, all trained on the Great Lakes and commanded by a serious, efficient young ensign from the Midwest named Don, controlled the armaments: a 4.5-inch gun, two Browning .50s, two twin Marlins, two Browning .30s, one Lewis gun, and one .303 rifle with a thousand rounds. The seventy-odd Philippine crewmen, perhaps remembering the ship's desperate escape from Manila just ahead of the Japanese conquest in December 1941, all carried .45 automatics and knives—light, razor-sharp blades in wooden sheaths. "If we are torpedoed I think we will go up with a large 'bang' and will not need to worry about spending endless days in a life boat," Cox mused.

OS.33 had a more rough-and-ready quality than the flotilla that had transported the Yanks to England. The *Doña* churned along at wing, the next-to-last ship on the group's western flank. "It is the usual thing, destroyers and corvettes plying alongside or back and forth in front of us, sometimes close but mostly small grey lumps on the horizon," Cox wrote. The fact that they didn't "dress by the right" in tidy columns, as the Halifax convoy had done, reflected, the British officers agreed, the paucity of English ships in this group. "Norwegians and Americans and Dutch and the rest English," Rob continued. "They are gloomy ships, low and ill-shapen; sometimes one sees rust breaking through the grey paint and when one doesn't see it, one feels it is there. . . . This convoy is the ragged irregulars, the tumbledown stonewalls of New Hampshire not the broad well-kept ones of Northern England."

Cox's concern about the future was well-founded. When the five excited Americans settled their trunks in the *Doña*'s cabins, they became part of a huge and complex resupply operation at a moment of great peril for the Allies. After eight months of bloodletting in the Libyan Desert,

Rommel's *panzer-armee* for the first time had crossed the threshold of the British Empire itself. Traveling in British trucks powered by British gasoline and eating British rations, all prizes captured at the fall of Tobruk, Axis forces were now in Egypt. The Royal Navy had abandoned the harbor at Alexandria, and trains leaving Cairo were filled with the wives and children of British functionaries. On the Eastern Front, the *Wehrmacht* continued to press forward into the Soviet Union, approaching ever closer to the bountiful oil fields of the Caucasus. It could be said without exaggerating that the future of Western civilization hung in the balance.

In America, government and industry had mobilized to build and equip an army, but it was not yet ready to take the battlefield. Meanwhile, diplomats and politicians jockeyed behind the scenes with the British to determine where American infantry first would fight—in Europe, opening a second front in France, or in North Africa, joining the campaign already in progress, but lately faltering badly.

The British 8th Army was dangerously depleted. America and Britain both hastened to resupply it, but Axis dominance of the Mediterranean meant that most everything bound for the battlefields of North Africa had to travel by ship around the vast bulk of the continent before heading up the Red Sea to Suez, a journey of some twelve thousand miles, made longer still by the necessity to follow a zigzag course to elude torpedoes.

"When we left, Rommel was 80 miles from Alexandria," Cox worried. "It is not at all unlikely that Egypt has fallen. If so, what for us? And we feel too that no one knows that we're on this boat anyway. I suppose they do."

Jack Brister fell into his cabin on the *Doña Aurora* as an exhausted reveler into bed. "Accommodations are luxurious," he noted in his little yearbook on June 29. The room he shared with Durkee had comfortable mattresses, sizable closets, and an adjoining bathroom where hot water abounded. The two Americans arranged their books atop the cleverly crafted bureau desk and tested the reading lamps over the beds. Durk was thrilled with the ship. "She looked a beautiful job," he wrote home, "a passenger freighter with the long, distinct lines of a sailboat."[3]

Brister, after days and nights of bliss and sadness taking his leave of Maureen, felt first and foremost tired. "Sleep, sleep, sleep," he recorded on day one of the journey, "how I miss you, Mavourneen." The next day, he salted his leisure with a book, choosing one that touched on the soldiers' most consuming current concerns, plumbed the character of the newest and now most beleaguered of America's allies, and promised to last longer than any other possible choice. "Up for breakfast—read, then went back to bed and damn near slept through lunch," he wrote. "Read all afternoon—WAR & PEACE. It must strike fear and awe into a writer's heart, so good, so unapproachable does it seem."

Once under way, the 60th officers were expected to assist the American navy gun crew in protecting the ship. They stood watch twice daily, two hours in every twelve, and they stood to on the circular gun deck in the very stern at sunset and sunrise, which, off the Irish coast and just days after the summer solstice, occurred only about three hours apart.

As the ship rode the great swells of the North Atlantic, plowing south, then southwest, the tension of keeping watch in the danger zone alternated with a monotonous calm. Brister captured the mix, along with reading and remembrance, in daily entries in his yearbook.

7/3 <u>Friday</u> In my watch from 2-4 a.m. I booted. Feel much better. Haven't missed a meal and don't intend to. Understand we had an emergency change of course. Wonder if Mavourneen is following us. The darling. Slept all morning.

7/4 <u>Saturday</u> Watch! Roving Red light. They didn't know what it was on the bridge. WAR & PEACE.

7/5 <u>Sunday</u> Watch! Flame—seems from funnel—flared up in the night on a ship across the convoy. WAR & PEACE. Wearing down to the ragged ends—the veneer of politeness is wearing off. Nerves give way easier—too much—must absent myself more from the difficult company.

7/7 Tuesday Watch! WAR & PEACE!

7/8 Wednesday Watch! WAR & PEACE! The moon is taken for a red light & causes great stir . . . until she rises high above the sea.

7/9 Thursday Watch, Sun, off Portugal. WAR & PEACE. Finished—first time. I hesitate to even attempt to find the appropriate words for this. It is a marvelous and miraculous living work of art.

Friday, July 10, marked the anniversary of the Yanks' departure from New York. A year had passed since they met Rex Benson at the St. Regis and began their odyssey. The action and knowledge they had dreamed of then, thinking that war was something you dived right into, like a swimming hole, had been supplanted in the event (as the British would say) by a subtler, more intricate knowledge. Cox wondered about how it had changed them.

"It is hard to tell when one is constantly with the same people," he thought. Cutting, who remained his closest friend, had obviously changed physically. He was bigger, and his manner more self-assured. Regrettably, the experience of becoming a British officer seemed to have reinforced many of his less admirable assumptions about taste and class and the importance of appearances. "His vanities have become his principles," Cox wrote, and then immediately remonstrated with himself for perhaps being unfair to his friend. Heyward would always be something of an enigma. They lived together; Cox used his soap. They shared common memories of a past life that Cox thought of as "the wheel of frivolity," and they confided in each other, Cox because doing so was as safe as telling his troubles to a stone wall, Cutting because Cox could speak his language. Cox understood and tolerated Cutting's assumptions, even if he didn't admire them. "He is rather like a bottle that is so tightly corked and so covered with vain but handsome labels that no one can see what its contents are."

As for the Dartmouth boys, Brister had grown less blithe, Cox decided, and Durk increasingly big minded and self-confident. Only Bolté remained pretty much unchanged.

"We don't laugh as much as we used to," Cox mused. "In those first days when everything was new, we turned the newness into something laughable. Now because we are so used to novelty, it no longer seems out of proportion; in fact, what causes us to laugh as a group now is when something is 'typical.'" When Cox and Bolté first went on leave to Ireland, they had laughed at Dickie Adare because he was utterly novel; the last time, because he seemed so familiar.

"And I do not think it is romanticizing us to say that our purpose in coming here has deepened until it is almost an essential part of our nature," Cox concluded. He knew this to be true of himself, and he believed it true for the others, too, although they might deny it. If someone had told him a year ago that America would come into the war in December, he would have stayed home. "But now I am glad I came," Cox wrote, "glad I didn't know that America would get involved so soon."[4]

As the days went by, *Doña Aurora* steamed south. Europe fell behind them. The sun grew hotter, the nights longer, the sea calmer. On board, the pace of life grew ever more leisurely, until one morning two English officers, Coleman and Wake, turned up for breakfast in their dressing gowns. The Philippine waiter took umbrage. "We are not savages. We are nice people," he said, and refused to serve them.[5]

Despite anxiety about the future and the fact that they literally were sitting on a powder keg—or perhaps as a result—the officers gradually were transforming the *Doña* into a floating literary salon, an Ivy League dorm room, an English men's club where the members spent four hours daily at the Brownings on the bridge and stood to briefly at sunrise and sunset. The young men's minds roamed as far and wide as the encircling horizon. The Yanks filled the space with talk and books: Tolstoy, Shakespeare, T. E. Lawrence, as well as new authors: Carson McCullers, Eric Linklater, Jerome Wiedman, A. E. Coppard. Conversation became arch, abstract, and speculative. Even the American ensign, Don, was drawn in. A product of the new V-7 program to train American college students as navy midshipmen while they pursued their degrees, he had graduated recently from Notre Dame. His Catholicism offered irresistible grist for the conversational mill, and he lent around one of his books, Clifton Fadiman's anthology *Reading I've Liked,* which introduced to the mix James Thurber, E. B. White, Somerset Maugham, and Bertrand Russell. So high-flown did the speculation become that Brister accused Durk and Bolté of arrogance:[6] "These boys . . . are doing this Philosophy stuff too soon. I always connected it somehow to wisdom and wisdom is got by living not by reading," he noted. "The Philosophy must be hollow and forced—'when a young man be as a young man.'"

"And always there is the sea," Cox wrote, "and the rocking of the ship and its lurching and its climbing up and up a wave, and sliding down again." A whale spouted. Flying fish leaped wave to wave. One day, a female peregrine falcon perched on the mast for hours, her presence put down as inexplicable by Cutting, the resident bird expert. Cox counted it a good omen for those who were going to hunt Rommel. Another day, a convoy of porpoises romped through the ships' wakes, as if enjoying the joke of men and war.

In the smoking room, the ship's captain sat in his undershirt, suspenders dangling about his haunches, playing solitaire, which the English called patience. Cox wondered whether he cheated.

At ten a.m. on the morning of July 11, *Doña Aurora* separated from the convoy. Bells to the engine room jangled. A shiver ran through the ship and the engines raced. The atmosphere grew festive. A misty morning rain had wet the decks, and they glistened in sunlight. The ship's officers stood on the bridge in pressed whites, hands clasped behind backs, rocking gently between toes and heels, eager and happy as their ship pulled out of line to starboard. Signal flags went up—"Thanks for your escort"—and the destroyer that had led them for ten days flashed back on the heliograph in Morse code: "Thanks. Good luck. May your voyage continue as quietly as it has been."

That evening, the news came over the wireless: a German U-boat had torpedoed one of the other ships of the convoy. Later that night, rockets flaring in the distance indicated that another still had been tracked down or ambushed.

The Yanks would never know the full extent of the losses that night, or how lucky they were to get through safely. Some two weeks earlier, between June 22 and July 2, six U-boats had left bases in France to rendezvous at a position in the South Atlantic east of the Azores, there to form up as the wolf pack *Hai,* or Shark, and await Convoy OS.33.

Of the forty-one vessels in the convoy's nine columns, six were bound for South America and five, including *Doña Aurora,* for South Africa. These eleven, along with one other ship, SS *Consuelo,* would detach from the protected group continuing together to Freetown and then proceed unescorted.

Not until three thirty that afternoon did the OS.33 escort receive a report from British admiralty that they had picked up a U-boat radio signal reporting a sighting of the convoy. By then, it was too late. Half of the vessels that had detached were successfully targeted and sunk, and before *Hai* patrol was finished, nine other vessels would be located and destroyed, at a cost of only one U-boat.[7] Some five months later, on Christmas day, a German torpedo would sink *Doña Aurora* herself.[8]

Yet for the Yanks the voyage to Cape Town remained an extraordinary period of leisure and reflection. "Many loose ends that had been quietly thrust in[to] the background were gathered into some kind of order," Durkee later remembered. "I don't suppose that we will ever again have a time like that."

Doña Aurora was a fast ship, and perhaps it was the great advantage of speed that saved her. Once released from the convoy, she could accelerate from the group's pace of eight knots to her own cruising speed of fourteen knots. She zigzagged on. For a torpedo to be aimed with accuracy, a submariner needed to take two bearings on the target, enabling him to predict its speed and course. The zigzag minimized the chance that a torpedo could be aimed with a good chance of a kill. Still, crew members aboard the *Doña* complained that the indirect course slowed them down too much.

The Philippine captain, confident and imperious, kept his own counsel. Paying no attention to admiralty orders, he followed a course of his choosing, certain he knew best. Sometimes he behaved like a monarch indulging in every whim. Sometimes he was all sailor. Sometimes in his khaki shorts he sat with the 60th officers as if he were chief passenger and all the ship being run for his convenience. "He, and all the crew, are closer to America in their point of view than English people are," Cox observed.[9] When the captain was feeling jovial, he sprayed water on anyone who approached the bridge, using the hose normally intended for swabbing the deck.

The weather grew stifling. "To move at all is to force a passage through invisible haze," Cox wrote, thinking of black ice and hockey skates. He wondered when next he might see some.

On the hot mornings the Philippine crewmen flooded the deck and rolled in the water like amphibious puppies. Sometimes a breeze broke the humid spell. "Nothing so clean as the wet deck in the mid-morning sun and a fresh wind blowing," Cox wrote later, feeling revitalized.

Left to themselves, the Yanks enjoyed discussing the British. "At times it is completely impossible for me to understand how England has become as great as she has," Cox began one night. "Consider Coleman. Pig-headed, narrow, selfish, rude, and lacking, I think, a sense of humor." Coleman seemed to contribute anything at all only when the talk turned to dogs and eating different kinds of game birds—not subjects of eternal glory in any case. Thinking of him and so many others like him, one could only wonder how Britain ever had produced the great explorer-adventurers Drake and Scott and Lawrence, or Shakespeare, or Milton, or any of a score of other great men.

In Cox's mind, much of England's greatness stemmed not from the landed gentry, but from the men who had revolted against the insularity of their fellows. "So that Rupert Brooke, if it was he who said it, was quite right in saying, 'They little know of England, who only England know.'" He found the best of England in two places: first, in the dreams and visions of its great poets and great doers, and second, in its yeomen, members of the rural middle class like his old sergeants Ives and Crouch. "It is not the public school boys or the Corporal Siths who are really the great ones," Cox believed, "but Sgt. Taylor and C.S.M. Marshall and, on a lower level, men like Corporal Lawrence whose ancestors saw [the French invader] William's ships in the channel and felt their eyes narrow with hate."

The great lack now, as the Yanks discussed it, was leadership. They had learned a few things about the English upper class, and they believed it had grown overcautious. "There are no leaders now because the class that has always produced the leaders is afraid for itself," Cox observed, "afraid that if it takes courage and leads these men, it will destroy itself, which is true because like overripe vegetables the aristocracy is moldy."

The greatest day for the English in the current war was the day France fell, Micky Heming believed. "Everywhere men lifted their heads and said with glad pride, 'Now we are on our own.'" When the bombs of the Blitz rained down, they laughed, he said, "for it was then that the heart of England was free of its sickened brain and Harold [who was killed fighting off the French at Hastings] and [Sir Francis] Drake walked through the burning streets of London."

Perhaps they flattered themselves, but it seemed clear to the Yanks that it would be America's portion to supply the imagination and the fervor necessary to destroy the German war machine. "We are the ones who must sacrifice," Rob wrote, perhaps with a frisson of self-aggrandizement.

"England has suffered and will suffer more and will endure but it is to us that the sacrifice will come, for some of us will perish going forward or survive victorious and to all will come in the end knowledge that they gave themselves not to create a new Jerusalem but to maintain an old and wretched order from which someday might spring a better time."[10]

On July 15 the dark silhouettes of another convoy slowly rose into view and grew larger. When *Doña*'s captain failed to heave to and identify himself, one of the military escorts slashed a shell across her bow. *Doña* slowed, stopped, and the crews exchanged greetings,[11] while the passengers savored the novelty of visitors at sea—the little corvette that pulled up alongside and the "cheery piratical-looking crew" that crowded her deck, "stripped and bronzed and motley dressed, months of weather in their skin."[12]

Two days later, the captain posted a sign on the notice board: the next morning, at seven fifty-four a.m., *Doña* would cross the equator. They had traveled about half the length of Africa.

On the day itself, "the sun rose up straight," Brister noted, "lingered, then settled as straight to bed."

For Cox, on watch that morning, passing from the northern to the southern hemisphere seemed a bit anticlimactic. "It was very different from crossing the Massachusetts–New Hampshire state line," he wrote home, tongue in cheek. "They do those things much better in America, with a hundred 'last chance filling stations' and such. One feels a bit awed when one sees 'last hot dog in Massachusetts.'" The equator, by contrast, slipped by unheralded. "Over the rim of the world we sail and there is not even a little sign post to say it," Cox mused.

Standing watch, his mind unfettered, Rob conceived a corrective. "When I have made my fortune and the power and beauty and riches of the world bow kneeling at my feet," he wrote home, "I will renounce them all and in a very small coracle will put to sea with a sufficiency of food, a barrel of beer, and an important parcel. Southward over the bounding main I'll bound until at last, food eaten and beer exhausted, I will come to latitude zero. There with my last strength I will unwrap the important parcel and throw into the sea the large stone and the long and rusty chain attached thereto. And from the other end of the chain, anchored by the stone, a little buoy will float and attached to it this. . . ." And then he drew a little picture of a signpost emerging from rows of waves and on the post a rectangular sign: EQUATOR.

For a while, two albatross flew along with them, evoking the spirit of Coleridge.

A British officer, Ransom-Jones, noticed while on watch how the beat of the engine almost coincided with the beat of the waves, making the waves an almost perfect visual representation of sound. Meanwhile, the continual weight of nature's grandeur—"The stars roll and sway—swing like lanterns—sparks fly up to join them, silly human sparks"—turned even Brister philosophical.[13] "Bertrand Russell on immortality after the crushing effect of scanning the heavens so full of worlds is very good," Brister thought. "There is a soul. Even I may have one."

Words filled pages. Bolté reread his journal and decided "it might amount to something."[14] Micky Heming insisted on reading Cox's journal of the Yanks' Atlantic crossing and reproved him: If he had the least grain of ambition he would write a book one day.[15] Cox strained to describe all the different colors that stars can be. He jotted down a strange, dreamlike vision touching on his summers in Vermont: "The boy in the night sitting above the boathouse and the sound of the waterfall, the grass wet with dew, and the stars; footsteps on the gravel of the dike, and a low secret laugh. Everything is so soft. Where is his father?"

Micky Heming was writing music. Intense, volatile, and impatient after two years of waiting in England to join the battle, knowing all the while that in peacetime he would have been apprenticing with a great conductor, he paced as he worked. Cox wished there were a piano on board, but Micky seemed to have all the instruments he needed in his own head.

"How does it go? I've forgotten my own tune!" he cried, when Cox stopped in at his cabin. "No. Oh, yes. All the strings multifortissimo—*dee-da-dad a da*." He moved his right arm in and out, his left bent up, fingers curled as if fingering the notes while his body turned and swayed. "Then the brass *taarrumph*. Then later on the faith theme. Then there's a march, and then something that matters and the faith theme and more that really matters."

"Have you written it down?"

"Some of it. The trouble is, I like to orchestrate too much. I'm more a conductor than a composer. I guess you have to be pretty old before you can resist doing things for effect. I wonder how old you should be before you do the Eroica."

"You mean before you conduct it?"

"Yes. At least forty, I should think. The Seventh, now that's absolutely elemental. The bloke who made a ballet of the creation to the music of it wasn't far off. I went through it twice when I was on watch. Absolutely grand."

One morning, dropping in, Cox found Heming exhausted. "I had a crisis last night," he explained. "Thinking, writing, reading. I feel rather spent as a result."

"What was it all about?" Cox asked.

"I don't know—life, big things. It hasn't happened like that since 1937 in Paris." He explained how that year, studying abroad, he had been forced to choose his future path from among three possibilities—learning the jewelry business, becoming a theatrical producer, or studying to be a conductor. His parents had decided already for the practical choice; he would go into business. But every part of Heming rebelled at the thought, and he pushed forward regardless with conducting.

"I've never had to go through anything like that, never had to make any decisions," Rob said. "I suppose I decided to do this war thing. But it doesn't seem that way. I just came."

"You're lucky that way," Micky said.[16]

After that, Cox thought more about why he had left home for the war and what exactly he intended to fight for. "What the war is about is economics and political theory, and dynamic democracy, and nationalism, and jealousy, and thousands of big words, but basically it is for the right to live," he wrote in his journal. "It is simply so that we may have the terrifying and glorious opportunity to say, This is I and about me is the world, and all that therein is [is] waiting for me to do what I want with it, to take this and reject that and make myself a part of such and such a pattern . . . to live in that way most true to our nature, for economics and politics and the like are only a way and a means to existence."[17]

Most of the time any war news that arrived by wireless was so mangled by the Philippine captain's broken English as to be incomprehensible. The officers knew that Egypt held and that the battle once again had stalemated along the El Alamein line. Generally, though, since the news was so little and so garbled, they ignored it, Cox noted, "as we ignore the stirrings of flesh when at night the warm wind from the equator blows over you lying on the deck."

But violence found its way into Jack Brister's vivid dreams. One night he witnessed a ritual homosexual gang rape perpetrated, in the nonsensical way of dreams, on a kind of altar elevated on a basketball court. He attributed it to dinnertime talk of T. E. Lawrence's brutalization in *Seven Pillars of Wisdom,* to a submerged memory of José Clemente Orozco's lurid fresco *Ancient Human Sacrifice,* which was part of a series decorating the Dartmouth Library,[18] and to the "repulsive mince and carriage of limb" that characterized a much-disliked British officer on board named David Fletcher. "Each minute with him is full of an atmosphere of drowning kittens," Brister wrote.[19]

Three days later, Jack was analyzing the problem of capturing another dream in writing.[20] "It is sad that when you wake, you must recall the dream with words for they are—in the conscious mind—the curators of all vision. A dream flows; words stop, arrest it to pick out a single picture. . . . The experience seems shattered. . . . Does the rest fade from focus because the pieces are brought into such sharp focus?"

Jack listed the words that captured his dream of war.

First parachutes, wire strung between them in the sky, then
the sky so filled with parachutes it seemed embroidery—and
it was—all lace and ruffles flapping down the sky.

Airplanes, flames, dark smoke, and a black fuselage . . .
drifting, as though down through water.

But we—a lot of people, I guess my present company, Bob
Cox I saw—were in a boat and yet a house for we steamed
through a forest thick enough to protect us from the bombers.
Bob looked up through a trap-door to the sky. I saw the trees
all around and wondered how we ever got through them.

Fighters machine gunning us and the Ambler high school,
too, so it was my house and the *Doña Aurora* in which we
steamed.

And throughout, no feeling of fear—only interest, mild at
that.

That same day, Brister started writing again. He was exultant. He
started a story called "The Scout Master" about a boy called Bristletop,
because his hair grew straight up, like Brister's in his freshman picture at
Dartmouth. He jotted down ideas for other stories, at least two a day for
some time. Each story had a point. "A kid can be too smart!" "If you want
to keep a secret, keep it yourself." "Man has more to lose than life." He
identified characters, listed incidents, toyed with point of view. Meanwhile, he and Durk studied Spanish with help from the captain and the
chief engineer. "It should give us the perspective on English that one
needs," Jack wrote.[21]

As the *Doña*, driving toward Cape Town, passed the unseen shores of
French West Africa, as the ship turned southeast and slowed in the head-
wind,[22] as the men relaxed and the bonds of military discipline fell away,

a festering conflict between the captain and the American ensign, Don, moved to the fore.

Right from the start, the captain had kidded Don for his insistence on military discipline. Worse, the captain withheld information, then talked behind Don's back about his youth and inexperience. Worst of all, he undermined Don's authority as the man in charge of ship's defenses.

Their differences resonated among the passengers. "Don, the 'little Ensign,' is worrying harder than ever," Brister noted on July 19. Don so feared U-boats that he slept every night in his cabin fully dressed, life belt in place, sitting upright in a chair with the door open and the lights on.[23] "This overkeenness which tries to anticipate fate is very sad to behold and uncomfortable to be near," Brister wrote. "It means that though he's a Catholic he's gotten very little from religion—in his own mind he can never find the still waters; he studied metaphysics and a lot of philosophy at school—it sure does him a lot of good—hah! It is not enough to study only."[24]

When the captain took a liking to the British officer Peter Wake, Peter, too, decided that Don was overkeen and that the captain was more important in all matters on shipboard.

All the KRRC officers had long found the necessity of standing watch to be a chore and a nuisance, and the captain encouraged their indifference. He invited the watchers to come into the deckhouse for coffee. He posted additional watches from his own crew so that the sleepy, bored British soldiers felt their work was redundant. One night, Peter Wake and David Fletcher fell asleep on watch, a breach of military discipline that clearly communicated disrespect for the ensign, right in front of his subordinates.

David Fletcher took up the issue with Don. Disliking Fletcher and feeling alien to the English, the ensign pointed out that no one should stand watch who didn't want to, since they would only be taking the place of someone who could be watching conscientiously. He suggested that

Fletcher, who, as a captain himself, held formal authority over most of the other 60th officers, should get them together and ask what they wanted. But Fletcher never did, knowing, as Cox interpreted it, that the officers would argue and that despite his rank he would be unable to control the argument.

Brister saw the events as a lesson in leadership. "David Fletcher thinks commanding is deciding questions for yourself and issuing the orders," he wrote. "He doesn't realize that if there are twelve men under command then you must look from twelve points of view, if one hundred, one hundred points of view, before deciding.

"Few men, I guess, realize the organic relationship any command must involve. The thought of the leader must go out and touch each person under his command as must his subsequent action."[25]

One day near the end of the voyage, Don encountered Fletcher in the smoking room with the others and asked him what decision they had reached. As predicted, everyone began arguing vehemently about whether or not they should stand watch. Personal feelings came into play, Fletcher's captaincy having become irrelevant on a ship where it was no longer necessary to subordinate them.

The captain's dismissive attitude, Fletcher's failure to cooperate, and the general lack of respect for Fletcher had created a messy and chaotic situation. "If two hours later we had to put into action some plan which required great cooperation in order to be successfully complete[d], we would have been unable to do so," Cox recorded. "We completely lost sight of the purpose of the watches and we completely lost sight of the fact that Don was responsible for the defense of the ship and that our function was to do willingly what he asked. . . . Everyone forgot the issue because they were more interested in comfort."

Each individual, it seemed, had forgotten his military role in favor of his own personal grievance. "It was like when a child looks through a microscope for the first time, not knowing what he will see but having been told that he will see a marvel," Cox thought. Placing his face too close to the eyepiece, he sees only his own eyelashes magnified in the microscope's mirror, but not recognizing them, he says "Ah, yes!" and marvels at what in fact has nothing to do with the question at hand, but is in fact just a part of himself. "I think," Cox concluded, "this is what is strangling the army."

"There ought to be a united front," Brister agreed, "but it seems a rule of nature that fronts must be united against immediate and not intangible enemies." Even U-boats, they had learned, could seem too intangible.

On the last night at sea, July 25, the conflict came to a head. The captain threw a party, and the men gathered in the smoking room at four fifteen to celebrate journey's end, dressed for the occasion in a motley assortment of military regalia—some in khaki drill, some in service dress, one officer named Palmer in patrols, Cutting in patrols and a cross belt. The captain and all the ship's officers wore best blue, as did Don. The captain held court. Later, Brister recorded one of his stories:

> The British at home are much different than the British abroad. In Glasgow, the local harbor pilot was nervous, hit two ships and was going for a destroyer before the captain gave him up ($250,000 damage). The captain gave him a chance. The pilot blamed the steering after saying "yes" to [the] captain; he blamed the ship when the underwriter came aboard.
>
> (Here in the story, David (f—ing) Fletcher said, "Who's the underwriter?" "Oh, well, you can't go wrong." And repeated it seven times throughout the narrative. God damn his tongue, reason, and eyes—and I'm afraid God has.)
>
> The captain said, "I give him chance, he tell me he got wife and three kids. I pity him, but then he betray me like Japanese."

Having been forced for nearly a month "to live only on food and water" (Cox remembered W. C. Fields's joke), the men partook freely of the captain's gin cocktails. At dinner, there were speeches. The captain stood and read very fast from three bits of paper a long and flowery toast. The men attended very closely, as it was all but incomprehensible—all but the final word, peace. They drank to it gladly.[26]

"By this time it was obvious, as indeed it should have been from the beginning, that owing to the limited choice of activity there was nothing for it but to get drunk and talk a lot of nonsense," Cox recorded. "I did so, and therefore missed the full import of the behavior and speech of Fletcher, who first refused to go on watch and then went up only to come down again. It was all rather hideous. But later he came in and I was sufficiently drunk to say, 'What do you think about? What do you believe in?' and he said, 'I was President of the Oxford Labour Union and we voted 80 percent to 30 not to fight for King and Country.' 'Why,' we said 'did you change?' 'I was president,' he said, 'and we voted 80 to 30 not to fight for king and country.' He was very drunk, sweat on his upper lip, and it so happened that we were sitting in a semicircle and he opposite at the open end under a light so that it seemed as if we had before us the personification of nihilism and we united, leaning forward together strangely fascinated by this skinny gibbering creature. At that moment the self of Fletcher was naked. It was not a pleasant sight."

"Poor David Fletcher has lost the 60th," Brister wrote. "Poor David Fletcher is lost. Something is wrong with him. There must be a key. Someone said he had an accident which hit him on the head. There is something more. Poor, poor David, lost, lost."

The next day, Saturday, July 26, Cox was "wearing a huge turban," as the young brilliants of Boston said when troubled by the aftereffects of overzealous conviviality. At midnight that night, heading on deck to stand watch, he was struck by a sight so unbelievable, "so magical that to tell of it is useless"—red and green navigation lights first; then on the horizon ahead the lights of Cape Town spread like a glittering necklace before the dark, flat height of Table Mountain. For Brister, "the excitement of land, lights, and other men and their works was almost unbearable." For the Englishmen, it was the first time in three years that they had seen city streets lit up at night.

CHAPTER 6

Lost in the Honeycomb

Cape Town, South Africa
July 27–August 15, 1942

> *I got the Cape Town blues*
> *I've got a belly full of gin*
> *I got a bet I won't get in*
> *Before they close the door*
> *You'll all hear the news*
> *I got the Cape Town Blues*
> *Waiting for my boat to leave.*
>
> —Jack Brister

In daylight, the glittering vision of Cape Town resolved into the purposeful hubbub of a working wartime harbor: a broad, seething crescent of wharves and warehouses, derricks, quays, and cargo, shipyards and car parks overlooked to the southwest by the tall, light gray rectangles of modern office buildings in the business district. Behind them, a crazy quilt of low, buff-colored houses and red roofs rose gradually, then faded into gray-green foliage hemming the sheer gray face of Table Mountain, its flanking peaks and the saw-toothed ranges retreating on both sides like a massive rampart separating the imperial outpost from the vast, unfathomed mystery of Africa spreading away and away behind it.

On the deck of *Doña Aurora,* Jack Brister tucked field glasses beneath his overgrown forelock and surveyed the view, tongue firmly in cheek. "Rough big Table Mountain is thrilling to see. I love mountains—the rough and challenging solitudinous mountain which taunts me to try its lovely strength, conquer its majesty, spit from its top. Here it should be easy—through the glasses I see a cable car."[1]

The commercial rumble and the earthy, industrial odors of the anchorage called to the new arrivals poignantly, almost domestically. The water had lost its briny Atlantic tang and shimmered blue, rather than green, in the harbor. But the soldiers were confined to the boat for the day. They ached to get ashore and hungered for war news. At last, a report came back: The 8th Army was still struggling to hold Rommel at the El Alamein line. Their high hopes turned to ashes. After a series of confrontations and skirmishes throughout July—a month of violence that historians would one day discuss as the First Battle of El Alamein—Allied and Axis armies once more would settle into familiar internecine rituals of reconnaissance, harassment, reinforcement, and entrenchment.

It was a good day for letter writing, in any case. Still no mail for the travelers—it had been nearly three months now without a word[2]—but the men at long last could anticipate their own messages actually being dispatched toward home. Brister wrote to his father and to the two women in his life, Betty Turner and Maureen Robins. In a letter to Ambassador Winant he emphasized the upside of military developments. "Today's dispatches from Cairo—we had no news for almost a month—dispelled all our fantastic fears and re-established the fact that there was a place waiting for us in the thick brown dust of a growing offensive.[3]

"I hope your girls are all well and happy as we left them," he went on, referring to the ambassador's wife, Constance, and to his housekeeper, Orol Mears. "The trip is only half complete, but already I feel like Gulliver and am anticipating Candide."[4] Then he revisited with a twist Winant's courtesy to the Yanks on the evening they first met. "If they want anything, like sand, or palm leaves, or Armenian rug merchants just send the word."

For one last time, the Yanks spent lunchtime in the conversational ether. "Today we talked about American poetry and about the old Franklin-Edwards streams which one can see today in Sandburg and McLeish," Cox recorded. "And we talked of the fact that McLeish and Sherwood have such a tremendous influence on American policy today, which is something to make one think."[5]

"I don't want to sleep so much to read so much to think about so much music," Micky Heming complained.[6]

On Tuesday, July 28, the officers of the 60th Rifles were at last released. Stepping ashore in Cape Town was like moving in one moment from paucity to plenty. The small city on the southern edge of Africa struck them as beautiful, exotic, and fecund. There were pleasures they had not tasted for more than a year—*milk* chocolate and fresh oranges[7] and bananas,[8] which they grabbed up and in some cases regretted; more than one officer gorging on fruit found that their stomachs, so long deprived, rejected it violently.

At the crowded train station, the Yanks encountered a group of American soldiers who had come to South Africa as guards on a ship. What did they think of Cape Town? A good one, they said, a good town "filled with willing amateurs."[9]

As the train racketed southeastward to the Yanks' next temporary home, the gangs of unattached men in transit, the novel variety of complexion and dress among the local people, the arid, ever-present mountainsides, the jarring mix of tall, modern buildings and old-fashioned arcaded facades with upstairs porches gave a frontier quality to the passing scene. They found Imperial Forces Transshipment Camp to be a vast grid of tents and tin-roofed huts spread over the flats approaching Muizenberg Mountain. Here some seventeen thousand men awaiting their fates as soldiers were amassed and dispersed and amassed again at the battlefront. New huts of brick and tin under construction nearby soon would increase the camp's capacity to twenty-five thousand.[10]

The Yanks dropped their belongings in their tents and rushed right back into town. After four weeks on shipboard, where the only thing female was a dirty white-and-gray cat, the most thrilling novelty they had encountered was women. "We'd caught the fever," Brister noted in his yearbook. "The way they looked at us set us burning—we didn't stop to think that every man got the same look."

But the first night ashore belonged to Micky Heming. Eager for a break from the group, he and Rob had agreed to dine together at the Mount Nelson Hotel, and Micky had invited Jack along, too.

The Mount Nelson commanded the boulevards of Cape Town as a Victorian dowager the head of the dinner table. Built for a visit from the Prince of Wales in 1899—a time when British dignity was about to be grievously tested by the South African war with the breakaway Boer Republics—the hotel was, and remains, an ornate, sprawling stucco grande dame cushioned all around by palm and hibiscus gardens, with Table Bay and the city spread before her and the awesome, rutted flank of Table Mountain standing guard at her back.

It was winter in the Union of South Africa, and dark had fallen by the time the three soldiers, again fortified by fruit purchased from a vendor near the train station, set off up Adderley Street, the main thoroughfare. At large after being so long sequestered, they felt their very nerve endings vibrate with the excitement of exploring an alien city—"of window shopping, of seeing the lazy blacks and the dapper blacks," Cox would write later, when he recorded his impressions. "Up the leafy avenue in the moonlight and the sound of thin women's heels on the asphalt, slow, walking, and lovers on the benches in the shadows and a pool of water under the warm electric light, the sound of 'When We Were Young in May' on the harmonica played by one of three soldiers on the bench by the pool, all the clean white buildings rising above the trees."

Inside the hotel, spacious, well-appointed lounges, thick carpets, and elderly couples in evening dress all spoke poignantly and reassuringly to Cox. "Good, good," he found himself thinking, "these people uphold the Empire, good old dress for dinner." The promise of good food and wine drunk, for a change, from glasses awakened a longing for other pleasures. "Ah, this is a lovely night, this is a beautiful place—this big, expensive hotel on the hill above the city," he would remember thinking, "and I will sit here and drink a little gin and vermouth and then eat the good food and romance will come if I sit and wait here in this quiet, rich, and friendly place."

After cocktails, the three young men ate heartily in the big, dark-paneled dining room, then returned to the lounge where there were young women to eye until Jack, who had arranged it, said that Micky could play the piano.

The dining room was empty now and Brister and Cox sat each at his own table, sipping the local Van der Hum brandy while Micky settled himself at the grand piano. Then the floodgates opened. "What it was he played I do not know," Cox wrote. "There were parts of the Eroica and the Sonata Pathetique and The Man I Love by Gershwin and the Wedding March played both right and satirically. But one knew that he was spending all that had been built up on the trip—getting rid of it and even in this thoughtless playing giving form to the broodings over the English dream and his sense of destiny, his necessity to make music."

From where Brister and Cox sat nearby, backs toward a corner, Rob caught sight of a woman sitting in the shadows across the room near the door. She looked tall and cool and very lovely in the dim light, and thinking she had been drawn in by the music, he crossed the room and whispered, "Do you want a drink?" She nodded. Rob ordered four more and sat beside her, still listening, intent on discerning the ideas and intentions behind Micky's torrent of sound. Jack soon joined them, but still Rob felt that each of them sat alone, thrilled by the music, and he, at least, awed. "I felt I was watching someone wrestling with his spirit," he would write.

Micky ended with a composition of his own called "Tamberlaine," then joined the others. As they talked, the woman revealed her situation, a not uncommon one in wartime. Her husband had just been killed in Libya. She had been visiting General Wavell in India when the news came, and now, with three young sons back in England, she was making her long way home.

The story was a sad one, but from inside the rapture produced by Micky's art, Cox found Mrs. Byars herself to be strangely petty. Hers were the qualities that irritated him most about the British, excepting Micky— a propriety that felt like coldness and, above all, a nearly debilitating restraint. "A bit of a bitch and a snob," he described her later, "and careful, talking nicely of Wavell with whom she had been visiting. One should have felt sorry for her, but one couldn't because one felt her capacities were small, that she did not suffer greatly because she did not enjoy greatly. She had carefully limited her desires and her emotions and her mind. She would turn her head if she saw ugliness and she would turn it from beauty because it is also painful. What needs came from herself she turned to hollow things like social prestige. Micky sensed this too and felt remorse that she should have heard him play as he did. He had broken all his fingernails."

The next day, after a stop at a barber, the three went with Durk to find a gramophone shop and play some records. They wanted to hear Beethoven's Ninth, but had to settle for Tchaikovsky, who had lately grown very popular among the British, possibly in tribute to the Russian people now suffering and dying by the tens of thousands for their common cause. No sooner had the Sixth Symphony begun than Micky announced, "Too slow."

"How do you know? You've only heard two notes," Durk said.

Micky threw him a pained look. Everything was wrong with the piece. It was too slow, then too fast, and above all the phrasing was wrong.

The line between sublimity and sentimentality is a fine one, Heming told them, and especially so with Tchaikovsky, who sits precisely on the border. He is great when played sincerely.[11] It was the one thing Micky said he really cared about—sincerity in music.[12] He had no such criticism when they listened to Delius's 1912 tone poem "On Hearing the First Cuckoo in Spring." To Heming, it was England, and he felt about it as Cox felt about a few lyric poems. "If he had not written it, I might have myself."

Despite having asserted his weariness with music before going ashore, Micky would spend the weeks in Cape Town making daily visits to the music shop and taking in every available concert, even though he nearly always left the performances infuriated.[13]

That night, the American friends discovered the Delmonico, a large, noisy hall fitted out as a nightclub where sailors, soldiers, and merchant seamen crowded in to drink, dance, eat a steak, and maybe find a woman to go home with. Cox, still under the spell of the sea voyage and Micky's emotional musical summation, once more found his fierce hopes for romance disappointed. Indeed, if sincerity were the value most to be cherished, here, he felt, was its opposite. The scene left him uncharacteristically cynical—"everyone pretending—intoxicated by the noise and the setting—to be alive, since they have made of living such a mess that only under the fake sky with the electric stars and manufactured clouds is love and comradeship and lusty drinking credible. Above the brawling hall on balconies, one eats thick juicy steaks and drinks a little and believes for a time in the illusion."

The next night, Brister investigated the illusion more closely. He got lucky—to a point. Jack left the Delmonico with two young women—a pretty blond named Sharon and a voluble, dull brunette, Doreen—and a half-drunk midshipman, who wandered away after Doreen, initially receptive and bubbling over with silly, flirtatious talk, drew the line at deep kissing. After seeing Doreen home, Jack and Sharon rode the train, leaning together and kissing and dozing, then walked to the simple house in the Cape Town suburbs where Sharon lived with her family.

That night, a full moon coincided with a six-hour trial blackout in Cape Town; the notion of establishing a permanent blackout to deny enemy U-boats and airplanes the advantages of backlit ships and geographical bearings had been a matter of local controversy for some time.[14] Sharon's mother had thrown a blackout party, and when Jack and Sharon arrived, she was wandering around the darkened house, tidying up and holding her head and groaning. She had been sick, she informed them, and she was annoyed. Her guests had left while she was in the bathroom.

Jack and Sharon settled themselves in the small parlor. From an adjoining room, Sharon's little sister called, "Can I have some cake?"

"Asking for cake at this hour?" the mother cried. "You'll get a good crack the first thing you know. Go to sleep."

Then she was in the parlor, fumbling with a candle. Sharon shouldn't be alone in the dark with a soldier. Before long, she reappeared with a lightbulb and insisted that Jack screw it into a socket. The garish light did no favors for Sharon, who had seemed beautiful by moonlight.

"Now you mustn't stay too long," the woman said, before stumbling into the next room. Jack and Sharon heard the bed creak and the little girl being threatened into silence. When a gentle snoring began, Jack's hopes rose.

But the sofa! It was too short, too lumpy, and it was filled by Sharon. Sitting beside her on the floor, Jack wondered what to do next. He had a good idea that given the right sign from Sharon, all discomfort would be quickly overcome by appetite.

Sharon wanted to talk.

Jack made the best of it. He liked to talk, he was full of longing, and he let his imagination run. He talked to Sharon as if she were what he wanted—undiscovered gold, a woman meant for a mountaintop, glorious in the sun, wind, rain.

"I used to climb the mountain every Sunday," she said. He wished she wouldn't interrupt.

And so it went on, Jack stoking the fires with poetry, she responding in a measured way, opening her mouth to his kiss, then jumping up to show him the books she had read—*The Sting of Love, Modern Warfare.* She invited him to a party the next day with her family. When he declined, she asked him to come again to the house; she'd be home alone. He said, "I don't think I'd better."

She snapped at him, "Oh, bugger you, then," and left the room.

Jack walked all the strange way back to transit camp, his imagination inflamed, thinking about the mysterious country around him. The next day he wrote in his yearbook: "A hell of a big moon to walk home by— eight miles, in a strange dark continent where the whites still hold the darks at bay with whips, hatred, and violence."[15]

South Africa's active alliance with Great Britain in World War II had not been an obvious outcome. Many white South Africans were of German descent and, at least initially, in sympathy with the German cause, but more significant still was the history of bitterness between Afrikaners, whose Dutch ancestors had first established the cape colony in the seventeenth century, and the British, relative newcomers whose practice of rounding up and removing civilians to concentration camps during the South African war (called the War of Independence by local nationalists) had left ineradicable scars. Nevertheless, one charismatic Afrikaner general, a hero of the War of Independence who became a favorite of Winston Churchill, had pulled together a coalition that favored active support for Great Britain. In 1939 Jan Christian Smuts was elected prime minister over an opponent who favored neutrality, and his charismatic patriotism, along with the British community's ties to the motherland, held South Africa to the Allied cause. As in Canada, conscription would never be practicable in South Africa, but volunteers for the army and the air force had been numerous, and they proved their loyalty with blood.

When the Yanks arrived in Cape Town at the end of July, details of Rommel's swift and devastating capture of Tobruk at the end of June still were filtering in. Most of the South African 2nd Infantry Division—two complete infantry brigades and most of their supporting units—had been lost. The defeated garrison had been commanded by South African major general H. B. Klopper. Of the nearly twenty-seven thousand men killed or captured by the Germans, roughly 45 percent were South African.[16] The *Cape Times* devoted its entire front page on July 27 to an appeal for donations to the Thank You General Smuts Fund, which would be used to provide comforts for the prisoners of war. "Never before has there been such need to support a cause . . . thousands of our brave men who have fought so gallantly up north are now prisoners of war in enemy hands. . . . In thousands of Cape Town homes there is untold grief and suffering for their loved ones." Shorter articles inside offered advice on what to do "If He's a Prisoner of War . . ."

The names of South Africans killed in the course of smaller calamities appeared in a regular column called "Roll of Honor" and in short news stories: Sixteen killed on April fourth in the sinking by Japanese dive-bombers of the British cruiser *Dorsetshire* in the Indian Ocean;[17] seventeen dead on a British aircraft carrier sunk in April in the Bay of Bengal.[18] On July 29 the list of casualties at Tobruk was printed in two groups: "MISSING" and "MISSING BELIEVED PRISONERS OF WAR." The type was tiny and the long columns of names filled two pages of broadsheet. The Avenge Tobruk Appeal, launched in June by General Smuts to recruit twelve hundred gunners to replenish the ranks,[19] was lagging badly behind goal. "Shame of Civilian Manhood" ran the headline for that story.[20]

Cape Town's Anglo community and its supporters extended themselves mightily to entertain visiting troops. Under the umbrella of the South African Women's Auxiliary Services (SAWAS), more than ten thousand white women organized work groups to send comforts to soldiers and planned entertainments for the men of visiting convoys.[21] Each morning, volunteers drove to the docks and the train station to pick up soldiers in search of hospitality. The Yanks were escorted to the movies and to the symphony. They went for drives in the countryside. They played squash. They played golf. On the links one day, Cox grew frustrated with his game and caused a stir. "[I] was so atrocious," he wrote his friend Goody Wigglesworth, "that after six holes, I let my eight-year-old

Negro caddy take the shots. He was excellent. All the English were hor-rified."[22] The American consul in Cape Town entertained them, along with his American friend in the oil business. The City Club, founded in 1878 and the second-oldest of the British men's clubs in town,[23] welcomed them to its lounges.

Everywhere the Yanks went, Brister collected stories.

The American oil man's young assistant had a beautiful wife. More than once her picture had appeared on the cover of the leading local magazine. But the assistant also had a beautiful case of asthma, which prevented him from dancing with his wife at parties and charity events, and he traveled often to visit agents all over South Africa. "What's she going to do?" Jack wondered. "The cards are all turned up!" He foresaw no happy ending.

The American consul, Denby, a thin man with a stove-in shirtfront, was "nice like sugar." His wife was pretty, but her face wore "the Cape Town brand," dark circles below her eyes. Their daughter, reputedly quite beau-tiful, had fallen from a train and fractured her skull, or perhaps she had jumped. "She is in trouble," people said. The event left her paralyzed.

Major Orr, his wife, and his daughter, Brigid, took Jack to the sym-phony, which played in a clublike setting where one could both drink and listen. Major Orr said, "Really!" and raised his eyebrows. "Oh, I love this bit," he said, of a Handel transition causing the orchestra to struggle.

"What are they playing now?" he asked, after fetching a fresh bottle of brandy. They were still busy with the Handel.

"Oh, Daddy!" Brigid said, embarrassed by her father, who was beyond embarrassing.

His wife, a pleasant, English-looking woman who always trusted her first impressions, seemed annoyed as well, her laugh forced. Lately, she had found the major taking sides with their daughter, countermanding her orders. They would form alliances in turns, and grow the girl up too quickly in the process.

Brigid herself, at sixteen, was courageous, spirited, poised on the crest.

Particularly fascinating to Brister were the stories he heard about black Africans, whom the British called Kaffirs and Brister perhaps imagined to embody a rare, primitive kind of vehemence or passion. He heard of an elderly Kaffir who posed as the father of a good-looking girl in order to sell her, for fifteen pounds, to young men in need of a wife. He would hand her over after receiving half payment, then take her away to await payment in full, which never came.

On one occasion, the girl liked her ostensible husband and decided to stay with him. In the dead of night, the old keeper crept to their hut and attacked the young man with his strong white teeth, almost biting his nose off. The girl ran away, never to be seen again. The young Kaffir was out fifteen pounds and half his nose. After the wound healed, however, he spoke of his disfigurement proudly.

Jack heard again the old story of the well-groomed, well-spoken English lord who had "gone native" and lived as a chieftain among the Kalahari bushmen. He tried to imagine the Kalahari Desert itself, where, it was said, the dry grass grew ten feet tall and so thick that a car passing through left no track, where the natives sucked water from secret springs using two hollow reeds and an ostrich egg, where you had to travel only by landmarks, and if you missed one, you were lost.

He heard of the two kinds of Africans—the faithful, unspoiled ones full of racial pride who would work in the city for three years, then return for three to their homelands, and the unfaithful, the "civilized" Cape Town Kurros, who took revenge for their losses with knife and razor.

But what impressed him above all was the general atmosphere of hysteria provoked in Cape Town by the coming and going of men from the military convoys. "The girls have gone crazy," he wrote. "Hospitality, competition, and amorality compete. The office girls can see the ships in the harbor from their work—not much work gets done."

On drives and hikes, the Yanks found the singular landscape of South Africa thrilling. In early winter, the many vineyards were brown and neatly manicured, the rows of sculpted vines, the broad, tawny fields abutting wild, precipitous hills. Craggy peaks—Lion's Head, Devil's Peak, the Twelve Apostles—towered above smooth sand beaches, all of it softened and colored by the confluence of sky and sea. "Among the vineyards the smooth white geometric houses with thatched roofs brown and the rounded gables on the façade and on the two ends" set Cox to wondering about the first Dutch and Huguenot settlers. He imagined them self-satisfied, "fatly looking over their juicy acres."[24]

But the country as a whole they found strange and, ultimately, frustrating, its complicated knot of race relations enforced by the code of white superiority. "All the English here are apologetic that South Africa is not England," Cox noted. "Fools. My god there is a beauty in the air of this country that makes England a shaded place. There is a promise here that would be fulfilled if the English were not so apologetic of themselves."[25]

Cox's romantic hopes revived on Saturday, August 1, when he and Bolté headed off to the suburbs for a dance at a country club called Kelvin Grove. Brister, stuck on picket duty that night, would see eight men drunk to unconsciousness carried across the Transit Camp footbridge instead.[26]

"We went to the party feeling maybe we will meet some women to intrigue us," Cox recorded, "so long in the Army and on the sea without even speaking to a woman." Here was a good party, he thought, with girls in evening dress, and he imagined the fun that used to be.

But the young Americans' efforts to engage the local girls at first fell flat. "We were intrigued and fascinated by the country," he would remember, "and we wished them to express the country, but they had no interest in it." They talked about parties and clothes and friends. Even Cox's usual coping strategy failed to satisfy. "One felt, to drink we go, but there was no pleasure in drinking, for they were unsympathetic even to the sometimes necessity of drinking." Rob and Chuck judged the girls small-minded—"those girls who wouldn't go to a cheap cinema to see a good film, but must go to a good cinema for a cheap one."

Then, as the evening wound down, Bolté and Cox moved in desperation to a livelier table. "I'm bored over there. Let me sit here," Cox said. That was better. Chuck struck up a conversation with a young woman named Myra who called herself Alabama, for reasons unexplained. Rob asked Yvonne to dance and enjoyed the waltz—"more than an athletic event," he wrote later, "and there was a promise of the time that was to follow."[27]

"Chuck and Bob meet 'Alabama' and Yvonne at Kelvin," Brister reported more bluntly in his yearbook. "Durk meets Vera. Chuck and Bob get it fast and heavy."

Yvonne Michau, a young woman of French and Austrian descent, had learned just recently that her fiancé, a flier with the South African Air Force, had been killed in North Africa. Her friend Myra apparently was distinguished only by her foolishness and her willingness. On August 2, Bolté unburdened himself to Brister in the latrine. "She's unbelievable, what corn! I just listen—she's a good piece, though."[28]

Over the next few days the two young women took Rob and Chuck out for drives and for meals, introduced them to their families, and talked to them about the country's interior, where both families owned farms. Soon Jack would be joining the party when Rob or Chuck wasn't along.

What occurred between Rob and Yvonne during "the time that was to follow"? To know precisely is impossible. His journal entries were characteristically circumspect about their sexual encounters, but it is not difficult to grasp the gist from the details that he recorded.

"Up by the first cable station. The many lights. Where can we go? This car is too small. Outside it is too cold. The empty house. Singing. Casey Jones and The Ruttin's. Now you sing [to] me in Afrikaans. Do you ever feel that you are more than one person—that a part of you wanted to do one thing very much—live a whole life perhaps—and that another part of you—a bigger part—said no you must live other deeds. Do you see what I mean? I want you to see that.

"When we drove over the winding downhill pitching road, the lights would come up to meet us on the sharp bends."

Yvonne and Rob talked often about Austria, which had captivated Rob during his European trip after prep school. He met Yvonne's mother, who claimed to love Americans. "They are so energetic and always carrying books. They like literature. I have tried to give my children literature and travel," she said. "If we'd known you were coming, we could have had a good meal. I like a meal with soup and fish to start. You like literature. Have you seen this *Reader's Digest?* Such literature all written by people who live in Chicago and New York. Oh, the Americans, they are wonderful. There was an American scientist who stayed in Cape Town—such lovely silk pajamas—he wore them at garden parties—it was very hot, you know—a different pair each time. He had come from India," she said.

"I didn't let you love me just because he was dead," Yvonne said, and: "I mean, I wouldn't let [just] anyone love me. I hope you go up north."[29]

Rob would remember one of the Afrikaans songs Yvonne sang: "Hurry and cut the corn—my love is caught in the wait-a-minute bush."[30]

"Yvonne really cares for Bob," Brister noted on August 9 in his yearbook.[31] And yet near the end of the Yanks' stay in Cape Town, Yvonne called Brister and invited him over on a night when she was home alone. Station picket duty prevented it. "There was the fateful chance all lost, all arranged for, what was never meant to be and thank god wasn't," Jack wrote. "It'd make little difference. I remember Mavourneen—there aren't many! There aren't any!"[32] He wrote a poem:

The loss of balance
The absence of values
There is no looking up.
The bright angel sticks her nose
In the newspaper, a cocktail glass
Or a teacup.
And if this [be] light
Send me back to the blackout.

How I do miss the home
I knew. Mavourneen, you were my last home.
Would Whitman sing so happily and
Surely of himself if he left his
Country.
Emerson said there was no need to
travel—it is indeed easy to be
self-reliant if you never imperil
your balance—never risk curiosity,
adventure, the call to the darkened
honeycomb.

Cox liked Yvonne, her directness and her unapologetic enjoyment of life as she found it. She liked her days at the university; she liked the communal life there, which excluded all others. She liked to swim and play tennis and squash, to dance, to drive to beaches or wine farms. She liked the way black feet pressed the grapes as her ancestors' feet had done in France. "A world of Yvonnes would be an easy world, for they merely want to live and enjoy the good things that are their heritage," he wrote. "But life is not as Yvonne visualizes it. The complications of modern man step in—not modern man but man always, man evil and warped, man intolerant—and her lover is killed and she is numb and must go back to her father's sheep farm to put on armor against life. There is no armor."

But Yvonne did not make Cox happy. Sexually inexperienced, he found fast love disorienting. "Yvonne has been lovely," he wrote, "but ah god the cruelty of it to say let us give each other joy as much as we can but do not think that such joy promises anything for the future. The form she desires is big and admirable and have I helped her or hurt her? And then all the business of Myra, warm-hearted and demented, always in the background and saying by her presence, You too are like me. Think not that what you are doing is any different from what I do. You also are insincere and your thoughts run crooked. But that isn't true, for all people are not alike, but the shades of difference are subtle and Heaven and Hell look very much alike."

Cox wished he could accept life uncritically. "What one wants so much is a unity to life and where does one find it? Where does one find unity and wholeness? Is it in submitting, submitting, submitting or in constant grasping?"

He had found purpose as a soldier, but now that goal appeared stymied. "I would be many things and I may be nothing. I have no identity. I see form here or form in a totally different place, but I may not pursue that form because I am pursuing what I do not even know. . . . We drift, unwilling. We did not ask to drift. We saw a form and understood its compulsion, and they deny us even when we are seeking. Always one sees promise but never fulfillment.

"Or is life just *now* always now and sometimes those nows are lovely and the rest of life is forgotten," he worried. With forward movement impossible, time began to hang heavy, then heavier. "The camp is like a prison camp, with no one belonging here and officers cut off from their units. Some going one way, some another. All of them forced to stay a time and listen to the sentimental music of the gramophone."[33]

Taken together, it seemed all just a tiresome waiting game. As resupply and reorganization proceeded in North Africa, as the Axis soldiers and the Allied soldiers in Egypt tested the lines and reinforced territory with barbed wire, gun sangars, slit trenches, and scores upon scores of land mines, the American British officers suspended in transit at Cape Town again grew restless, after three months without mail feeling often homesick, cut off, trapped betwixt and between.

"One reads oneself into surroundings so much," Cox wrote on. "When we first came to Cape Town we thought it was an eager country because we ourselves were eager. We saw promises that could be fulfilled because in us there was promise. Now, when we want to go on to Egypt, we feel frustrated and so feeling see frustration around us. The English here are frustrated because they cannot impose Anglicism on the Afrikaans. The Afrikaans are frustrated because they are snubbed by the English and do not find the growth that is inherent in their country. The blacks are frustrated because they are worse than slaves. And within these divisions are smaller divisions of tinier purposes. Truly this place now seems to be one of several purposes each thwarting the other.

"So much time wasted, so little time," Cox thought. "Let us get down to it. It is hard to be a soldier without a war."[34]

Feeling untethered, Cox found his thoughts turning homeward, as Brister's had done. Settling down with his journal, he began to draft a letter to his mother that was unlike any of the many others he had written, or would yet write. "I have thought infrequently of writing this letter," he began, "and each time shied from it; first because it is like all the sentimental heroics which prevent clear thought, and secondly because I'm quite certain that I shan't be killed." It was for her to open in the event of his death. "On the other hand," he continued, "I think that you would like a last letter if anything should happen, a letter to tell you what I hope you know already—how glad a time you have given me—and to try and say what I think about life. About the last I'm afraid I'm not very articulate. But I believe—oh yes I do believe."[35]

A couple of days later orders came. The Yanks prepared to ship out. Rob and Jack said good-bye to Cape Town with Micky over a drink at the City Club. Then they joined Durk and Chuck and Heyward and the countless other soldiers crowding onto gangways, heading to sea again.

CHAPTER 7

Interlude *Duchess of Atholl*

Cape Town, South Africa, to Suez, Egypt
August 15–September 2, 1942

> Queen of four thousand souls: they are in you and you
> become more and more in them. The very air of your passages
> becomes the very air they breathe—in & out—it stinks!
>   I said four thousand souls—but the question is when is a
> soul not a soul—or when is a soul?
>
> —Jack Brister

Aboard the refitted ocean liner *Duchess of Atholl*, Rob Cox awoke in pitch dark and found himself trapped in a coffin. The ship, designed for a thousand passengers at most, now contained four times that. The air had a sour, stale weight—a quality of lavatories, sweat, exhalation, of layer upon layer of tired human flesh—and the weight was crushing. His wooden bunk, one of eighty packed at two-foot intervals four to a stack in a windowless hold, allowed six inches of airspace between his nose and the planking above. Were he to spread out his arms, his fingers would fall on the bodies of men sleeping in bunks beside him. His muscles began to tense and quiver. He fought back a compulsion to shout, to flee. Through the earliest hours of morning he lay awake in the narrow bed and the blackness, shame compounding claustrophobia, and breathed in shallow gasps until, at last, sleep freed him.

The next day, Rob felt abashed by his reaction to the constraints of a crowded troop transport, and he wrestled with the question of whether or not he should try to force himself to adapt. "Why should we be slaves to our bodies?" he asked in his journal. Would it be weakness to give in to his fear? Why did he mind so much? Then he thought, "But is it not more foolish to say, I will lie in that living coffin just to show I can?" Being an officer bestowed certain luxuries; much as he enjoyed the camaraderie of the riflemen and believed in their essential equality, that was a fact he had accepted. He found a place for his camp bed in the small cabin shared by Micky Heming and Peter Wake. One thing was clear: "The idyll is over now. It is hard getting back to machinery of army."[1]

Duchess of Atholl was to *Doña Aurora* as Philadelphia to Ambler, Jack Brister observed. "The drama has more quantity but the quantity dulls the perception, perhaps mercifully.[2] . . . There's little room to breathe and still less room to find yourself alone for even a minute. The boat is teeming."[3]

On this sea voyage, little time or ink would be spent on wonder, except occasionally at the density of soldiers packed into the vessel and, later, the relentlessness of the heat. The *Duchess* was far larger than the two other ships the Yanks had known, and faster. The twenty-thousand-ton liner was 582 feet long and 75 feet wide, with two tall, straight funnels, a mast front and back, and many vent hoods carrying air to the vast hive belowdecks. When built in 1928 for the Canadian Pacific Co., she was the first of four new luxury liners—also *Duchess of Bedford, Duchess of Richmond,* and *Duchess of York*—considered to be in a class by themselves. Plying the Atlantic between Montreal and Liverpool, she for a time held the record for an eastbound crossing—six days, thirteen hours.[4] In 1940 she had crossed the Atlantic filled with women and children seeking security from war and delivered them safely to Quebec and Montreal. But now every hint of luxury had been erased. To the Yanks the routines and risks of traveling in convoy had become commonplace. As the *Duchess* plowed northward through the Indian Ocean toward the horn of Somaliland, the equator would go by unremarked.

Four days into the journey, on Wednesday, August 19, news passed through the crowds of men like a gentle breeze across a wheat field: The British had landed in France. "The news moved slowly for we were not anxious to be swept by rumor and no one seemed to know the source," Cox wrote. Amid guarded speculation—"But there were tanks. Tanks must mean the second front"—the men hoped, dared not hope that the liberation of Europe was at last at hand. That night, everyone went to bed anxious.

The next morning the officers returned to their habitual pursuits in the lounge, but they set them aside when the chimes rang and moved quickly toward the loudspeaker. "Now that the raid on Dieppe is over . . . ." The men fell silent. "No one said anything, no one showed very much disappointment," Cox noted. It was just another place name for the familiar list of failures that began with Dunkirk and ran through Greece, Crete, Singapore, and, lately, Tobruk. "We have become hardened to waiting, to defeat and disappointment," Cox wrote. But, he added, "we are eager. . . . How quietly, how swiftly, how lightly walking did the whole lounge put down their books and cards. Slowly walked back to them, reluctant."

It was perhaps best that the officers on board *Duchess of Atholl* did not stop to dwell on events at Dieppe. The cross-channel raid on the French seaport would with time accrue all the bitterest labels of military history: disaster, catastrophe, calamity, fiasco, debacle. Near dawn on August 19, nearly five thousand Canadian troops itching for action after a long wait in England, some one thousand British personnel, and fifty U.S. Rangers eager to gain experience attacked near dawn at four points along a ten-mile front to complete a "reconnaissance in force" and test defenses at the German-occupied port.

Almost from its inception the endeavor had been troubled. An earlier attempt on Dieppe code-named Rutter had been canceled after the Allied flotilla was discovered and attacked by German bombers while still moored off England. Despite opposition from other British commanders and the security risk inherent in remounting an operation after its objective had been revealed to the troops, the new chief of combined operations, Vice Admiral Louis Mountbatten, proceeded to reorganize it under the upbeat, and later sadly ironic, code name Jubilee.

En route from England, British ships encountered a German convoy and the critical element of surprise was lost. Landing craft labored to reach shore and attacking soldiers struggled up steep, pebbly beaches raked by machine gun fire. Gun positions in cliffs flanking the beaches rained down slaughter. Of fifty tanks intended to support the infantry attack, only twenty-seven reached shore, with two "drowned" in the shallows, and of those landed only fifteen managed to progress a short way beyond the beaches. The commanding general compounded disaster by ordering reinforcements ashore when the situation already was lost. Allied casualties exceeded two-thirds of the attack force.[5] The Royal Navy lost one destroyer and thirty-three landing craft to no obvious purpose, and of sixty-six squadrons of fighter planes from nine nations sent to engage the Luftwaffe, one hundred sixty Allied aircraft were lost, to the Germans' forty-eight.

Lord Mountbatten would assert that the lessons of Dieppe made possible the Allies' later war-winning amphibious successes; nowadays, the defeat might be termed a wake-up call. But by August 1942, the British high command had surely experienced a surfeit of those. Dieppe illustrated convincingly the Allies' unpreparedness for a cross-channel invasion. If it highlighted the essentials for success in the new and complex style of warfare that Winston Churchill called "triphibious,"[6] because it demanded intimate cooperation among air, sea, and land forces, it did so by their absence. Planning was slipshod, intelligence faulty or absent, equipment inappropriate, surprise lacking, personnel inadequate, timing off, communication poor, and so on. It was the sort of enterprise that might possibly be valued by aficionados of noble British failures; certainly the ill-led ground soldiers could not be faulted, and several Victoria's Crosses and Distinguished Service Medals were won. But it was not an episode to gladden the hearts of men biding their time as best they could en route to the battlefield.

Oddly, the huge, teeming quantity of men everywhere around them threw the Yanks back on one another for diversion and company. "I wonder if I ever impressed on you what a splendid group I have been wandering with," Cox wrote his mother. It had dawned on him that, excepting two leaves spent with Tony Van Bergen in England, he had been with at least one of his compatriots 95 percent of the time, nearly every waking moment. "The best thing about all of us is that we all respect each other's individuality and leave each other alone when we want to and talk only when we want to," he continued. "We kid each other a fair amount, and all in all, it is a rather good thing. I don't know any other place where you see the same people so constantly."[7]

He ran his mind over them. Cutting, always at the ready with Band-Aids and soap, was to Cox the least interesting, though, like the rest, he was very good-hearted. Brister: an intense yet private man who kept his dearest thoughts to himself. On the first night in Cape Town, returning to transit camp a bit drunk, Rob had told him he was like Old Man River, a slow-moving force who would get there if anyone would.

Durkee, Cox considered to be the most mature of the lot, with a mind disciplined to fact and fairness. It rather quashed conversation at times, of course, as in argument or discussion Durk hastened to identify the essential question, then refused to discuss what he had no facts to support.

Then there was Bolté, hardest of all to describe, though also the easiest to laugh with. He was so full of contradictions, walking the line between facile and brilliant. At St. Paul's he would have been called a "feign," someone interested in art and ideas, the opposite of a "techno." Like Cox, Bolté had a gift for "feigning," but he was also genuinely smart. His head was gigantic, which Cox supposed went along with being brainy. He could put on Chuck's officer's cap and spin it around as if his head were a gatepost. Bolté wasn't a fake, but it was hard to tell what he really believed. "He refuses to commit himself to himself," Cox thought. Perhaps that accounted for his success as a newspaperman at Dartmouth.

When Rob and Chuck were staying in Ireland together, a female dinner guest had turned to Rob one evening after dessert and said, "Tell me about your friend." Rob asked what she meant. "Well, he has the most interesting face I've ever seen," she answered. "It's so bitter and so affectionate, both at once." Later, when Cox told Brister the story, he said that she was seeing into the future.

For Micky Heming, there was, as always, the devouring preoccupation of music. On the gramophone in the cabin, he played Berlioz's "Le Carnival Romain," Delius's "Cuckoo," and conducted as if there were a real orchestra. When Brister watched, the intensity tied him in knots.[8] Micky was composing a new work—"Threnody," or mourning song. He explained to Jack the importance of color in music. Debussy had it, Mendelssohn did not, and on down the line. Jack hazarded a definition. "Color seems to mean a more sensitive use of the tonal qualities (or color) inherent in the instruments themselves." But don't go labeling passages, instruments, or chords as definite colors, Heming warned. Consider the difference between intensity and excitement—good and mediocre.

Others found relief from monotony as they could. At night on deck, the drunks fought one another for sleeping space on the benches. "The men lie in the passageways," Cox wrote, "on the stairways, in the corners of the stairway landings, stripped to a pair of shorts but sweating always. At night there are hundreds of them close against the walls of the staircases, often invisible in the darkness, sometimes their strained faces lit up as they inhale a cigarette. In the early hours of the morning one stumbles over the prone bodies."[9]

Bolté, who liked his drink, sometimes joined in with the men when he spotted a bottle. One night Heming found him passed out cold. "It's almost tragic, really," Jack noted, but he could not sympathize completely. "Not enough sensitivity," Jack judged. In his eyes, Bolté was compromised by his easy enthusiasms—"too ready to appreciate with no inner moral fibre, which makes most good people understand first and then appreciate." Jack grew impatient with his friends at times, as he did with himself. "Heyward is talented but almost blind," he noted in his yearbook one day.[10] Cox, on the other hand, had risen in his estimation. After a long talk on August 24, Brister wrote, "I'm beginning to understand and consequently like him a hell of a lot. He is sincere. I didn't realize." Only one person, it seemed, had never rubbed him the wrong way and that was Maureen. "Dearest M. you are too far from me," he pined. "I shall always remember happily our short time in the sun. We are luckier than most for we two have had, have shared a memory, of complete and lazy delight."

Ten days into the journey, on Tuesday, August 25, Micky and Jack started work on a play, pooling their common intensity, energy, and wholeheartedness, Heming's volatility steadied by Brister's firm focus. It would be a comedy, called *Hope Town*. Brister had been reading E. M. Forster—*A Passage to India* and *Howards End*—and, feeling inadequate by comparison, took a while to get rolling. But a full day of work on Wednesday left him buoyed: "Should be a good, funny play," he noted.

As they worked, Micky's small cabin filled with cigarette smoke. In the upper bunk, Cox lay immersed in *Moby-Dick*. The maritime fable of conquest and obsession and their costs, of the symbolic meanings behind natural experience, enthralled him. "There is something of Ahab in Micky," he thought.[11] "I feel like Stubb most often," he wrote home, more lightheartedly than he often felt. "'I do not know, but I am Stubb, and Stubb has had his history,'" he quoted. "'But I vow now that Stubb has always been jolly.' Of course he hasn't. But whenever he thinks about it, it seems as if he has.

"Melville must have been quite a boy," he mused on. "I don't know much about him. . . . But he speaks in a letter to Hawthorne of Heaven as containing lots of very good champagne. I hope he's right."

But Cox was not really lighthearted. At night he paced the deck, and not just in search of fresh air. He was brooding about a rumor that the 60th officers on board would be transferred to a different regiment upon arrival in Egypt. "It's just a rumor and no point worrying about it," he chided himself, but he still couldn't clear the thought from his mind. Surely, being Americans, the Yanks wouldn't be transferred from the former 60th Royal Americans, and he felt certain that the colonels commandant Davidson and Wake would never stand for it. But still, it would mean more time wasted. "How ironical it would be," he wrote home, "when all last year we wished to be treated just like the others instead of being displayed as phenomena, [if] we should now be treated or maltreated as if we were not Americans." The fact was, though Cox perhaps was unaware of it, the past months of training and discomfort and tight quarters and open spaces and subservience and freedom had wedded him to his regiment, just as they were intended to. "It's the same fight in brass buttons as black," he continued to debate himself. "But I like my black ones." He remembered a rhyme, written in the last war about the men of the KRRC.

> He honestly thinks that his corps is unique.
> That all other regiments are horribly weak
> Is the text of his barrack room sermon.

"He honestly does, too," Cox thought, "whether he's a rifleman or Lieutenant Colonel."[12]

For the balance of the journey, Brister and Heming were absorbed in their work. By Friday, the twenty-eighth, they had blocked out all three acts and a prologue. Brister felt hopeful about *Hope Town*. "I think it has the stuff of a play in it. All that remains now is to polish and write it," he noted. When one of the thousands of soldiers aboard died and received a sea burial, it caused only a brief interruption. "We just dropped a man over the side, gave him three volleys and a few fake flowers," Brister noted, "then rejoined convoy."[13]

Cox, meanwhile, began to think about doing some real writing himself. It was what people had always said he was meant for—his mother, the masters at school, even his uncle Max. But he himself had found the notion of such a sedentary, inward-looking occupation off-putting. And what would he write about? Now, with time on his hands and no more-active tasks available, his thoughts turned toward the place and the people he knew best—the Vermont small town Windsor, where his large extended family had been leading citizens or summer visitors for four generations. From this great distance, he saw the place itself as the hero, and all the little places in it as symbols of different forces. He thought of the two waterfalls in the dike that bordered the pond on the way to Paradise, for instance. The distant one, near a farm, seemed an evil thing—slow-moving, very slimy and dirty, with a stagnant smell, dark and sinister. One didn't like to be near it. The closer waterfall near the boathouse was, by contrast, fascinating. It rushed and roared and sprayed down into a white, foaming pool splendidly exciting from a distance. But if you got right down by the spray and the foam, you could detect the same dank stink that you smelled at a distance from the far one. Writing home, he asked his mother "to do a preposterous thing"—to jot down all the facts she could think of about Windsor and the many relatives, known or unknown to him, who had shaped it. He admitted he didn't know when or if he would get to the project. "Let the whole thing be a secret between the two of us," he told his mother. But it would be there, his family and its history all recorded in a neat package, when he was ready for it.[14]

Near the end of August, the *Duchess of Atholl* turned westward into the Gulf of Aden. Behind was the Arabian Sea. "Our first view of the East,"

Durkee wrote to his parents, "was impressive in the intensity of the bare land and deadly sun. The inevitable camels, natives, and mud huts are there. The land and people seem to have existed from the beginning of time." Scrawny, hook-beaked birds of prey called Bromley kites hovered and dived around the ship. "Great vulture-like birds flying in never-ending circles only emphasize the complete negation of active life,"[15] Durkee thought. Jack Brister thought of Ronny, the stuffy British officer in *A Passage to India*, hearing near Aden that his mother was dead. "A bird goes after a fish and the shark goes after the bird, or are the sharks and the birds both after the fish?" Cox mused.

They headed north again, into the Red Sea. An unrelenting offshore wind intensified heat and discomfort. A match cupped in the hand seemed to burn like a bonfire; an electric lightbulb was a radiator. At lunchtime, the men felt drops of sweat slide down their chests, gather in their navels. When their khaki shirts turned black, they took them on deck and hung them up in the sun. They soon were dry, but no cleaner.

Cox struggled to maintain a cheerful outlook. He blamed the long journey, the endless reading, the desperate effort to amuse themselves with talk. "We are all being a little small minded," he wrote. "We've come to that awful stage of thinking despair the attribute of a great mind."

One hot night, going on deck for some air, he confronted the evidence that individuality and free will were indeed mirages, that any man was interchangeable with every other. Under a gibbous moon, ropes, winches, derricks, and lifeboats cast shadows across the bodies of sleeping men. Booms, masts, halyards, and funnels stood in sharp relief against deep blue sky. "On all the decks they were sleeping. Privates, corporals, sergeants, lieutenants, laid out in neat rows like the dead—all their different cravings, needs, and beliefs made identical by sleep . . . with only a slight odor to show they were men."

By day, with his journal, Cox wrote to anchor himself with specifics, cataloging the things that made him feel alive and unique. "Moments like the steel-edged sing of skis on the corn snow of Tuckerman's headwall, tight-laced skates firm about my arches, black ice in November . . . headlighted rain on Madison Avenue at six p.m. in December, sailors on Boston Common in May nights . . . the third old fashioned and getting friendly intoxicated, good food, salt . . . my friends, so many good ones— waltzes, swimming at night, little breezes snaking through long grass, corners of eyes. . . . I could go on forever remembering what I have liked. Sometimes I have felt a thrill of excitement because I am able to place one foot in front of another and move over asphalt."[16]

Returning to the cabin one afternoon, Cox found Peter Wake lounging in the upper bunk, the gramophone resting on the lower along with the re- cord *On Hearing the First Cuckoo in Spring.* Cox played it once, then started to close up the machine.

"Would you mind playing that again?" Wake asked. They listened once more. Wake said, "It's almost too much to hear that."

"How do you mean?"

"Well, here, cruising up the Red Sea and everything."

"It's very much England, isn't it?"

"I go on countless long and lovely walks through the countryside while I'm listening."

Wake's comment struck Cox as strange. The weeks at sea had been a dark night for him in some ways, but he felt now a new sense of auton- omy. He wanted to see certain people and places. He felt hungry or thirsty for them. But he felt no longing or sadness. "About America, I have more of it in me when I am cruising the Red Sea than I had in America," he wrote. "I do not deny the thrill of at last returning. But it will be a long time before I shall need to return."

As if to formalize the sentiment, Cox wrote a poem apparently ad- dressed to Kit Motley. It memorialized his decision to leave home and the end of that seemingly long-ago passion.

A Song

"All roads must have their forks," you said,
"What way runs the road for you?"
The left fork led to an unknown shape
By a path too narrow for two.
The other the twisting path of love
But always the river in view,
That alone I must stumble the single way
The two of us always knew.
But we toyed a time on the edge of the road
I wove you a daisy chain
"A time for honour . . . a time for love,
O wait, I'll be back again"
But I knew when I left I had asked too much
I knew you would not remain,
For a silent cry sprang out of your eyes
And your mouth was twisted pain.

Meanwhile, Heming and Brister pressed to finish their play. As *Duchess of Atholl* approached the Gulf of Suez, they worked on act one and act two. On Tuesday, September 1, with port at long last in view, it was done. "Finished it!" Jack crowed in his yearbook. But his joy was short-lived. "It stinks. Chuck gave some good catty-cornered—but good, I say—criticism. I'm afraid I knew it though. Aren't I a conceited ass? It was a good attempt at collaborating anyway. Poor Micky!"

As the *Duchess* steamed into harbor, fresh war news arrived. It, too, was disappointing, at best. "Supposed to disembark tomorrow," Jack wrote. "Rommel is advancing in south, whoopee!"[17]

PART 3

Desert Rats

"But what's this long face about, Mr. Starbuck; wilt thou not chase the white whale? Art not game for Moby Dick?"
"I am game for his crooked jaw, and for the jaws of death too, Captain Ahab, if it fairly comes in the way of the business we follow. . . ."

—Herman Melville, *Moby-Dick*

CHAPTER 8

Into the Blue

Egypt
September 3–October 24, 1942

> When I consider the way I have come here to what is the center of the world really, or near it, I am filled with wonder. "From Winchester where the round table waits, we come to seek the Holy bloomin' Grail, Brisk cockney Lancelots, with rifles at the trail."
>
> —Rob Cox

Among British and commonwealth troops in the Western Desert, rumors abounded to explain the German soldiers' seemingly uncanny superiority in battle. In one version, men headed for the Afrika Korps had trained in enormous greenhouses constructed in Germany to prepare them for the terrible heat. In another, huge fans blowing sand simulated the particular discomforts of enduring a North African *khamseen*, or sandstorm. But while the Nazis certainly applied technical ingenuity in unexpected—and sometimes unimaginably heinous—ways, these notions said less about actual training methods than they did about the high regard, sometimes approaching awe, that many Allied soldiers felt for their enemy, even as they prepared themselves to kill him.

More objective observers, such as the Australian journalist Alan Moorehead, formulated more prosaic, but certainly more useful explanations for the Allied retreat that by the end of July 1942 found the Axis army encamped just one hundred fifty miles from Cairo and the Suez Canal, unable to realize the killing blow thanks only to the tenuousness of their supply lines and the utter exhaustion of the troops.[1]

For three years, Moorehead followed the ebb and flow of the desert war, often at his peril, from the first Italian advances on the Egyptian border in September 1940 until the end of the North African Campaign, nearly two thousand miles westward on the plains and beaches near Tunis. His three-book narrative *Desert War* makes as vivid the grinding day-to-day of life in the trackless desert as it does the heart-stopping chaos of battle. In July 1942, after fighting along the El Alamein line had ended in stalemate, he sat down to try to tease out the reasons for the British armies' continual failures, even when they fought, as did the 8th Army in Egypt, from well-protected positions less than a day's drive from their own advance base. "The fighting had been close and very bitter," he wrote. "There had been casualties of up to ten thousand on the line in these July battles and still neither side was able to get anywhere."[2]

Back in England, people were beginning to ask similar questions. In Parliament, a foredoomed vote of no confidence in the prime minister and "the central direction of the war" was proposed and defeated, but a growing number of voices supported the position that a new minister of defense, one who was not also the prime minister, was needed to temper Churchill's single-minded domination of war planning.[3]

On August 3, the prime minister, still in charge, flew to Egypt with General Sir Alan Brooke, chief of the Imperial General Staff, to look over the situation there himself. When he left a week later, the command structure had been reorganized and new men put in charge. Persia (now Iran) and Iraq were removed from Middle East Command, as was General Auchinleck. Replacing him as commander in chief was General Harold Alexander, "a dynamic little man who had done well at Dunkirk and as well as possible at the fall of Burma."[4] The new commander of 8th Army was to be a man beloved of the King's Royal Rifle Corps and the regiment's most successful World War II commander. Lieutenant General William H. E. Gott, known as "Strafer," had gained his nickname in 1915 while an officer of the 2nd Battalion in France; it referred to the German prayer "Gott Strafe England"[5] ("May God punish England"). His experience in the desert was unparalleled. He had risen quickly from commanding officer of the 1st Battalion to become commander of the 7th Armoured Division—the famous Desert Rats—and then of 13 Corps. But just one day after he accepted his new commission as commander of 8th Army, at the age of forty-two, the Luftwaffe put an end to it. As Gott's plane, a Bristol Bombay troop carrier loaded mostly with wounded, headed over the desert to Cairo, six attacking Messerschmitt 109s shot out its engines. The pilot managed to guide the severely damaged aircraft safely to earth, but the German fighters returned. After three strafing passes, the plane was consumed by flames. Among nineteen passengers killed was General Gott.[6] His replacement was a little-known protégé of General Brooke's named Bernard Law Montgomery, another World War I veteran, son of an Anglo-Irish missionary, whose paucity of experience with desert warfare was counterbalanced by the enormity of his belief in his own competence.

Alan Moorehead, like many historians and commentators since, placed blame for British defeats not at the doorsteps of the generals, however. He identified a broad and sometimes dauntingly amorphous range of problems, all related to the Allies' general unpreparedness for a new type of warfare, which they long had hoped they could avoid. The Allies had inferior equipment of all kinds, from guns, tanks, and aircraft and the support systems for maintaining them to the relatively fragile water and fuel containers—no small matter for an army in the desert—that made "jerrycans" prized booty. (British petrol cans, tellingly, were referred to as "flimsies.")[7] In the German talent for organization at all levels, in speed and directness of control, in morale, in training, the 8th Army suffered a disadvantage. But above all these, it was cooperation between the tanks and the antitank gunners that was, in Moorehead's mind, the Germans' best achievement.[8]

> It was in the control of tanks [Moorehead wrote] that the Germans revealed their greatest gifts. They were tank technicians pure and simple. They were the elite of the Afrika Korps, as compact, as neat and efficient as a team of acrobats. They had been trained to the nth degree and as a group, a group that could be controlled very nearly as easily as one tank. They were self-contained. Stukas, tanks, recovery vehicles, petrol wagons, anti-tank gunners, all went forward together and their senior officers were often in the van. . . . We could not hope to marshal and drive our tanks as the Germans did. We were simply not trained to it and they had years of practice.[9]

Throughout the summer of 1942, nevertheless, the Allies' situation was brightening. "I see no reason for pessimism in this thesis which seeks to prove that not only the generals but the British army, as a whole, was at that time inferior to the German army," Moorehead wrote.

> In every department, I saw we were making huge improvements. . . . There had been no such improvement on the German side. . . . On our side we had the new Grant tank and there were even better tanks arriving; we had the new six-pounder gun and hundreds of them were beginning to flood into the Middle East. The new Spitfires [fast and nimble fighters beloved of RAF pilots in the Battle of Britain] were starting to come in at last. The Americans, headed by their air force, were taking their positions in the desert.[10]

As the five Yanks and their multitudinous companions steamed uncomfortably toward Suez, Rommel was putting the 8th Army's new commander in chief to the test. Despite suffering several untreated physical ailments, including severe sinusitis and stomach pain, the German field marshal hazarded one more desperate thrust toward Cairo. On the night of August 30, two German panzer divisions, as well as 243 Italian tanks, rumbled forward across the southern end of the El Alamein line, expecting to find the British side only lightly defended. Meanwhile, a feint launched in the north was intended to prevent the 8th Army from consolidating. Rommel planned his main thrust to roll with typical speed through British defenses, swing northeast toward the coast road, and cut the 8th Army's supply lines.

But in fact the attackers encountered strong defenses behind dense minefields. Aided by intelligence gleaned from decrypted enemy messages, Montgomery had foreseen the attack and prepared for it. Leading German elements met dense artillery rounds, machine gun and mortar fire. Vickers Wellington bombers lit up the night with flares and blasted Nazi tankers with bomb loads of up to four thousand pounds each.[11] In a hugely significant change from past tactics, what did not confront the attackers immediately were British tanks.

When at dawn the panzer divisions found themselves still twenty miles short of their goal, the main thrust was redirected northward toward a long, low ridge called Alam Halfa—precisely where Montgomery expected them. By now, a sandstorm had further embroiled the battlefield, and patches of soft sand strained tank engines, gobbling fuel. Axis troops approaching the ridge ran into a firestorm from dug-in tanks and concealed six-pounders and twenty-five-pounders. Through artillery concentration and self-restraint, bolstered by well-coordinated aerial support and directed via an improved radio network,[12] the 8th Army sprang its trap effectively. After two days of repeated attempts to capture the ridge, Rommel, now short on fuel and tanks, ordered his forces to withdraw.

On September 3—the third anniversary of the British declaration of war and a day of prayer in Britain—the 8th Army counterattacked, pushing the Germans and Italians back toward the original El Alamein line. There, after a few more days of skirmishing, it stabilized.[13]

As the Yanks disembarked in Suez to await the train to infantry base depot, they saw all around them the evidence of change—crowds of reinforcements spilling out of lighters from the troopship, armaments piling up, ready to be delivered to the front. The sight of spanking-new General Sherman tanks being driven ashore off a barge thrilled Cox patriotically. The new American-made tanks would at last erase the mortal disadvantages of the older models—Cruisers, Matildas, Valentines, Churchills—all of them effectively obsolete against the faster, better-armed, and better-armored German war machines and their variety a frustrating complication in the logistics of maintenance.

The afternoon was very hot with just a faint breeze.[14] In the distance, cliffs of yellow sandstone glinted fiercely along the shimmering gulf. The air felt strangely gritty—there seemed to be a fine layer of dust on everything—and it had a new land smell one rifleman described as being reminiscent of scorched linen.[15] For hours the soldiers milled about on the quay waiting in the hot sun for their train to load, with only tea for sustenance, and Brister was cursed with stomach troubles, a condition the English called "gyppy tummy," which made it sound far merrier than Jack felt. He had been plagued for two days. "Without exercise and sleep and regularity the body soon enough perishes," he recorded. "As I find to my pain and [private] internal delight, I let everything [go] for the damn play."[16]

The new arrivals amused themselves commenting on the crowds of querulous local men in traditional long cotton galabiyyas, whom all the soldiers called "wogs." The lighter pilot seemed to take childish delight in sounding his steam whistle, and Cox later wrote of a "great laughing, punching-each-other crew of rascally Egyptians" who lurched down the pier with paper caps on their heads, rattles, tin horns, and old *New Yorkers* in their hands, "very happy in their dirty nightgowns." They must have been unloading an American ship where there had been a party, the Yanks concluded, perhaps wistfully.[17]

It was growing dark by the time the officers had tossed their valises into boxcars—"cattle cars," Cox called them for obvious reasons—and the train moved out. It groaned forward some hundred yards, then wheezed to a halt. Someone announced there was a break in the track. The train stood still for a few more hours. To pass time, the men sang, banging time on the steel walls of the train cars. It surprised Cox to hear his British companions bellow "Marching Through Georgia," an old American Civil War song that was a family favorite. But then, he thought, it fit in well with the General Sherman tanks.

With Peter Wake, Cox walked the length of the train, then walked back. They smoked and talked until Peter's cigarettes ran out; then they hunted for places amid the sprawling crowds on the boxcar floors. Cox tucked his revolver under his hip, gas mask under a shoulder, and rested his head on a suitcase. "Thus I kept most of myself off the cold steel floor," he wrote later. "There was a dullard who kept talking all the time."

The troop train pulled in at infantry base depot the next morning at seven, after a twelve-hour journey to cover thirty-five miles. Clambering down, stiff and cold, from the boxcars, the men had to acknowledge that everyone would have arrived cleaner and sooner had they walked. Some things army didn't change.

Infantry base depot at Geneifa sat on the southern rim of Great Bitter Lake, part of the string of waterways that link the Suez Canal with the Red Sea. Here had sprung up a vast village of canvas where new arrivals got a first taste of life in the desert, slept for the first time on the sand "in wind-slapped tents,"[18] as Brister put it, and rubbed shoulders with the sunburned, sandblasted vets who passed through quietly, nursing desert sores, dysentery, or jaundice, beginning or ending a long-postponed leave, or returning to the front from casualty stations and hospitals.

In the crowded mess tent, lean men in khaki shirtsleeves and baggy shorts hunched over shaky tables writing airgraphs home or slouched into low-slung, broken-springed chairs and sofas by the fireplace. Cox managed to strike up a conversation with a vet of the 2nd Battalion who was recuperating from wounds received at Alam Halfa, where both the KRRC 1st and 2nd battalions had fought with the 7th Armoured Division to hold up Rommel's southern advance. "He had been on a standing patrol for five nights or something," Cox noted, "and the next thing he knew he was in an ambulance."

Glancing around as if to check who might be listening, the vet took Cox into his confidence. He shared his deep regret over Gott's death and his lingering distrust of Montgomery, the new commander, despite the recent victory. And he offered Cox some practical advice: Don't shoot at a dive-bomber that is definitely headed for your section; bury yourself and it won't touch you, but fire at any heading for the next section over. He went on: "You are fighting the desert so much more than the Germans and are so thirsty that you don't hate them and both sides treat prisoners well. Indeed, you feel the only person tolerable in the world is someone equally thirsty."

"Sounds true," Cox thought.

Then the old soldier launched into reassuring anecdotes—how Rommel himself had told a British tank captain that the Cruiser was the best tank in the desert, but the British misused it; how General Ravenstein, Rommel's second in command until he was captured in November, said that if his troops had our morale, he could go through Europe like a knife through butter.

"All of which made me eager," Cox told his journal later, though "a little worried about lack of technical knowledge."[19]

"Excitement!" Brister crowed in his diary on September 8. "Fulfillment at last! Small anxiety."[20] After four days of acclimatization and hardening, which involved long marches and PT exercises, Brister, Bolté, Durkee, and Cutting received orders to move off and join battalions near the front. By the next day, Durk and Brister were living with the 1st Battalion in open desert. They discovered "the slit trench custom" by which men dug themselves individual shallow trenches to sleep in, for protection in case of attack—"necessary" but "curious" in Brister's view, "men digging corpse pits before sleep." On September 10 they reached battalion headquarters, learned to nose their jeeps into a protective square "in leaguer" for the night. Brister found the atmosphere here "more human, to take the edge off the unflinching desert." But still military. One night, eating his simple dinner in the colonel's mess, he watched the battalion commander himself drive up, shouting for drinks and smokes: "Whiskey and soda and twenty Player's!" The colonel got them.

Bill Durkee was all but wild with enthusiasm.[21] While Brister, the writer-observer, maintained some critical distance, Durk embraced regimental life in the desert unreservedly. Even the tiresome train ride to IBD, he told his parents naively, "wasn't pleasant—but a good introduction to real fighting."

Durk's first letter home from the desert on September 10 fairly glows. "Our regiment has been doing a tough and successful job," he wrote. "In every battle they have distinguished themselves and in the last push did a major part of the work. The Army is confident and will push 'Jerry' out of the desert."

Seated on the sand in the shade of a truck "deep in the desert," Durk described the novelties and the strange excitement of his new life. Lifting field glasses to his eyes, he could see the enemy himself, positions shimmering in the sun across the great flat waste of no-man's-land.

"We are fortunate to come at this time," Durk wrote. "The worst heat is over. In the early morning and evening the air is clear and mild. At midday the sun is still very warm and night brings a really heavy dew and penetrating cold." He noted the surprising ways in which the desert resembled the sea. During the drive to the front, the sight of many "softskin" supply trucks back in echelon milling about in all directions on the stony ground had reminded him of sailboats maneuvering for position before the start of a race. And wayfinding in the absence of distinctive landmarks was like ocean navigation. "Movement and direction must be almost entirely done by compass," Durk explained. "Since spaces are great it is imperative that navigation is exact; if it isn't, you are liable to get lost or run into the enemy.

"The places you read about in the paper, most of them," he continued, "are fictions. Probably the only thing to mark, say, Knightsbridge is an old gas tin. The base essential of fighting here is not ground occupied but enemy armour destroyed."

But for all Durk's ardor, he could not overlook the desert's greatest irritation and frustration, the flies. "Nothing is immune," he wrote. "If you set a cup of tea down for five minutes, a whole family is sure to be out swimming. The normal action is, lift them out and continue drinking. At first this seems difficult, but the desire for the tea and the unsuitability of the fly soon overcome your natural repugnance." Still, he managed to find a silver lining. "The great thing is their bravery. You can shake, swat and push but they won't move. Their tenacity is a lesson for any soldier."

On September 12 Brister, updating his yearbook, recorded his reaction to a first experience of air attack—"indirect, interesting, chilling but not really frightening." This time, the bombs fell harmless. The answer from the Desert Air Force took down four.

On September 18, the 1st Battalion moved north to Burj-el-Arab on the Mediterranean coast. "A rest by the sea," Brister wrote acidly. "The moment we got there a programme is gotten out—times to bathe, and clean up, maintain, go to shows, drink beer, etc. An organized rest. 'What the men are suffering from,' says the general, 'is boredom. We must give them a rest from boredom.'" On Saturday night, September 19, the New Zealanders put on their famous show featuring a female impersonator. Days, Brister and Durk swam in the cold, bright sea and it was grand.

"Instead of being with Roland, I am not even with Charlemagne but somewhere back in Charlemagne's echelon where I can't even hear the music of Roland's horn," Rob Cox moaned in a letter home. Left behind at IBD without his countrymen for the first time in well over a year, he felt as low as he ever had in his life. No one told him why he alone re-

mained behind—if for more training, then why on the eleventh had he
found himself on a course not of vital, new information, which he was
eager, even anxious to learn either by instruction or experience, but of
the same old stuff he had heard one thousand times in England and knew
by heart? "Sitting listening to it while the others go merrily on their way,"
was, he grieved, "almost too much to stand."[22]

At night, the continual movement of trains and equipment and men
toward the front deepened Rob's melancholy. "S[herman]s going through
on tank carriers—carriers and tanks on trains silhouetted," he wrote in
his journal. "The train stopped and the trucks rolled up to load the kit
bags; the troops were already in the train; they were singing the usual
songs and 'Carolina Moon,' which seemed unusual. In different cars the
singing was different; in one, lively; in another 'When They Sound the
Last All Clear' and 'Rose of Tralee.' Oil leaking from some part of the engine had caught on fire and was burning in gusts like a blow torch, brightening the night for about forty yards around and intensifying the sounds
of the scene. There are lonely sounds here sometimes, any sound of movement is lonely; lorries through the night rumbling, and footsteps even
when you lie in your tent at 11 p.m."

Come Saturday night, unable to sleep, Cox wandered over to the officers' club at lakeside, which someone had optimistically dubbed the
Lido. "The moon was very bright, [a] full, Ramadan moon," he wrote, in
what would be his last journal entry. "The distant palms on the sweet
water canal were clearly outlined and as I walked down I heard the sound
of the orchestra in the distance." His hopes rose.

The rooftop dance floor, open to moon and stars and overlooking Great
Bitter Lake, was a lovely spot. But the scene disappointed. Despite the
presence of several visibly tight officers, there was no liquor to be had, and
beneath the rhythms of the small orchestra—accordion predominating—
was a grating tattoo like the sound of fingernails on a blackboard, the effect of leather and hobnails scraping across the concrete floor. Even the
women, nearly all of them nurses, were uniformly unappealing, though
Rob felt uncharitable at the thought. "The nurses were ill-shapen and thir-

tyish, undoubtedly wonderful people, and all the officers were undoubtedly very brave and the flower of manhood," he wrote later, but he left quickly. Walking back to his tent in the dark, he at last found something captivating: "two Arabs on slim and tall white camels whose hooves were silent on the asphalt, moving ship-like under the moonlit palms."[23]

Cox shared a tent with his two best British friends, Peter Wake and Micky Heming. Peter, son of one of the regiment's two colonels commandant, was even more miserable about their stranding than Rob was. His brother Toby had been at the front for some time as a company commander with 1st Battalion and had just won the Military Cross at Alam Halfa.[24] But with time, their spirits rebounded. Cox was constitutionally incapable of remaining morose while exercising, and he enjoyed the morning training course and swimming in the lake in the afternoons. In one letter home his description of the morning outings reads like a page of T. E. Lawrence. "The principle feature . . . was a 'walk' that went across the plain for about a mile towards an escarpment and then up through a gully with high cliffs on each side. Going through the gully one felt as if at the end of it one might find anything from Bedouins to Wisemen to a buried city or a lost city where crystal streams lined the streets. Instead one found a path up to the top of the escarpment and one went along the edge of the cliff for a couple of miles until, coming to a place where there was not a vertical drop but only a thirty degree slope, very sandy, one ran down, feeling like a camel as the sand cushioned your tremendous strides.

"Peter Wake and I used to do the five miles in just under an hour," he told his mother. "We deemed it pretty rapid going. Everyone else deemed us crazy."

Among the riflemen at IBD were soldiers Cox and his friends had known at Winchester. All of the squad he had had as a lance corporal were there, and he still relished the endemic good cheer of the London cockneys. They recalled Cox goading and cursing at them: "What'll you be like when you meet the Germans if you're such a bloody show'er now?"

"Oh, Corporal, they won't send us against the Germans, we're too old," they had said then, all being about thirty. Well, it gave them a good laugh now, remembering how Corporal Cox had been more right than he knew.[25]

Cox and Wake shared a batman named Harrington who remembered the American volunteers at Winchester because of the excitement when Eden and Winant came to visit. "Apparently we were more prominent figures . . . than we knew," Cox wrote home, jokingly but also this time somewhat proudly.

When Cox asked Harrington whether he was ready to move to the front, the answer delighted him. "Yes, sir, I get browned off down here. Them that's been there say it's better up there than here. It's a picnic up there, I reckon it is."

Before long "the old fancy" was running free again, and Cox was quoting Yeats, almost precisely, in a letter home.[26]

> It is weird how peaceful it is here. I am very happy these days, something of the wide spaces makes one feel early morning-ish, something of the sun and the blind wind gives one the same feeling that Maine lakes and Tuckerman's Ravine and a long walk in the rain give. . . . I would change Ireland to New England if it scanned and say 'I am of Ireland, and the holy land of Ireland, and time runs on said she, come out of charity and dance with me in Ireland.' I have something to say I think but it is mine and must be mine or else I can not say it . . . but perhaps there'll come a time.

In her letters Fanny Cox had suggested a private code by which Rob could let her know his movements without alarming the censors. The signal for a move toward the front was drawn from fairy tales. At long last, the order came. "Now I am off," Rob wrote home happily, "to see— three guesses—Snow White and the Seven Dwarfs!"

———

By Wednesday, September 23, Brister and Durkee were back in the line in the southern sector with the 1st Battalion,[27] overlooked by the twin peaks of Himeimat, a long ridge seven hundred feet high that bordered the escarpments and salt marshes of the Qattara Depression.[28] They were getting to know their new platoons—"Some good men and some worthless ones," Brister noted. "Shifty ones give me the creeps. Can't endure them at all. But the army calls forth any latent shifty ones as a poultice pus." And they were learning the lay of that rough, undulating desert land in detail, patrolling, discerning and mapping enemy positions and minefields, and practicing with maps and compasses and guns the new gospel of all-arms cooperation. From his yearbook, it is clear that "Jerry" was never far from Brister's mind. Was the Qattara Depression truly impassable? Amid the stillness of the desert, Jack thought, "He must be working on something."

On October 1 a second air attack ripped the sky. This time, German bombs found their mark, destroyed a gun portee, killed two, and left one who lived badly burned. "I felt sick," Brister noted. "The burned man was courageous. I wished that he should live. Howell, his name."

October 2 was a quiet day, until Brister, on patrol in his jeep, strayed into an Allied minefield. Suddenly, the sand exploded beneath him with a deafening clap. His jeep jumped, then settled back on a tilt, one tire and one wheel gone, the vehicle riddled by shrapnel. Brister himself—the medic could hardly believe it—suffered only a punctured eardrum. "I was very lucky," he wrote. Even a peaceful reconnaissance had its dangers.

The burned man, Howell, was buried, as were some other dead, on October 3. Brister described it: "The padre came, draped a bit of ribbon about him[self], read words from the book while a score of us stood by and we called them buried (in the minds of men). Afterwards the padre stuck the bottles with their particulars upright in the sand."

That morning, a Saturday, Bill Durkee sent home an effervescent and informative report. "[After] three weeks on the desert I feel like a veteran and look like one for that matter," he wrote proudly. "On a gallon of water per man per day one's washing is sadly diminished, you should try to bathe on a couple pints. The real old timers are a leathery brown, the sand, wind and sun have blasted, torn and dried up their skin so that they have practically given up washing; water can do no more."

In his systematic way, he described the fauna and the flora and the weather. "The only vegetation in this spot is a small shrub, something like our tumbleweed, the only color as far as you can see is brown. There are lizards, bugs that look much like large beetles, scorpions, and sand snails that live on the shrubs." He did not tell his family that the soldiers sometimes gathered up the snails and fried them. Surprisingly, they made quite a nice change after day after day of eating "bully beef," or corned beef from a can.

Two days earlier, the new arrivals had experienced their first winter storm. About noon, the sky to the west grew black and the constant wind stilled. Slowly the darkness advanced toward them across the vast plain of desert, heralded by whirling sand spouts. When it was a few miles away, they could determine that what they saw was a solid wall of dust, nearly two thousand feet high and blocking the horizon for miles. When it hit, sand blasted everything, forcing them to cover any bit of exposed flesh against the sting. The storm made compasses go haywire, and anything metal might become shocking to touch.

"It only lasted about ten minutes," Durkee wrote, "and then it started to hail. The pellets were the size of bird eggs. We all knelt behind the trucks to protect ourselves. It was quite an experience; they tell of some that last three or four days."

But despite the challenges of the climate, Durk went on, "Everyone is agreed that this is the place to fight a war if it must be. There are no cities, forests, gardens or green fields to destroy, only the opponent. The military mind is in its element, pure tactics and maneuver are the order of the day. Cities, civilians, and civil authority do not exist to confuse their minds."

The next day Durk and his machine gun platoon of thirty-six moved off with the rest of 1st Battalion to form up in column, while Brister boarded the train to base hospital at El Qantara on the Suez Canal to have his ear treated. "I'm afraid I'm missing something," he recorded, and as days passed, his frustration only grew. The treatment was straightforward and the diversions of reading, playing chess, talking, and walking were undeniably pleasant. He enjoyed the peculiar tableau presented when a ship moved across his field of vision through the Suez Canal; it looked like a vessel advancing steadily through a sea of sand. The wireless brought news, some welcome, some not. On October 17 Berlin Radio triumphantly reported the sinking of *Duchess of Atholl.* But Brister's sense of being left out of the very events for which he had traveled so far and given up so much grew ever more painful. "Will there ever be contentment from now till I die?" he implored in his yearbook. "Now, I'm held in hospital withdrawn from the fight."

When the great day came for Cox to leave IBD and join the 2nd Battalion, he and Harrington loaded their possessions onto a jeep and set off very early on the road toward Cairo. It was the first trip of any length that Cox had driven in a long while, and it excited him to travel on his own for a change. The morning air was cool, the sky slowly brightening to a crisp, sharp blue, like a fall morning in New England. He felt migratory. With all his belongings strapped onto the jeep and Harrington crammed in atop old boots and blankets, it seemed briefly like the Windsor trip that his family made twice yearly, moving between New Jersey and Vermont.

As Cox headed west, the Nile delta opened out before them, startlingly green, wide, and fertile. The land was absolutely flat in a way Cox found unsettling. He was aware that he had yet to experience "the blue" as the fighting riflemen knew it, but he had spent considerable time contemplating the brown wastes around IBD, and to his continual amazement, being a man who had always thought trees and lakes and mountains important, he loved them. Possibly it was their geometric barrenness. Perhaps in May, when conditions were dryer and hotter, he would not have loved them so well—"the lone and level sands stretching far away." He remembered "Ozymandias" and Shelley's traveler from an antique land, which could certainly have been Egypt. There, as they neared Cairo, were the three great pyramids, punctuating the perfect line of the horizon like an ancient geometry lesson.

Still, for all its flatness, the greenness of the delta would have been—if he could be allowed for a moment to consider the unthinkable—an unbelievably beautiful sight to the Afrika Korps, should they ever see it. "This is a good war out here in that respect," he wrote home a few days later. "He has a lush green land as a goal and we have our goal ever west which is the direction of home and the traditional American direction." He had been looking forward for a while now to spending Christmas in Benghazi, and he thought that after that a springtime leave skiing in the Alps would be nice, the Swiss Alps—if neutrality laws allowed—or, better still, the Italian.

All army vehicles in the desert had their windshields removed to prevent reflected light from catching the enemy's attention. This made driving challenging, and when the wind kicked up and the sand, too, which had proven nearly inevitable, it was painfully so. "I will look Oriental probably when I get home," Cox wrote his mother, "for to keep moving one narrows one's eyes to slits when driving, to slits also against the sun. But so far I see no change."

The violence of sand and wind against his face took Rob back to the fall of 1938, when he and his mother, quite unknowingly, had migrated home from Vermont through the great hurricane that would be remembered as the Long Island Express. They had dropped off his younger brother Louis for his first year at St. Paul's in the rain—it had been raining for days—then returned to Windsor. They were aware that the rivers were rising and that flooding was occurring in western Vermont, but that hadn't seemed particularly ominous; flooding was a regular part of the change of seasons and happened like clockwork when the ice broke up in the rivers each spring. The family in Windsor had been anxious about their safety, but no one said the word "hurricane," and Rob and his mother were eager to get home. The next morning, before they left, Uncle Louis made them promise to stop if the water got too high and, whatever happened, to telephone him that night at nine.

They pulled out of the gravel driveway onto Route 5 in pouring rain, but by lunchtime, when they reached the little town of Simsbury, Connecticut, northwest of Hartford, the rain had stopped. His mother, memorably, bought him a nice rare steak for lunch. "Honestly, you have been driving me around for about three days; you really deserve a good lunch," she said. "Just have anything you want."

For a while after they'd finished, they stood on the porch with the restaurant owner, looking around at the stillness. Not a drop of rain, not a breath of air disturbed it.

The wind started up at about the same time they did— "absolutely terrific," as his mother would say, the rain whooshing and lashing the car as if thrown down from huge buckets. The wild weather, far from alarming them, made them feel exhilarated. They were having a wonderful time! As they fought their way south through Connecticut, Mamma asked Rob whether perhaps they should stop. They knew people in nearly every town along the road. Rob didn't want to, and Mamma didn't either. They drove on.

Then bad got worse. Everywhere cars had stalled out or stuck; the sluicing road was littered with them. But Rob and Mamma sailed on and on, feeling wonderful.

Looking back later, the hurricane's unexpected destructiveness had become confused with the growing menace in Europe—Hitler annexing Austria in March 1938, then moving on Czechoslovakia in the fall—and with the strange stasis that seemed to follow, like the eye of a hurricane, each frightful act of aggression. They heard Hitler's voice on the radio and were chilled that fall when the war almost started but didn't.

When Rob and Mamma reached home, they still hadn't grasped the full extent of the storm damage. Plainfield had been windy, but less so than other places. When the telephone rang with news that his sister Molly, visiting relatives near Boston, was fine, Mamma couldn't understand why they were calling. Later that night, when Uncle Louis finally got through, they gained some sense of the damage. He had had to leave his house and fight his way to the telephone office to get a line. All along Main Street, big old elms had fallen. The virgin pine forest in Paradise was wrecked. The woods, Mamma would say later, looked "as if giants had been playing jackstraws!" Everywhere ruin, and Paradise never again the same.

That had been Rob's personal family loss. It would be nearly two years more before all hell broke loose around the globe.

Cox reunited with Cutting and Bolté under canvas at Khatatba, a permanent camp northwest of Cairo that had showers, a well-stocked NAAFI, and cinemas the men called Shafto's Shuftis;[29] Shufti, the Arabic for "look and see," was also the local slang for reconnaissance.[30] Shafto was the entrepreneur who ran the picture shows. Heyward and Chuck were training to lead machine gun platoons, learning which was the business end of a Vickers. Sweetening the reunion was a large pile of mail. One of Cox's letters had been fourteen months en route. Posted in August 1941, it was from Kit, explaining that she was engaged to be married.

After a few days, Cox received orders that made all the hated waiting and uncertainty worthwhile. "Life has definitely turned for the better," he wrote home on October 7. "I'm with the 2nd Battalion now and have one of the most cherished types of platoon to command, what I really wanted but never thought I'd get because I hadn't any knowledge." He would have charge of a platoon of six-pounders, the new antitank gun that everyone hoped would bring the British artillery into something like parity with the German. His men being all away on their first leave in eight months gave him time to learn the job.

The six-pounder was a long, heavy gun surprisingly crude in its controls, but wonderfully devastating in effect. The greatest improvement was its armor-piercing qualities; at a thousand yards, the six-pound shells could penetrate two and one-half inches of armor, where the two-pounder, until then the British mainstay, was powerless against anything thicker than about one and one-half inches. To aim it horizontally, you leaned against a leather-padded metal arm, while elevating or depressing the nine-foot barrel was accomplished by turning a cogged wheel with your left hand. The sight was a simple crosshairs with very little magnification; when the gun was aimed at twelve hundred yards, the thick wires all but concealed the target. The ranging device was a brass quadrant with notches and a lever that you moved one notch for every fifty yards of distance.[31] "Different guns have different characteristics and genders," Rob reflected. "The rifle is a man, the Bren gun a very well-bred lady." The six-pounder was huge and crude and yet responsive and powerful. "My guns are mastiffs."

When the gun was fired, the barrel recoiled up to thirty inches along the gun cradle and the entire ton-plus machine moved back and dug itself a bit deeper into the sand. As Cox leaned against the shoulder piece and pressed the firing lever, the gun pushed him back on his heels in a way he could not for some time identify. Then it came to him, a clear memory of football practice, of crouching forward ready to charge much as he crouched into the gun, and of his coach reaching forward with both hands and shoving his shoulders sharply to test his stance. That's how it was firing the gun.

Cox learned this about the six-pounder, along with countless details involving parts and mechanisms, repairs and maintenance, the commands connected with exactly how the five-man crew needed to work together to unload the huge gun from its portee, to site and range and load it—taking care to keep fingers out of the semiautomatic breech—then fire. He learned something about how to place his guns and about the new tactical approach to working in concert with the armor. It was this last that turned out to be the hardest part to convey effectively to his men, who had come up working independently in column, each platoon a piratical force unto itself.

"As far as facts or tactics go, all the time I spent in England is wasted," Cox wrote home, and then, characteristically, inverted the situation to find the good in it: "but not ultimately since it's a way and basis for thinking."

Gradually, like the others, Cox came to know the peculiar ways of the desert. He found his battalion area by compass bearing and speedometer. When he arrived, there was only a single truck; everyone was out on a divisional scheme, and when they went out, their homes went along with them; their vehicles were home. Peering into the distance, he gradually made out about seven others, well camouflaged against the pebbly, barren landscape, within an area of about five square miles. Continuing on for a mile more, he found his company mess, a three-ton lorry cut down to little more than its bed, to make it less conspicuous. It would be another quarter of a mile from the company mess to his platoon area, and when his men and their vehicles returned, they spread out, each about 150 yards from the next. The next company was more than two miles away. Dispersal made the positions harder for enemy planes to detect and to target.

Cox enjoyed the solitude and the self-contained feeling that came from this arrangement, but there also was a congenial sociability about company life, isolated as they were in the desert. At day's end, the six officers of Company D ate together at the officers' mess, and sometimes friends from other companies drove in for a visit. There was whiskey to be had, and in the evenings they would sit around and drink a little, and when Bolté came to call, they drank a little more, Chuck unleashing his magnificent gift of gab, making the English roar with laughter not only at his jokes and observations, but also at the American way he told them.

Cox grew accustomed to the locally made smokes, "V" cigarettes, which one lit with peculiarly brittle matches made in India.[32] He marveled at the transformation wrought by the occasional rain: ants and other insects emerging everywhere and a sudden invasion of sand martins, trim little black-and-white birds that pecked at the insects, which he supposed were in turn aided by the moist earth, hunting for—what?[33] He learned how desert soldiers made tea, one of their few reliable pleasures, on makeshift stoves they called "Benghazis," filling empty petrol tins with sand, wetting it with petrol, then carefully lighting it—a practice that worked well as long as none of the dimmer riflemen took it in mind to add petrol while the sand was still hot and reduced themselves to blazing torches.[34] He learned how to make a cap for his mug from an old ration tin,[35] and why it was important always to replace the cap between sips so as to avoid a mouthful of drowned flies. He learned not to be surprised when, after a long day outdoors, a wet comb raked through his hair emerged covered with mud.

At the end of September, the 2nd Battalion began staying up nights practicing with the 1st Armoured Division a scheme in which they traveled single file through three dummy minefields, then took up positions in "open country" beyond them. At first, they thought it was just one more exercise. But when every night the procedure was exactly the same, the three minefield gaps with the same code names, the mock British minefield, no-man's-land, and two mock German minefields always equally deep, the men began to talk. No one told them it was rehearsal for the coming battle, but everyone supposed so.

It has been said that as men prepare for battle, they draw into themselves. There is likely to be a flurry of letter writing, which is a kind of withdrawal, but also an affirmation of individuality and an escape from a hostile environment into a comforting personal world.[36] When Cox next wrote home, he was lying in the shadow of his jeep on the hard sand, well aware of the imminence of battle and well satisfied. He had recently proven himself as a desert navigator, something he had been nervous about. The orders were to lead the entire company for eleven miles from gun range back to company lines—a trivial matter where roads exist, a vital challenge on the unmarked desert, and his first time in the lead. He calculated angle and mileage on the map and set out, all too aware that a mistake would land him and, worse, some one hundred and fifty others in the middle of nowhere. When the company mess shimmered into view in the distance ahead, he was filled with joy, and when he turned around and saw the long string of vehicles following, it seemed the biggest thrill of his life.

"Yesterday I discovered why I liked the desert," he wrote home. "It's because you can go wherever you want."

Lately, the stars had seemed brighter, and always sleeping outdoors, he had begun to notice their movements. When he lay down on his blanket nearly under his jeep—a precaution against being run over at night— the Pleiades were in the east and Orion not up yet, but if he awoke at about four, the constellations would be right overhead. They seemed closer, too, in the desert. He could almost feel the movement.

"Yesterday we passed a well," he wrote home. "There was a tree there and a windmill pumped water so that a few things grew. I wondered what it would be like to live there. Not bad really—one would be grateful for the tree since it was the only tree and one would have water and enough food." He had moved into a place of essentials. "I have nothing here I don't need.

"It seems to me that since I've been away I've been more alive—noticed things more," Cox wrote. "Perhaps that's growing up but I think too that it's because one is perpetually hungry for what one left behind. When all is said and done there's only one thing anyone wants and that is to go home."

But going home, of course, was not an option. "The other night we had a sand storm," Cox wrote, "and somebody pointed out the ridiculousness of the whole thing. The immense effort and wealth that is spent on bringing two armies to the desert. Perhaps the most ridiculous part is that none of us would stop and go home if we could until it's over."

Cox ended his letter home with an important P.S., using the code suggested by his mother for when he moved into action. This time it was a morale-building cliché. "I am sorry I've been so poor about mailing these," he wrote. "Don't expect me to be any better in the future. Stamps are hard to get and V for Victory." He underlined the crucial phrase twice. "Please never worry," he added, "as if I felt you did it would spoil my glorious time."

———

At first light on Tuesday, October 20, Cox, Cutting, and Bolté moved their platoons with the 2nd Battalion to a point northwest of Khatatba and some twenty miles south of the coast, with the whole 1st Armoured Division in the neighborhood.[37] The days of solitude were, for the time being, over.

On Wednesday, October 21, all the officers assembled after lunch to hear the plan. The attack was to begin on Friday, the twenty-third. The battalion commander, Colonel Heathcoat-Amory, passed along what he had learned directly from General Montgomery, aided by an enormous map, at a conference the previous day. Monty prided himself on explaining clearly his overall plans and expected every single man of his army to understand them. The attack, he had said, would be launched along the whole of the forty-mile line, with the main thrust in the north, the German strongpoint, to maximize surprise. A simultaneous attack in the south would prevent the enemy from consolidating and mislead him about the location of the main thrust. Ranged along the front from north to south were eight divisions of infantry—the Australians, near the sea, below them six divisions of commonwealth infantry, then the Fighting French. Four armored divisions would come on behind the infantry, the 1st Armoured Division to go in behind the Australians and the 51st Highland Division just to their south.

Monty assured them of the 8th Army's superiority in numbers of both armor and men and guaranteed them absolute supremacy in the air. At 2140 hours on Friday, October 23, nine hundred guns of every caliber would open up the biggest barrage yet laid down in this war, from the sea to Himeimat. The infantry would attack all along the line and create bridgeheads for the armor to pass through, so they could join up in open country behind the enemy line. The role of the armored divisions was to hold off the enemy tanks while the German and Italian infantry were wiped out. That done, the Axis armor would be destroyed. It would take seven to ten days, Monty expected, before the enemy would break and run.

At last light on the twenty-first, the 2nd Battalion moved with the 1st

Armoured Division to El Imayid station, some twenty miles east of the El Alamein line. Precautions to maintain secrecy were elaborate. So that recce planes would not realize that an armored division had moved up during the night, dummy vehicles were erected in the vacated area, tanks were disguised as three-ton lorries, and all guns had camouflage nets flung over them. That night, no fires could be lit, no slit trenches dug. At about 0100 hours, the men bedded down in their final concentration area on the hard sand. Well aware that the density of vehicles, gun carriers, tanks, and men at El Imayid made them a heaven-sent target for enemy bombers,[38] the men found reassurance in the fact that no planes disturbed them that night.

At ten o'clock on the morning of October 22, company commanders passed on the plans to the riflemen. Then the battalion commander, after some morale-boosting words, read out the order of the day issued by General Montgomery for October 23: "When I assumed command of the Eighth Army I said that the mandate was to destroy ROMMEL and his Army, and that it would be done as soon as we were ready. We are ready NOW."

CHAPTER 9

El Alamein

Egypt
October 21–November 30, 1942

> Rivers of blood were poured out over miserable strips of
> land which, in normal times, not even the poorest Arab would
> have bothered his head about.
>
> —Field Marshal Erwin Rommel[1]

W hen Jack Brister returned to his battalion on October 21, he
found them encamped on the hard sand with the 4th Light
Armoured Brigade, 7th Armoured Division, about seven
miles behind the El Alamein line,[2] the singular jagged peak of Himeimat
signaling the line's southern end in the hazy distance. The headquarters,
an ingenious graft of truck and canvas, hummed with purpose. He saluted
Colonel Consett and announced himself recovered and returned. The battalion commander responded with surprise, then annoyance; traveling
unauthorized to the front was a clear violation of army regulations. Finally, he relaxed and welcomed Jack back, pleased to see him.[3]

Dispatched to rejoin his platoon in A Company, Jack felt the change
of atmosphere that had overtaken the battalion since he'd left for the hospital three weeks before. It had seemed then that the vast, flat desert

could accommodate any number of men and tanks and vehicles with elbow room to spare. Now it teemed.

The boys back at platoon greeted Jack with surprise, too, and pleasure. He had worried a bit about how they would receive him, and the reaction was gratifying. They were keyed up, and his unexpected reappearance seemed another piece of the excitement. He had arrived just in time for the show.

Recently, the riflemen's routine of patrolling by night and observing the enemy by day had gained interest from new occurrences on their own side of the line. At night, when they took up their positions or prepared to enter no-man's-land, they could hear the sounds of the 44th Divisional Reconnaissance Regiment practicing mine clearance a few miles to the rear. Dummy tank battalions sprang up, equipped with amplifiers that mimicked the roar of tank squadrons on the move. Fake supply dumps and mock wireless networks appeared to support them.[4]

For the last two nights, the men had rehearsed an advance through minefields, the KRRC motor companies leading single-file columns comprising tank squadrons, Royal Engineers, and gunner observation posts.[5] The air was full of plans and preparations.[6]

The next day, October 22, Jack gathered with Durk and the other officers and NCOs beside a fifteen-cwt truck on whose side hung a large map showing the desert along the El Alamein line from the Mediterranean to the Qattara Depression. Overlaid in red and green on the loose contour lines were the locations of enemy troops and minefields.[7] A murmur of satisfaction moved through the group as they recognized in graphic form the information they had gleaned on patrol.[8]

Colonel Consett explained. As the map illustrated, enemy defenses were much deeper and more elaborate in the north. Consequently, the bulk of Allied forces had been deployed there, although much work had been done to conceal this fact from the enemy. In the southern sector, only 7th Armoured Division and the 1st Free French Brigade southeast of Himeimat would be employed in breakthrough and exploitation.[9] Brister and Durk's brigade, the 4th Light Armoured, would form the spearhead

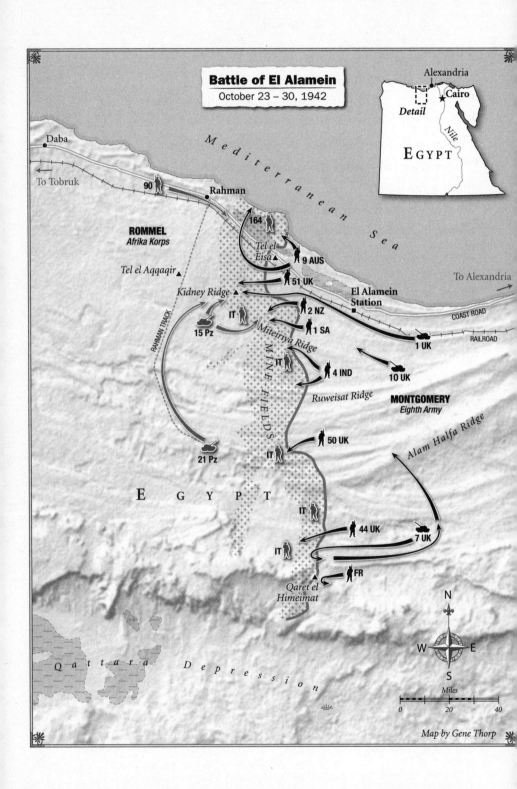

Battle of El Alamein
October 23 – 30, 1942

Alexandria

Cairo

Detail

Nile

E GYPT

M e d i t e r r a n e a n   S e a

Daba

To Tobruk

90

Rahman

164

Tel el Eisa ▲

9 AUS

ROMMEL
Afrika Korps

Tel el Aqqaqir ▲

Kidney Ridge ▲

51 UK

To Alexandria

El Alamein Station

COAST ROAD

RAILROAD

IT

2 NZ

1 SA

RAHMAN TRACK

15 Pz

IT

Miteiriya Ridge

1 UK

M I N E   F I E L D S

IT

4 IND

10 UK

Ruweisat Ridge

MONTGOMERY
Eighth Army

Alam Halfa Ridge

50 UK

21 Pz

IT

E   G   Y   P   T

IT

44 UK

7 UK

IT

FR

Qaret el Himeimat ▲

Q a t t a r a   D e p r e s s i o n

N

W ✦ E

S

Miles

0   20   40

Map by Gene Thorp

of the southern attack,[10] with each of the four KRRC companies leading a column of the 7th Armoured Division down cleared paths through the minefields. The outcome, on the map, was as plain and simple as two broad black arrows, one in the north and one in the south, which swept across Allied and Axis minefields, penetrated German and Italian troop positions, then curved inward to meet up on the far side of enemy lines.

Having performed the patrol and reconnaissance work behind the maps, the men of 1st Battalion had a fair notion of what awaited them. Even in the southern sector, Axis defenses were dense and deep. Two minefield belts, each about half a mile in depth, were separated by a nearly mile-deep swath interspersed with infantry. Behind the minefields waited a third deadly belt of dug-in tanks and antitank guns. "Not a nice proposition to attack," one officer summarized dryly.[11]

What was more, unlike their two American lieutenants, many of the riflemen were battle veterans who had learned for themselves the price of combat. Durk's C Company, under the command of Peter Wake's deco- rated brother Toby, was made up of men from the old 9th Battalion, the Rangers, who had seen hard struggle and bitter loss in 1941 amid the winter-locked hillsides of Greece and in retreat during the Germans' dev- astating airborne conquest of Crete. Those who survived had joined the dispiriting contest with Rommel on the Gazala line this May and June. In July, in one glorious last hurrah, a single company of the 9th had pulled off a daring raid on Fuka aerodrome, eighty miles behind German lines. But by midsummer the battalion's ranks had thinned out to the point where, without reinforcements from England, the Rangers had had to be disbanded, and the soldiers were reassigned to 1st and 2nd battalions. Durk's men's bond extended back even farther, to prewar days when they had worked together in the London Gas Works. They still talked proudly of their old battalion.[12]

Now, after nearly two months when the enemy had had little to do but dig tank traps, string barbed wire, plant land mines, devise booby traps, and dig in their antitanks, machine guns, and mortars, the men of 1st Battalion must have awaited with profoundly mixed feelings the return to action. But what they expressed to one another were high hopes and great confidence,[13] in line with the "Personal Message" that General Montgomery circulated to his army in advance of the battle, which relied on the homely and familiar terminology of cricket to bring war's mortal grappling into the realm of the commonplace.

"All that is necessary," Monty wrote, "is that each one of us, every officer and man, should enter this battle with the determination to see it through—to fight and to kill—and finally, to win.

"If we all do this there can be only one result—together we will hit the enemy for 'six,' right out of North Africa." To hit for six is roughly equivalent to hitting a home run in baseball—the ball flying out of play, the best possible score.

On the morning of Friday, October 23, the padre administered the sacrament of Holy Communion.[14] "Let us all pray that 'the Lord mighty in battle' will give us the victory," Monty's message said. As the day wore on, weapons were recleaned and repolished, vehicles scrubbed and serviced and stocked with water, food rations, petrol, ammunition.[15] Jack Brister took a moment to record in his yearbook the event he had so long anticipated: "Tonight's the night. Over the orders once more, and then at 5:20 [p.m.] we moved off to the battle."

As dusk fell across the vast, stony plane of the Western Desert, ten thousand–plus men of the 7th Armoured Division mounted their vehicles and began jockeying for their places in column. The thunder of tank engines throbbed in their ears. Four lines comprising gun carriers, troop carriers, jeeps, tanks, antitank guns, and trucks lengthened gradually across the pale sand. The columns lurched forward. The advance began.[16]

The army passed slowly into narrow lanes cleared earlier through the Allied minefields by the sappers of the 44th Reconnaissance Regiment, aided by tanks newly equipped for mine clearance. "Scorpions" were fitted at the bows with mechanical flails, rotating cylinders studded with heavy chains that whipped the earth ahead, triggering antitank mines before they could do any damage. White cotton tapes delineated the pathway edges, and lighting the lanes at regular intervals were improvised streetlamps made from petrol tins, the symbol for each path glowing dimly where it had been cut out of the metal on the eastern side, the western side kept dark to prevent enemy detection.

Nearly four and a half hours later, at nine forty, just as planned, the sky behind the advancing men caught fire. The crack and boom of the opening barrage piled noise upon noise along the length of the horizon, so that the force of sound rushing up seemed to propel them. In the desert now a man could shout or laugh or scream or cry and no one would hear him.[17] The power of it was overwhelming, thrilling. A man might feel puny and yet immense, both at once.

The full moon rose. The hard ground cooled, and the steady advance of the 1st Battalion churned it to dust. Each driver could only follow mechanically the black silhouette of the vehicle three yards in front of him.[18]

As the columns progressed, activity ahead of the men increased. Machine gun bullets traced streaks of light against the night in all directions. Armor-piercing shot skidded to earth like lightning and ricocheted upward in brilliant parabolas.[19] Near the heads of their columns, Brister and Durk and their men reached the end of the Allied minefields and passed into no-man's-land. Here, soldiers of the Reconnaissance Regiment were going about their business like moonlit phantoms, escorting prisoners, salvaging weapons and ammunition from a knocked-out vehicle, helping back the wounded. Some lay wounded themselves; others just lay awkwardly where they had fallen, bodies fractured and, amid the cacophony, strangely and utterly still.

As the British columns rolled forward into the marked gaps in the first enemy minefield, the men took some comfort from the rushing sound overhead of friendly fire. The opening barrage had been lifted and retargeted farther on to protect them. But their route grew ever more hazardous. On every side, enemy shells droned. Shrapnel whirred and sliced

202 ★ INTO DUST AND FIRE

around the red gashes of shellburst. Antitank and small-arms fire increased. It became clear that the second enemy minefield was the seat of fierce opposition.

Now the seemingly mechanical flow of Allied vehicles began breaking down. Halts became increasingly frequent, and confusion and anxiety about the causes spread. As the leading men approached the second enemy minefield, a terrible fire rained down. Armor-piercing shot streamed across their paths in wide, focused arcs. The enemy had the lanes in their sights.

Troops of tanks ordered to the fronts of the columns forged gamely ahead, but even their thick armor could not withstand the concentrated fire. Soon flaming hulks blocked the pathways, illuminating lead vehicles for the enemy gunners. From behind and to the flanks, the leading men heard bursts of machine gun fire and rifle shots, awakening the fear that hostile fire now surrounded them. They could not know that what they heard were in fact the last complaints of enemy soldiers being rounded up between the minefields.

Each unexplained halt fueled new anxieties. "Holy havoc reigned," Brister would write. By one a.m. on Saturday, October 24, his column was stymied. "The usual muddle—we were to turn back—we were in the wrong gap."

Since they plainly would not penetrate the enemy minefields before dawn, the tank squadrons received orders to return through the first enemy minefield before daylight made sitting ducks of them. One by one, the drivers turned back, so that before long two lines ran alongside each other in the narrow lanes, only the eastbound in motion.

Durk's machine gun company was instructed to form strongpoints behind the first minefield to protect the tanks. For company C, October 24 was a day for digging in and wondering what the second night of battle might bring.

Brister's company followed orders to assist the 44th Reconnaissance Regiment in clearing up between the minefields and consolidating the night's gains. First light found them struggling to round up prisoners and clear and occupy enemy pits and trenches while continuing to endure, in Brister's words, "most concentrated shellfire." Although low-flying Allied aircraft laid down smoke continuously to screen them, the ground between the minefields was crowded with troops, and the enemy retained good observation posts on the high ground of Himeimat. The plan for the Fighting French to capture the peak had failed. Although an initial nighttime assault had gained the objective, they had been driven off again in the morning.

Losses were inevitable. In Brister's platoon alone, Rifleman Beeton took a shot in the stomach, but lived. Five others—Roden, Warren, Pearse, Mitchell, Duffy—and Sergeant O'Leary were killed.

The second night of the Battle of El Alamein, October 24–25, brought another attempt to penetrate the second enemy minefield in the southern sector. Again, Durk and Brister ordered their platoons to form up in column and drive through the marked lanes, which, they had been told, would be completed that night. Yet, again, the intensity and accuracy of Axis antitank fire as they reached the second minefield spelled certain destruction for any vehicle that hazarded the paths. Soon burning hulks again blocked the way, and the men again were ordered back. "Two dancing fires gave us away to bomber and shell fire," Brister recorded. "Fiendish!"

On the next night, no new attempt on the gaps was made, but steady shelling continued. The enemy, the men learned on the afternoon of the twenty-sixth, had the lanes through the second minefield so well covered as to render them useless. Instead, two secret new gaps would be cleared that night by the Royal Engineers, working in silence and protected by small patrols of the Reconnaissance Regiment. The new plan, or hope, was to pass through these gaps on the night of the twenty-seventh–twenty-eighth. In the meantime, Brister's company was relieved by men of the 44th Infantry Division and after dark moved back into reserve positions behind Durk's company, where they held the right flank of the bridgehead through the first minefield.[20] Still enemy fire continued. Brister's friend Peter Mortimer lost four gunners to one shell. Few men slept that night, as they hastened to dig in as best they could before daylight.

At dawn on the twenty-seventh, Durk went forward with the other officers of B and C companies to inspect the ground ahead. Ordinarily, enemy positions could be tough to spot, dug into the earth and protected by piled-up rocks and sandbags, camouflage nets, and the gray-beige dust color that quickly characterized anything and everything in the desert. But in the slanting light of morning, with the sun casting long shadows behind them, Durk could see the enemy clustered around their guns among camelthorn tufts and stony outcrops to north and west, as if the broken desert had been colonized by some huge, malevolent variety of prairie dog. The nearest group was just five hundred yards away. Durk and his friends began to plan. The rough, undulating ground promised adequate cover. Why not seize the position? Fight back. Make some headway. But Colonel Consett vetoed the notion. He had orders to conserve the battalion's strength for more important operations ahead.[21] So Durk's machine gun platoon found protected vantage points for their two three-inch mortars and four Vickers medium machine guns and contented themselves with firing accurately and effectively onto the enemy strongpoints.

Brister took his platoon and their three-inch mortars north and bombed another enemy outpost at about eight hundred yards. After a couple of hours, their accuracy was rewarded. A white flag fluttered into view above the stoneworks. They honored the flag and ceased fire while the enemy carried out their wounded. The enemy resumed firing briefly, then fled. Brister wanted to stalk them with his platoon, felt confident they'd succeed, but Sandy, the company commander, told them they had to move on.

That day, word came that Beeton had died of his stomach wound. There also was news about the progress of the minefield gaps. Maintaining silence and secrecy had slowed down mine lifting—a painstaking, if adrenaline-fired, process in any case. The engineers would need one more night to finish.

By the morning of the twenty-eighth, the men were told, the two new gaps had been completed. One of them, however, had "roused the enemy's alarm."[22] The soldiers' hearts sank at this news, as they remembered the inferno they had confronted during the first two nights. Clearly the breakthrough in the south would be held up for some time.

Frustration began to fester, souring into discouragement and corroding the men's customary wry heartiness. They needed good news, and, fortunately, reports began trickling in from the north. The Australian division had pierced nine enemy minefields to advance along the coast. After very hard fighting, the 51st Highland Division and the New Zealand Division were well into enemy defenses. Still, that didn't change their own situation. Without another infantry assault to take out the enemy's many and lethal antitank guns, any breakthrough in the south was doomed to failure. No one was surprised, therefore, when 7th Armoured Division was ordered out of the line. They were to reorganize and prepare to exploit if a new attack by 44th Infantry Division should prove successful.

On the night of October 28–29—the sixth night of battle—the exhausted men of 1st Battalion KRRC moved back across no-man's-land into their own minefields and the forgotten luxury of safety. Heads nodded as their vehicles ground back along the dust-clogged track. The next morning they slept on into daylight. "All awoke refreshed," Peter Wake would recall with astonishing cheeriness, "for a day of cleaning and polishing of weapons, careful checking of reserve rations, and—last but not least—a quick letter to those at home."[23]

That night (October 29–30), 44th Infantry Division made a final attempt on the second enemy minefield. A fierce and successful counterattack by Italian infantry put an end to any plan to break through in the south.

About thirty miles to the north on the afternoon of October 23, Cox, Cutting, and Bolté went over orders one last time with their men: Be ready to move into position at last light, bed down until 0015 hours, then move at 0030, with the rest of 7th Motor Brigade, for sixteen miles through British minefields to the El Alamein box, just behind the front line. Three tracks—Sun, Moon, and Star—had been well marked, not only by petrol tins with the appropriate symbol cut out of them, but with great cairns at thirty-yard intervals.[24] In plan, the infantry—in this case the 51st Highland Division—would go ahead to force a bridgehead. Then KRRC motor companies would advance beyond the last enemy minefield, dig in, and form an antitank flank to defend the armor, coming on behind them.

In the event, of course, things went differently. The Battle of El Alamein, like all planned offensives, depended on a series of complicated, error-prone, and unpredictable operations progressing smoothly. Under a bright bomber's moon, the vehicles of 2nd Battalion KRRC closed up into columns, and when they reached their start line, the men got down and tried to sleep. But the opening barrage beginning at nine forty set the western sky ablaze and produced a crescendo of noise that, after a brief pause before zero hour at ten o'clock,.would continue all night and, with variations, form the nerve-jangling backdrop of the sleepless nights and days to come. "The whole of the western sky was lit up with a succession of flashes as far to the south as the eye could see," wrote one officer. "It was eerie, uncanny, tremendous."[25] Unsurprisingly, sleep proved elusive. Monty's promise of air cover notwithstanding, an exploding bomb raised a huge plume of dirt and smoke just four hundred yards to their north.

At about 0115 hours on October 24, the column snaked off again down the by now extraordinarily dusty track. After about three hours, progress halted, the way blocked by a huge scrum of men and vehicles. Word came that Australian and New Zealand infantry, to the north, had succeeded in reaching their objectives, but the Highlanders ahead were struggling.

Dawn painted the huge, unbroken sky the palest possible blue. Bostons, Baltimores, and Mitchells roared by overhead, with Hurricanes as escorts and Spitfires as top cover. The men watched as antiaircraft fire found two medium bombers. They flared briefly, then arced downward. Tiny figures tumbled from the cockpits, the promising white flowers of their parachutes blooming above them—all but one, whose sickening plunge continued.[26]

Caught nose-to-tail and hemmed in on the cleared track by enemy minefields, the men of 2nd Battalion couldn't help but consider what gratifying targets they would make for an enemy bomber or a strafing Messerschmitt. In later life, the commander of Cox's gunnery company, David Graham-Campbell, would concur bitterly with one of the officially recognized lessons of the battle. "It is a serious criticism of Montgomery's generalship that we were moved forward and had to sit between the first two minefields within shelling distance of the enemy suffering useless casualties (especially us in our unarmoured vehicles)," he wrote in his memoir. "And it is a criticism of Montgomery's character that, to his dying day, he claimed that everything had gone according to his plan, and roundly cursed our tanks and their Corps Commander because they did not fight their way out."[27]

Cox, new to battle, was unsure what to make of the shelling. His men were experienced, having been for about a year in the desert, and he supposed they found it familiar. He kept his anxiety to himself for fear of appearing a coward. But as shellbursts continued on all sides, they grew more and more nerve-racking. Cox's pride broke and he turned to the men beside him. Was this the usual thing? Their reply brought both relief and anxiety. This much shelling was as new to them as it was to him. Turned out he was being quite calm, even if only through ignorance.

A rumor circulated that 2nd Battalion would attack that night, but the waiting went on. The soldiers bedded down as best they could on the dusty ground. The circling German bombers droned. Their dropping bombs boomed and rattled, most, fortunately, in the distance. But sleep remained elusive, what with the bombings and the shellings and the anxious hope of a coming order to move.[28]

At two thirty a.m. on Sunday, October 25, the advance slowly ground forward again, the columns moving along Star track through British minefields until, just before first light, they halted between first and second enemy minefields. There was desultory shelling, always the odd burst of machine gun fire, otherwise the usual quiet before the feverish activity of men and tank crews at dawn. The soldiers attempted to disperse, moving offtrack as they could. Then, again, waiting. As another dawn spread, a German plane flew over. The sun glinted silver off a cylinder that dropped from its belly. In reply, a terrific barrage erupted, tracer from the Bren guns glowing a lovely pink against the delicate blue sky.[29] Many of the keyed-up, frustrated men shot off their guns just for the joyous release of it.[30]

Soon the scope of the traffic jam became clear. The vast gallimaufry of tanks, guns, and transport vehicles was being held up by a third enemy minefield. Dispersion was impossible, and when shells from the Germans' powerful eighty-eights began to fall steadily, "brew-ups" and casualties resulted. Stuck in place, the gunners answered back in kind, successfully attracting even more counterbattery fire. Bolté, restless, went to inspect his platoon. Remembering *War and Peace,* he strove to emulate General Kutuzof's calm under fire and his glad acceptance of bad news as if it were all part of the plan. The method worked. "I really think you're enjoying this, sir," his batman said, not unaccusingly.[31]

In late afternoon, new instructions arrived: prepare for attack that night. Cox brought the news to his men. "Major Blundell thinks we may move out here tonight"—he pointed to the spot on his map—"and so maybe we'll have some fun."

Cox was fond of all his men, but the rifleman who spoke up then was, he thought, a prince of a fellow. "Why do the officers always think it's fun?" he reproached. "It's not our idea of fun, sir."

"It's not theirs, either," Cox replied, surprised perhaps to find himself explaining the English to the English. "But it's a way of talking, so that you sort of make little out of something unpleasant."

"We don't like hearing it called fun though, sir," the rifleman persisted, and Cox could only allow as he was probably right.[32] And when the men, now more than ready, leaguered at last light, they learned that the attack was called off.

About seven hours later, at around two a.m., Cox and Cutting received orders to join a two-company advance following an infantry attack on antitank gun emplacements on Kidney Ridge, a feature about two miles

ack Brister, at five, poses shyly for a 1925 Christmas portrait of the clan. His five sisters and two
brothers are grouped around the table. His father, Dr. Frederick Brister, stands fourth from left
n the rear. Courtesy of Tom Watkins

The Cox family in 1936 at their home in Plainfield, New Jersey. Rob, seventeen, sits at far right,
with Rowland and Betty between him and his mother, Frances. Archibald, called Bill, sits at far
left, behind Louis and beside Max, then Molly. Cox Family Archive

Rob Cox sent this postcard of a cheerful yet determined Winston Churchill to his youngest brother, Rowland, from Halifax, Canada, on July 12, 1941, three days before he sailed for England. Jokingly addressing his brother as "Ronald," Cox sent him birthday wishes and much love to all the family. COX FAMILY ARCHIVE

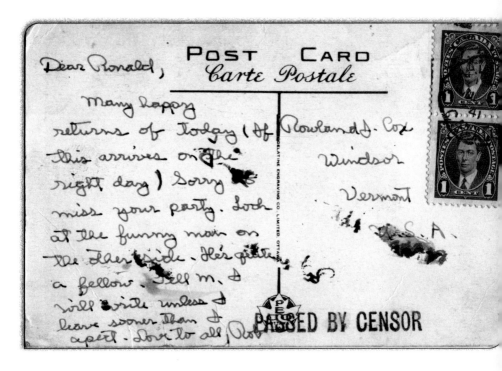

On the rifle range at Bushfield Camp in Winchester, England, the five American volunteers get acquainted with their weapons along with other new recruits to the King's Royal Rifle Corps. Rob Cox, Jack Brister, and Chuck Bolté (*left to right*) practice at the tripods, while Bill Durkee (*far left*) and Heyward Cutting (*left*) observe. THE ROYAL GREEN JACKETS (RIFLES) MUSEUM

Chuck Bolté grabs a smoke during field training exercises at Bushfield. Jack Brister is behind and to the right of him. THE ROYAL GREEN JACKETS (RIFLES) MUSEUM

Concentration registers on Chuck Bolté's face as the riflemen practice the march-at-ease. Cox is behind him, Cutting behind and left.

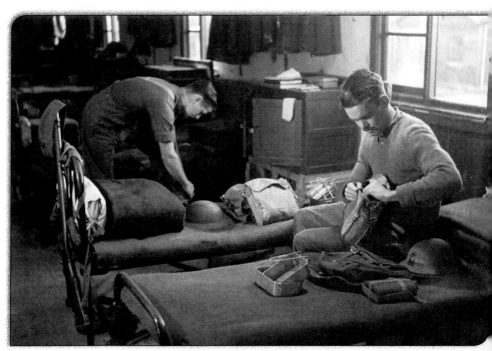

Chuck Bolté (*foreground*) and Jack Brister organize their kit in the barrack room at Bushfield. Canvas pouches containing respirators were carried around the neck almost constantly for fear that the German Luftwaffe might bomb England with poison gas.

Rob Cox, captured by a British Office of War Information photographer in October 1941. After his death, Fanny Cox kept this photo framed in her bedroom. Cox Family Archive

In service of the King: The five Yanks consider the foreign currency in their pay envelopes for the benefit of an Office of War Information photographer. The Royal Green Jackets (Rifles) Museum

In a scene staged for Office of War Information photographers, the American volunteers demonstrate hard-won mastery of the drill, with rifles at the trail. Bolté, Durkee, and Brister lead the section. Cox commands. Cutting reviews.

Brister (*center*) and Bolté leap a trench in the Hampshire countryside during bayonet training staged for War Office photographers.

Jack Brister greets the American ambassador John Gilbert Winant during his visit to Bushfield with British foreign secretary Eden on November 1, 1941. Winant later would describe the American volunteers as "my contact with life." Cutting watches at left.

Taking in the sights of old England, Durkee (*left*) and Bolté visit the Hospital of St. Cross, a charitable home for elderly men in Winchester founded in 1136. They receive the "wayfarer's dole," a gift of bread and ale from the porter, who wears traditional medieval garb.

Cutting helps Bolté don his rain gear when the weather turns bad. Cox is to his right, with Brister, looking miserable, behind him (*far right*).

Lance Corporal Bolté dishes up a typically starch-heavy meal for his squad at Bushfield. Tea was plentiful, but vegetables, eggs, and dairy products were all but nonexistent.

In Egypt, ancient and modern mingle as Allied reinforcements stream toward the El Alamein line in autumn 1941.   LIBRARY OF CONGRESS

British soldiers, probably mugging for the camera, demonstrate the seriousness of the fly problem in the Western Desert by wrapping their heads in protective netting.
LIBRARY OF CONGRESS

A Vickers medium machine gun and its crew in action amid the stony wastes of the Western Desert. A condenser can connected to the gun muzzle reclaimed precious water from steam for reuse in the weapon's cooling jacket. LIBRARY OF CONGRESS

The crew of a British six-pounder prepares to answer an enemy shell. Supplied in North Africa beginning in 1942, the powerful new antitank guns greatly improved the 8th Army's chances of knocking out German panzers.
LIBRARY OF CONGRESS

The dreaded German 88 served the Axis well in both antiaircraft and antitank capacities. "We were all afraid of the 88," wrote Chuck Bolté, who lost a leg to one.   LIBRARY OF CONGRESS

German prisoners from the 90th Light Division are searched for weapons by their British captors south of El Alamein. (Note the Afrika Korps armband on the second soldier from left.) The battle netted some ten thousand German prisoners and twenty thousand Italians, 29 percent of Rommel's army.   LIBRARY OF CONGRESS

The detritus of battle attests to effective targeting of an Italian ammunition column by British artillery. "You learn to shut your eyes to carnage and refuse to let it register in your brain," wrote one veteran of the desert war. LIBRARY OF CONGRESS

In early November 1942, heavy rain hampers Allied pursuit of retreating Axis forces in Libya. The Grant tank (*foreground*) was among the many new American-made weapons that helped rebalance the scales in favor of 8th Army.
LIBRARY OF CONGRESS

Jack Brister and Rob Cox meet General Montgomery, at rear in his trademark black tanker's beret. The 8th Army commander visited 1st battalion KRRC on March 19, 1943, to rally troops for the Battle of Mareth. THE ROYAL GREEN JACKETS (RIFLES) MUSEUM

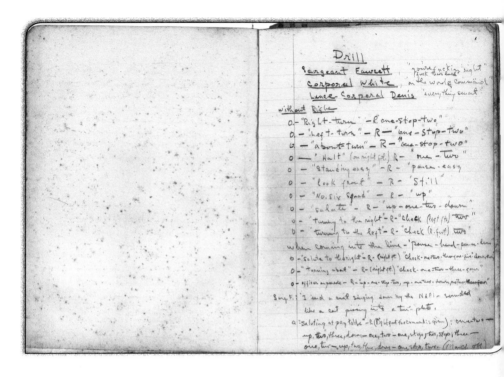

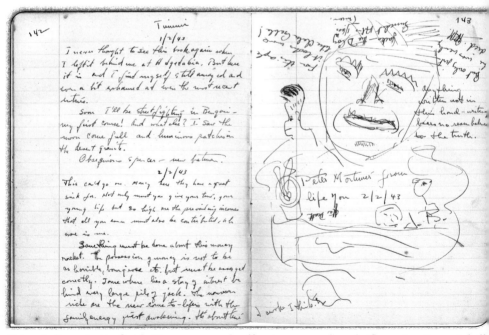

Brister's diary start to finish: Page one records officer's commands and rifleman's actions at drill along with choice quotes from the sergeant; on page 143, nineteen months later, Jack scrawled a portrait of his friend Peter Mortimer, who added his own comments. Courtesy of Tom Watkins

At 64th British General Hospital in Alexandria, Heyward Cutting (*center*) visits with Bill Durkee, in sunglasses and with tented legs. COURTESY OF VAUGHAN DURKEE MCTERNAN

Charles and Mary Bolté on their wedding day, July 24, 1943.

COURTESY OF BROOKS BOLTÉ RANDOLPH

Bill Durkee, his wife, Mary, and their three children at Mary's parents' house in Denver, circa 1954. The children (*left to right*) are Vaughan, Edward, and William Porter IV.

COURTESY OF VAUGHAN DURKEE MCTERNAN

ahead named for the shape of its contour line on the map, even though in fact it was a very shallow depression. In bitter cold, their platoons moved off down Moon track, then halted at the end of the third enemy minefield for about two hours, shivering under fairly heavy shell fire inspired by the infantry ahead of them. But the infantry were stymied. The KRRC companies retreated for another day of staying put and taking fire, a heavy sandstorm now adding discomfort on discomfort.

After three nights of waiting, at about seven fifteen p.m. on the night of Monday the twenty-sixth, Colonel Heathcoat-Amory arrived from brigade headquarters with new plans. Although repeated attempts by the armor to advance had been repelled by heavy antitank fire, efforts to locate the enemy guns had been successful. The KRRC companies would soon join a two-battalion assault on two strongpoints on Kidney Ridge.[33] KRRC 2nd Battalion, on the right, would attack a position code-named Woodcock. The 2nd Battalion, the Rifle Brigade, would attack a position code-named Snipe on the left. Cox's and Cutting's B Company and Bolté's C would take the lead for the 60th. "The orders were so detailed and unrealistic that I stopped taking notes from the commanding officer after three pages," Bolté later remembered.[34] Nevertheless, the brigadier had given assurances, the colonel said, that they should have no difficulty in reaching their objective.

As the fraught dark gathered and Colonel Heathcote-Amory wound up his talk, a few enemy planes drawn by a nearby fire scored a direct hit on an adjacent antiaircraft gun emplacement. Three wounded and one dead did not seem a good omen.[35]

With just two hours to prepare, the officers rushed to check vehicles, replenish supplies, and give out the long, complicated orders to their men in the dark. At about nine p.m., with the moon, now past full, rising behind them, the companies drove forward slowly in column through the last enemy minefield, halted briefly in open country, then spread out in "open order" to attack. Just before zero hour of 2330, a series of flashes again lit the sky behind them, followed by a succession of thuds and then the whistle of shells overhead. Within five minutes, three regiments of twenty-five-pounders had joined in, and for about twenty minutes the battalion advanced beneath a comforting canopy of whistling shells. Under the brilliant desert moon, visibility was "quite two hundred yards," as the British would say.

"It was an impressive sight," Colonel Heathcoat-Amory later recalled, "carriers in front, motor platoons next, and mechanized machine-gun trucks and anti-tank gun portees bringing up the rear, all moving on a compass bearing and marching by the center."[36]

They had covered about a mile and a half when Cox got his first good look at the enemy in the flesh. Out of the dust and confusion wandered about two dozen German soldiers with their hands raised, ready to give themselves up. They were young, and though he spoke no German, they seemed to Cox to be nice enough fellows. But they also were an interruption and a nuisance. Uncertain whether or not they'd been searched, Cox felt compelled to go through their pockets to ensure they were unarmed. Beyond that, no one seemed to know what to do with them. Certainly taking them along would be unhelpful, so Cox chose one rifleman to escort them back to the gap in the minefield.[37]

As the company drove on, a thick cloud of smoke and dust kicked up by the shells of the barrage hung before them, then enclosed them, visibility dropping to near zero. When the gloom lifted a little, the order came to advance on foot. The men stopped and began to jump down from their vehicles. Just then, heavy machine gun and antitank gunfire ripped into the leaders from a range of only seventy-five yards. Dust and smoke again closed in. An ammunition lorry, now in flames, cast a lurid glow over the sudden chaos. Bright tracers streaked the darkness. Occasionally, exploding mortar shells shook the air. Soon, the resonant popping of small-arms fire amplified the din.

When the Allied barrage ended, the dust cleared gradually. All around him, Cox saw men struggling with their vehicles. The commanding officer's eight-cwt had gotten caught in a barbed-wire fence protecting the enemy strongpoint, while the adjutant's vehicle had broken down toward the rear and was being towed in circles in an attempt to revive it. Other men returned enemy fire. Cox attempted to move forward with his gun portees, but they, too, became entangled in a jumble of barbed wire. Bolté, in his jeep, saw him signal them on with a wave and a shout, shells banging around the blazing lorry. A few minutes later, Cox hit the ground, a bullet through his back. A German machine gunner had let the Tommies pass so he could shoot up their rear.

Cutting led his machine gun platoon onto a low rise, where they became pinned down by heavy fire drawn by the silhouettes of his vehicles against the firelight. He got his platoon out of the hole, picked up a wounded officer, and started to a flank in his jeep, but soon drove into a hail of machine gun bullets. With both legs damaged, one arm hit, and, somehow, his two front teeth knocked out, he managed to drive back to B Company area. Then he collapsed.

Bolté and the rest of C Company had remained in their vehicles and motored ahead toward the right flank, benefiting from the advantage of surprise and the cover of the dust cloud. He and his fellows fared better. Some reached the objective, scattering the German defenders, though not defanging them. Bolté survived the night. But his company was isolated, and at dawn he turned his field glasses to the rear in hopes of sighting reinforcements. Suddenly, astonishingly, someone hit his thigh very hard with a baseball bat, or so he felt. He heard the screech of an .88 shell as he fell, telling his company commander what even he himself, afterward, found almost unbelievable—"They got me."[38] A shell fragment had ripped into his right thigh, high up, and knocked him flat until medics could retrieve him.

On October 30 the men of 1st Battalion KRRC got wind of a change of plan. Conjecture, speculation, and rumor were the conversational currency of the battlefield, but in this case, few doubted the central fact that Monty's Operation Lightfoot was failing. The sequence of necessary actions had been disrupted by the depth and complexity of Axis minefields and the intractability of the antitank gun screens protecting them. The infantrymen leading the way had advanced the line, most notably in the north, where the Australians had pushed effectively toward the coast road, and around Kidney Ridge, where advance positions on Snipe and Woodcock, despite grueling counterattack, had been held.

After six days of hard combat along the forty-mile length of the El Alamein line, the Allies could be said to have made progress. They had worn down the enemy's strength, and his reserves of fresh troops had been shallower than were the Allies' from the start. By drawing his tanks into battle, the 8th Army had depleted his armament and reduced his essential supplies, particularly of petrol, which was now growing desperately short. But 8th Army armor, behind the infantry and the supporting motor battalions, had been unable to follow up. The promised breakout behind enemy lines had not occurred. As Major Graham-Campbell of 2nd Battalion 60th later would put it, "The work of the gunners, Royal Engineers, and infantry was absolutely magnificent but, through no fault of theirs, [they] were unable to establish themselves beyond the third minefield, so the lanes through it could not be cleared and we could not get out into the open ground; to that extent the battle had not gone according to plan, and we should not have been called forward until there was something that we could usefully do."[39]

As if to emphasize the stalemate, on the afternoon of October 30 a sandstorm blew up, grounding planes, disorienting compasses, silencing the blinded gunners. It "spread like a great shroud over Egypt, half-burying the dead, and hid for a brief moment the hate and passion of war," one participant wrote.[40] The commanders of 8th Army took advantage of the lull to continue crafting a new plan. The new offensive would resemble Lightfoot, but on a smaller scale, and would be code-named Supercharge.

The order came down on October 30 for the men of 1st Battalion KRRC to move behind the lines with 7th Armoured Division to the northern sector. According to reports, attacks there had penetrated far, and the 1st and 10th armoured divisions had been committed so heavily that they no longer were available for their intended role as the "corps de chasse."

The 7th Armoured Division and a New Zealand brigade, taken out of the line for the purpose, would move north to replace them. The infantry divisions now would launch a new attack oriented just north of the original center line near Snipe and Woodcock and toward a shallow knoll, Tel el Aqqaqir. When they succeeded in gapping the enemy line, 4th Light Armoured Brigade and the New Zealand brigade would follow behind and exploit, securing the way for the tanks.[41]

On the afternoon of the thirtieth and for most of the thirty-first, the 7th Armoured Division traveled north some five or six miles behind Allied lines. Late afternoon of the thirty-first found them leaguered about a mile and a half behind the battle, near El Alamein rail stop, the indifferent Med now not far off on their right. "Excitement was high," Peter Wake wrote later. Rumors began to spread that the breakthrough was made and armored cars already were pursuing the enemy through the open desert.[42] The enormous fireworks display lashing the sky to the west and south seemed to give the lie to this hope, however. Indeed, Axis resistance remained formidable. The weary men of the 7th once more attended to the housekeeping duties of war. Replacement troops arrived needing to be schooled in platoon ways. Brister worked in the new riflemen Mitchell, Flood, Vizzard, Francis, Dempsey, and Layton. Vehicles maintenance. Weapons cleaning. Rations, petrol, and ammunition replenishment. They tended to all the tasks that would ease a long march, which they now had good reason to believe lay soon ahead of them.

On the night of November 1–2, a heavy barrage again rocked the desert on a scale not far short of the opening night. At 0105 hours the second great attempt to penetrate enemy lines began.[43]

The next day Colonel Consett called together the officers of 1st Battalion and ordered them to prepare to advance through one of the northern minefield gaps at short notice. When Brister and Durk passed along the news to their men, it affected them like a shot of adrenaline. The Battle of El Alamein, it appeared, was won![44] Men who had fought back and forth across the northern edge of Africa for months, even years, could all too easily imagine the victorious road ahead, the battle at last again mobile, the Western Desert open to any and every maneuver of the 8th Army's choosing. The old, bitter lessons learned in Jock columns and on two previous advances to Benghazi seemed suddenly and joyously important again.

By November 2, Field Marshal Rommel had indeed set in motion the process of withdrawal. His ranks were depleted, his tank squadrons eviscerated, his petrol and ammunition supplies all but exhausted. Behind the lines at El Alamein, panzer units and the Italian infantry had been moving steadily south to north. Sixty-odd miles to the west along the coast road, preparations already were afoot for a stand at Fuka, where a steep coastal escarpment to the south prevented tank movement and funneled pursuing troops into a narrow defile.

But still the battle of El Alamein raged on. Australian infantry in the north drew *panzer-armee* reserves into a frantic *danse macabre*. Further south, 9th Armoured Brigade, the spearhead of Operation Supercharge, battered itself against the German antitank screen, to be followed by 1st Armoured Division. A German counterattack on the morning of November 2 produced "the greatest clash of armour seen at El Alamein," according to historian Niall Barr. "In these few hours, the battle of El Alamein was decided."[45] That night, 7th Motor Brigade, including 2nd Battalion KRRC but without its American officers, made a second attempt to punch a hole through the gun screen. On the afternoon of November 3, reports began to arrive that the coast road to the west was solid with retreating Axis traffic.[46] That night the 5th Indian Brigade attacked at Tel el Aqqaqir, followed by the 7th Argylls, aided by another creeping artillery barrage. On the morning of November 4, twelve days later than General Montgomery had planned, a gap at last was opened for the British armor to drive through enemy lines.

On the evening of November 3–4, the riflemen of the 1st Battalion KRRC mounted their trucks with beaming faces. As the march began, the cry was, for the third time in two years, "On to Benghazi!" "No one suspected," Peter Wake would remember, "that Benghazi was merely to be a stepping stone on the victorious advance to Tunis. At most Tripoli was talked of as a goal to end all goals."[47]

The night ahead proved to be both exhilarating and frustrating.[48] As the 1st Battalion KRRC led the 4th Light Armoured Brigade down two lanes dimly marked BOOMERANG and HALF MOON, bottlenecks, crowding, changes of plan, and uncertainty continued to beleaguer them. The real moon, now in its last quarter, cast only a pale light, and the minefield lanes by now had been reduced to a gluey state that one chronicler described as "a colloidal solution of sand, petrol fumes, and personal irritation."[49] All around them, as the men labored forward, for three miles lay the wreckage of the enemy's defenses: vehicles gutted and racked, charred tanks and guns tossed at peculiar angles, equipment and clothing scattered in arbitrary, ruined mounds, and everywhere the simple wooden or metal crosses overlooking the fresh-dug soil of shallow graves and the reeking, contorted husks of dead men who still lay where they had fallen, some with their rifles still clenched in their hands.

But victory brooked no contemplation. The way was forward and the pace was quickening. As the sun turned the turgid desert haze to silver, the whole of 4th Light Armoured Brigade, free at last of the minefields, spread out in open desert formation, racing westward.

"What a lot of kit!" Brister noted later in his yearbook, impressed by the quantities of clothing and other gear left behind by the fleeing enemy. For Brister and Durk, the last of the five American friends still in action, the early days of pursuit were a disorienting welter of exhilaration, apprehension, and fatigue. Driving, scavenging, coping with prisoners—most of them Italian infantrymen left without transport when the German *panzer-armee* retreated and now terrified by the prospect of being abandoned without water or food—made up a routine fractured violently and unexpectedly from time to time by air attack and enemy fire.

On November 4, after a fast ride across the desert toward the coast road, Brister's jeep with one tire flat and shredding, Brister's platoon ran into a German patrol, which opened up with machine guns and antitanks from about five hundred yards. They were driven off, just a few British vehicles damaged, but the confusion that resulted was sobering.

After moving off at first light the next morning, as they approached the coastal town of Fuka, they found the way blocked by a minefield that extended the line of the Fuka escarpment southward for ten miles. Later, the minefield was discovered to be a British dummy laid during the summer withdrawal, but for the moment the armored brigade had to aim for a gap, and covering artillery fire delayed them. Shell fire from the enemy rear guard landed close, frightening Tug, Brister's driver and batman. Through the minefield at last in the late afternoon of November 5, Brister's A Company moved to the lead in the pursuing pack.

On the sixth a new, quite unexpected complication developed. Clouds rolled in, and in the early afternoon, the skies opened. The freak downpour "soaked the sand into deep slime."[50] Flooding ensued. Jeep and carrier tires spun without purchase; only the tanks could move reliably through the quagmire. The remnants of Rommel's *panzer-armee*, moving back on the hard surface of the coast road, were handed a reprieve, their escape assured, at least in part, by a chance rainstorm.

On the eighth Durkee's C Company caught up with Brister's, and 1st Battalion struggled on along the coast toward Sidi Barrani. "The race continued for days," Jack wrote later, "through muck, mud, and rain." They met the enemy again at Sidi Barrani, then at Buq Buq, at "Hellfire Pass" on the escarpment at Sollum, then at Capuzzo just past the Libyan frontier, whence they traveled by desert track into the old Gazala battlefield. When the sun at last broke through, it seemed a benediction. The desert steamed and grew warm again. Brister seized an opportunity and, after weeks without bathing, had a good wash in a rain pool.

As the leading edge of the advancing 8th Army progressed beyond established Allied airfields, the danger of attack from the air increased. Few events were as alarming as the high-pitched scream of a diving Stuka or the sight of a Messerschmitt dropping out of the sky, cannons blazing.

On November 9, as Durk and Brister led their platoons toward Gazala with 4th Light Armoured Brigade, it was a Messerschmitt 109 that found them. Sandy Goschen, Brister's company commander, was wounded, and the exploding shells from the cannon smashed into Durk's knees, leaving him all but helpless.

Being lead element in the chase was a source of pride for 1st Battalion, but for an injured soldier in urgent need of medical help, it was a tragedy ready to happen. Finding a doctor among the countless vehicles scattered across the desert was a daunting task, but Toby Wake, Durk's company commander, set off to find one, and after some time his jeep reappeared with a truck beside it—the doctor. He took a look at Durk's wounds, but had nothing in the truck to help him, so Durk was lifted painfully inside and they rushed off in search of a Casualty Clearing Station, where the process of removing shrapnel from his knees could begin. "In all this game of bumping in ambulances, being hauled about on a stretcher, filled with M&B tablets, operated upon, etc., there wasn't much pleasure," Durkee later stoically recalled. (M&Bs were a multipurpose sulfa drug manufactured by the company May & Baker.) It would take five days of excruciating transport, fever, and delirium for him to reach No. 8 General Hospital in Alexandria, which proved just the starting place for another long, painful journey back to health.

Now only Brister remained. After they'd lost Sandy Goschen, what remained of Company A was sent back, and Brister took over a platoon in Company C, under Toby Wake. On November 13, they reached Tobruk, having covered 376 miles in ten days of pursuit.[51] They hugged the coast until Derna, then turned inland, the land rising, to Giovanni Berta. There was more rain. "I slept in a rocky sheep pen," Brister would remember, "the pouring rain creeping through to me bones—it seemed. It wasn't sleep—merely a restful shiver."

Heading southwest, 1st Battalion traveled overland through the Djebel hills, where they met the enemy twice. They fought again for Benghazi, arriving at last in the harbor town that for so long and so often had been the focus of British aims and hopes. The seaside streets, surely once picturesque, and the once-white stone buildings had been ravaged by conquest and reconquest. Not entirely destroyed, though: Brister managed to find a hotel, where he enjoyed the unspeakable luxury of spending the night between sheets.

They went on, now to the south along the Gulf of Sirte. They reached Adjabiya, 778 miles from El Alamein, on November 23, one month after the artillery barrage that had launched them westward. They continued on through the marshy wastes around the old German stronghold of El Agheila—the westernmost point ever reached by British forces in two years of shuttling battle. Here they found the enemy dug in, and they paused. Preparations were being fine-tuned for the unprecedented advance that lay ahead, while Rommel gained some time for his operation to continue the retreat still farther westward.

Jack Brister, the last of the five Yanks remaining, closed out his yearbook, apparently exhausted. His last entry is as disjointed as the days it describes. "All this took a long time. Unfortunately I forget the dates. Toby was unbearable most [of] the time. Slept my platoon in a cave."

CHAPTER 10

Recovery

Egypt after El Alamein
October 27, 1942–January 1943

> Now, this is not the end. It is not even the beginning of the
> end. But it is, perhaps, the end of the beginning.
>
> —Winston Churchill, November 10, 1942

When the doctor in the surgical ward at 63rd General Military Hospital, on the edge of Cairo, told Bolté that he was getting too dopey and cut back on his morphine, reflection stopped. His mind contained little but the pain in his festering knee and the struggle against it.[1] Decades later, looking back, what he recalled most vividly about that time was the noisiness of his ward—the groans, cries, shouts, the calls for nurses (whom the British called sisters), and the pissing on the floor when the sisters didn't bring the urinals fast enough. Fortunately, a long, open porch ran along one side of the ward, and as soon as Chuck could be moved, he spent as much time there as possible, to get away from the noise.

One day two nuns visiting the hospital stopped by Bolté's bed for a chat. When they saw what remained of his right leg, they offered to pray for him. Bolté had long considered himself a confirmed atheist, but he accepted the offer. When he told this story to another visitor, a friend from battalion named Harry Charles, Harry misted up a bit. "I think I'll say a little prayer for you myself," he said.

The sister who attended Bolté was tough and experienced. She brought him his prelunch tot of whiskey—the doctor thought it might help wean him from painkillers—in a coffee mug. "Mustn't arouse jealousy in your neighbors," she quipped sagely. After a week or two of changing his dressings, she advised him one day not to look at the stump. Then came the day when she herself blanched at the sight and turned quickly away.

Cox also was laid up at 63rd GMH. The bullet that found him that night on Kidney Ridge passed into his back and out his left side, grazing his elbow. He felt sure the wound itself was not grave—"If I'd broken an ankle skiing or something, it would be a more serious injury," he reassured his family—but it seemed to take a long time to heal, and in the meantime he contracted jaundice, not uncommon among the North African troops, which robbed him of appetite and made him depressed. "I suppose I would have had jaundice whether I'd been wounded or not so that it's the jaundice more than the wound which is bad luck," he wrote home on November 9, 1942. "It's so unpleasant having no appetite. I sit and think of all the good things there are to eat and how I wouldn't enjoy them even if I could get them and it makes me very sad, which does seem foolish of me."

Not that he lacked reasons to feel terrible anyway. There was Bolté's plight, for starters. "Poor Bolté—I do feel so sorry for him," he wrote home. And he worried about his other compatriots. From Cutting's batman, who had been in the same ambulance as Cox going back to Cairo, he learned that Heyward had been hit in the knee, but no further news could be had. He felt powerless. He felt disappointed. He didn't like to think back to the days before the battle of El Alamein; the contrast was too painful. "Everything afterwards fizzled out into such a personal anti-climax," he told his mother, "that you didn't really want to remember the fun it was the month before the battle started."

Meanwhile, back in New York, Fanny Cox endured one of the most harrowing moments a war mother can face. None of Rob's coded messages concerning his moves to the front had yet reached her, but the action there filled the New York papers—"Allied Attack—Desert War Flares"; "Counter-Attacks Met by Allies at Gaps Torn in Foe's Defenses; Six-Hour Cannonading Sends Allied Troops Surging Over Foe's Strong Points—Sky and Earth Ablaze."[2]

On November 9th, a Western Union messenger arrived at East 66th Street, where the Coxes had moved into a less costly apartment. By comparison with the fear that coursed through Fanny Cox when she saw him, the telegram he brought could only be called good news:

REGRET TO INFORM YOU OF REPORT RECEIVED FROM MIDDLE EAST THAT 2/LT RH COX KINGS ROYAL RIFLE CORPS WAS WOUNDED IN ACTION ON 27TH OCTOBER 1942. LETTER FOLLOWS SHORTLY

UNDERSECRETARY OF STATE FOR WAR

It would be nine more days, during which Fanny Cox worked frantically every contact she had in Washington and Boston to try to learn what had befallen her son, before a second telegram followed:

WOUND VERY SLIGHT PLEASE SEND 20 POUNDS TO MY ACCOUNT AT BARCLAYS BANK CAIRO TO REPLACE LOST CLOTHING LOTS OF MAIL LOVE AND CHEERS.

ROBERT COX

Cox's temperament required that he make light of his wound, and he had never imagined the War Department would bother telling his mother about it. It is unclear exactly how he learned of her distress—possibly through his English cousin Bill Streeten, whose young son was living with Fanny Cox in New York while Bill was in Cairo with the Royal Engineers—but it clearly shamed him. Indeed, he found the whole situation—being tied down in bed while his battalion pursued the enemy, having trained for months only to see action for just a number of hours—deeply dispiriting. Later that month, in a letter to Nancy Adare, the lady whose Irish estate he had visited during training in England, he likened the situation to a hockey game, and the anger one felt "when the hockey coach put in another line and took you out of the game just when you were getting warmed up and then put you back in and just when you were getting warmed up, out you came again." Otherwise, after El Alamein, the war-as-game metaphor had lost much of its luster. "Then there was the battle which was pretty intriguing," he wrote, leading up to his wounding, "except for some things that made you realize it wasn't as much of a game as you first felt it was."[3]

Visits with Bolté only discouraged Cox further, although he went regularly and strove to be cheerful for his friend's sake. When the wireless played in the wards to keep the men entertained, they followed the war news avidly. That, at least, was heartening. On November 9 reports came over that American soldiers had landed in French Morocco. The Yanks at last had joined the fight. In an astonishing feat of logistics, seamanship, and secrecy, thirty-five thousand GIs had crossed the Atlantic all the way from Norfolk, Virginia, to assault the North African beaches. And they were not only in Morocco. Another thirty-nine thousand landed in western Algeria, and ten thousand more joined twenty-three thousand British soldiers in storming Algerian shores. "I'm so glad we're really going places now," Cox wrote home. "I do wish I wasn't in bed."

In Libya, Axis forces continued to fall back. On November 10, Winston Churchill celebrated the El Alamein victory and the joint Allied invasion of northwest Africa with a rousing speech: "Rommel's army has been defeated. It has been routed. It has been very largely destroyed as a fighting force." On November 13, the 8th Army recaptured Tobruk. And on November 15, Feast Sunday, church bells pealed throughout Britain; excepting one false invasion alarm in September 1940, it was the first time they had rung out since war began.

One day Bolté watched Cox saunter toward him, rangy and rumpled and seemingly eager as ever in his hospital robe, with an extra-wide grin on his strangely yellow-tinged face and a book in one hand, which he waved triumphantly. He had been scrounging in the hospital library, poor pickings as it was, and had found some Hemingway. They both enjoyed Hemingway. The book, *The Fifth Column and the First Forty-nine Stories,* was full of men like them—men who carried guns, men far from home, close to death, wounded, in pain. Bolté read it, and the story about the gambler, the nun, and the radio gave him an idea. No matter how much pain he felt, he had never dared cry. But the character with the broken leg explained that crying relaxed him. So Bolté let himself try it, softly under the blankets, and he found that it helped.[4]

They shared a good laugh about the British brass's handling of Cox's loss of his kit. His shirt had been sliced up by the doctor, but what had become of the rest was a mystery. To the British powers-that-be it was as if they had lost track of his overcoat at a dinner party: They were apologetic, of course, and politely solicitous. "I had a letter from the adjutant yesterday," Rob related. "He apologized for the 'bad hosts' they'd been to the Americans and said we were missed and that he was glad to hear I'd be well and was *willing* to come back. That type of Englishman is really marvelous. They can't talk about anything except as if it were a game or amateur. Of course I am not only willing but anxious, but supposing I wasn't. It really wouldn't matter if I was willing or not. Still, it all makes for a cheery atmosphere and I do it myself I guess."[5]

But Cox inevitably came away from visits with Bolté feeling sad and diminished. "He's having a pretty grim time," he wrote home, "and my little wound makes me feel like a slacker."[6] Yet despite Cox's native optimism, his recovery dragged on. The jaundice waned gradually, until on November 20 he could report, "I have the most colossal appetite and am now investing in and eating a grapefruit daily, so that with my cornflakes and honey [which he also paid for himself], breakfast is now quite a festive meal." But his spirits flagged. "I don't know why I bother to write all this drivel but really there is very little one can write about when one just lies in bed all day. I'm getting more bored each day and at present have nothing to read." He felt cut off not only from home but also from his friends in the army.

Had Cox known of Bill Durkee's condition, his worries would have mounted. After five days of bumping across North Africa some 175 miles from front line to Casualty Clearing Station to hospital, Durk had undergone a second operation to remove shrapnel from his severely damaged legs at No. 8 General Hospital in Alexandria. The biggest problem was his right knee, where dusty metal fragments had penetrated the tibia. He settled finally at 64th British General Hospital, an orthopedic hospital in Alexandria, where he could be treated by the chief specialist in the Middle East, a wonderful Australian called Colonel Armstrong.[7] By then, the wound in Durk's right knee had become thoroughly septic; the bones themselves were infected.

For weeks, Durk lay flat on his back with his bad leg in traction, waiting for the infection to subside. A rubber ring like a miniature swimmer's tube supported the base of his spine to prevent bedsores, and every evening a sister swabbed his back with a solution to toughen the skin. As if to make matters worse, he received disturbing news from his family. They had sold the house on Balboa Island that Durk thought of as home and moved into less luxurious quarters in the coastal town of San Marino. But what worried him more was his father. A big, vital man who loved boating and fishing and business, he had been stricken by malignant high blood pressure. The details remained hazy, but he needed an operation and was losing weight fast. As Durkee in Egypt wasted away from illness and lack of exercise and appetite, his father in California was doing the same.

Then the younger Bill Durkee took a turn for the worse. He, too, contracted yellow jaundice, and combined with the poisons in his knee, it overwhelmed him. One afternoon while chatting with a visitor he slipped into unconsciousness. The doctors and nurses did all they could to revive him, but the wounded soldier remained unresponsive. After four days, the matron, or chief nurse, anticipating the worst, penned a letter to Bill's parents. "We are sorry," it began, "but we did everything we could do. . . ."[8]

Then, on the fifth day, Durk woke up. Wondering where he was and what had happened to him, he tried to take a sip of water, but couldn't lift the glass. He was so tired, he remembered later, that he couldn't stop yawning. After a few days more, a letter arrived and, hoping it brought news from home, he tore it open. "We are sorry," it began, "but we did everything we could do..."

By some mischance, Durk had received the letter that told of his own death. Enraged, he rang the bell for a sister. "Just what the hell is this?" he roared, precipitating what the British called "a terrible flap." The sisters were distraught that such an upsetting thing could have occurred, while Durk worried that his parents might have received the same letter; they had troubles enough. In the end, he assured the sisters that he would get well if only to calm them, and the story eventually was transformed into an anecdote, his outrage becoming connected in the telling with his subsequent improvement, as if the adrenaline unleashed helped lift him over the hump.

"From that time on I got better every day," Durk wrote to his parents much later, "although there were times I never expected to get up and you would never believe how horrible I looked." Before long, the hospital would become a sort of home. "I knew everyone in the place from the C.O. (Commanding Officer) and Area Commander to the bootblack," he recalled. As other wounded men recovered and he became the most senior patient, "all visitors, official and otherwise, were shown to me first. Before I left my doctor told me he had never seen anyone go so far and still live—they nicknamed me the 'resurrection patient,' but quite honestly at no time did I realize how ill I was and the thought of not getting well never occurred to me."[9]

By Christmastime, Durk had been moved from his private room into a ward, so he could enjoy the festivities with the other men. The bone infection and the jaundice both were nearly gone, although his leg still was in traction. As the "up patients," who could walk, enjoyed a simple banquet on tables set up in the middle of the plain, high-ceilinged room, Durk struggled to feed himself Christmas dinner on the sidelines with the other bedridden soldiers. "It was wonderful to see so many people and to have so many laughs," he wrote home. "My only curse was and still is that I can't sit up. What a great day it will be when I can roll over on my side to go to sleep!"[10]

Rob Cox's jaundice continued to improve, as well, but the bullet wound in his back festered, becoming septic and oozy, and in the third week of November he was transferred to No. 2 General Hospital, a collection of tents and Nissen huts near the Suez Canal. X-ray photographs showed no metal left in his wound, but the consensus was that some other bit of stuff—"pullovers, khaki, worsted" in army parlance—was still in there. Rob enjoyed bantering with the friendly orderly who regularly applied heat to the wound, successfully eliciting great quantities of pus. When Rob told him that the doctor intended to operate, the orderly bristled. "We'll beat him to it, sir," he asserted, and began to recount the many and various other infections his heat treatments had cured. Then one day his tone changed. "I'm afraid it's no use, sir," he lamented. "We'll never clear it up."

Cox cajoled and urged and cross-examined doctors and sisters alike in the effort to get his wound attended to quickly. He even indulged in anger that it hadn't been made right yet—only to remonstrate himself with the memory of so many others who were so much worse off. Surgery must wait, he was told, until the jaundice was gone entirely, because the anesthetic affected the liver. Possibly in desperation, he began to write a story. "It passes the time and stops you from thinking about nothing or at least you think a little differently," he told his mother. He wrote letters and read more Hemingway. "I read *A Farewell to Arms* again yesterday," he wrote home, "but although it is very good I'm afraid parts of it read too well now because when [the hero] is wounded, I kept thinking that I was reading about Bolté and it was nearly too strong."

At the end of November Cox received news from Bolté.

Dear Rob:

Your letter came a few days ago and I've read it several times with increasing enthusiasm. How right you are about things: the hospital making us old-womanish; the reminiscing about our strange, good year of education and fun that suddenly went sour for both of us when we began to lose men; and the feeling you had about my leg but couldn't say (as if you had to say it: I felt it and that was better). Well, don't tell anybody: but you can write. You can write anything you want, any time. I suspected it, from how well you talked, in Ireland and other places where we talked; but this letter proves in writing that you can write. I'm proud to know you.

I am feeling some better. The second amputation was very clean and neat, and hasn't infected. I have no temperature and everyone says I look much better. The only trouble is I feel lousy and have a lot of pain still. But I'm eating a lot and sleeping better.

I promoted myself to lieutenant because we've been commissioned more than 6 months, and I refuse to go home a 2/lt. I promote you too. . . .

I'm for South Africa around Xmas. Hope to see you before

then. Anyway after the war we'll visit each other in Vermont and Connecticut, and someday go to Ireland with our wives and see Dicky and Nancy. Anyway, we will keep in touch.

Yours Ever—

Bolts

Cox sent on the letter to his mother. "The part about writing is quite amusing—but I don't know—I never feel as if I can and anyway it is something I don't like to talk about much, and never do anymore." But he couldn't mail his letter until the paymaster brought money to buy a stamp, and in the interim, his news improved. On December 1 the surgeon went ahead and opened up his wound, installing drains for the abscess, which made Cox feel much worse for two days, until he felt much better. "Everything is healing now and I think I'll be able to get up in a day or two," he finished off his letter breezily. "I've just learnt that Cutting is down the road about half a mile with both legs broken. I'll go see him as soon as I can."

On New Year's Eve, when 1942 turned to 1943, Bolté would learn just how delicate a matter his second amputation had been. That night, talking with the assistant head of surgery on the porch, both of them a bit drunk, the doctor explained the art and instinct of determining just when the knife should fall. "Dr. Jack saved your life," he said. "He has the best sense of timing of any doctor I know. It was a race between the gangrene moving up and the wound in your thigh healing fast enough so he could operate. If he'd amputated above the knee one day sooner, the wound wouldn't have healed enough; if he'd waited one day later, the gangrene would have gone up over your knee and he couldn't have operated at all. You owe him your life." They clasped hands, Bolté later remembered, shed a quiet tear each, and had another pull from the bottle.[11]

This time when the guillotine fell, Bolté lost his knee, the empty air now beginning at the very same spot that Nobby Clark's leg had been severed that night at Kidney Ridge, clean above the knee. Chuck would hang on to Nobby's memory. In the months to come, it would prove a useful antidote to melancholy and nostalgia, the times when, despite everything, he missed the field and the fight and his men and his friends and the simple, clear imperatives of army life, and believed he should be back there.[12]

But the pain and trouble he'd endured made Bolté feel more relieved than mournful when he lost his knee, and as the stump began to heal, he took a pride that he knew to be ridiculous in the speed with which he passed the next milestone—nineteen days from amputation to crutches, only two days behind the ward record.

Now that the pain had eased, Bolté could begin to think about the road ahead. In his darkest hours, he had envisioned himself a perpetual invalid—"weaving wicker baskets" was the current shorthand for a pathetic lifetime of useless indolence. His surgeon, Dr. Jack, had reassured him that he wouldn't "be a vegetable," but no tonic could have equaled the effect of the cablegram that arrived one day from Robert Sherwood in New York. He was by then the head of the overseas branch of the Office of War Information. Guy Bolté, Chuck's father, had called him to report Chuck's wounding, and Sherwood sent word to Chuck to hurry up and get well. "We need you at the OWI," he said. Chuck had a job waiting for him in New York at the Office of War Information.

Then there was Mary. When Guy Bolté had written Chuck's sister, Linda, he asked her to tell Mary about the amputation. Linda later would describe reading her father's letter; it was, she said, "as though I had been kicked in the stomach, literally."[13] Passing along the news could not have been easy. Mary had spent most of the previous year hunting for a way to join Chuck in England. When they spoke, Linda tried to ease into it, beginning with the good news: He's coming home. Then she told Mary why.

Chuck felt it was unfair to hold Mary to their engagement under the new circumstances. Or perhaps he needed to know that she didn't mind marrying a man with only one leg. Maybe he simply didn't feel up to facing all the ramifications of pursuing their engagement when things were so changed. Whatever the reasons, he wrote her a letter offering to free her from their secret agreement to be married.

Chuck had observed the importance of morale in combating the effects of major surgical shock. When his friend Peter was brought into the ward from the desert with one hand blown off, the doctors tied up Peter's wound, put him to sleep, and predicted an early recovery. But Peter loved two things in the world: playing the piano and caressing beautiful women. When he awoke and saw the stump where his hand had been, he turned his face to the wall and would speak to no one. He died quite quickly.[14]

So Bolté counted himself lucky. He had a job waiting for him with Robert Sherwood, a man he greatly admired. He still felt a keen interest in current affairs and the world situation. Another of his visitors, the American minister in Cairo, Alexander Kirk, brought him bundles of American newspapers and magazines. "Nice to see the old bread and butter again," Chuck told his father, but what he read somewhat alarmed him. "Everyone seems to be sniping at everyone else," he wrote. "Rumors fly, Roosevelt still a big target, Washington lambastes manufacturers, manufacturers and Luce [publisher of Time and Life magazines] attack labor, and army and navy claim credit for air victories, inflation threatens, people bully the army for not opening a second front; and over all, in every publication, is Alexander de Seversky [early advocate of strategic aerial bombardment] saying 'I told you so' about airplanes. No doubt things aren't as bad as I read them—or are they?"

After a few weeks, Mary's reply arrived. "I got engaged to a man, not a leg," she wrote, almost indignantly.

"Everything is still clean and almost completely knit," Chuck wrote home exultantly. "I've practically no pain and haven't had any dope for a week, not even to sleep. All this seems miraculous, after the first six weeks. I am back to wisecracking, and all the old familiar vices that go with it. Had a cigar after dinner last night."

The cigar was a gift from one of Bolté's new American friends, a big bomber pilot everyone called "St. Louis," because that was where he came from. He had moved in with the Brits when the new American hospital in Cairo ran out of space. There was also Guy Ramsey, a forty-year-old railroad expert from Chicago with shrapnel in his legs who had come over as supply officer for a diesel locomotive outfit of the Royal Engineers. "He cheered me over some bad times," Bolté would remember, "and we had endless talks about home, families, meals we'd like to eat, football players, and jobs—all the real important things that seem to lie closer to the heart than wars, for instance."

One Saturday word got around that some American army men were staging an exhibition softball game across the street from the hospital. Bolté found St. Louis and another American called Georgia—real name, Wade Claxton—who had been shot down on a strafing mission in his P-40, rescued from enemy territory by a couple of 8th Army armored cars, and brought back to 63rd General Hospital by automobile, hospital ship, train, and ambulance. Georgia was "a quiet man with a good laugh who couldn't help bragging that his old school would be going to the Rose Bowl."

Georgia and Bolté hobbled across the street on crutches, while St. Louis pushed himself along in his wheelchair behind them. From seats on the first-base line, they shouted and cheered just as though they were home. The score was lopsided, the officiating casual in the extreme. The all-English spectators watched politely, apparently awed by the players' noisy effusiveness, although they managed to applaud two home runs. The American soldiers in the audience didn't care about the quality of play or the Britons' diffidence. They were elated to be outdoors, watching something like baseball. All they wanted was a hot dog and some soda pop.[15]

Even after his operation, it seemed to Cox that the doctors and nurses conspired to keep him in bed forever. When the surgeon stopped by one day, Cox inquired, "Sir, can I get up today?" The doctor allowed only that Cox could put on a dressing gown and sit in a chair. The young lieutenant replied that he had been in bed quite long enough; he didn't see that he'd ever get healthy lying on his back all the time. Taking the surgeon's mumbled reply to mean "all right," that afternoon Cox got up, dressed, and went off to find Cutting. When he returned, the sister was furious. Cox again made his case—he felt fine; his wound was healing. Between his arguments and the "fait accompli" which he presented, he was allowed to get up every day after that. It made a big difference.

Visiting Heyward was good. They talked over everything, including their shared bad luck. When Fanny Cox sent Rob the letter from Sir Hereward Wake to Rex Benson extolling the young Americans' success as officer candidates, their virtues as men, and their contributions to the regiment, they surely were proud, but when Heyward finished reading it, the two invalids burst out laughing. Big assets, indeed! They laughed and laughed at all they'd done for the regiment, lying in bed for weeks.

He found Heyward, Cox wrote later, "in excellent spirits, although he had a pretty tough time. Both legs broken but not badly and they are no longer in casts." His tendency to minimize bad health news was again asserting itself. Making Heyward's legs operational again would be a long, complicated, and undoubtedly painful business. Decades later, his sister Patricia would remember reaching him by telephone in the hospital and being told, "I've had eleven operations so far and I have two more to go."

Visiting Heyward soon became a mainstay of Cox's daily routine, along with eating and drinking coffee or tea. After breakfast in bed, he would go to the YWCA—an institution intended to serve the many nurses in Cairo but in fact nearly always filled with convalescing male officers—where coffee and biscuits could be had. At noon came lunch; at three, a cup of tea and some cookies. Then he went back to the YWCA for more tea. He would visit Heyward, then return to the hospital in time for supper at six, followed by a visit to the NAAFI at eight for fried eggs, baked beans, and tomatoes, returning to the ward in time to get into bed and drink Ovaltine. On days when Heyward wasn't feeling up to a visit, he would return to the YWCA for another tea instead.

News drifted back from the front. Eighth Army continued to advance.

Benghazi fell, without Rob, on November 20. Axis forces retreated to El Agheila, the high-water mark of past British advances, where the deep gorge called Wadi el Faregh, backed by salt marshes and dunes much like those of the Qattara Depression, created a natural defensive line. Rommel was reinforced with two armored divisions, the Luftwaffe reinvigorated by new Messerschmitt squadrons.[16] Everyone expected a stand. And yet in the event Rommel fell back again, to a new defensive line about 150 miles east of Tripoli, along the Wadi Zem Zem.

"Apparently the R.A.F. simply blasted what was in Agheila out so that no real battle was necessary," Rob told his family, "although there's always more to these patrols than the papers make out. The papers said that it was the biggest 'blitz' they'd ever given out here. If you had seen them the first two days of the 'Alamein show' you would know it must have been pretty terrific to be bigger than that."[17]

But not all news was good. Cox and Cutting learned of Durkee's plight—badly machine-gunned in both legs and hospitalized in Alexandria. They heard of many individual losses. The Battle of El Alamein had cost the 8th Army just over 13,500 men killed, missing, or captured,[18] including nearly half of their battalion.[19] Hardest to take was the death of Micky Heming. He had arrived at the front just in time for operation Supercharge and been killed within days while loading a six-pounder. "To say he would have been a great conductor some day is one of those banal things people say," Rob wrote home. "He would have been but it doesn't matter. He was a very rare and vivid person."

As 1942 drew to a close, those healthy enough in Cox's ward hung red Christmas balls and festooned the room with gaudy streamers made up of small Allied flags, provided by the hospital staff, and, for a bit of holiday greenery, palm branches. On Christmas Eve, nurses swept through the wards, passing out sheet music and gathering an ever-growing number of carolers, who walked from ward to ward, singing by lantern light under the velvety black Egyptian sky. The next morning, Christmas services were conducted in the wards; then Christmas dinner was served at long tables lined up and down the middle of the room. Whiskey was poured, and Heyward kept a bottle of Champagne at the ready, which Cox looked forward to sharing.

Cox received two Christmas letters, plus a parcel of honey and chocolate from home. He felt grateful for the contact from his family. He felt grateful to be alive. Now that he was healed, he realized what a near miss his wound had been. He could feel just where the bullet went in, and it was not a question of inches but of millimeters as to how far it had been from his spine. He might easily have been even worse off than Bolté—more Jake Barnes in *The Sun Also Rises* than Frederic Henry in *A Farewell to Arms*. The difference between success and failure was minute, it now seemed to Cox, with everyone walking a hairline between triumph and disaster. It was astonishing how many somehow managed to avoid both.

Chuck Bolté found that walking with crutches was trickier than he had assumed, given the lopsided way his body swung through between the two supports and the difficulty of balancing on his extant leg as he moved the crutches forward. Just after Christmas, he was practicing next to his bed when in strode Jack Brister. It was extraordinary, Chuck thought, the way people sometimes popped up out of nowhere in North Africa. He hadn't seen Jack since late September, before the battle, when he and Durk had headed south with the rest of 7th Armoured Division while Bolté and the others in the 1st had gone north.

Jack now was sunburned and desert hardened in the way they had noticed early on in battle veterans—the quiet, proud Desert Rats who had been chasing Rommel back and forth across Libya and Egypt since September 1940. Bolté supposed Jack could now count himself among them. But he still had the familiar warm grin as he thrust his big hand toward Bolté in greeting. Brister had only just heard about Bolté's casualty; their mutual friends at the front hadn't wanted to upset him.[20]

Jack said, "Now you're bound to be a genius." It struck Bolté just right.[21] Typical of Jack—no hemming and hawing and avoiding the obvious, but no depressing excess of sympathy, either. Chuck caught him up about the others, and Jack shared what he knew from the front. He had chased the Germans west as far as Adjabiya, a thousand miles from Cairo, in less than six weeks, before his battalion had withdrawn for some rest. Jack was back in Cairo for treatment of a "poisoned toe." The two friends could only laugh about that—flown hundreds of miles to the hospital for athlete's foot.

It was his second war wound, Jack reminded Chuck; the first was the punctured eardrum that had sent him into the hospital in early October. Jack then told the story of his desperate return to the front just before El Alamein, which left them in stitches. After his release from the hospital, he'd missed the regular army train back to base depot and been commanded to await orders. Having thereby been forced, he stressed, to take matters into his own hands, he hitchhiked to Cairo, bluffed his way onto the Alexandria train by insisting he was a porter, enjoyed a luxurious night in a hotel in the city, then took a taxi the sixty-five miles to transit camp and a canteen truck back to battalion. The colonel there hadn't known whether to reprimand or to welcome him, so he did both.[22]

Laughing with Jack, Bolté began to feel for the first time in a long time that everything, anything, was doable. The two friends left the hospital, flagged down a taxi, and sped through the crowded, noisome Cairo streets to the fabulous Nile island retreat of Gezira. There they basked in the sun beside the British Sporting Club pool and downed the first of what Chuck felt sure would be a great many more beers to come.[23] The Germans were in retreat, and America at long last had joined the fight. Chuck told Jack his plans. He would be sent to South Africa, where the climate was more conducive to convalescence and the army had become expert in crafting and fitting prosthetic limbs. That would take a few months, but then he would go home to take a job and be married. Jack told Chuck that he was thinking seriously about transferring to the American army. Rob, too, would be back at the front before long. The Yanks were on the move again, three of them, anyway, with Bolté, at least, headed home. Maybe not right away, maybe not as he had been, maybe not for a very long while. But still, home. America, at last.

For Bill Durkee, still on his back in the orthopedic hospital, the road home would be long and painful. In mid-January, he was hoping to be out of bed by the end of the month. His legs, so long idle, had grown extremely thin—"like canary bird's ankles," he told his parents.[24] Now, after two months, he was gaining weight rapidly. The only thing that prevented him from eating more was the fact that he still ate lying down. "My stretched-out stomach is most uncomfortable when overfilled," he wrote. But he was sleeping without the help of medication, which everyone said was a very good sign. It seemed the only lasting effect of his wounds would be a stiff right knee. He felt very grateful to the doctor for saving his legs.

But after yet another month he still lay in bed. By February 20, his right leg was no longer in traction; it simply rested in a splint, raised at the foot, and he could lift it, straight legged from the hip, which he practiced to strengthen it. Only when the knee bent was it still very painful. Best of all, he now could sit up for the first time in three months. He wrote to his father, who similarly had lost fifty pounds but also was expected to recover, "It will take more than either of us have had to knock us out."[25]

There were complications, however. His right foot wouldn't flex; he could only point it. The necessary nerve, it seemed, no longer functioned. Even the application of a twenty-volt electrical current failed to stimulate it. What was more, the sepsis in his knee had destroyed the lubrication and the proper fitting of the joint. And there were still five pieces of metal embedded in the tibia at the knee joint, the largest of them a quarter-inch in diameter.

Still, at the end of February, Durk was predicting cheerfully to his family that he would be out of bed soon. "They are making a caliper for my leg (a brace)—so I should be able to get up and learn to walk in the very near future." But after yet another month, he remained supine. Each time the doctor pronounced his bad knee fully healed, it would act up again, the metal shards irritating the surrounding tissue and causing new flare-ups. In surgery again on March 3, the doctor tried but failed to remove the largest piece of metal. If his knee didn't heal this time, Durk was told, the doctor might have to operate again. "When I finally do get up," the wounded soldier wrote home, "I swear I will sleep in an armchair rather than go back to bed."[26]

Cox was released from the hospital shortly after New Year's. As was customary, he was assigned to a convalescent home for two weeks of sick leave in Cairo. He wandered the bazaars, visited the pyramids, rode a camel, played squash, and passed time socializing—at a dance with cousin Bill Evarts of the Royal Engineers; with an old friend from home, Buddy Stillman, who was in Egypt with the American Field Service; in conversation with whoever seemed amusing in the famous Long Bar of Shepheard's Hotel, where a framed graph on the wall plotted the course of a two-day bender: up from "normal" through "ga-ga" to "blotto," plunging to "terrible," then back up slowly through "good," followed by a slight downturn back to "normal."

Meanwhile, Cutting's health took a worrisome turn for the worse. One leg swelled up, full of blood; a problem had developed with internal bleeding. His blood wouldn't clot properly. The hospital test for hemophilia proved negative, but in time Cutting confessed that clotting had long been a problem. Cox didn't know whether to be anxious or angry, and was both. "The idiot is a hemophiliac," he wrote home. Cutting had known it when they all first met up in New York, but he told no one for fear of losing the chance to join up.

Cox himself was growing desperate to get back to the front. One night at Shepheard's, when he met Buddy Stillman for drinks, an event arose that seemed to crystallize the shallowness of life in the fleshpots of Cairo. As the two Americans headed out, two New Zealand soldiers boisterous with drink were trying to enter. The military policemen at the front door insisted that enlisted men were not permitted. The Kiwis appealed to the Americans, and Buddy backed them up.

Rob felt caught between his egalitarian principles and his job as an officer. He flashed the MPs a friendly smile, clapped one of the Kiwis on the shoulder, grabbed his hand, and complimented him heartily. "Best soldiers in the desert, let me shake your hand, you and us are the only decent people out here."

"Yes, sir, thank you," the Kiwi answered, "but we beat Rommel, and they won't let us in there to drink. They throw us out."

"Sure," Cox replied, "but it's filled with stuffy fools and you don't want to go there anyway. Come on." Then he whisked them swiftly out onto the sidewalk and into a taxicab.

"I think the poor Kiwi was so surprised by my unorthodox behavior that he couldn't stop to collect his wits," he explained later in a letter home. "Actually, I'm quite proud of the little episode, but the reason I tell it to you is because if you think about it, the whole difficulty of being a British officer is there. I too would like to take the Kiwis into Shepheard's and drink with them. I would like everyone to mix with everyone, but they can't, and sometimes you feel as if you were a little of each nation, but not all of either and were being crushed between the upper and lower millstones. This is not true but you feel that way at times. That's the bad side of it, but the good side is very, very good and miles away from Shepheard's, as are the good people."[27]

Jack Brister returned to his men on February 2. The 1st Battalion had retired from Adjabiya to Tmimi, on the eastern edge of the Cyrenaica peninsula, to rest, refit, and train with the 7th Motor Brigade, 1st Armoured Division. To his surprise, there, too, was his journal. "I never expected to see this book again when I left it behind me," he wrote. "But here it is and I find myself still amazed and even a bit ashamed at even the most recent entries."

As the 1st Armoured Division awaited new orders, Jack grew ever more restless and disconsolate. His journal, characteristically, combines notes on his high-calorie literary diet with pitiless self-criticism. By the end, a new tone would be struck—wistfulness, regret, even exhaustion, and a wan hope.

"Michael Fyfe came over from brigade about tea-time," he wrote on February 13, two days before his twenty-third birthday. "Brought *Childhood Boyhood and Youth,* Tolstoi, which has a most excellent preface. Gave him *Orlando* in return. A most charming woman Virginia Woolf.

"I hate myself for desiring to write yet lacking energy enough to decide what, how, etc. enough to excite the latent energy which comes to life seemingly from nowhere. Sometimes I think I should stop kidding myself. But what else would I enjoy doing? The right sort of people are so important for composition. One can hardly be a recluse and still do one's job."

Letters from Turner poured in. She reminisced about their three weeks together during the summer of 1940—three weeks in time, "much longer the way we filled them," Jack remembered.

"Then came a letter saying she had almost married one of the 'noble men' off to the wars, in a frenzy of patriotism. She'd reached the quiescent stage still rather hesitantly asking me to come home that way. She's reading Proust which I think should help her maintain a more even keel. We speak in an effort at honesty, and a shrewd mood of noncommittal that we cannot be sure 'til after the war.

"She's so far from me now I remember without pain all we did and realize it shall never come again—yet there's always 'perhaps.'

"I'm almost certain it would be far better to have committed oneself—I go out now in so many directions. Not unscathed, I preserve freedom which by itself is nothing, unborn, waiting, and how impatient I am with waiting."

CHAPTER 11

Spring

Medenine, Tunisia, to Argoub el Megas, Tunisia
March 15–April 28, 1943

> In the words of the old hymn, you have "nightly pitched
> your moving tents a day's march nearer home."
>
> —Winston Churchill, address to the army at Tripoli,
> February 3, 1943

B y mid-March Cox and Brister were back in the field, their days
circumscribed by the bright blue dome of open sky, their peace by
the soft boom and crump of distant shelling. After the long pursuit from El Alamein, Montgomery's 8th Army had crossed the Tunisian
frontier on February 2,[1] captured the small agricultural market town of
Ben Gardane, and sprawled northward over the coastal plain, to their left
the jagged rampart of the Matmata Hills, to their right, as always, the sea,
and the Libyan border now some forty miles behind them.

The North African campaign had turned a corner, literally and figura-
tively. Having driven the enemy some fifteen hundred miles westward, the
hunt wheeled north, its sights reset onto the port city of Tunis some five
hundred miles ahead. Not only was Tunis, capital of the French protector-
ate, the symbolic seat of power, it also was, like Bizerte, Hammamet, and

other ports, an obvious exit point for Axis forces abandoning North Africa. Most important, though, after the Casablanca Conference in January, Tunis would be a vital jumping-off point for the planned Allied invasion of Europe by way of Sicily and Italy, which was scheduled to commence in July.

The land had changed dramatically. Instead of gentle rises and shallow depressions in a broad, flat waste, here mountains and hills defined the battlefields. And here the troops enjoyed the luxury, and the inconveniences, of water. In the north, winter rains had transformed the clayish soil into a sucking paste that made progress impossible. Now, as the rains abated, wildflowers painted the hillsides. Irrigated fields shimmered with spring wheat and young barley.

And the 8th Army no longer fought alone. More than one hundred thousand American soldiers who invaded Algeria and Morocco in early November had battled east at great cost and now maintained the southern end of a long, rough line of Allied forces that extended to Tunisia's northern coast at Tabarka, near the Algerian border. The French in Africa, after initial resistance, had joined sides with the Allies, and French units occupied south-central Tunisia around the mountains of the Grande Dorsale. To their north fresh British and commonwealth troops filled Lieutenant General Kenneth Anderson's new 1st Army.[2] The British sector began at El Aroussa on the southern slopes of the Monts de Teboursouk, the range that defined the northern edge of the Medjerda Valley, a broad, tank-friendly plain that formed the entranceway to Tunis from the west.

But the enemy, too, had reinforced positions. Although the Allies had succeeded in preserving the secrecy of the Torch landings, the Germans, once aroused, wasted no time in responding. Within days German and Italian troops were pouring into Tunisia—a relatively straightforward proposition from bases just eighty miles across the Sicilian Channel. All but surrounded, with their backs to the sea, they seemed doomed to eventual expulsion. Yet since November, as the Allies labored east through the Atlas Mountains of Morocco and Algeria and west across the desert wastes of Libya, Axis weapons, ammunition, and supplies had been landing at Tunisian ports and airfields.

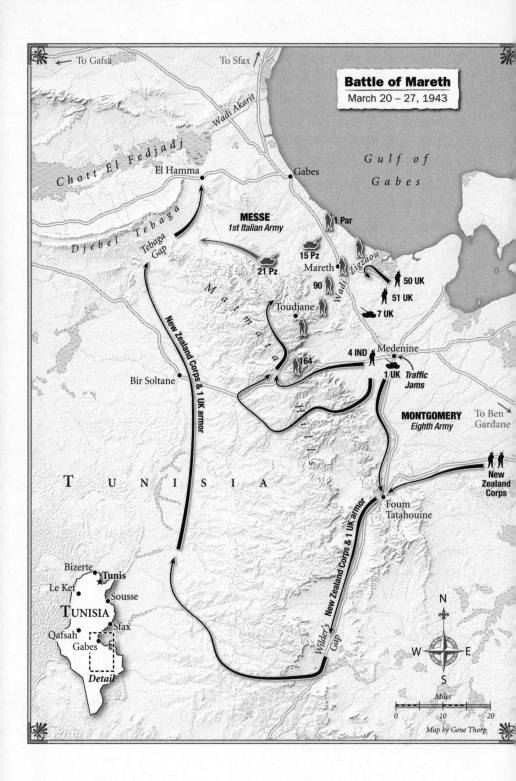

Battle of Mareth
March 20 – 27, 1943

To Gafsa

To Sfax

Wadi Akarit

Chott El Fedjadj

*Gulf of
Gabes*

El Hamma

Gabes

Djebel Tebaga

*Tebaga
Gap*

MESSE
1st Italian Army

1 Par

15 Pz

Mareth

21 Pz

90

Wadi Zigzaou

50 UK

51 UK

7 UK

Toudjane

New Zealand Corps & 1 UK armor

Matmata

164

4 IND

Medenine

1 UK *Traffic
Jams*

Bir Soltane

Hills

MONTGOMERY
Eighth Army

To Ben
Gardane

T U N I S I A

New
Zealand
Corps

Foum
Tatahouine

Wilder's Gap

New Zealand Corps & 1 UK armor

Bizerte

Tunis

Le Kef

Sousse

TUNISIA

Sfax

Qafsah

Gabes

Detail

N

W   E

S

Miles

0   10   20

Map by Gene Thorp

And having arrived first, the roughly two hundred thousand troops of Rommel's and von Arnim's combined armies[3] were able to occupy the high ground, siting guns and establishing observation posts so as to control the approaches to their final North African redoubt. As the Allies struggled to set the stage for the long-awaited invasion of Europe, Axis forces dug in to delay them. Tying up the Allies through the summer in Tunisia would postpone the landing in Europe for another year and buy the Germans time to shore up their adventure in the Soviet Union, which that winter was faltering badly.[4]

They applied a full range of lethal ingenuity to preparing the way. Snipers infested the Tunisian hillsides: Every olive grove might conceal a gun; booby traps and mines larded valley floors and mountain passes—anyplace that a carrier, a jeep, a truck, or a tank might drive. To the Desert Rats in Montgomery's army, it soon became apparent that their accustomed style of warfare, maneuvering freely in diffuse formations across wide-open spaces, was now defunct. Even the tanks, ill suited to Tunisia's soggy valleys and narrow gaps, had lost much of their potency.

Moving into the line from the south, 8th Army nevertheless prepared for one more old-style frontal assault at Mareth, where the Germans recently had reinforced a neglected line of defenses that stretched for twenty-two miles between mountains and sea. Taking advantage of the natural impediment of a seasonal watercourse called Wadi Zigzaou, the position originally had been fortified by the French to keep their Italian neighbors at bay. Now the aging string of blockhouses had been further reinforced and diabolically embellished to create a deadly gauntlet of yawning tank traps, concrete dragon's teeth, dense minefields, and barbed-wire snares[5] backed up by well-dug-in guns and tanks.

On March 15 Jack Brister and his comrades of 1st Battalion KRRC awoke in a basin of land full of palm trees and fig trees and wildflowers; yellow mustard, red poppies, yellow and white daisies, blue cornflowers, and purple iris enlivened the hillsides.[6] They had moved the night before into

244 ★ INTO DUST AND FIRE

the reserve position of 7th Motor Brigade, 1st Armoured Division, along the coastal road connecting Ben Gardane to Mareth—their mission to cover the gaps between the three large hills that formed the basin.[7]

In another contrast to the desert environment, this location had been lived in and cultivated, although it now was all but deserted. Toby Wake set up camp around a small Arab village of flat-roofed stone houses and cisterns and narrow stone streets, which boasted one remaining inhabitant, soon dubbed Town Major. The elderly brown-skinned man revealed an amazing facility for aircraft identification. He could name an approaching plane, friendly or hostile, by the sound of its engine long before it was visible. The British officers marshaled every argument they could think of, and communicate, to persuade the old Arab to leave, but even the threat of imminent battle could not move him. He refused to budge.

Atop the largest of the three hills stood a small white stone house, now deserted. To the Scots Guards, who had preceded 1st KRRC in the position, it was Edinburgh Castle. The officers of the 60th, so many of them Eton men, promptly rechristened it Windsor Castle, which lent the spot a homey air. Here, after a half-hour climb, they spent much of each day poring over maps, plotting in their location, studying the Mareth positions across the plain to their west, and identifying the surrounding peaks—a novel process, one 60th officer mused, "after some two years of never having seen a hill."[8]

From this hilltop vantage point, they also could see the battlefield near the important crossroads of Medenine, about fifteen miles down the coast from Mareth, where nine days earlier three panzer divisions had been decisively stomped by 8th Army. Some of the men went to investigate.

There was little to see now but cindery wreckage. Later, military analysts and historians would reconstruct what happened during Axis operation Capri, the last of Field Marshal Rommel's attempts to disrupt and delay Montgomery's advance before returning, ill and discouraged, to Germany. But they would remain baffled by Rommel's conduct of the battle. "There is no satisfactory explanation of why such a master in the handling of tanks as Rommel could have attacked in this way," Alan

Moorehead wrote in the last volume of his North African trilogy. "He deliberately broke his own strict rule—which we had learned from him at such cost—never attack fixed positions with tanks."[9]

When the panzers advanced at dawn on March 6, the 8th Army was ready. Having received advance warning through intelligence decrypts, Monty had dispatched three hundred tanks, 817 artillery and antitank guns, and three now well-seasoned divisions to the twenty-five-mile front near the crossroads of Medenine, where they laid an elaborate and various trap. Gunners and tankers dug in and ranged their sights. A seemingly primitive ploy—scattering bully beef tins to simulate a minefield—channeled attacking panzers into the 8th Army's field of fire. A dummy gun line enticed the German panzer chiefs forward. As the British gunners leaped from their trenches, seeming to abandon their weapons, the German tanks moved irresistibly onward—into the devastating fire of the actual gun line, well protected, reinforced with new seventeen-pounder antitank guns, and full of expectancy. Roughly fifty German tanks were lost that day—nearly one-third of the armor. British tanks were scarcely used, none destroyed. Within four hours, the armored attack had stalled. An infantry assault that afternoon fared no better. By evening the enemy had pulled back to harbor behind the Mareth defenses near the coast.

That night, patrols from the Scots Guards, an infantry unit that had borne much of the brunt of the Medenine attack, crept through the field of carnage. Eighth Army had suffered one hundred and thirty casualties to the Axis's six hundred and thirty-five. The Scotsmen wanted to make certain that the crippled panzers never would be used again. They blew them to smithereens.

It gave the soldiers of 1st Battalion KRRC a comforting feeling. "From what we heard, it did appear that 10th Panzer Division, who had made the attack, had been curiously inept," one officer wrote. What was more, the warming glow of superiority now extended beyond their longtime enemies to encompass their new American allies as well; in mid-February the green American troops had suffered disheartening setbacks at Sidi

Bou Zid, Gafsa, and Kasserine Pass, to the northwest. "Perhaps," wrote Major John Hogg, second in command of 1st Battalion KRRC, pondering the German defeat, "they had been unduly inflated by previous successes against our allies."[10] Alan Moorehead would count the Battle of Medenine the turning point of the Tunisian campaign. "The Germans lost the offensive on that day, and they never again recovered it."[11]

It seemed for the moment just the sort of life a soldier wanted.[12] Operational commitments were few. Patrolling by night and day kept things interesting and gave the officers a good way to break in new subalterns. "By dint of saying 'Ssh! Ssh! The Germans are just over the hill,'" Hogg remembered, "we even managed to instill a little liveliness into our early morning stand-to—all most necessary to our future well-being."[13]

But it was nevertheless plain that the day of combat was approaching, and the officers looked carefully at the country ahead that everyone expected would be their next battleground. "Peaceful unrest" was the way Jack Brister, always an enthusiast of paradox, described it—this apparently pacific atmosphere that presaged an explosion. Even the few enemy planes that flew over continued on to target the "soft-skin" vehicles and the command area to the rear.[14]

On March 17, a steady wind blew in a cloud of fine sand that put an end to patrolling, and Brister, in a contemplative mood, settled down to write a letter to Bolté, who was convalescing with his new tin leg among the legion of amputees at Baragwanath Hospital in Johannesburg. Jack was a gunner now, commanding a platoon of six-pounders. "Battle Number Two is gradually shuffling and shaking itself into a fit position to shiver the night and cast about the men and materials of war in climax," he told his friend. "And Chuck, I'll be there. If possible I'll get the job of ringing the great long chimes. Chimes always go well with a climax. Shall we call it Monty's orgasm?"

Recent letters from Ambler had brought news about an old Brister family friend named Hamilton, a middle-aged engineer who had enlisted in the American army and shipped out for North Africa. It pleased and inspired Brister to think that they might encounter each other, perhaps in Tunis after the victory was won. But even more than this, he was moved by the selflessness that Mr. Hamilton's commitment implied. "He left a wife and two grown daughters to go. He left everything he'd made, and built, and loved for the past twenty-four years," Jack wrote. It filled him with something that could only be called patriotism, before morphing into a less generalized kind of love. "The heroes don't die in a democracy even as crazy as ours," Jack told Bolté. "I am proud. So proud of everyone I feel responsible for and responsible to: you, Durk, Bob, Heyward, Mr. Hamilton, my father, etc. It's a hell of a list—once borne to understanding the golden fetters are fitted for ever. Hail, Ahab, you fetter of gold, you."

For Rob Cox, the return to the front in Libya at the end of January had been another kind of ecstasy. It felt wonderful to be out of the hospital, out of Cairo bars, out-of-doors. With his khaki shirtsleeves rolled up, the warm sun on his forearms felt wonderful, and the cold nights were fine for sleeping. After months of feeling useless, disappointed, and, on the worst days, disappointing, he felt renewed by the responsibility and the good fellowship of his men. The English had a word for it that Americans lacked. These men were his *mates*, and their *mateyness* was a balm.

It had been a bit of a letdown not to rejoin his old platoon. This new one already had lost two commanding officers in the three months since El Alamein. Dick Wood, a son of Lord Halifax, the British ambassador to the United States, had lost both legs after a bomb, strange as it sounds, literally fell in his lap. That it failed to detonate saved his life, but the weight crushed his legs. His successor, Dennis Grier, had lasted just eighteen days before he was killed in the advance on Tripoli. When Cox arrived, a lieutenant who knew nothing about the guns had been commanding for two days, and he remained as second in command. The situation was awkward; Cox disliked it intensely and felt sure his subordinate did, too. But he took an instant liking to the marvelous platoon sergeant, Wilding, and to his new batman, a fine redheaded Irishman,[15] and proceeded to take command regardless.

Cox and the 2nd Battalion moved now ahead of Brister and the 1st, who still were resting and refitting at Tmimi. They entered a new country of stimulating freshness and variety after the monotony of the Egyptian and Libyan deserts, at a pace that allowed time for exploring. One bright afternoon Cox followed a watercourse up through beehive-shaped hills of sand and marble and onto a plateau where about a hundred sheep grazed on patches of grass and the ground ahead sloped down to a valley sparsely dotted with palm trees and native huts. A couple of crashed planes lodged in the sides of the beehive hills, and when Cox heard voices, he picked up his field glasses. Two Senussi, the Libyan natives, walked over the hills about two miles away toward the road he had come from. They carried *eggas* (eggs) to trade for *chai* (tea) with the westward-moving army.[16]

Two days later, Cox and his platoon entered Tunisia. Among the men, this welcome progress inflamed rumor and speculation about the ever-improving proximity of home. In one popular but improbable claim, the 7th Armoured Division, so long in action, would never be sent onto another battleground without a return to England first. One day Sergeant Wilding, grown tired of the "monopolous" quality of their days in transit, picked up a map of Europe and North Africa and described his particular vision of the future after the Boche were driven out of Bizerte. "The old 2nd 60th, the old corps, the desert rats, the old jerboas" would continue to move forward along the North African coast, then into Spain. There they would enjoy a delightful internment with "all them senoritas" until one day Generalissimo Franco himself would come along, and learning who they were—"the old corps," the world-famous old jerboas of the desert army—he would pop them all onto a plane and send them home to England. Meanwhile, the First Army, the Americans, and the rest would carry on a "most colossal offensive" in Europe.[17]

Cox relished the sergeant's whimsy, and it amused him to consider the complications entailed by his own thoughts of home. The men and even the officers spoke so often and so warmly of going home to England that he often thought that way, too. But of course for him, like his four American comrades, England would be only step one. In a sense, he thought, he was lucky. He had twice the pleasure to look forward to. After the joy of seeing the green hillsides of England again—somehow the long-absent bright green of an English meadow had become synonymous in his mind with home—he would be able to savor the anticipation of yet another, American homecoming.

But that was all, he had to recognize, just wishful thinking. He sympathized with his men, especially the married men and the many who had become engaged before leaving; too many had had to be taken to see the legal officer after receiving cheerful letters from their wives saying that they were now quite happy with someone else. He himself couldn't take the speculation seriously. He wanted to go home when the war was over.

All in all, it was indeed a restless time. Nevertheless, Cox savored his encounters with a foreign world and the whole, competent feeling that he always got from living outdoors or from taking a long walk. When the platoon rested near a village, he enjoyed the peculiar, halting exchanges with the natives. One week, a hospitable old man named Ali brought them mint tea each morning, pouring it from a small blue teapot into a single tiny glass, each man sipping in turn. On the afternoon that Ali turned up with a meal, Cox couldn't help feeling that he set a fine example of good manners and open-mindedness for his English fellows, who could be oblivious to the niceties when foreigners were involved, by downing the entire dishful of a really disgusting, greasy, peppery grain stew. No one else would touch it.

When children were involved, making friends was even easier. Most spoke some French, and one boy named Bilgassam—they all were boys—called him "Monsieur Ro*bear*" in a piping voice as he boosted the boy onto the seat of a gun or let him try his hand at steering the jeep. "Never say soldiers are hard-hearted," he wrote home on March 5. "We are in an oasis and there are a lot of little children around. What they haven't been given isn't worth giving and every morning and evening now there is one aged four and one aged seven who come down, salute, shake hands, and receive crackers from us."[18]

But it was his men and their guns that mattered most. They had managed to salvage a number of German weapons—spandaus and lugers, especially, were prizes—and on lazy afternoons they liked to try them out, but the platoon's four big six-pounders and the trucks that pulled them required constant and consistent attention to keep them clean and well-oiled and working smoothly despite the continual grit in the air and the spewing sand, and to keep the teams of gunners, five men to a weapon, in practice. Cox longed to apply their skills to some Germans; his experience to date had been frustrating. But in the meantime he led the men in search of practice targets, which could be challenging to locate in the desert wastes.

One cloudless day when they went out with the guns to practice, they could find only a single palm tree. Silhouetted against the sharp blue sky at about six hundred yards, it made a nearly irresistible target. Yet it also illustrated perfectly clearly the rarity of such living, growing organisms, and Cox well knew how the shade of a single tree could transform a spot of blazing sand into a small oasis. "Trees are rare and precious," he explained later, writing home. "I'd no intention to destroy the palm tree. I only thought I'd slightly bruise the palm tree. I cannot lie. I am afraid my men shot down the palm tree with antitank guns."

Real action as they made their halting way forward was at best sporadic and at worst deadly to no real effect. The biggest problem was land mines, which the retreating enemy had left behind in quantity. The battalion's second in command, Pat Sykes, ran over an antitank mine and had to have his foot amputated. Two other officers, Tim James and Tom Miller, were killed outright.

Meanwhile, speculation and foreboding increased. The men got up earlier, breaking leaguer in the dark at five thirty. After a wash and a shave and a second cup of morning brew, Cox would drive to headquarters and try to learn some news. The colonel knew the plan—everyone agreed on that much—but he wasn't passing along any details. So rumor and gossip filled the void, and after dark each night the soldiers watched the bright moon rise a sliver bigger and recalled the huge, brilliant disk that rose over El Alamein on the night of battle and wondered what the March full moon would bring and whether it might possibly be their last full moon in Africa. Cox waxed poetic to pass the time in his letters home. "Many the moons—the harvest moon, the hunter's, and the moon that shines on the first nights of summer when a man learns that warm eyes shine in moonlight." He remembered Kit and wondered for a while about that. "Is it the eyes that shine, or is it moonlight in them, and the eyes were empty mirrors that reflect the moon?" But he soon came back down to earth. Really, he decided, the situation reminded him most of a waterfall in a Vermont river where he liked to swim, and the first time that he had stood above it, "wanting to jump and not wanting to."[19]

By then, war drums were beating loudly, and General Montgomery, who held a strong belief in the importance of meeting his soldiers face-to-face to rally them for battle, planned a visit to 1st Battalion. He was particularly interested in meeting the regiment's American officers.

Thus Cox arrived at the 1st Battalion position near Medenine uncharacteristically attired in his battle dress, ankles neatly gaitered, web belt and braces scrubbed bright. He was surely curious about the general. Although Monty was known to have inspired strong, widespread loyalty, the regiment had found it hard to transfer their long-standing allegiance from Strafer Gott.

On a well-trodden patch of open ground surrounded by gentle hills and overlooked by a single palm, Cox and Brister found places side by side in a semicircle of neatly attired lieutenants, and then there he was, big black tanker's beret distinguishing him instantly from the battalion and company commanders around him—compact, wiry, slightly stooped yet alert, his face, with its slim mustache, long nosed and pointy in a way that inspired frequent comparison to animals—vulpine, ferrety, foxlike—interviewing with apparently genuine interest the men whose lives he was about to fling onto the killing ground. Brister, no doubt to Cox's affectionate amusement, seized the opportunity to learn all he could and engaged the general in a conversation of notable length—the regimental history characterized it as "splendid"[20]—while a photographer recorded the encounter between the American British officers and their British commanding general.

That night, 1st Battalion took over a position in the line proper from a British battalion of the Indian division, whose earnest preparations for night patrol—from face blackening to the ritual dispensing of rum—amused the old jerboas, who were accustomed to a more casual, and ascetic, approach. The next morning, as German gunners responded swiftly to the riflemen's impromptu excursions to investigate their new territory, they began to consider whether the Indian infantrymen might not have been onto something.

On the next day, the twentieth, Brister wangled the job of driving Humphrey Woods from 1st over to 2nd Battalion, positioned some twenty miles to the southwest in the hills, where Major Woods was to take over as second in command. When they arrived, a few inquiries soon led Brister to Cox, and the reunion was again splendid. What did they discuss on the day of battle? They often compared notes about their compatriots: From what they had heard, Heyward was at long last on crutches and Durk mending, more slowly but cheerfully. They always liked to talk about books. Cox had recently reread *Seven Pillars of Wisdom,* finding it less thrilling but more interesting than the first time around, and had run through *The Red Badge of Courage,* which, under the circumstances, held little interest for him, although he knew it to be good.[21] They might have enjoyed speculating about the name of Bolté's hospital in Johannesburg—*Baragwanath*; what could it mean? They must surely have discussed the latest war news—from the improving situation on the Soviet front to the battle that lay just ahead of them.

That day, the plan for the Battle of Mareth was at last laid out. The main blow, code-named Pugilist Gallop,[22] would be struck that night at the northeastern end of the Mareth line near the sea. A barrage in the style of El Alamein would cover the advance of infantry and Valentine tanks of the 50th Division across Wadi Zigzaou and through the bristling fortifications beyond. Brister and the rest of 1st Armoured Division would remain in reserve, ready to burst through the resulting hole in the Axis line. Meanwhile, the New Zealand Corps, recently created by Monty from Freyberg's New Zealand Division, 8th Armoured Brigade, and a recently arrived contingent of Free French,[23] were making their way west and north in a wide outflanking maneuver through the Matmata Hills. Second Battalion KRRC, along with the Rifle Brigade, had been dispatched a few days earlier into the hills at the western end of the Mareth line to probe for weak spots and exert "all possible pressure" on the enemy's right flank in order to confuse them about British plans and prevent them from concentrating at the point of attack.[24] The work had proved, as Major Woods put it, "altogether a new kind of fighting."[25]

Monty's message to his army on March 20 was typically clear, direct, and aggressive. He invoked the personal demon of Rommel (although the German field marshal had already returned to Germany), outlined a vision of the upcoming battle as the first step toward total victory in Africa, and cast that victory—if each man did his duty and pulled his full weight—as inevitable. "The Eighth Army NEVER WITHDRAWS," he asserted. "FORWARD TO TUNIS! DRIVE THE ENEMY INTO THE SEA!"[26]

Moving forward four days later from positions on the eastern edge of the Matmata Hills, Cox and his men got a full sampling of the complexities entailed by the new kind of close mountain warfare that was becoming their standard fare. Launched into the mountains with the task of seizing a series of razor-backed ridges, the battalion moved forward in a leapfrogging pattern whereby one company would advance and occupy a position through which the others could then move ahead to the next. It was a logical, but not a foolproof approach. On the first night the advance company encountered no enemy opposition as it occupied the first objective, only to discover at sunup that they had settled down in full view of the enemy. The first rule of mountain warfare—"gaining the second-highest peak is of little value"—was proven to be all too true.[27] A "very uncomfortable"[28] day of taking heavy mortar fire ensued. In the hilly Tunisian terrain the mortar, with its highly arced trajectory, was coming into its own.

As the rest of the battalion progressed past this ridgetop toward the next objective, a variety of hazards confronted them. Besides the ever-present risk of arousing enemy fire, they seemed to be swimming through a sea of land mines. The variety and ingenuity of Axis devices had increased with time, and here they encountered the fiendish German S-mine, loaded with ball bearings, which sprang up to chest height before exploding.[29] More than likely, as if that weren't enough, the explosion then would attract a hail of enemy gunfire.

On the second night, a team of sappers led the way, some sweeping mine detectors before them—a slow and tedious process at best—and others marking the route with tape for the trucks, machine guns, and artillery OPs, or observation posts, that followed. Often, they had also to improvise a passable track, as the way led over the banks of sunken wadis or through axle-cracking hummocks of rock and sand.

When the advance had arrived some five hundred yards from their objective, reconnaissance parties crept forward to investigate the ridge. Finding it "clear of enemy,"[30] two platoons occupied the high point. Here, observation lines were everything. The position suffered from a blind spot; to look down one edge was to come into full view of an enemy strongpoint one ridge beyond. And so it was here that the enemy made a stealthy counterattack, crawling up to within sixty yards of the British defenders. Suddenly, hand grenades and sniper fire tore the air and roiled the ridgetop. Ducking behind rocks, the riflemen fired at anything that appeared on the skyline and lobbed grenades in a frenzy of mortal peril, eventually driving off the enemy. But the afternoon brought shelling from German 75mm guns. The British OP was shelled out and two signalmen were wounded. Continuous sniping kept the enemy at bay, but retribution followed. Under fire, the enemy would send up red Very lights, bringing down a heavy barrage on the riflemen.

That night, by moonlight, replenishment parties arrived and the wounded were carried back—an impossibility under the day's heavy shelling and machine gun fire. Machine gun and mortar platoons managed to capture the hill from which the enemy had been directing fire, laying themselves open in turn to a morning of continual mortar fire and exchanges of hand grenades. But that afternoon, March 27, soldiers on the high points noticed the first clear signs of an enemy withdrawal. Several German gun tractors and three-tonners were sighted moving west and south. At first light the next morning, the riflemen found they could walk about in the open without drawing fire. When they mortared a ridge shoulder, thirty Italians appeared, each waving a white flag. Another hillside produced a group of three, one of whom, having been reassured that he would not be shot at, went back and brought out fifty more. By day's end eight officers and 143 other ranks had surrendered, and a sizable cache of vehicles and weapons had been seized.

German and Italian units began to withdraw from the Mareth line on the night of March 26–27, but not because Monty's plan had succeeded. The frontal attack on the north end of the line began on March 20 with a thunderous three-hundred-gun barrage, the infantry crossed the rain-swollen Wadi Zigzaou and gained a shallow bridgehead, and forty-two Valentines managed to trundle across the wadi on improvised causeways. But it was not nearly enough. "Of such battles are myths made and empires lost," wrote military historian Rick Atkinson, who characterizes Mareth as "a valorous attack of regrettable ineptitude."[31] Bad weather robbed the attackers of needed air support, antitank guns and other vehicles were unable to follow the tanks across the flooding Zigzaou, and when 15th Panzer Division counterattacked on the afternoon of March 22, the watercourse "became an abattoir, with bodies beached on the mud or floating heavily in the stream."[32] Monty's army had disclosed its intention and point of attack without capturing any significant ground.[33] In the meantime, the New Zealanders had been moving around south as unobtrusively as possible, directed on El Hamma, an oasis town to the north and west that guarded the narrow passage between the coastal city of Gabes to the east and the Tebaga mountains to the west.

On March 23, Cox managed to drive east out of the hills and check on Brister where he awaited orders in reserve with 1st Armoured Division. Cox found him, happily, in very good health and good spirits, but the visit was short. The long-awaited movement order arrived, and it was not what the soldiers expected. The battle of Mareth, like El Alamein, would take longer than anticipated and be redeemed by a change of plan. The 1st Armoured Division was to reinforce the New Zealanders' long left hook, which now would carry the main force of attack. Brister had to get busy and pack up. Had he known that he would never see Cox again, would he have lingered?

That afternoon, Brister's platoon hitched the six-pounders to their trucks and handed over their position to the Gurkhas of 4th Indian Division. But no sooner was the transfer complete than the Gurkhas' orders were countermanded; they, too, were told to move on, down the same road as 1st Armoured Division. The resulting confusion was epic.

"The German bombers were a bit active that night and we had visions of a most unpleasant night ahead," wrote one KRRC officer. "However, it developed into a boring night instead."[34] First Armoured Division led off at nine thirty, and an initial leap forward—"a five-mile run at terrific speed"—cheered them.[35] Then progress stopped for four hours. It was the start of a bungled and frustrating flog, fruit of "a first-class staff bog-up"—two different corps moving down the same road at the same time, apparently having failed to consult each other. The Medenine crossroads was a sea of traffic, as the 4th Indian Division headed westward to outflank the Mareth line through the hills. By daybreak Brister and his men had covered all of eleven more miles. "Browned off" put their feelings politely.[36]

The blockage continued until about midday on Wednesday the twenty-fourth, when they lunged forward again "like a bat out of hell." That afternoon at about two thirty they left the road to travel cross-country, and by teatime they had arrived at their dispersal area, only twelve hours behind schedule. They were told to eat and "get cracking," and so the flog went on. Through the hills, the going grew mucky, and frequent bottlenecks and wadis slowed them further. That night they covered twenty-two miles total and became even more browned off. Just after first light they reached a "super bottleneck," where they sat for more than six hours, until pulling out at two thirty. By now they had to cope with "really bloody going"—grass and hillocks with soft sand in between—until at about five o'clock they struck the east–west road from Medenine, still clogged solid to the east of them. They had flogged some 150 miles to cover about thirty as the crow flies. On March 26, after a night's welcome rest, they pressed on for about five more hours and at last achieved their final halting place.

It was a terrible day. The sand of a full-blown *khamseen* (or *quibli*, as sandstorms were called in Tunisia) bit the men's skin, burned their eyes, and reduced visibility to less than ten yards. Here and there, wreckage hulked in the gloom, suggesting that the New Zealanders, who had gone before and marked the track, had done so at a cost.

So it was without much enthusiasm that the men of 1st Battalion KRRC learned upon arrival that they would see action that evening. The New Zealanders had breached one minefield, but the enemy held a line at Tebaga Gap, an opening between the Matmata Hills and the Djebel Tebaga, which ran westward about fifteen miles southwest of the important crossroads oasis El Hamma. "The idea was that the New Zealanders, with 8th Armoured Brigade attached to them, should make a hole in the Huns' present line just before last light, and that 1st Armoured Division should then pop smartly through the hole in the dark and make a bee line for El Hamma."[37]

Thus Major John Hogg cheerily summarized General Montgomery's remedy for the failed assault at the Mareth line. In a talismanic reference to the successful second phase of the Battle of El Alamein, the new operation was code-named Supercharge II. "The blitz attack went in twenty minutes after the last vehicle of 1st Armoured Division had arrived," the general later bragged.[38] By then some forty thousand soldiers and 250 tanks had successfully assembled, and Monty, taking a page from Rommel's book, sent them forward as the sun set behind them, temporarily blinding the enemy. It was a blitz as defined and demonstrated for more than three years by the enemy, comprising an overwhelming mobile force concentrated on a single point of attack, capitalizing on the power of surprise, and integrating land and air forces to devastating effect.

At about three p.m. of that very long day, Brister and his men began to form up. They moved forward through the teeming air—dust kicked up by the vehicles joining dust from the sandstorm—and swung into place behind 2nd Armoured Brigade to pass through the breached minefield. Then again they waited, but this time with senses abuzz from apprehension and expectancy and, possibly, Benzedrine, which the 8th Army dispensed to counter drowsiness.[39] At three thirty the first wave of low-flying British and American Hurricanes, Kittyhawks, and Bostons broke over Axis targets. At four o'clock the Royal Artillery launched a thunderous creeping barrage, and fifteen minutes later the first tanks rolled forward. Past abandoned slit trenches and gun sangars, Brister and his men drove steadily ahead until just after dark, when they hit the road to El Hamma, which was to be their axis of advance. Halted, as prescribed, to await the moonrise, they partook of some welcome refreshment. From the padre's truck emerged that rare elixir the soldiers called "B Echelon," or whiskey. It cleared and warmed their dusty throats wonderfully. The padre had been ordered to defend it with his life.

From the Kiwis passing to and fro along their track, they learned that the battle was proceeding satisfactorily. The Axis line had been penetrated. Yet they were hardly popping smartly through the hole. The air grew colder. Midnight came and went. The moon rose. Nobody could find out what was happening up ahead, and rumors spread of fifty tanks from 21st Panzer Division lurking hull-down somewhere, which gave way, as the moon rose higher, to horrific visions of being caught in the road "bonnet to tailboard"[40] as the Germans returned to their guns at first light.

After about three hours, however, the men began to sense movement and in no time they were driving hell for leather, five tidy lines of traffic centered on the road, compressing into a single line to circumvent the obstacles posed by frequent wadis, then fanning out into position again at high speed, the evidence of strife everywhere around them—trucks in flames, prisoners moving to the rear unescorted—and "the rumble and clatter of heavy machinery on the move"[41] carrying them forward in the dark.

Progress stopped five miles short of El Hamma, though the riflemen would not know just where they were until days later. At first light on the twenty-seventh, they were jockeying to form a defensive perimeter amid masses of tanks, armored cars, trucks, and carriers. "Had they been sheep, they would have been bleating in their most lost fashion," Major Hogg remembered. "For half an hour chaos reigned supreme." But by full daylight, they had sorted themselves out, and the day passed quietly save for a few incoming shells, the men listening to the sounds of a tank battle farther south with 21st Panzer Division, which had moved west to meet the new threat at Tebaga Gap.

What the riflemen also could not know was that the retreating Germans had improvised an antitank gun screen two miles ahead. It would successfully hold up the 8th Army while a flank screen was organized to cover the withdrawal from the Mareth line. For the next two days, "we might have been at Mena for all the war there was," Hogg wrote, referring to command headquarters well behind the lines near Cairo. Beside the early morning stand-to, the occasional reconnaissance plane to shoot at, and the omnipresent project of repairing and maintaining vehicles and guns, there was nothing to do. El Hamma did not fall until the morning of March 29. The pause had enabled General Messe, commander of the Axis army in southern Tunisia, to reinforce sufficiently to hold the very narrow gap south of the town and to pull out at his leisure on the night of the twenty-eighth–twenty-ninth. Monty's long left hook had succeeded in turning back the enemy, but not in blocking his escape.

Whether or not 1st Armoured Division should have continued on the twenty-seventh to assault the German gun line would become a topic of frequent speculation among KRRC riflemen, as it would remain among military historians and armchair generals ever after. "In the light of later events, I think it is a great pity that we did not go on to El Hamma," Major Hogg wrote, "though it would have been a bold—and war-winning— man who would have taken that decision at 0500 hours that morning."

Having slipped through the Tebaga Gap, Messe's forces now withdrew about thirty-five miles north to the next, and the last, line where Axis forces could hope to stop the 8th Army in southern Tunisia. Between the Mediterranean and a string of impassable salt marshes called Chott el Fejaj, the Akarit position, as at Mareth, was anchored in the east by a steep-sided seasonal watercourse reinforced with tank traps and minefields. Five miles to the west, the coastal plain broke upward, first into the humpbacked Djebel Roumana, about five hundred feet high, and then into the forbidding jumble of rocky peaks and ridges of the Zouai heights and Fatnassa hills, which offered vantage points at up to nine hundred feet overlooking the plains.

Brister's men began to move again at three a.m. on March 30 and continued in fits and starts to a new position in the southern shadow of these formidable hills. Patrol work revealed an equally formidable enemy dug in there, yet despite the enemy's commanding vantage point, and with the exception of one unfortunate company whose antitank guns were targeted, the battalion experienced only random shelling. The enemy, it seemed, was conserving its resources, reserving them for identified gun positions and suspected observation posts.

The main assault on the Akarit position was scheduled to begin at four thirty a.m. on Tuesday, April 6, with the Highlanders advancing in the east across the plain and 4th Indian Division and a brigade from 50th Division in the hills. Brister and his platoon, like the rest of 1st Armoured Division, prepared to burst through any gap torn in the enemy line.

As night fell on Monday, April 5, and a sickle moon rose, two battalions of Gurkhas, experts in mountain warfare, picked their way silently up the hillsides overlooking the route of advance. It was still pitch dark when the 496-gun barrage shattered the night at four fifteen a.m., resounding and echoing against the stony hillsides. All along the line, fighting was intense, bloody, and sometimes valorous. Montgomery would estimate his casualties for the one-day battle at about two thousand, of which five or six hundred were fatalities.[42] Two Victoria Crosses would be awarded, one to the Gurkha officer Lalbahadur Thapa, who led the charge up Djebel Fatnassa, and the other, posthumously, to a medic in the East Yorkshires of 50th Division, who returned again and again to the field of fire, single-handedly rescuing three wounded men before being fatally wounded himself as he prepared to pick up a fourth. "We had on this day the heaviest and most savage fighting we have had since I have commanded the Eighth Army," Montgomery recorded in his campaign diary.[43] "Certain localities and points changed hands several times."

Yet in other ways, the assault "had run like clockwork," in the words of military historian James Holland. By seven thirty-five, all of the Indian Division's objectives had been taken. By ten a.m. on April 6, they were about to break out into the plains behind the enemy line. "The path was clear for the British armor," Holland recounts. "The surprise had been total and now a decisive victory was there for the taking."[44] Here was the chance they had been waiting for—to kill the beast instead of just shooing it onward. Yet almost nothing was done to capitalize on the battle's initial success.

The official *Annals of the King's Royal Rifle Corps*, though less blunt in its assessment, effectively agrees with Holland's judgment. "It would appear that if some of the expertise of air and artillery control, which had been so recently displayed in breaking through the Tebaga gap, had been applied to neutralizing the few anti-tank guns covering the pass exits, an overwhelming torrent of armour might have been unleashed on to the plain and the 1st Italian Army destroyed before it escaped into the hills far to the north."

The laconic 1st Battalion account of what in fact occurred tells a quite different story:

6 April. Battalion warned to move at 1000 hours 7 April.

7 April. No orders received.

8 April. Orders to move at 1300 hours. Actual move after dark.[45]

The overcautious plan that emerged in response to the morning's successes called for another attack behind air bombardment and artillery barrage nearly a full day after the 50th Division breakthrough. But by then the enemy was already gone, having slipped away again on the night of April 7–8, practically under 8th Army's noses. "Here in this spot," wrote a deeply frustrated Major General Francis Tuker, commander of 4th Indian Division, "the whole of Rommel's [sic] army should have been destroyed and Tunis should have been ours for the taking. Again the final opportunity and the fruits of our victory have been lost."[46] It is hard not to wonder how a more courageous and flexible response from the high command might have changed the course of all that followed.

In the event, Brister and his men motored unmolested through the mountain pass on the night of April 8, part of a long procession of vehicles and weapons. Eighth Armoured Brigade took the lead, "and even they were not seriously engaged," wrote Major Hogg, sounding almost wistful. A kind of nostalgia seems to have affected the men, lately so often keyed up yet so little employed. "As for us," Hogg remembered, "we had nothing more formidable than the going to compete with, and this varied considerably."

North of the Gabes gap, the Tunisian countryside opens up, for a distance, into a broad, fertile plateau interlaced with wadis, known as the Sahel, an Arabic word for "coast" or "margin." It has since the time of the Phoenicians in the ninth century B.C. been a source of agricultural bounty and an enticement to successive waves of colonists—Romans, Arabs, Ottomans, French. As Brister and his men progressed north about twenty-five miles inland and parallel to the coast, they passed through almond groves and cornfields. Row upon row of olive trees flashed slender, silver-gray leaves in the sun. The roads improved. Better still, they reached a region of chicken farms—the "egg belt," the men called it—which improved their breakfasts remarkably.

Alan Moorehead likened an armored division on the move to prehistoric beasts: "this vast procession of steel lizards . . . grumbling and lurching and swaying" up the road.[47] As the men of 1st Battalion, 60th Rifles, 7th Motor Brigade, 1st Armoured Division enjoyed a few days of relative comfort and calm, some of the old-timers nevertheless remembered the old days in the Western Desert nostalgically. As the vast numbers of Allied soldiers closed in on Axis positions, the amount of territory per man diminished and crowding increased. "In many ways this war is far less fun than it used to be," Major Hogg complained. "There is none of the business of the next company being 15 miles away. Everyone is hugga-mugga, and it is often with great difficulty that we can find an untenanted spot to lay one's head. We seldom move less than a Brigade strong, guns never fire in troops; they seem to have regimental tasks as a minimum with divisional concentrations as the normal. Effective to judge by results, but much less fun to us, who are really much more like lorried infantry these days than motor battalions."[48]

Nearly two months earlier, having assumed command of the amalgam of American, British (including commonwealth), and French forces known as 18th Army Group on February 19, General Harold Alexander outlined his plan for destroying Axis forces in Africa. As described by General Sir

William Jackson, who wrote a respected history of the North African campaign some thirty years after serving there as a field squadron commander with 6th Armoured Division, it entailed two distinct phases: "first, to unite his Army Group by passing Eighth Army through the narrow 'Gabes Gap'; and second, to tighten a land, sea, and air noose around the Axis forces in Northern Tunisia and so weaken them by naval and air blockade that a 'coup de grace' could be delivered by Anderson's First Army without excessive loss of life."[49]

With the retreat of Messe's forces from Wadi Akarit, the first of these goals had been accomplished. At the end of the first week of April, moreover, Axis forces were withdrawing not only along the coast but also from other southern passes, where they had been locked in intermittent combat with American troops since February. On April 7, General George Patton's American II Corps, who had been holding off two panzer divisions that would otherwise have menaced Monty's men, advanced east and made contact with the extreme western patrol of 8th Army's armor car screen on the Gafsa-to-Gabes road. "Eighth Army had been passed successfully through the Gabes Gap," wrote military historian Jackson, "and the two great Allied armies, one from the eastern end of the Mediterranean and the other from the Atlantic coast . . . met exactly five months to the day after the TORCH landings."[50] On April 10, the advancing line of 8th Army reached the prosperous port city of Sousse, from which in the ninth century A.D. the great Arab Aghlabid dynasty launched its conquest of Sicily. Here the land ahead once more begins to bunch together in hills, and 8th Army began to prepare for its last Tunisian set-piece assault at Enfidaville.

As Messe's army retreated into von Arnim's northern Tunisian bridgehead, Allied naval and air forces pressed to starve them into submission. "Axis tonnages landed in Tunisian ports dropped from 70,000 tons in January to 29,000 in April."[51] General von Arnim, contemplating his last stand, was short of ammunition of all kinds, without tank or gun replacements, and so short of fuel that he could contemplate only local counterattacks.[52] What was more, as Allied forces took control of airfields abandoned by the Luftwaffe, the Allies gained supremacy in the air. Meanwhile, Hitler and Mussolini reaffirmed that Tunisia was to be held at all costs. "It was clear to everyone except Kesselring and Hitler," writes W. G. F. Jackson, "that they should have been evacuated while there was yet time to save at least part of Panzer Army Group, Africa."[53]

On April 12, as 8th Army was advancing past Sousse, Alexander released his plan for prosecuting the second part of his strategy for driving the Axis out of Tunisia. While 8th Army sustained pressure and drew enemy reserves to the eastern end of the Allied noose, 1st Army would advance on Tunis, and II (U.S.) Corps, in the north, would capture Bizerte while protecting 1st Army's flank. First Army's attack was to begin on April 22.

What did not change as the balance of power in Tunisia had shifted was the challenging character of the landscape, especially when Axis soldiers remained dug in on the heights. While Allied troops had drawn the noose tighter, they had not yet commandeered the passes through the mountain fastnesses that protected Tunis, and while a sweep down river valleys and through mountain defiles was not in itself a difficult thing, the overlooking hills and mountains had to be conquered first. "German skill in combining a few anti-tank guns, mines, and infantry astride the best defile into a savagely effective flank or rear-guard was from now on to be the dominant frustration of our armour until the end of the war," state the annals of the KRRC. Meanwhile, Axis morale had, if anything, hardened. "Both the German and the Italian soldiers knew they were holding the 'last ditch' with their backs to the sea, across which there was no escape," wrote Howard.[54] Dislodging them was not at all an easy thing.

After the Battle of Mareth, Rob Cox and the 2nd Battalion KRRC had settled down briefly to a period of rest—their first since El Alamein. The weather was glorious, and the wildflowers scented the Medenine valley with honey. "All were very tired and battle weary, and this was just what the Battalion needed to get into shape for the final fling at Tunis, if we were required," wrote Major Woods, the second in command. For a short while, it seemed they might not be needed. "At present we are resting," Cox wrote Bolté on April 6, "and everyone doubts if we will be used at all."

The next day, however, as the enemy streamed north from Wadi Akarit some fifty miles up the coast, the order came to prepare to move out in twelve hours. Cox and his men packed up their few possessions, hitched their guns to the trucks, and on April 8 moved north as the advance guard for the 4th Armoured Brigade, to find their places in 7th Armoured Division on Montgomery's extreme western flank.

With the brigade moving overland, it was the riflemen's role to reconnoiter the route ahead, usually by night so that the tanks could follow by daylight. "There is an excitement in reconnaissance like nothing else," Alan Moorehead wrote. "For the most part you are in perfect safety . . . but you are never sure and you keep looking round the horizon and listening, and you have a fine sense of discovery and adventure."[55] The 8th Army's quarry had fled to the next viable defensive position in the mountains and hills some 150 miles to the north, but they had left a harvest of mines behind them, and from time to time Cox's men encountered a rear guard, who greeted them with shelling and occasionally required a skirmish, but inevitably withdrew before long.

For a time after passing through the Gabes Gap, Cox's and Brister's battalions marched in parallel, still some twenty miles apart, up the Sahel, "across the open country in which they were most at home," as the annals put it, "glorying in the green corn, fresh eggs and olive trees, but with the knowledge of hills ahead hanging over them."[56]

When Alan Moorehead reached the Tunisian front after a breather in the United States and England in early 1943, he was at first disoriented by the enormous changes that the landscape had wrought. "For a month I could not get used to this front. The geography baffled me. The tactics were an endless riddle. It was, I suppose, a kind of claustrophobia, for I could not accustom myself to the nearness of everything, the fact that while you sat on one hill there was the enemy just across the valley sitting on the next hill. Sometimes you could lift your glasses and actually see the Germans walking about." Here, he wrote, "The two armies seemed to be forever clutched in a tight embrace. . . . If you advanced a thousand yards it was considered a great achievement." And, he concluded, "this compression of the fighting seemed to me to call for much quicker wits and much more vigilance than the desert."

The pastoral quality of the days soon gave way again to the rigors of patrolling through the Tunisian mountainsides, and as Rob's men approached the mountains, Axis resistance increased. Soon each enemy position they encountered required platoon attacks like those in the Mareth Hills to dislodge it. "Shelling increased and mines as usual were everywhere." On April 15, Lieutenant J. L. Cowley, who commanded a carrier platoon in Cox's company, was killed by a shell while trying to retrieve a badly wounded comrade from his Stuart tank—"a very gallant action," as noted by the regimental history.

The country grew more impenetrable, dominated seemingly everywhere by the four-thousand-foot peak of Zaghouan, one of Tunisia's tallest. "It was becoming increasingly obvious that any advance on this front was going to be slow and costly."[57]

On April 16, the 7th Armoured Division probed forward between 4th Indian Division, to the east, and French 19 Corps in the hills to their west, due south of Tunis. Second Battalion was ordered north to relieve a motor battalion of the rifle brigade with the 1st Army. They captured part of the tiny village of Djebebina, still overlooked by knife-edged Zaghouan.

The soldiers had grown comfortable with the role of patrolling by night and infiltrating by day, but their exposed position now opposite the German 164th Division brought casualties daily. The weather turned bad. All morning on April 19, Cox's company was harassed by a German 75mm gun firing at fairly close range. No one could spot it. When Lieutenant Radclyff was ordered forward to find it, Cox volunteered to go, too, and help.

The two officers covered nearly half a mile of rough, scrubby ground on foot before the nerve-jangling stutter of a machine carbine broke from a haystack just fifty yards ahead. Cox felt the skin around his left armpit grow warm and wet. The two lieutenants raced for cover. Back at their own lines, Cox's comrades cut away his bloody shirt and took a look. Red blood oozed freely from three ragged bullet holes in his left shoulder and upper arm. They pressed field dressings onto the wounds, and that appeared to stanch the bleeding. They helped Cox into his jeep and set off to find help.

Amid the jagged hillsides and narrow passes of the Tunisian Dorsales, it was easy for a division's component units to get separated, battalion from brigade, company from battalion, platoon from company. Cox's company had threaded its way forward between the hills until it was isolated at least four miles from battalion headquarters. So the driver headed for the nearest aid post, which was located at Royal Dragoons headquarters about two miles away. The terrain was very rough and progress slow, but they found it, only to learn that the doctor had left to go forward and attend Dragoon wounded. It would take two more miles of frustrating jostling to reach the brigade's advanced dressing station. There, fortunately, the doctor was in.

By then, Cox had grown very weak. Recognizing the effects of substantial internal bleeding, the doctor immediately gave him an infusion of plasma, which was really all he could do; in a place where human blood was the soldiers' daily harvest, no whole blood was to be had for a transfusion. Cox complained of feeling very tired and soon slept. The driver continued on, directed to the main dressing station, where they would be able to transfuse him. But that proved a trip too far. After traversing the ocean from Halifax to England, surviving U-boat-plagued waters on the North and the South Atlantic; after enduring the soul-crushing heat of Cairo's southern approaches to lead a platoon of gunners nearly two thousand miles across some of the most inhospitable country on earth; just six days after his twenty-fourth birthday and an equal number before Easter Sunday; about thirty miles south of Tunis and less than a month before the Allied conquest of North Africa, Rob Cox died on the way.

On April 13, Jack Brister received word that 1st Armoured Division would be transferred north to Anderson's 1st Army for the final drive on Tunis. A few days of orders and counterorders ensued, brightened for the men by the laughable cloak-and-dagger atmosphere that surrounded the planning—all deadly secret, to be performed under cover of darkness— and the paternalistic efforts of their commanders to reduce any rivalry between 8th and 1st armies through the issuance of defensive-sounding memoranda, which the officers of the 8th found to be for the most part hilarious. "Arabic terms are not customary in the First Army," but French slang was.[58] The officers speculated as to how they could stop the riflemen from speaking of *chai* and *eggis*, from saying *maleesh* for "doesn't matter" and *sayeeda* for "hello" and instead summon up some phrases from the last war—"Mademoiselle from Armantiére," perhaps. "The final sentence was the masterpiece," Major Hogg remembered: "'It should be brought to the notice of all ranks that the 6th Armoured Division and the 46th Division have both fought extremely hard and well, and that the First Army is extremely sensitive'!"

The other matter of concern in preparation for the transfer was paint. The vehicles of 1st Armoured Division still wore their yellow-brown desert camouflage, not 1st Army green. New paint was to arrive by plane from 1st Army under escort by a special American team of sprayers. Painting parades were planned, then postponed when the Americans failed to appear, until at last they arrived with their flat accents, their capacious helmets, and their paint guns, only to discover that they hadn't brought nearly enough paint. They did what they could, the process proved messy enough to be quite amusing, and eventually two companies, including headquarters, were transformed. The rest would have to go on clad in 8th Army yellow.

Perhaps as a reaction to the prospect of transferring from one British army to another, perhaps in anticipation of the end of the North African campaign, or perhaps simply because he had recently had enough leisure time to think it over, Jack Brister penned a letter on April 14 to Sir John Davidson, KRRC colonel commandant, communicating his decision to transfer to the American army. He reminded Sir John of the Dartmouth men's June 1941 visit to Colonel Benson in Washington, when they had been assured that they could transfer should America ever join the fight. Jack was as loyal as any Englishman to his regiment, to his officer friends, and to his men, or almost—thus he began, "Now, and with great regret, I feel, when our present campaign ends, I must transfer."

Jack was not an Englishman. There were practical enticements for joining the American army of which the British soldiers were well aware; the superior pay and generally higher standard of comfort frequently were discussed, any feelings of envy generally ennobled as disdain for the Yanks' relative softness. Money had often been a real issue for Jack, but the decision reflected above all the patriotic solidarity that he had voiced in his last letter to Bolté. "For 23 years," he wrote now, "I have been pledging allegiance to the United States of America. The time has come to turn those words of allegiance into action of allegiance."[59]

On the night of April 17, Brister and his men began the long flank march to join Lieutenant General John Crocker's IX Corps in the Bou Arada area near the bottom of the Goubellat Plain, about thirty miles south of Tunis. Their route carried them behind the lines through the mountain byway of Kasserine Pass, which still bore the gruesome detritus of the American humbling by Rommel there in February, then north to their dispersal area just beyond Le Kef, an attractive French hilltop town used by General Alexander for his headquarters, whose Arabic name, meaning "the rock," suggested its historical role as guardian of the approaches to Tunis. They encountered American troops moving north to occupy their battle positions facing Bizerte. The whole Allied front, it seemed, was on the move, preparing for the final push. In Le Kef a large sign on a café wall greeted them: WELCOME TO THE TROOPS OF THE EIGHTH ARMY. They later learned that some of their group who had driven through earlier with the tanks on transporters had announced their arrival unsubtly, vehicles plastered with signs: MONTY'S DESERT RATS.[60]

Over the next three days, the rest of the 1st Battalion vehicles were repainted 1st Army green, and while the men of Brister's platoon tended to the chores attendant on preparing for battle, they also savored their new position near the banks of an actual river teeming with actual fish, which made for excellent bathing as well as for excellent fishing, once the fish had revealed their enthusiasm for the age-old anglers' fallback of bent pin and lump of bread. The padre took to wearing his bent pin in his hat as if it were a fly he'd tied himself. Only the cruder efforts of the Royal Engineers encamped nearby could spoil the fun. Making the most of their ample store of explosives, they took to tossing charges and grenades into the river, capturing dozens of stunned fish at one go.

Though withholding judgment of their new 1st Army colleagues, the riflemen found at least one aspect of their new military affiliation to be decidedly admirable. The NAAFI was stocked abundantly, especially by contrast with the supplies of a desert army on the move. "The cigarette situation was getting acute with the Eighth Army as we had gone too far and too fast for anything but the bare necessities of life and movement— rations and petrol," Major Hogg remembered. "Here were lashings of cigarettes and real Scotch whisky, a thing we had not touched for an age, as the Middle East [had] for a long time been supplied only with Canadian 'whisky.'"[61]

But the pleasures of the day soon gave way to the order of battle. Alexander's Operation Vulcan would begin on April 22, and on the pitch-black night of April 21–22, Brister moved his platoon up to their battle station behind a high hill near El Aroussa, the battered township from which, since January, 6th Armoured Division had been making periodic, indecisive forays up the pass toward Pont du Fahs. The traffic en route was dense, and as they arrived at their position rain was falling.

Crocker's IX Corps was to make the first strike, their immediate goal to capture the German-occupied hills that effectively barred the way to the Goubellat Plain.[62] At midnight, more than two hundred guns opened up in support of an infantry attack by 46th (Br) Division, whose task it was to create an opening for the advance of 6th and then 1st armored divisions against the fabled Hermann Göring Division, which soon would be joined by 10th Panzer on the southern flank. After listening to air attacks, artillery, guns, and shelling as night turned to day and the day dragged on, Jack and his men heard finally that the advance had been only a very partial success, though some progress had been made. It was the dinner hour, about six p.m., when the order arrived for a "rush move" to take over a reserve position from some Welsh Guards of 6th Armoured Division. The colonel and company commanders went ahead to reconnoiter the territory before last light, while Jack and the other platoon leaders hurried their men to decamp and form up in column.

The night was pitch. The road was narrow and, after another cloudburst, slippery, and it was clogged with the rear echelons of 6th Armoured Division moving forward. But the ways parted—the 6th turning off onto "Coventry Street," the 1st going on to "Piccadilly," and Brister and his men stumbled forward to rendezvous with their commanders.

The handover from the Welsh Guards at first light the next morning provided considerable merriment for the riflemen and their officers alike. The guards, "men of good performance and fine record in these parts," according to Major Hogg, nevertheless were "of a somewhat different school of thought from ourselves. They all wore tin hats and almost slept in equipment." They also were cranky and resentful, as they had settled into their position just two hours earlier. The helmetless, disheveled men of 1st Battalion KRRC were, by contrast and for no easily explainable reason, "in terrific form and finding life very funny indeed." Sandy Goschen drove up "to find these immaculate and tin-hatted figures awaiting us, and vastly surprised them by the order of debussing: first of all the Section hens (providers of the breakfast eggs), then the platoon dog, and finally some rather scruffy, unshaven, and sleepless riflemen."[63] The handover was a success, nonetheless, and the riflemen rested until early afternoon, when they once again lurched forward to a position just west of the Bou Arada–Goubellat road.

Here for two days they waited, as advance units slowly forced back 10th Panzer Division toward the Tunis plain. At night, the Luftwaffe, despite much-diminished potency, kept the men on edge. Suddenly, a blinding yellow light would flare, to be followed by the firecracker pop and sizzle of antipersonnel weapons known, incongruously, as butterfly bombs, because they whirled earthward in flocks, each with two yellow wings, each little bomb releasing its detonator as it spun so that sometimes it exploded on impact and sometimes it lay harmlessly until a vehicle ran over it or a man kicked it with his foot. Not far away, three heavy antiaircraft guns stood guard, their air raid siren screaming a warning at regular intervals, to be followed by deep, majestic booms, the antiaircraft rounds rising to great heights and, in the riflemen's mind, identifying themselves and their neighbors like bull's-eyes on a target. No reprisals ensued, though, and they may have felt lucky to lose only a few men to strafing.

By April 25 the armor had advanced all of about six miles, and rather than crumbling German defenses, they had found resistance stiffening. Further progress would require more hill clearing, most particularly of the high, double-peaked cone called Djebel Bou Kournine, or among the riflemen, "Twin Tits,"[64] which towered some twelve hundred feet above the Goubellat Plain, providing the Germans with outstanding observation from nearly impregnable posts.

On the morning of April 26, 1st Battalion KRRC received orders to move forward that night some two thousand yards and take over an advance position of 7th Rifle Brigade on a low ridge, Argoub el Megas, overlooked by Bou Kournine. The Argoub ridge had the shape of a tilted table, its southern side lower than the northern and only its broken edges offering any cover from Bou Kournine. The northern end was still strongly defended by Germans, who could hide by day behind the steep northern edge, then attack by night with Spandaus and stick grenades. As the battalion formed up for the move at last light, sudden bombing and shelling killed two riflemen.

That night, as the riflemen dug in at their new positions on the southern end of the ridge, the men of 7th Rifle Brigade picked their way down the steep side and into hellish danger. Flares lit up the ground around

them and German tanks fired on the carriers from the east. As they struggled forward along a single passable track, the final blow came just before
first light. The rifle brigade's antitank guns ran into six massive new German Tiger tanks armed with 88mm guns and shielded by nearly four
inches of armor, at its thickest. Two six-pounders together could not penetrate the Tiger's front, and the British guns were knocked out. The rifle
brigade fell back into reserve, and the bulk of the 1st Battalion KRRC
moved back, too, leaving Jack Brister and the rest of B Company as an
"unenviable outpost" on the southern edge of Argoub el Megas.[65]

The riflemen, all too aware of their exposed positions as daylight approached, dug feverishly to improve the slit trenches bequeathed to them
by the rifle brigade, enlisting their soup-plate helmets to dispose of the
spoil. That morning, April 27, brought continual harassment by shell and
mortar, sniper, and air attack. At B Company headquarters, Jack Brister
hunkered over a map with the company commander, John Hope, and
another officer, presumably discussing the best next step from their unfortunate position. A chance shell whined over the lip of the ridge and
found them. Brister was instantly killed. His companions were wounded.
Two hours later, papers arrived confirming the change Jack had been
waiting for: His transfer to the American army was approved.

CHAPTER 12

Home

USA, London, North Africa
May 14, 1943–

> . . . of wandering forever and the earth again . . . of seed-
> time, bloom, and the mellow-dropping harvest. And of the big
> flowers, the rich flowers, the strange unknown flowers.
>
> Where shall the weary rest? When shall the lonely of heart
> come home? What doors are open for the wanderer? And
> which of us shall find his father, know his face, and in what
> place, and in what time, and in what land? Where? Where the
> weary of heart can abide forever, where the weary of wander-
> ing can find peace, where the tumult, the fever, and the fret
> shall be forever stilled.
>
> —Thomas Wolfe, epigraph, *Of Time and the River,* referenced
> in Cox's last letter to Bolté, April 6, 1943

By the time the telegram found Jack Brister's father in Ambler, the battle for North Africa was won. On May 8, Tunis and Bizerte fell. Newspapers, radio, and newsreels all trumpeted victory. Remaining Axis forces surrendered by May 13, the afternoon when General Alexander famously telegraphed to Prime Minister Churchill, "Sir, it is my duty to report that the Tunisian campaign is over. All enemy resistance has ceased. We are masters of the North African shore."

Two days later, when the Western Union messenger appeared at his door, Dr. Fred Brister may have feared that he brought news of his older son, Dick, away with the coast guard. He tore open the telegram. It was Jack, his youngest child, the one whose birth had coincided with the death of his wife. Jack was gone.

Brister's death resonated through the small hometown where his sisters once had enjoyed riding their family horse bareback down the dirt main street. On May 20, the *Ambler Gazette* carried on its front page Jack's high school graduation photo. His thick hair was cropped so it bristled straight up, and he wore a bright grin on his face. The headline read, "Ambler Officer Killed in North Africa Action." The story summarized the origins of the King's Royal Rifle Corps in U.S. history and recounted Jack's high school successes in football, basketball, drama, band, yearbook, and academics. The paper pronounced him "one of the most popular members of the younger set of this community."[1] There was no mention of a memorial service. His father, an iconoclast by nature, eschewed ceremony as a salve, even for this.

Dr. Brister took some comfort from the letters that arrived from Jack's commanding officers and from his friends in the regiment, but their praise must also have cut. "He was the most remarkable person of my own generation that I have ever met," wrote fellow 1st Battalion officer Michael Fyfe.[2] "He was one of the few people about whom I feel, very sincerely, that he was a really great loss to the *world,* as apart from those who already knew him and loved and admired him for his deep understanding, kindness, genuineness, moral courage, and energy. His sense of humour was infectious and cheering, and he had that sympathy—in the real sense of the word—which goes with what I consider a right sense of values. Above all this, and this is what I mean when I spoke of his being a loss to the world, I think he possessed the energy and ability to turn these qualities, and the ideas which resulted from them, into practical achievements."

Fred Brister stayed in touch for some time with Jack's beloved wren, Maureen. They had begun a correspondence after the Yanks left England for the front. Addressing her letters to "Jack's Dad," Maureen had passed along letters from Jack and confided details of their romance. She wrote of her hope of visiting the family in Ambler, but she was posted to Egypt in August 1943, and the meeting never occurred.

Maureen, like Jack, had become fast friends with the American ambassador in London. In November 1942, when news reached her that Jack had been wounded—a reference to his burst eardrum in early October—she rushed to Gil Winant's apartment near the embassy. Mrs. Roosevelt was visiting at the time, and the ambassador talked with Maureen for two hours while the first lady slept. "I wish I had time and room to tell you all that he said," Maureen told Jack's dad. "He was so nice and so interested and sympathetic, so understanding of the woes of a girl in love with a soldier in the middle of a desert battle; and all this when he has his hands full of a nation's trouble, when he takes no time for rest for himself." Walking Maureen back to her hotel, Winant confided, was the first time he had been out since fighting reignited in Egypt. "It was cool and dark and very very late," Maureen wrote, "and the streets were deserted in that London town that in the same day had been celebrating the Eighth Army's victory. All the bells had rung throughout the land for the first time since the war began." Six months later it would fall to Gil Winant to tell Maureen of Jack's death.[3]

The posting to Egypt cheered Maureen somewhat. "I'm lucky really to get the chance," she wrote Fred Brister. "It might have been anywhere else in the world where he had never been—and then some of the colour would have gone out of the land. Now I have a great aim and object—I'll even be able to see the desert he loved so well—the blue sea—I shall feel all the time nearer to him—you can see that, I know. But again I must say that my only regret is that it will delay for a while *our meeting*. Wouldn't it be wonderful if you could come with me? But you'll be there in a sort of a way, all the time."

Maureen poured out her heart. "Oh Jack's Dad—the days are sometimes so long—and the nights unbearable—there seems no end to all this, but I remember that you say the 'sunrise will always come again.' I try not to let anyone else know what I feel inside because there is enough sadness in the world—so I pretend all the time, and I can be happy like that too, but sometimes things are too much for me, and I have to run away and hide till I'm good again—you see there are so many ghosts about—in the same streets and town and country. I go into a book shop and suddenly remember that here we bought such and such a book or here Jack said— and it all comes flooding back, and I know how much I still miss and need him. People always say 'time will help'—maybe it will—there will I know be new people and things—but there can never again be a Jack for me. If you love as completely as I did, it can never be recaptured again. I'm self- ish about all this—my sorrow can be nothing to yours—and yet you never question or give way to it. You have been so fine and Great and Strong about it all—that I would never let you down by being anything that you and Jack would not love—and so I try hard to be all that you would want me to be."

But, in fact, Fred Brister never really recovered from the loss of his youngest son and died himself only three years later, at the age of seventy- five.[4]

Gil Winant was deeply grieved himself by Brister's death. "There was no boy that I have met in my stay here who meant as much to me as Jack Bris- ter," he wrote Fred Brister in what for the taciturn diplomat was an excep- tionally long letter, "not only for what he was but for what he would be in building a world of the future. He has gone in helping to save what we have got, in protecting what was given to us. I believe Benét was right when he said 'We who are alive today did not make our free institutions. We got them from the past, and we hold them in trust for the future.' Jack has joined you in paying that debt. In all that was human he was above re- proach, whether it was eating griddle cakes or making love or giving life.

"The little group he came on here with used to get leave together, and when their money ran out they used to come up and camp in my apartment. They were my contact with life, with all that youth and fineness means [sic] in the world of today. Knowing them helped me keep faith with America, and faith in its ultimate willingness to sacrifice and fight.

"He loved you as few sons have ever loved a father. Your garden, your house, your caring for people as a beloved physician, are as real to me as anything in my life.

"Thank you for Jack. He lifted life here as he did for others at home and abroad."[5]

A few months later, Winant suffered the ordeal of learning that his own son, John Gilbert Jr., a pilot in the U.S. Air Force, was missing in action after his Flying Fortress, en route home from bombing Münster, encountered a flock of Focke-Wulfs and Messerschmitts at twenty-five thousand feet. A long month later, in November 1943, word came that John was alive in a German prisoner-of-war camp. A consciousness of his son's suffering, the fear that his own prominence might have caused especially cruel treatment, and, after John's liberation on May 5, 1945, the memory of it all haunted Winant. By 1946, with the war ended and Harry Truman the new president, he was, in the words of Averell Harriman's biographer, a "troubled and brooding figure, no longer appreciated in Washington as he had been during the Roosevelt administration."[6] He returned to the United States in January 1947 at the age of fifty-eight to write his memoirs, a project he found laborious at best. The first copy of the small volume was en route to his Concord, New Hampshire, home on the evening of November 3, 1947, when he retreated to his son's bedroom, pulled a gun from the pocket of his dressing gown, and shot himself in the head. Downstairs, Orol Mears, still his housekeeper, heard a crash. She ran at the sound, but could not save him.[7] He was buried in the St. Paul's School cemetery. In 1948, the Winant volunteer program established in his memory sent the first American volunteers to help rebuild bombed-out churches and community centers in London. Now called Winant Clayton Volunteers, Inc., the program continues to sponsor American-British cultural exchange and community service.

In New York in the spring of 1943, Fanny Cox organized a requiem mass for her son at the Church of the Resurrection on East 74th Street, a high Anglican house of worship whose rector, Father Gordon B. Wadhams, had become a beloved friend and spiritual guide. On Monday evening, May 10, the whole family and countless relatives and friends gathered before the large, ornate crucifix suspended over the nave, where priests in black vestments celebrated Rob's sacrifice. Among the mourners was Kit Motley Emmet, who had married Cox's rival in February 1942 and borne a daughter by the end of that year. Willy Emmet was training with the Army Air Corps. He would receive his pilot's wings in May 1944 and go to England in January 1945 to pilot a B-17 bomber, the famous "Flying Fortress." He was shot down and killed shortly before the war's end.

The U.S. Army granted Rob's younger brother Max two weeks' leave to attend his brother's service. Louis and Rowland came down from St. Paul's. Two months later, Louis also would be inducted into the U.S. Army and in early fall of 1944 would ship out for Europe, where he went into combat with the infantry in France, fought through the bitter winter in Alsace, and was wounded in late March 1945 on the Siegfried Line near the Rhine. He was flown home safely.

Ten days after the Cox family mass and half a world away, the 1st Battalion KRRC marched with the 7th Armoured Division in the victory parade on the Rue Gambetta, Tunis, to celebrate the successful conclusion of operations in Egypt, Libya, and Northwest Africa—three years of warfare back and forth over nearly two thousand miles from the Citadel in Cairo, peacetime home of the 1st Battalion when it served merely as the pivot group of the mobile division, to the port of Tunis, by which time the mobile division had become the 7th Armoured Division and "the most famous of all divisions in the desert war."[8] Of those who left the Citadel in August 1939, two officers and ninety-nine enlisted men—"other ranks" to the British—saw the end of the campaign with the battalion, while of those who left barracks in the Nile delta in May 1940, three officers and 109 other ranks had the honor of being present when the battle was won."[9]

The 1st Battalion spent eleven months training and refitting in North Africa before landing in Italy in April 1944. They took part in the advance up to the river Po and the invasion of Austria.[10]

The 2nd Battalion KRRC, after four months in western Libya training and refitting, in September 1943 landed in Italy and fought with the Allied army there until January 1944, when they returned, at long last, to England. In June 1944 the battalion landed in France. From then until the German surrender on May 8, 1945, it took part in all operations, including the final Allied offensive through Holland and Germany to Hamburg.[11]

In November 1943 the Rifle Depot barracks in Winchester, where the five American volunteers had trained, were handed over with all appropriate fanfare to the American 60th Infantry Regiment, who trained there for the invasion of France.[12] (Depot operations were moved to York with the KRRC 10th Battalion.[13]) In a formal letter of welcome, the King's Royal Rifle Corps and the Rifle Brigade saluted the soldiers of the American army. "Greatly as the members of both Regiments may regret the necessity of temporarily leaving their Depot, they are proud it will be in the safe keeping of American troops who have come across the sea to help defeat the common enemies of the human race."[14]

Field Marshal Erwin Rommel, who had inspired both fear and admiration among his British adversaries in the desert, accomplished the German occupation of northern Italy by August 1943 in preparation for the Allied invasion of Italy, which began on September 3. He oversaw the improvement of coastal defenses in Western Europe and established Army Group B headquarters, preparing to repel the expected Allied landings. In July 1944 he was badly wounded during an aerial attack, and that autumn became caught up in the aftershocks of the July twentieth plot to kill Hitler. Implicated by a conspirator, he was given the choice of standing trial for high treason or swallowing poison, his reputation intact. He chose the latter course.

During four months of recuperation in South Africa, Chuck Bolté learned to walk with a tin leg and enjoyed the salubrious effects of the mild climate and the convivial local social life. His friend Alexander Kirk, the American minister in Egypt, had offered to arrange a flight straight home from Cairo, but Bolté hadn't felt ready. "I wanted to come home under my own steam," he later wrote, "and hated the thought of my girl and my family meeting me, in a stretcher or on crutches, at the airport."[15] Bolté's lack of a passport caused complications; the U.S. consul said he couldn't give a U.S. passport to a British soldier. A few days of hobbling between British and American consulates ensued, until an imaginative British vice consul resolved the dilemma much as the American volunteers' trip had begun—with an elaborately stamped and beribboned document, this one attesting that Bolté was *not* a British subject.

The journey south, when it finally came, proved worth the wait. During four days on a big, four-engined Empire flying boat, Bolté looked down on the vast length of Africa, along the Nile to Khartoum, across the rising land to Lake Victoria Nyanza, past Kilimanjaro and the green uplands of Kenya to the sea at Mombasa, then down the coast through Zanzibar to Lourenço Marques, and inland to the big lake behind Vaalbank Dam outside Johannesburg.[16]

One day at Baragwanath Hospital in the spring of 1943, Bolté sat rereading *Seven Pillars of Wisdom* in the head nurse's office, which doubled as the library. The mail arrived, including a letter with the news that Cox was dead. When he read it, Bolté burst into tears. "Oh, come along," the head nurse said crossly. "He can't have meant that much to you." But, Chuck thought, he had, he had.[17]

When he went north again in June 1943, Chuck took the hospital's copy of *Seven Pillars of Wisdom* along with him. He returned to Cairo to await a plane home, and while stopping at Infantry Base Depot to make arrangements, he learned of Jack Brister's death.[18] "It's made me pretty unhappy," he wrote to Gil Winant on June 15, "but not bitter, as I thought it would if it happened." Speaking of both Brister and Cox, he went on: "I feel lucky to have known them, and as if I have to work very hard to try to make up for what they would have done."

That weekend, Bolté went to Alexandria to visit Cutting and Durk. By June, Cutting was fully recovered and content with a new staff job as town major for Alexandria, which had entailed a promotion to captain. Durkee, walking now with the aid of a brace and a stick, was still in the hospital and, in Bolté's estimation, "low in his mind."[19] All three young men were painfully conscious of the two empty places in their once tight-knit group. "It was not a happy reunion," Bolté later remembered. Bill and Heyward had heard of the deaths only a few days earlier. The survivors talked of Jack and Rob, of what good guys they had been, "but only a little."

"I guess each of us had his own thoughts," Bolté reflected. "I had counted so much on the years of peace, when we wouldn't live so far apart but what we could see each other often. We had even planned an annual reunion, a Hill-climbing Day we called it, when we would meet at the house of whichever one of us settled in Vermont first, and race each other up a hill, and bore our wives and children with reminiscences that would grow gaudier with the years."[20]

Durkee had gotten up out of bed in mid-April, five months after his wounding. "Slowly I am learning to use crutches," he wrote home on May 1. "In fact, I amazed everyone by standing on my good leg the first day." A wheelchair with an extra-long seat to support his bad leg enabled him to propel himself around the hospital grounds, and he learned to walk with a caliper that transferred the weight off his knee to his right hip. But his knee still hadn't quite settled down, his foot was no better, and the doctor still talked of another operation in a few more months. Some time convalescing in South Africa seemed likely, though he himself wanted to return to England "to get things settled." Whether or not the army would keep him, he wanted above all else to contribute to the war effort. "While the war is on I want to be in it doing the best I can. It would be wonderful to get home," he wrote his parents, "but with this thing still on, I wouldn't feel right about it."[21]

Durk's life, while still closely circumscribed, had expanded a little. Cutting visited regularly, and for the first time in more than five months the California boy who loved fishing and sailing and swimming could at last go outdoors. The hospital was located quite near the ocean, and friends sometimes pushed him down to the waterfront. "It is most enjoyable and makes a great change," he wrote home. "We stay for tea at a hotel and arrive back here about 6:30 in time for dinner. My tan is improving daily and believe me the sun is very hot. The cool ocean breeze saves the situation, however."

It took some time to grow accustomed to being vertical, a strange experience at first. "After months on your back you develop a new sense of proportion that is destroyed when you get on your feet again," Durk wrote home. "Even stranger is the fact that I have grown at least an inch."[22]

When Bolté arrived unannounced in New York on a Saturday night in late June 1943, he telephoned Mary from Grand Central. "This is Chuck," he said. "You got a date tonight?" Mary and Chuck's sister, Linda, and his stepbrother all convened in Greenwich. His father and stepmother, away on a fishing trip in the wilds of Maine, returned immediately upon learning Chuck was back, and the reunion was joyous.

On July 6, Bolté wrote a letter to Fanny Cox, asking whether he and Mary might visit her during their short honeymoon in New England. He had stopped in to visit Max Perkins at the Scribner's offices in New York, and he also asked her about Rob's story, which Chuck had read when they met up in Cairo in January. "Mr. Perkins said he thought Rob's story written in hospital was in your hands now. I hope you want to publish it. If it's as good as I remember it from one reading in Shepheard's, it's the valedictory of all the boys in the world who volunteered for the war, remembering their youth and gladly leaving it for whatever the war gave them."

At three p.m. on Saturday, July 24, Fanny Cox attended the wedding of Chuck Bolté and Mary Elwell at Dwight Memorial Chapel on the old Yale campus in New Haven. Bolté wore his KRRC uniform and leaned on a wooden walking stick. It was the last day before his medical discharge from the regiment.[23] For the organ prelude, his high school music teacher played Dartmouth songs, and hearing them resonate from the walls of the Yale chapel amused Chuck.

Back in New York, Bolté enjoyed his job at the Office of War Information (predecessor of Voice of America), and he worked hard. He and Mary rented a one-room walk-up in Greenwich Village. She found a job as an assistant editor at *Mademoiselle* magazine, which helped pay the bills, but meant they saw less of each other than they might have preferred: She worked days, while he went to the office at three p.m. and worked late into the night preparing the military news for early broadcast to Europe. One afternoon, heading off to work, he abandoned his cane. Suddenly feeling tired by the sight of it, he found he didn't need it anymore.[24]

It wasn't long before Bolté was campaigning again, this time for the cause of veterans' rights and international peace. He became director and spokesman of a new organization, the American Veterans Committee, which aimed to offer a more contemporary and inclusive alternative to the Veterans of Foreign Wars and the American Legion, which were organized after the Spanish-American War and World War I, respectively. Bolté described it in a letter to Winant as "a new veterans association for the men and women of this war, pledged to progressive politics at home and sound internationalism abroad."[25] His first book, *The New Veteran*, published in 1945, carried the dedication "For John Frederick Brister and Robert Hill Cox—brave men who died fighting and were their own memorial."

The book articulated the needs and aims of the twelve million veterans of the U.S. armed forces whose cause, Bolté felt, was being usurped and exploited by politicians who overlooked the individual "needs and fears and confidences" of returning soldiers in favor of a generic, sentimentalized portrait of a returning hero who needed only some coddling and Mom's apple pie to satisfy him. "Many of us, still in uniform or luckily out of it, are determined to continue working for what we fought for," Bolté wrote. "We know the war doesn't end with the firing of the last shot—but we also know the old men may come out again and take our victory from us."

It was the image conjured by T. E. Lawrence in 1920 in *Seven Pillars of Wisdom*:

> We lived many lives in those whirling campaigns, never sparing ourselves any good or evil: yet when we had achieved, and the new world dawned, the old men came out again, and took from us our victory and remade it in the likeness of the former world they knew. Youth could win, but had not learned to keep, and was pitiably weak against age. We stammered that we had worked for a new heaven and a new earth, and they thanked us kindly, and made their peace. When we are their age, no doubt we shall serve our children so.

And it was a phenomenon that the five American volunteers often had discussed among themselves, back when they were still together—what sort of world would remain after the scourge of war was ended, and what their parts might be in shaping it. It had been the focus of many rapt discussions with Ambassador Winant, for whom peace and social justice went hand in hand.[26]

In Bolté's book, and in the many newspaper and magazine articles leading up to it, Chuck adopted a tone that was at once idealistic and slightly ominous. "With the knowledge we have gained of living with each other, with our new skills and disciplines, we can certainly give much to our families, our neighbors, our country, and our world. We have the best reasons to hate war and to work for peace, at home and abroad. But we can only give the good things we have learned in a society where we can take our places as normal and productive citizens. We cannot give in a society where we are regarded as half heroes and half problems. . . .

"The new 12 million are a standing challenge to the existing order of things," he continued. "We can use our great power to diminish the evil of that order, or we can use it to diminish the good. Which course we choose will be determined as much by what civilians do now as by what veterans do in the future."

Recalling the many long talks he had had with his friends as they came to grips with the devastation in London or evaded U-boats en route to Africa, he remembered Bill Durkee's words: "It's all our fault," meaning the fault of everyone. "'We've got to go into politics, somehow. If the decent guys won't do it, the bad guys will—and if we let them, we've got nobody to blame but ourselves.'" Bolté became an organizer. In his first editor's note for his first bulletin of the American Veterans Committee, turned out on a borrowed mimeograph machine, he wrote: "We are concerned with the military problem of security, the political problem of freedom, the economic problem of welfare, and the moral problem of justice. The problems are inter-related; their solution adds up to peace."

With his new job, and his unfailing ability to frame his beliefs and actions in a newsworthy style, Bolté gained fame as a spokesman for American veterans. As they went about fund-raising, Charles and Mary quickly became a golden couple, taken up by New York society, dined and brunched in Hollywood, and received in Washington by Eleanor Roosevelt, who put them up one weekend in the Lincoln bedroom and took Mary swimming in the White House pool.[27]

By July 20, 1943, Bill Durkee was well enough to be evacuated to England by air, even though sea passage now was a matter of only two weeks, not two months. Ambassador Winant found him a job with the Economic Warfare Division at the American embassy in London. The job gave Durkee contact with the ambassador, and a great day was one when Winant dropped in to chat and perhaps told a couple of stories about his experiences with Prime Minister Churchill. Sometimes Durk would pass an evening with Miss Meers, who continued to pamper him with butter, steak, and vegetables. On weekends when he went to stay with friends in the country, he enjoyed pastimes of a peculiarly English sort. "We built hen coops, ploughed fields, planted wheat, played poker and I even gave a talk to the Home Guard on the 'battle of Alamein,'" he told his parents.

"The past few months have been very confused ones," he wrote home in January 1944.[28] "My walking has improved so that I feel quite natural with a peg leg although any great speed is quite impossible." One small wound in his knee was still draining, but the emergence of a pinhead of metal gave him hope that the rest might with time work its way out without another operation.

He found London much changed from the days when he had discovered it on leave with his four American countrymen. "The old quietness and strain are almost gone," he wrote home. In 1941 the five volunteers had themselves composed "a great portion of the Americans in the city." Now, "the thousands of American Army boys give it more of a Times Square atmosphere," he said. The city was in many ways a better place— the old tenseness gone, the people gay and confident. "But for me it is not the same," Durk wrote, "nor I suppose will it ever be, but then that's that."

Durkee was a civilian now, having been released from the British army for six months to work at the embassy, and he expected a permanent release on medical grounds. But his workaday clothes and the desk job made him feel like a fish out of water. "Concentrating for any period of time is still difficult and sitting at a desk all day is not much to my taste at the moment," he wrote. He had hoped to transfer to the American army, but even with Winant's help, the transfer was rejected on account of his leg.

Nearly every day, it seemed, he heard of someone else he knew in the regiment or had met in London or in Egypt being killed. An RAF man with whom he had played cribbage by the hour in the hospital was sent away and lost in North Africa.

"It's so damned hard to lose the people you really care about, fellows you would like to have as friends for years," he wrote home. In a condolence letter to Dr. Brister, he addressed his grief at losing Jack. "Because I know what Jack was to me," he wrote, "I know in a small way what his loss must have been to you. And yet, you know, it doesn't still the pain to know that others miss him more than you—it is something taken away—a part of you torn out so that one is less than he was. For Jack was a brother as well as a friend. I learned—learned from his words and feelings and deeds—he was the rare life friend. Others more expressive than I Dr. Brister have, I have no doubt, written you about Jack and the true man he was; for me please just know it was the terrible loss of a man I loved and respected above all others."

In London, Durkee could enjoy the companionship of other battle casualties who understood his experience. They would gather at what he called "old crock's" parties. "Wooden legs, bad arms, limps all over the place," he told his parents, "but none of them really mind—they have too much courage."[29]

Durkee was angry, too. What he read in the news made him angry at America and at Americans, especially the "so-called statesmen" who were impugning the integrity and determination of the British war effort. "It makes me so angry that you at home don't really get a true picture, there seems to be so much anti-everything from so many people," he raged. "To impute such things to this nation after all they have done is not dishonest, but shows that we may not even know for what we and they are fighting."[30]

By April 26, 1944, he could write home more cheerily, "I am quite recovered physically." But eighteen months after his wounding, he still felt unready to return to the States. He was thinking about what to do next, "and even more about how to do it."

"These three years of war have influenced me a great deal, as they must anyone at my time of life," he explained to his parents, who were understandably eager for his homecoming. "One is constantly meeting people and forces not to be understood without a relaxing and indeed a complete re-examination of what one believed and thought before. This in some ways accounts for my lengthy silences." He felt he needed to work things out for himself. "I could have come home some time ago, I suppose, but in a sense I would have been running away; even more the one lesson I know by heart is that you can't go back to the 'good old days' or any other days, what's been has gone, I've seen too many old boys over here trying to relive the last war and it doesn't work. So, if I had come home right away, as much as I want to see you all, I would have been most unhappy and restless." He asked his parents for time and understanding. "Please don't have the impression that I have any delusions of grandeur or that I am pitying myself over what I've been through, what has happened is so much less than to so many others. All I ask is that in confidence you give me your patience for awhile longer in the knowledge I will do my best to be home before the summer is out."

He sweetened the request with a bit of humor and a look to the future. "My leg has at last completely healed so the only lasting trace is a stiff leg which is a very small handicap. Only when it is damp does it hurt a bit to walk so I see nothing for me except to be a crotchety old man able to predict the next rain."

Bolté went to San Francisco in April 1945 as an adviser to the founding conference of the United Nations. In September, in an address written for delivery on ABC television, he commented on the bombings of Hiroshima and Nagasaki and, on behalf of the American Veterans Committee, asked President Truman to take the lead in guiding the world toward international government by strengthening the UN. He began with his own experience. "I lost a leg . . . when I was hit by a high-explosive shell from an 88-millimeter gun. We were all afraid of the 88. It was a very good weapon, and we always had casualties when we ran into one. But for the past few weeks, I've been going around feeling as if I'd been shot by a cross-bow, or wounded in a skirmish against the Indians up in the Mohawk Valley. That's the way the atomic bomb is likely to make a veteran of this war feel.

"Because the veterans of this war know the tragedy of war and understand the price of peace, the American Veterans Committee has now called upon President Truman to take the lead in guiding the nations of the world toward this hopeful destiny. . . . It is simply because we do wish to prevent [America's] destruction in some future and far more terrible war that we now call upon our fellow citizens to join with us in asking for the establishment of a true world governing body.

"The discovery of the atomic bomb demonstrates the commanding lead which science and technology have taken over government and the art of human relations. . . . It is now, literally, a matter of life or death with us to catch up to the scientists."

Greatly complicating Bolté's work at the AVC was a growing struggle to prevent its takeover by the Communist party. At first dismissive of the AVC as an elitist liberal organization, the Communists set their sights on it after finding the American Legion impervious. At the same time, accusations of Communism became the weapon of choice among Bolté's detractors. In 1947, exhausted by organizing, Charles and Mary moved back to England for a two-year Rhodes scholarship at Oxford. In a letter of support for Bolté's application, Gil Winant remembered the five young volunteers who had arrived in London six years earlier. "They were as gallant a group as I have ever seen, and able and self-sufficient. I realize you are asking for the recommendation of one man, but their reaction on one another and their extraordinary morale under unusual circumstances was [sic] part of all of them. . . . All of them made you very proud to be an American."

After returning home, Chuck went into publishing. He became a vice president of Viking Press and executive secretary of the American Book Publishers Council. He and Mary moved to the suburbs and adopted three children, two boys and a girl. The first son was named after Chuck's father, Guy. The second was named John Cox Bolté.

Bolté's second book, published in 1956, was *The Price of Peace: A Plan for Disarmament*. In 1966 he left publishing to become executive vice president of the Carnegie Endowment for International Peace. All his life, he would speak out about issues of peace and war. When he appeared in 1973 at a career symposium at Dartmouth, where he also received an honorary degree, he was billed as a "worker for peace." The Dartmouth senior who escorted him around the newly coeducational campus—the first Dartmouth student who ever kissed him, he joked, after she kissed him good-bye—asked him how there could ever have been a war that seemed worth fighting. He recalled his provocative assertion at another Dartmouth symposium two years earlier on organizing the peace after the war in Vietnam: "Vietnam has given war a bad name."[31]

In 1973, Chuck and Mary Bolté moved to Dresden, Maine, where he worked briefly at the Natural Resources Defense Council of Maine and edited the *American Oxonian*, the magazine for Rhodes scholars. They both contributed articles to magazines ranging from *Down East* to the *New Republic*—a life Chuck described as a combination of total independence and total insecurity. Mary died suddenly of a brain tumor in 1980. Chuck edited a collection of her writings called *Portrait of a Woman Down East,* for which he wrote a warmly affectionate introduction. For fourteen more years he continued to live in their old, slightly run-down farmhouse, until he died in 1994, aged seventy-four.

Throughout his life Bolté lived with two disabilities, and he made the best of both of them. His prosthetic leg was often uncomfortable—terribly hot in the summer and frequently the cause of pain and illness as areas of skin rubbed raw became infected. But he never suffered from embarrassment. In the early years after he returned home, he worked with other amputees to help them adjust to their condition. In this he often collaborated with Richard Wood, son of British ambassador Lord Halifax, who had lost both legs in North Africa when a bomb fell in his lap. Chuck's sister, Linda, still remembers Dick Wood's visit, accompanied by his batman, to the Boltés' home in Greenwich; how charming and positive and competent Dick was, and how much work it was attending to all the needs of his batman. Bolté's daughter, Brooks, remembers family trips to the beach with her father, who would park his artificial leg in plain sight near their blanket and enjoy the curious, admiring questions of the little boys it attracted. But Chuck Bolté did suffer, and, perhaps understandably, alcohol—the same palliative he enjoyed in Cairo and South Africa and a favored source of entertainment before that—became a constant and abundant part of his life. Perhaps he would have accomplished even more without it, perhaps less.

"Yet an ending neither defines a life nor erases it. And a final silence cannot drown out what preceded. Charles Bolté's whole life spoke clearly and with meaning to others. Even time will concede that," wrote Pyke Johnson Jr., of Old Greenwich, retired managing editor of Doubleday & Co., in a letter responding to Bolté's obituary in the *Greenwich Times*.[32]

When Maureen Robins arrived in Alexandria, where she had work as a mail censor, in September 1943, she contacted Cutting, with whom she shared a great many memories. "I have been seeing rather a lot of Robin during the last few days," he wrote Gil Winant on October 1. "We have been very close, and I like to think it has been a good thing—for both of us." Soon thereafter, Cutting was transferred to Allied Forces Headquarters in Italy. "It has given our morale an enormous boost to see Eighth Army on the move again," he told Winant.[33] "Ammunition, food and petrol: I dream about them now!"

By August 1945, Cutting, now a major, was preparing to return to the United States from England. The war had ended in Europe on May 8, in Japan on August 15. With Winant's help, he was released from the British army on August 29. His mother was ill, and his arrival at home the day after her surgery for breast cancer cheered up the family immensely. He toyed with the idea of entering the foreign service, but decided instead to finish his degree before committing to a career. After a month at Harvard, however, Heyward learned that his mother's health was taking a turn for the worse; cancer had spread to her brain. He took a leave of absence, and on March 16, 1946, he confided to Gil Winant his fear that she did not have much longer to live. He saw Chuck in New York and Bill Durkee, by then a law student at Yale, in New Haven. On November 12, 1946, Winant sent Cutting his condolences, having just learned of his mother's death.

Heyward rediscovered his long-standing interest and ability in art. He lived in California for some time, married a beautiful redhead whom he met in the art world, then trained to become a planner and architect. In 1959 one of his room designs published in the *New York Times Magazine* featured "the newest look—the conversation pit." He raised three children in the Boston area, though his first marriage ended in divorce. He too struggled with alcoholism. Now in poor health, he lives quietly with his second wife near Boston.

After D-day the mood in England changed again. Many expected the war to end very soon. At the House of Commons on June 6, 1944, the prime minister announced "the liberating assault . . . upon the coast of France." He detailed successes in Italy; Rome had been liberated by General Alexander after five months of dreadful combat. And he proudly and cautiously described the initial success of the Normandy landings by the huge Allied liberating armies, with General Montgomery commanding the British Expeditionary Force. "Complete unity prevails throughout the Allied Armies," Churchill reported in his sonorous, inspiring tone. "There is a brotherhood in arms between us and our friends of the United States."

"As much as I want to be here when it is over," Bill Durkee wrote home in July 1944, meaning the war, "I think it is probably time that I come back." That fall he enrolled at Yale Law School. There he met a willowy, dark-haired drama student from Denver, Colorado, named Dorcas Mary Dunklee, who had served during the war as a Red Cross volunteer in India. When they married in 1947, Heyward Cutting was best man.

In 1949 Bill joined his father-in-law's law firm, thereby creating the unlikely sounding partnership of Dunklee, Dunklee, and Durkee. But his interest remained in the field of international relations, and he went on

to a distinguished career with the U.S. government and various international organizations, including the State Department, the CIA, and the
Defense Department. He and Mary raised two sons and a daughter. During a stint in Paris in the 1950s, when the family lived next door to the
Cubist master Georges Braque, he took up oil painting and pastels, which
remained a serious, sustaining hobby for the rest of his life. From 1968 to
1975 he was president of Radio Free Europe and a member of the Council
on Foreign Relations. He suffered a stroke in 1976 and retired to Colorado, where he died in 1982.

The body of the Americans' musical fellow-officer Micky Heming was
never found in Egypt, but his personal possessions reached home, and
his mother found the musical sketches he had made en route from England to Egypt. The conductor who would have trained him, had he lived,
engaged the composer Anthony Collins to craft them into a finished
work. "Threnody for a Soldier Killed in Action" premiered at City Hall,
Sheffield, on January 14, 1944, the day that Heming would have turned
twenty-four, with Barbirolli conducting the Hallé orchestra. It continued
to be performed throughout England—including in 1945 at St. Paul's Cathedral in London at a service of thanksgiving for the end of the war—
and in Italy, Greece, and Palestine, into the 1960s at least.[34] Heming's
name also endures at the British war cemetery at El Alamein, where it was
carved into a panel of pale stone brought from Portland, England, along
with the names of 11,873 other soldiers and airmen who died in the Western Desert, the Middle East, East Africa, and Greece and have no known
graves.

During the weeks after Rob's requiem mass, as the Allies prepared to invade Sicily, Fanny Cox devoted herself to learning the facts of her son's
death. Two weeks after the service, at the end of May, she went to Washington, hoping to see Dick Wood and talk with other contacts at the

embassy. In September she received a long letter from Lieutenant G. A. Lyon of 2nd Battalion KRRC, to whom she had written in June. Like Rob, Lyon was a lieutenant in D Company, the antitank gunners, and he and Rob had been very good friends. In the letter he vacillated between the two names for her son, Robbie and Bob—the American and the British. It had taken him some time to collect all the facts, Lyon explained, as both Bob's batman and his driver had been killed, and his platoon sergeant badly wounded, four days after Bob.

Lyon told Mrs. Cox how well liked Bob had been and how he had won the confidence and respect of his men, "no easy thing to do with a lot of hard-bitten veterans." Lyon knew this, he said, because Rob commanded Lyon's own platoon at El Alamein, while Lyon was in hospital. He described the events of the afternoon of April 19 in detail. He had spoken to the doctor who attended Bob at the brigade advanced dressing station, and he reassured her that Rob had never suffered greatly. "He was perfectly coherent the whole time, he only complained of feeling very sleepy and tired. I am absolutely convinced that he had no idea how seriously he had been wounded. The doctor told me that the only thing he said was that he felt quite comfortable and very sleepy and shortly after, he did go to sleep, never to wake up again."[35]

Lyon described the precise location and the appearance of Rob's temporary grave near the main dressing station eleven miles south of Djebibina, Tunisia—"On his right lies an officer of the Derbyshire Yeomanry, on his left a Rifleman of this Battalion."

He told her that all Rob's kit and personal belongings had been sent back "through the usual channels, so in theory you should, sooner or later, receive everything safely." But he added a caveat. "I must tell you, that based on past experience, it is very doubtful, due to the extreme difficulties of transport, the great distances, and, as always, to the general and perpetual uncertainties of war.

"This is the full story, Mrs. Cox, and I feel sure that you will be glad to have it. Robbie died a soldier's death, which I know is the way he would have chosen himself, and although that is poor consolation, I should like you to know it. We—his fellow-officers—are very proud to have known him; it is people like your gallant son that have made the Eighth Army what it is today.

"By the way," he added in closing, "I think you would like to know that what little was left of the German 164 Division surrendered to this Battalion on 13 May 1943. Our Brigade fired the last shot in the final African battle." What consolation Fanny Cox took from this, we cannot know.

Condolence letters poured in. Joyce Heming, Micky's mother, sent a radiogram on June 15:

ALL MY LOVE SYMPATHY THOUGHTS AND PRAYERS
ARE YOURS STOP OUR BOYS ARE TOGETHER AGAIN
SO HAPPILY HAVE COURAGE.

Fanny Cox answered many of them, in some cases initiating family friendships that endured for her lifetime and beyond. In response to a letter from one old family friend, Judge Learned Hand, who summered near Windsor and had employed Rob's older brother, Bill, as a law clerk, Fanny Cox confided, "I know, hard as it is, that Robbie's going, and his living and dying as he did for his own and our integrity, made his life more complete than anything else could have done—though I must confess that that age-old cry 'my son—my son' is always in my heart. So Bob was worthy of his Father, and I just can't say anything better than that."[36]

She found comfort in the consistency of Rob's life and the idea that its ending was consonant with how he lived it. That a man so passionately in love with life also could be so reckless with it seems hard to accept. But he had been a young man, only twenty-two, when he made the decision to go to war.

During the summer of 1942, when Rob and his compatriots traveled around the Cape of Good Hope, Fanny Cox's letters to Rob had been returned to her unopened and officially stamped: "IT IS REGRETTED THAT THIS ITEM COULD NOT BE DELIVERED BECAUSE THE AD-

DRESSEE IS REPORTED DECEASED." Aside from the alarm those words must have inspired, one can only be moved by the love her letters contained. She addressed him as "my dearest and my best." At one point she told him how, in a paradoxical way, it had been easier to see him go knowing that he had been "a perfect son."[37] Perfection may have been born of distance: Her granddaughter Elizabeth Weber remembers her saying that Rob had been nearly impossible to handle after his father's death. But Fanny Cox crafted for her son an image that was easy to love and still possible to give up for the sake of something higher. The sentiment would be engraved on his headstone when the Commonwealth War Graves Commission moved Rob's remains to the large, peaceful cemetery at Enfidaville, Tunisia. The words come from Psalm 122: "For my brother and companions' sakes I will seek to do thee good."

A book fund was established in Rob's memory at St. Paul's, to which Fanny Cox donated regularly, noting that since he never had had the chance to become a writer, books were the closest thing to preserving his memory.[38] Friends and family also made enough memorial contributions to endow a fund at Harvard.

In time, Rob's effects did arrive home from North Africa. Among them was the story he had written in the hospital in Cairo, titled after an A. E. Housman poem, "We'll to the Woods No More." As Chuck Bolté advised, Fanny Cox made some effort to have it published, but without success.

Among Rob's possessions there also was an envelope with his mother's name on it. Inside was the letter he had written in Cape Town to be read in the event of his death:

Dearest M—

I have thought infrequently of writing this letter and each time shied from it. First because it is like all the sentimental heroics which prevent clear thought and, second, that I'm quite sure I shan't be killed, which makes the writing a bit of emotional self-indulgence, undignified. Lately I am strong for dignity—not

pompousness but dignity in the sense "worthy of a man"—
whatever great or little worth man has.

On the other hand, I think you would like a last word if
anything did happen, a letter to tell you what I hope you already
know—how glad a time you have given me—and to try to say
what I think about life. About the last I'm afraid I'm not very
articulate, but I believe. Oh yes, I do believe.

Really the two are mixed—what one believes and for what
one is grateful. The me that is today is what I saw and touched
and heard and smelled and tasted yesterday, and what I thought
about sensation. Our will is but somewhat free—Therefore I am
grateful for my yesterdays. Do you know, I think no other
children ever had a home like ours. Were we very spoiled? It
seems now as if nothing we wanted was denied us excepting the
$500 electric automobile I saw in the Schwarz catalogue and
wanted for Christmas. I suppose things were denied us in such a
way that we felt no resentment. That's the real point, isn't it? The
absence of resentment. Possibly it was all too pleasant so that
the trees we climbed and the paths we prowled in "the jungle,"
the brook we dammed and the secret places we found in Paradise
made us soft dreamers. I do not think so. I think it near
miraculous to have had such a childhood.

This letter was to have been my "credo." Somehow I am
bogged. But I would have you know this: that although I am not
very old or wise I have at least touched the greater part of
human experience. I am not complacent. I have known little
deeply and I would know it all deeply. I have seen the forms of
things and in other people many of the accidents. . . . Often I
have felt that through me might one day be reflected the life I
have perceived. If I wrote, it would be because there was a
necessity in me which I could not avoid. There is no joy in
writing. I think there would be nothing but misery in seeing the
empty words into which one turned oneself. But lately I have felt

there will be a necessity for writing even as there was a necessity for coming here.

I do not need to tell you why I came. I doubt if I could tell you fully. Billy said when I talked to him about it that as far as he could see there were four reasons for going: nothing better to do; adventure; curiosity; and belief. I came for all four. But mostly for shame. I was ashamed of America. I love America, and I could not sit mediocre while America was being attacked. For America is not just a place between two oceans. America is a faith and because it is a faith must be dynamic or perish. Do you know what is written on the Statue of Liberty? I did once but I have forgotten. I will write what I would put there. "Send me your oppressed, for I will give them freedom. Send me your despised for here they shall be ennobled." One day the dream will be fact.

A child who loves a ball throws it in the air. A miser reveling in his gold clutches a handful and holding it aloft lets it stream gleaming downward in the sunlight. Even thus, I, who love life, know that my life is worth nothing if not worth risking. Evil has come amongst us saying "Put yourself in the balance with me." Are you not glad to do it? I am. You are glad, too, for I am happy.

"Bless the friends I love so well," but above all you, M. "Life is good, brother, there's a wind on the heath."

> *All my love,*
> *Rob*

ACKNOWLEDGMENTS

Without the generous and enthusiastic support of the families of all the Yanks, this book would not exist. Tom Watkins, a nephew of Jack Brister, arrived on my porch in Washington, D.C., in 2007, a rolling suitcase beside him, and announced, "Here's your book." The trove of diaries, letters, and photographs he brought forth allowed me to think he might be right. John Winslow Brister, named for his uncle Jack and now the grandfather of a fifth-generation Jack Brister, told me how to find Tom.

Brooks Bolté Randolph, John Cox Bolté, Marsie Frost, and, most especially, Linda Whitlock shared their memories, and materials from the Bolté family archive, with great warmth and good humor.

Ed Durkee and Vaughan Durkee McTernan were forthcoming with memories, facts, old photographs, and a thick sheaf of photocopied letters—priceless. Barbara Durkee Parker, now nearly ninety, contributed a lucid and entertaining account of Durkee family life.

Patricia Cutting Glenn surprised me with a phone call and filled in gaps in my intelligence about her brother in her comfortable London home.

Several people who were friends of Uncle Robbie in his youth met with me and shared their memories: our cousins Bill Streeten, Sarah Geary Connor, and Ned Thomas, along with his wife, Marjorie; Tony Drexel Duke Sr.; Dick and Mary McAdoo; and the incomparably warm-hearted and charming Kit Motley Emmet Lee, whose relief upon learning that Rob Cox had had another lover before his death was touching proof that real love never dies. It was an honor and a pleasure talking with all of them.

At the beginning of the path stood Charles "Baldy" McLane, longtime and beloved family friend, who died before I could ask him all my questions, but whose robust gallantry, playful wisdom, and waggling eyebrows live on in memory.

Two men offered indispensable insights during my travels in North Africa. In Tunisia, Mr. Hammadi, an Oxford-educated classics scholar who yet radiated the wisdom of the ages, gave me a flavor of how the war between European nations both impacted and depended upon the local population. He recalled the sound of guns and bombers as his Tunisian Jewish family fled the Germans from Gabes to Bizerte. Today, he loves a German wife. James Holland made vivid the human drama of the struggle for Egypt with charm and fervor and never lost patience with my endless questions, whether unanswerably general or frustratingly picayune. He pointed me toward invaluable books and shared materials from his own extraordinary collection. During long hours on the motor coach, Mark West and Denis Montgomery also shared useful books.

It is tempting for a first-time author to acknowledge everyone who has ever encouraged, either wittingly or un-, their writing habit. May I just mention some? Hortense Tyroler, best high school English teacher ever; B. Frantz; Marion McCollom Hampton; Alice Leccese Powers; my brilliant editors Tom Colin and Susan Morse; Michele Brourman; Deborah Shelkrot Permut; Lynda Stein; the astute and enthusiastic women of my reading group—Holly Hexter, Chris Healy, Betsy Gardner, Ellen Rich, Elizabeth Lewis, Patricia Adelstein, and Mary Hickey; my effervescent and easygoing travel buddy Nancy Lazear; the ever-positive Nancy Deck; loyal friends Cathy Hart and Kyle Carney, who buoyed and believed long before this book took root; and, obviously yet most profoundly, my mother, Mary Cox Golden, whose irrepressible curiosity, affinity for the unconventional, and native creativity were essential starting points. My two beloved sons, Aaron and Jonathan Berger, fall into this category, too, although they also are in a class by themselves. They never doubted the value of this project and often prodded me to get to work. Jonny pitched in with warp-speed typing and valuable editorial insights at critical moments. Janie Abernethy, Claudia Schwartz, and Ethan Foote contributed skilled research and typing, and the book benefited considerably from Ethan's discerning editorial eye.

Art Powell, my wise cousin-in-law on my mother's side, brought to his assessment of the first draft of this book great intelligence and skill as both a historian and an author. I am hugely grateful for his careful reading, which was both useful and inspiring.

The publishing professionals who have ushered this work from idea phase to publication have been to a one pleasurable to work with and exemplary in their persistence and expertise. My thanks go to Dedi Feldman, Sarah Burnes, Andrew Stuart, and Brent Howard.

Of all the experts I consulted for this project, none was more crucial to its completion than Lieutenant General Sir Christopher Wallace, chairman of the Royal Green Jackets Museum trustees, president of the Green Jackets Association, military historian, and author. I myself am a journalist, not a military historian, and the difference must surely have given General Wallace pause. But he responded with patience, clarity, and even wit to all my inquiries, eased the way at the regimental museum and in the photo archives of the Imperial War Museum, and made himself available by e-mail for last-minute checks. His generous reading of the first draft surely saved me much embarrassment and enriched the final product.

At the Royal Green Jackets (Rifles) Museum, the archivist Major Fred Gray generously provided materials and photographs that fleshed out the historical narrative. In the early stages, George Washington University professor of history and international affairs Ronald H. Spector got me oriented. At St. Paul's School, David Levesque was a generous and responsive guide to the archives. At the FDR Library in Hyde Park, Kirsten Carter passed along a trove of letters between my soldiers and the American ambassador John Gilbert Winant. I might never have discovered them without the friendly advice of Lynne Olson, to whom I was directed by my dear friend Liz Durfee Hengen, whose own high standards as a writer and researcher have long been an inspiration. Professor Bill Nasson at the University of Cape Town pointed me to unfamiliar resources concerning that fascinating region.

When World War II at last drew to a close, my grandmother, Frances Bruen Perkins Cox, gathered together her three sons' letters home, hired a typist, and had them typed up, then assembled into three books bound in red leather. From her act of preservation and remembrance sprang my first inklings of this story. My cousin Elizabeth Werner dug out Uncle Robbie's original letters, parts of which had been redacted from the typescripts, along with other useful family correspondence. She provided an insightful review of my first stabs at writing this book, as well as the family photo albums, and her usual warm interest and enthusiasm. My brother, Robert, Uncle Robbie's namesake, resurrected another part of the family archive, including Rob's journals and a few personal letters. I must thank him also for not writing this book himself.

My grandmother maintained ties with many of the people in England who had known my uncle. The family of David Graham-Campbell, my uncle's commanding officer in North Africa, has maintained and nurtured those ties with extraordinary loyalty and generosity. I cannot adequately thank Major Graham-Campbell's son, John Graham-Campbell, for welcoming me to England, sharing his father's papers and memoirs, befriending my son, and being a dedicated, enthusiastic, and enjoyable companion in the hunt. Without him, I never would have found General Wallace, nor learned countless fascinating details about the life of a gunnery company and their fortunes in battle. To John's wife, Maggie, too, go thanks for her warm hospitality, patience, and friendship. May the connection endure into the third and fourth generations.

One of the unexpected rewards of this endeavor has been discovering the generosity with which people on the far side of the Atlantic whose lives were touched by the Yanks came forward with their memories. The five young Americans' heroic gesture had not been forgotten. Charles Amory, son of my uncle's battalion commander, moved me deeply by placing a cross with my uncle's name on it in the "Garden of Remembrance" at Westminster for Remembrance Sunday, November 11, 2007. The late Sir Peter Laurence and Peter D. L. Way sent photographs and letters very early on that helped to bring my subjects to life. Their dedication to the values of continuity and loyalty and the depth of the bond that military sacrifice entails are impressive indeed. I shall remember you.

SOURCES

PRIMARY SOURCES

Bolté, Charles G., "Letter to a Niece: A Personal Narrative of the 1940s," unpublished, November 1973.

——, "Letters from Bolté," digests of letters from Bolté to his family published in *Dartmouth Alumni Magazine,* November 1941, December 1941, February 1942, March 1942, June 1942, August 1942, December 1942, January 1943, February 1943.

——, "Letter to the President," *The Dartmouth,* April 24, 1941, and other articles and letters in *The Dartmouth.*

——, ed., *Mary Bolté: Portrait of a Woman Down East,* Camden, ME: Down East Books, 1983.

——, *The New Veteran,* New York: Scribners, 1945.

——, "The White Whale," Senior Fellow Pamphlets 7, Dartmouth College Publications, 1941.

Cox, Frances B., as transcribed by Nancy Krause, *Grandma's Memories,* 1983, privately printed.

Dartmouth College Broadcast to Dartmouth, England, November 20, 1941, script and text of remarks by President Hopkins, Dartmouth College, Rauner Special Collections Library.

"Diary and Military Study Book" of John F. "Jack" Brister, 145 pages, dated August 21, 1941–February 13, 1943, unpublished.

Journal kept by Robert Hill Cox II, sixty-three pages, dated July 7, 1942–
September 18, 1942, unpublished.

Letters (1941–43) home of Robert Hill Cox II, compiled by Frances B. Cox, 203
pages, unpublished. Fifty-three letters, with related telegrams and letters
from British authorities and officers.

The papers of John Gilbert Winant, Franklin D. Roosevelt Presidential Library,
Hyde Park.

Letters home (July 13, 1941–July 11, 1944) of William Porter Durkee III, unpublished.

Miscellaneous letters of Robert Hill Cox II, unpublished: April 6, 1942, to Mary
Wigglesworth; November 15, 1942, to Paul Moore.

Miscellaneous unpublished letters of British officers Brister, Bolté, Durkee, Cutting, their friends and relatives, and Maureen Robins, ninety pages, September 20, 1937–June 26, 2007.

"National Service Year Book" of John F. "Jack" Brister, as transcribed by Hope
Brister Watkins, twenty-three pages, diary entries dated April 24, 1942–
November 10, 1942, unpublished.

"Record," journal kept by Robert Hill Cox II, seventy-two pages, dated July 10,
1941–August 15, 1942, unpublished.

Randolph, Jeff, transcription of an oral history of Linda Whitlock.

"St. Paul's School 1941," videodisk of the 1941 boat races, supplied to the school
by Hugh MacRae II.

ACCOUNTS BY OTHER SOLDIERS OF THE
KING'S ROYAL RIFLE CORPS

Chronicles of the King's Royal Rifle Corps, 1941, 1942, 1943.

Ellsworth, Ted, *Yank: The Memoir of a World War II Soldier (1941–1945),* New
York: Thunder's Mouth Press, 2006.

Graham-Campbell, David J., *The War Years: Memoirs,* unpublished family
document.

Jameson, Geoffrey, *To War with Friends: The War Diary of Geoffrey Jameson
K.R.R.C., September 1941 to September 1943,* privately published, York, England: Wilton 65, 1996.

Mills, Giles, and Roger Nixon, *The Annals of the King's Royal Rifle Corps,* volume
6, London: Leo Cooper, 1971.

Wake, Major General Sir Hereward, and Major W. F. Deedes, eds., *Swift and Bold:
The Story of the King's Royal Rifle Corps in the Second World War, 1939–1945,*
Aldershot: Gale and Polden, 1949.

INTERVIEWS

Brister, Dick (Brister's brother).

Connor, Sarah Geary (Cox's cousin).

Cox, Louis (Cox's brother).

Duke, Tony Drexel Sr. (Cox's prep school friend).

Durkee, Edward (Durkee's son).

Glenn, Patricia Cutting (Cutting's sister).

Graham-Campbell, John (son of Cox's commanding officer).

Lee, Kit Motley (Cox's girlfriend).

McAdoo, Mary Wigglesworth, and Richard McAdoo (Cox's friends).

McLane, Charles (friend of Brister, Bolté, Cox, Durkee).

McTernan, Vaughan Durkee (Durkee's daughter).

Parker, Barbara (Durkee's sister).

Randolph, Brooks Bolté (Bolté's daughter).

Streeten, William (cousin of Cox, who lived with his family during the war).

Thomas, Ned (Cox's cousin and childhood friend).

Wallace, Lieutenant General Sir Christopher (chairman, the Royal Green Jackets Museum trustees, and president, the King's Royal Rifle Corps Association).

Watkins, Thomas (Brister's nephew).

Whitlock, Linda (Bolté's sister).

SECONDARY SOURCES

Books

Abramson, Rudy, *Spanning the Century: The Life of W. Averell Harriman, 1891–1986,* New York: Morrow, 1992.

Atkinson, Rick, *An Army at Dawn: The War in North Africa, 1942–1943,* New York: Henry Holt, 2002.

Bacon, Admiral Sir Reginald, Major General J. F. C. Fuller, Air Marshal Sir Patrick Playfair, *Warfare Today: How Modern Battles Are Planned and Fought on Land, at Sea, and in the Air,* London: Odhams Press.

Barr, Niall, *Pendulum of War: The Three Battles of El Alamein,* New York: Overlook Press, 2004.

Bellush, Bernard, *He Walked Alone: A Biography of John Gilbert Winant,* The Hague, Paris: Mouton, 1968.

Bickford-Smith, Vivian, Elizabeth van Heyningen, and Nigel Worden, *Cape Town in the Twentieth Century: An Illustrated Social History,* Claremont, S. Africa: David Philip Publishers, 1999.

Bierman, John, and Colin Smith, *War Without Hate: The Desert Campaign of 1940–1943,* New York: Penguin, 2002.

Brown, James Ambrose, *Retreat to Victory: A Springbok's Diary in North Africa: Gazala to El Alamein 1942,* Johannesburg: Ashanti Publishing, 1991.

Carver, Michael, *Out of Step: Memoirs of a Field Marshal,* London: Hutchinson, 1989.

Childers, Thomas, *Soldier from the War Returning,* New York: Houghton Mifflin Harcourt, 2009.

Dear, I. C. B., and M. R. D. Foot, eds., *The Oxford Companion to World War II,* Oxford: Oxford, 2005.

Douglas, Keith, *Alamein to Zem Zem,* London: Faber and Faber, 2008, copyright 1946.

Duke, Anthony Drexel, *Uncharted Course: The Voyage of My Life,* Northport, NY: The Bayview Press, 2007.

Eden, Anthony, *The Reckoning,* Boston: Houghton Mifflin, 1965.

Edmonds, John B., ed., *St. Paul's School in the Second World War,* Saint Paul's School Alumni Association, 1950.

Fletcher, David, *The British Tanks, 1915–19,* Ramsbury: Crowood Press Ltd., 2001.

Fussell, Paul, *Wartime: Understanding and Behavior in the Second World War,* New York: Oxford University Press, 1989.

Glanfield, John, *Devil's Chariots: The Birth and Secret Battles of the First Tanks,* Stroud, Gloucestershire: Sutton Publishing, 2001.

Glenn, John G., *Tobruk to Tarakan: The Story of a Fighting Unit,* Adelaide: Rigby Ltd., 1960.

Gormley, Ken, *Archibald Cox: Conscience of a Nation,* Reading, MA: Addison-Wesley, 1997.

Griffith, Paddy, *World War II Desert Tactics,* New York: Osprey, 2008.

Heckscher, August, *St. Paul's: The Life of a New England School,* New York: Scribner's, 1980.

Holland, James, *Together We Stand: America, Britain, and the Forging of an Alliance,* New York: Hyperion, 2005.

Jackson, W. G. F., *The Battle for North Africa, 1940–43,* New York: Mason/Charter, 1975.

Kaplan, Justin, *When the Astors Owned New York,* New York: Plume, 2006.

Latimer, Jon, *Operation Compass, 1940: Wavell's Whirlwind Offensive,* Oxford: Osprey, 2000.

Martin, Albert, *Hellfire Tonight,* Lewes, Sussex: The Book Guild, 1996.

Merry, Robert W., *Taking on the World: Joseph and Stewart Alsop—Guardians of the American Century,* New York: Viking Penguin, 1996.

Mills, Giles, and Roger Nixon, *The Annals of the King's Royal Rifle Corps,* volume 6, London: Leo Cooper, 1971.

Ministry of Information for the War Office, *The Eighth Army: September 1941 to January 1943,* London: His Majesty's Stationery Office, 1943.

Montgomery, Bernard Law, *The Memoirs of Field Marshal Montgomery*, Cleveland, OH: The World Publishing Co., 1958.

Moore, Honor, *The Bishop's Daughter: A Memoir*, New York: W. W. Norton, 2008.

Moore, Paul, *Presences: A Bishop's Life in the City*, New York: Farrar, Straus and Giroux, 1997.

Moorehead, Alan, *Desert War: The North African Campaign, 1940–1943* (originally published 1944 as *African Trilogy*), New York: Penguin, 2001.

Mosse, George L., *Fallen Soldiers: Reshaping the Memory of the World Wars*, New York: Oxford University Press, 1990.

Nelson, Nina, *Shepheard's Hotel*, London: Barrie & Rockliff, 1960.

Ogorkiewicz, Richard M., *Armoured Forces: A History of Armoured Forces and Their Vehicles*, London: Arms and Armour Press, 1970.

Olson, Lynne, *Citizens of London: The Americans Who Stood with Britain in Its Darkest, Finest Hour*, New York: Random House, 2010.

Ordonez y Montalvo, Jose A. G., *St. Paul's School: A Pictorial History*, Concord, NH: St. Paul's School, 1991.

Panter-Downes, Mollie, *London War Notes, 1939–1945*, New York: Farrar, Straus and Giroux, 1971.

Parrish, Thomas, *To Keep the British Isles Afloat: FDR's Men in Churchill's London, 1941*, New York: HarperCollins, 2009.

Ranfurly, Countess of, *To War with Whitaker*, London: William Heinemann, 1994.

Roberts, Andrew, *"The Holy Fox": A Biography of Lord Halifax*, London: Weidenfeld and Nicolson, 1991.

——, *Masters and Commanders: How Four Titans Won the War in the West, 1941–1945*, New York: HarperCollins, 2009.

——, *The Storm of War: A New History of the Second World War*, New York: HarperCollins, 2011.

Samet, Elizabeth D., *Soldier's Heart: Reading Literature through Peace and War at West Point*, New York: Farrar, Straus and Giroux, 2007.

Stoddard, Brooke C., *World in the Balance: The Perilous Months of June–October 1940*, Dulles, VA: Potomac Books, 2011.

Tree, Ronald, *When the Moon Was High: Memoirs of Peace and War, 1897–1942*, London: Macmillan, 1975.

Wallace, Lieutenant General Sir Christopher, *The King's Royal Rifle Corps . . . the 60th Rifles: A Brief History: 1755 to 1965*, Winchester: The Royal Green Jackets Museum Trust, 2005.

Watson, Bruce Allen, *Exit Rommel: The Tunisian Campaign, 1942–43*, Westport, CT: Praeger, 1999.

White, David Fairbank, *Bitter Ocean: the Battle of the Atlantic, 1939–1945*, New York: Simon & Schuster, 2006.

Wilmott, H. P., Robin Cross, Charles Messenger, *World War II*, New York: DK Publishing, 2004.

Winant, John Gilbert, *Letter from Grosvenor Square: An Account of a Stewardship,* New York: Greenwood Press, 1947.

Wortman, Mark, *The Millionaires' Unit: The Aristocratic Flyboys Who Fought the Great War and Invented American Air Power,* Public Affairs, 2006.

Periodicals

"After Four Months," *The Pictorial,* Commencement, 1941.

Bolté, Charles, "The New Veteran," *Life,* December 10, 1945, pp. 57 and ff.

——, "Business in Britain," *Fortune,* October 1941, p. 91.

——, "The Crusader," *Eighth Army Weekly,* November 9, 1942.

Sherwood, Robert E., "America . . . A Soul and a Purpose," *Vogue,* February 1, 1941, p. 60.

Newspapers

Kukka, Christine, "Amvets Leader Writes in Maine," the *Times Record,* Brunswick, Maine, June 20, 1984, p. 12.

New York Times, Concord Monitor, Manchester Union, Boston Globe, Cape Times

Web Sites

http://www.bbc.co.uk/ww2peopleswar: Forty-seven thousand stories and fifteen thousand images contributed by the public to this British Broadcasting Company archive between June 2003 and January 2006.

www.krrcassociation.com/swiftandbold/maufe_a_full_life.pdf.

www.samilitaryhistory.org: The site of the South African Military History Society includes many fascinating personal accounts of the war years.

www.secondworldwarforum.com: The Web site of historian James Holland includes transcriptions of his interviews with veterans of the North African campaign.

Literary Sources

Holy Bible, Standard Revised Version

Melville, Herman, *Moby-Dick*

Tolstoy, Leo, *War and Peace*

Graves, Robert, *I, Claudius*

Lawrence, T. E., *Seven Pillars of Wisdom*

Films and CDs

BBC History of World War II

Desert Victory

Long Voyage Home

A Yank at Oxford

NOTES

Prologue

1 Bolté, *The New Veteran*, p. 8.
2 Robert Hill Cox II, Journal, p. 56.
3 Brister, Yearbook, p. 17.
4 Bolté, "There Were Five of Us," reprinted from *American Legion Monthly Magazine* in *Chronicle of the King's Royal Rifle Corps 1943*, p. 19.
5 Bolté, *The New Veteran*, p. 8.
6 Ibid.
7 Ibid.
8 Ibid, p. 9.
9 Ibid, p. 8.

Chapter 1: Decision

1 Richard E. Barkhorn, "War Referendum Vote Split as 'Defenders of Democracy' Circulate Convoy Petition," *The Dartmouth*, April 24, 1941, p. 1.
2 Bolté, "Letter to the President," p. 1.
3 Charles G. Bolté, ed., *Mary Bolté*, p. 1.
4 "Vox Populi," *The Dartmouth*, April 28, 1941.
5 "Hold Debate on War Tonight; Nazis Bomb Escaping British," *The Dartmouth*, April 29, 1941, p. 1.

6 "Vox Populi," *The Dartmouth,* May 1, 1941, p. 3.

7 Interview with Charles McLane.

8 Interview with Kit Motley Lee.

9 Dorothy G. Wayman, "Memorial Day Keynote Is National Security," *Boston Globe,* May 31, 2007, p. 1.

10 "Winant Returns; Silent on Mission," *New York Times,* May 31, 1941, p. 1.

11 "Defense Firm Adds Guards at Laconia," *Manchester Union,* May 31, 1941, p. 1.

12 Carl Zebrowski, "Your Number's Up!" *America in WWII,* December 2007, accessed at www.americainwwii.com/stories/yournumbersup.html.

13 Interview with Richard McAdoo.

14 Interview with Charles McLane.

15 Anthony Drexel Duke, *Uncharted Course: The Voyage of My Life,* pp. 124–125.

16 Ordonez y Montalvo, *St. Paul's School,* p. 67.

17 RHC Journal, p. 41.

18 Cox Letters, p. 32.

19 Interview with Kit Motley Lee.

20 Interview with Charles McLane.

Chapter 2: Convoy

1 "And What Is So Rare?" *New York Times,* July 10, 1941, downloaded from NYTimes.com archive.

2 Linda Whitlock, "Memoir for My Family," unpublished, p. 6.

3 Ibid, p. 3.

4 Interview with Linda Whitlock.

5 Ibid.

6 "After Four Months," *The Pictorial,* Commencement, 1941, p. 4.

7 Oral history of Linda Whitlock by her son-in-law Jeff Randolph, p. 2.

8 Bolté, "Letter to a Niece: A Personal Narrative of the 1940s," p. 8.

9 Robert E. Sherwood, "America . . . A Soul and a Promise," *Vogue,* February 1, 1941, p. 60.

10 Bolté, "Letter to a Niece," p. 8.

11 Ibid.

12 Ibid, p. 10.

13 Ibid, p. 13.

14 RHC Record, p. 3.

15 "Heyward Cutting, Flier and Explorer Dies in Auto Crash," *New York Times,* June 7, 1926, downloaded from nytimes.com archive.

16 RHC Record, p. 1.
17 Dear, et al, *The Oxford Companion to World War II*, p. 50.
18 Ibid.
19 Parrish, *To Keep the British Isles Afloat*, p. 212.
20 White, *Bitter Ocean*, p. 61.
21 Ibid, p. 60.
22 Ibid, p. 61.
23 Ibid, p. 100.
24 Willmott, H. P., et al, *World War II*, p. 81.
25 Ibid, p. 82.
26 Parrish, pp. 211–212.
27 White, p. 289.
28 Ibid, p. 72.
29 Parrish, p. 212.
30 www.warsailors.com/convoys/hx139.html.
31 www.warsailors.com/convoys/hxconvoys3.html.
32 White, pp. 7–11, 50–56.
33 RHC Record, p. 4.
34 Ibid.
35 Ibid, p. 6.
36 Ibid, p. 7.
37 Ibid, p. 8.
38 Ibid, p. 9.
39 Ibid, p. 11.
40 Ibid, p. 9.
41 Ibid, p. 14.
42 Ibid, p. 11.
43 Ibid, p. 15.
44 Ibid, p. 16.
45 Ibid, p. 15.
46 Ibid, p. 17.
47 Ibid, p. 26.
48 Ibid, p. 27.
49 www.baseball-almanac.com/feats/feats3.shtml.
50 Olson, *Citizens of London*, pp. 126–127.
51 Ibid, p. 135.
52 White, pp. 122–123.

Chapter 3: Riflemen

1 Jack Brister to Frederick Brister, August 9, 1941.
2 Nugent, Frank S., "The Screen: Robert Taylor Appears as 'A Yank at Oxford' at the Capitol—'She Married an Artist' at Criterion," *New York Times*, February 25, 1938. Downloaded from newyorktimes.com archive.
3 JB–FB, Ibid.
4 RHC Letters, p. 5.
5 RHC Record, p. 35.
6 Bolté, *Dartmouth Alumni Magazine*, November 1941, p. 17.
7 JB–FB, September 29, 1941.
8 Bolté, *Dartmouth Alumni Magazine*, November 1941, p. 17.
9 RHC Record, p. 37.
10 Bolté, *Dartmouth Alumni Magazine*, November 1941, p. 18.
11 Ibid, p. 17.
12 RHC Record, p. 41.
13 JB–FB, August 9, 1941.
14 Jack Brister, Diary and Military Study Book, pp. 1–2.
15 JB Diary, p. 2.
16 RHC Record, p. 41.
17 Durkee letter home, August 9, 1942.
18 Ibid.
19 JB–FB, August 9, 1941.
20 Bolté, *Dartmouth Alumni Magazine*, November 1941, p. 18.
21 John G. Winant, *Letter from Grosvenor Square*, p. 178.
22 Bolté, *Dartmouth Alumni Magazine*, November 1941, p. 18.
23 RHC Record, p. 37.
24 Ibid, pp. 37–38.
25 Bolté, *Dartmouth Alumni Magazine*, November 1941, p. 18.
26 JB Diary, p. 12.
27 RHC Letters, p. 7.
28 Bolté, *Dartmouth Alumni Magazine*, November 1941, p. 17.
29 RHC Record, p. 41.
30 Heyward Cutting to John Gilbert Winant, October 1, 1943, FDR Archive.
31 RHC Letters, p. 13.
32 JB–FB, September 8, 1941.
33 RHC Record, p. 38.
34 RHC Letters, p. 15a.
35 Jack Brister to Tom Littlefield, August 21, 1941.
36 RHC Record, p. 39.

37 JB Diary, pp. 25–26.

38 Ibid, p. 40.

39 Ibid, p. 34.

40 RHC Record, p. 39.

41 JB Diary, p. 27.

42 Ibid.

43 Ibid.

44 Bolté, *New Veteran,* p. 85.

45 JB Diary, p. 17.

46 Bolté, *New Veteran,* p. 85.

47 Ibid.

48 JB–FB, September 8, 1941.

49 Ibid.

50 Ibid.

51 Ibid.

52 Bolté, *New Veteran,* p. 85.

53 RHC Record, p. 42.

54 Robert Cox to Frances Cox, September 13, 1941.

55 JB Diary, p. 39.

56 JB–FB, September 8, 1941.

57 RHC Letters, p. 25.

58 Ibid.

59 Bolté, *Dartmouth Alumni Magazine,* December 1941, p. 12.

60 Ibid.

61 RHC Record, p. 43.

62 Bolté, *Dartmouth Alumni Magazine,* December 1941, p. 12.

63 Ibid.

64 JB–FB, October 4, 1941.

65 JB Diary, pp. 43, 45–46.

66 Ibid, pp. 45–46.

67 JB–FB, October 1, 1941.

68 JB Diary, pp. 44–45.

69 Durkee letter home, October 8, 1941, p. 3.

70 RHC Letters, p. 16.

71 Durkee letter home, October 8, 1941, p. 5.

72 Ibid, p. 6.

73 Bolté to Winant, November 2, 1941.

74 Ibid.

75 Durkee letter home, October 30, 1941, p. 4.

76 RHC Letters, p. 18.

77 Charles Bolté, "Charles G. Bolté '41 Reports on Ireland," *Dartmouth Alumni Magazine,* January 1941, p. 4.

78 RHC Letters, p. 18.

79 Kaplan, *When the Astors Owned New York,* pp. 43, 163.

80 JB Diary, p. 62.

81 RHC Letters, p. 33.

82 JB Diary, p. 67.

83 Ibid, p. 64.

84 RHC Letters, p.37.

Chapter 4: Officers

1 RHC Letters, p. 37.

2 Glanfield, *The Devil's Chariots,* pp. 219–221.

3 Charles F. Horne, ed., *Records of the Great War, Vol. V,* National Alumni 1923, cited on www.firstworldwar.com/source/cambrai_hindenburg.htm.

4 http://southernlife.org.uk/south_tidworth_htm.

5 Charles Bolté to President Hopkins, November 22, 1941, Dartmouth Archives.

6 "Dartmouth to Dartmouth Broadcast," November 20, 1941, Rauner Library archives.

7 RHC Letters, p. 38.

8 Ibid.

9 Bolté, *Dartmouth Alumni Magazine,* February 1942, p. 8.

10 Ibid.

11 Ibid.

12 Durkee letter home, December 9, 1941, p. 1.

13 RHC Letters, pp. 49–50.

14 Ibid, p. 45.

15 Brister Diary, pp. 105–106.

16 RHC Letters, pp. 51–52.

17 Durkee letter home, January 25, 1942.

18 RHC Letters, p. 58.

19 Ibid, p. 63.

20 Ibid, pp. 65–66.

21 Ibid, p. 70.

22 Ibid, p. 81.

23 Ibid, p. 79.

24 Bolté, *Dartmouth Alumni Magazine,* June 1942, p. 7.

25 RHC Letters, p. 80.

26 Bolté, *Dartmouth Alumni Magazine,* June 1942, p. 7.
27 Robert Cox to Frances Cox, April 6, 1942.
28 McSmith, Andy, "Last Orders at the Café Royal," *The Independent,* December 23, 2008.
29 RHC Letters, p. 91.
30 Ibid.
31 Brister Yearbook, p. 8.
32 KRRC Chronicle, 1942, p. 120.
33 RHC Letters, p. 108.
34 Ibid, p. 109.
35 Holland, *Together We Stand,* pp. 129–130, 137–138.
36 *Encyclopaedia Britannica,* Fifteenth Edition, 1995, p. 1004.
37 Holland, p. 187.
38 Atkinson, *An Army at Dawn,* p. 15.
39 Ibid, p. 150.
40 Ibid, p. 151.

Chapter 5: Interlude *Doña Aurora*

1 RHC Letters, p. 95.
2 www.convoyweb.org.uk/os33/index.html?os33.htm~mainframe33, accessed June 16, 2010.
3 Durkee letter home, August 8, 1942, p. 2.
4 RHC Journal, pp. 7–8.
5 Ibid, p. 6.
6 Brister Yearbook, p. 11.
7 www.convoyweb.org.uk/os33/index.html.
8 openjurist.org/206/f2d/651/de-la-rama-ss-co-v-united-states.
9 RHC Journal, p. 17.
10 Ibid, pp. 12–13.
11 Brister Yearbook, p. 12.
12 RHC Journal, p. 20.
13 Brister Yearbook, p. 12.
14 Bolté, *Dartmouth Alumni Magazine,* December 1942, p. 19.
15 RHC Letters, p. 109.
16 RHC Journal, p. 21.
17 Ibid, p. 22.
18 Brister Diary, p. 123.
19 Ibid.

20 Brister Diary, p. 82.

21 Brister Yearbook, p. 13.

22 Ibid.

23 Bolté, "Letter to a Niece," p. 15.

24 Brister Yearbook, p. 13.

25 Brister Diary, p. 130.

26 RHC Journal, p. 28.

Chapter 6: Lost in the Honeycomb

1 Brister Diary, p. 132.

2 RHC Letters, p. 117.

3 Brister to Winant, July 27, 1942, FDR Archive.

4 Ibid.

5 RHC Journal, p. 30.

6 Ibid, p. 29.

7 Ibid, p. 30.

8 Brister Yearbook, p. 14.

9 RHC Journal, p. 30.

10 Brister Yearbook, p. 14.

11 RHC Journal, p. 49.

12 Rob Cox to Joyce Heming, December 10, 1942.

13 Ibid.

14 *Cape Times*, July 30, July 31, 1942.

15 Brister Yearbook, p.14.

16 Moorehead, *Desert War*, p. 381.

17 *Cape Times*, July 27, 1942.

18 Ibid, July 28, 1942.

19 Bickford-Smith et al, p. 94.

20 *Cape Times*, July 27, 1942.

21 Bickford-Smith, et al, p. 96.

22 Rob Cox to Mary Wigglesworth, August 28, 1942.

23 Capetownclub.org.za.

24 RHC Journal, p. 34.

25 Ibid, p. 33.

26 Brister Yearbook, p. 14.

27 RHC Journal, p. 34.

28 Brister Yearbook, p. 14.

29 RHC Journal, pp. 45–46.

30 Ibid, p. 44.

31 Brister Yearbook, p. 15.

32 Ibid, p. 15.

33 RHC Journal, pp. 35–36.

34 Ibid, pp. 36–38.

35 Ibid, pp. 38–42.

Chapter 7: Interlude *Duchess of Atholl*

1 RHC Journal, p. 44.

2 Brister Yearbook, p. 16.

3 Ibid.

4 www.derbysulzers.com/birkenheadships.html.

5 Roberts, *Masters and Commanders,* p. 273.

6 Dear et al, *The Oxford Companion to World War II,* p. 25.

7 RHC Letters, p. 121.

8 Brister Yearbook, p. 16.

9 RHC Journal, p. 56.

10 Brister Yearbook, p. 17.

11 RHC Letters, p. 125.

12 Ibid.

13 Brister Yearbook, p. 17.

14 RHC Letters, pp. 126–127.

15 Durkee letter home, September 11, 1942, p. 1.

16 RHC Journal, pp. 52–53.

17 Brister Yearbook, p. 17.

Chapter 8: Into the Blue

1 Moorehead, pp. 389–391.

2 Historians now place casualty levels at ten thousand German and nearly thirteen thousand British. Watson, *Exit Rommel,* p. 6.

3 "Great Britain: The War and Winston Churchill," *Time,* July 6, 1942, downloaded at www.time.com/time/magazine/article/0,9171,932063,00 .html.

4 Moorehead, *Desert War,* p. 421.

5 Wallace, *The King's Royal Rifle Corps,* p. 170.

6 Holland, *Together We Stand,* p. 208, and interview with James Holland. Although Gott's death long was treated as a matter of happenstance, recent research, including Holland's interview with the British pilot,

indicates clearly that the plane had been targeted and the death was an assassination.

7   Moorehead, *Desert War,* p. 261.

8   Ibid, p. 410.

9   Ibid, p. 410–411.

10 Ibid, p. 420.

11 Watson, *Exit Rommel,* p. 10.

12 Ibid.

13 Wallace, *The King's Royal Rifle Corps,* p. 171.

14 RHC Journal, p. 61.

15 Martin, *Hellfire Tonight,* p. 25.

16 Brister Yearbook, p. 18.

17 RHC Journal, p. 61.

18 Ibid.

19 RHC Journal, p. 62.

20 Brister Yearbook, p. 18.

21 Ibid, p. 19.

22 RHC Letters, p. 130.

23 RHC Journal, p. 63.

24 Mills, et al, *The Annals of the King's Royal Rifle Corps*, p. 284.

25 RHC Letters, p. 132.

26 Ibid., pp. 134–135.

27 Mills, et al, *The Annals of the King's Royal Rifle Corps*, p. 288.

28 Ibid, p. 266.

29 Jameson, Geoffrey, *To War with Friends: The War Diary of Geoffrey Jameson K.R.R.C.*, p. 67.

30 http://peek-01.livejournalcom/7133.html.

31 Martin, *Hellfire Tonight,* p. 164.

32 Mills, et al, *The Annals of the King's Royal Rifle Corps,* p. 95.

33 RHC Letters, p. 138.

34 Graham-Campbell, David, Memoirs, p. 20.

35 Mills, et al, *The Annals of the King's Royal Rifle Corps,* p. 6.

36 Martin, *Hellfire Tonight,* p. 166.

37 Jameson, *To War with Friends,* p. 69.

38 Ibid.

Chapter 9: El Alamein

1   Barr, *Pendulum of War,* p. 349.

2   Mills, et al, *The Annals of the King's Royal Rifle Corps,* p. 294.

3 Brister Yearbook, p. 22.

4 Mills, et al, *The Annals of the King's Royal Rifle Corps*, p. 297.

5 Ibid, p. 294.

6 Brister Yearbook, p. 22.

7 Mills, *et al*, *The Annals of the King's Royal Rifle Corps*, p. 295.

8 Wake and Deedes, *Swift and Bold*, p. 101.

9 Mills, et al, *The Annals of the King's Royal Rifle Corps*, p. 295.

10 Ibid.

11 Wake and Deedes, *Swift and Bold*, p. 99.

12 Brister Yearbook, p. 19; Wallace, *The King's Royal Rifle Corps*, pp. 162–169.

13 Mills, et al, *The Annals of the King's Royal Rifle Corps*, p. 297.

14 Brister Yearbook, p. 22.

15 Mills, et al, *The Annals of the King's Royal Rifle Corps*, p. 297.

16 Ibid.

17 Wake and Deedes, *Swift and Bold*, p. 104.

18 Ibid.

19 Ibid.

20 Mills, et al, *The Annals of the King's Royal Rifle Corps*, p. 305.

21 Wake and Deedes, *Swift and Bold*, p. 107.

22 Ibid, p. 108.

23 Ibid.

24 Jameson, p. 74.

25 Ibid, p. 75.

26 Ibid.

27 Graham-Campbell, Memoirs, p. 29.

28 Ibid.

29 RHC Letters, p. 147.

30 Ibid.

31 Bolté, "Letter to a Niece," p. 15.

32 RHC Letters, p. 166.

33 Mills, et al, *The Annals of the King's Royal Rifle Corps*, p. 302.

34 Bolté, "Letter to a Niece," p. 16.

35 Jameson, p. 79.

36 Wake and Deedes, *Swift and Bold*, p. 111.

37 RHC Letters, pp. 150–151.

38 Bolté, "Letter to a Niece," p. 16.

39 Graham-Campbell, p. 28.

40 Barr, *Pendulum of War*, p. 371.

41 Wake and Deedes, *Swift and Bold*, p. 108.

42 Ibid.
43 Barr, *Pendulum of War,* p. 383.
44 Wake and Deedes, *Swift and Bold,* p. 109.
45 Barr, *Pendulum of War,* p. 390.
46 Ibid, p. 395.
47 Wake and Deedes, *Swift and Bold,* p. 109.
48 Carver, *Out of Step,* p. 142.
49 Jackson, *The Battle for North Africa,* p. 364.
50 Mills, et al, *The Annals of the King's Royal Rifle Corps,* p. 317.
51 Barr, *Pendulum of War,* p. 408.

Chapter 10: Recovery

1 Bolté, *The New Veteran,* p. 14.
2 *New York Times,* October 25, 1942, p. 1; October 26, 1942, p. 1.
3 Robert Cox to Nancy Adare, November 24, 1942.
4 Bolté, *The New Veteran,* p. 14.
5 RHC Letters, p. 166.
6 RHC Letters, p. 149.
7 Durkee letter home, April 26, 1944.
8 Ibid.
9 Ibid.
10 Ibid, December 31, 1942.
11 Bolté, "Letter to a Niece," p. 17.
12 Ibid, p. 9.
13 Linda Whitlock, interviewed by Jeff Randolph.
14 Bolté, "Letter to a Niece," p. 17.
15 Bolté, "Bolte Letters," *Dartmouth Alumni Magazine,* February 1943, p. 23.
16 Bierman and Smith, *War Without Hate,* p. 360.
17 RHC Letters, p. 171.
18 Barr, *Pendulum of War,* p. 404.
19 RHC Letters, p. 171.
20 Bolté, *The New Veteran,* p. 15.
21 Ibid.
22 Ibid, p. 16.
23 Ibid.
24 Durkee letter home, January 11, 1943.
25 Ibid, February 24, 1943.

26 Ibid, March 24, 1943.
27 RHC Letters, pp. 179–181.

Chapter 11: Spring

1 Carver, *Out of Step*, p. 150.
2 Moorehead, *Desert War*, pp. 504–505.
3 Ibid, p. 505.
4 Ibid, p. 543.
5 Atkinson, *An Army at Dawn*, p. 420.
6 Wake and Deedes, p. 121.
7 Ibid.
8 Ibid.
9 Moorehead, *Desert War*, p. 547.
10 Wake and Deedes, p. 121.
11 Moorehead, *Desert War*, p. 547.
12 Wake and Deedes, p. 121.
13 Ibid.
14 Ibid, p. 122.
15 RHC Letters, pp. 182–184.
16 Ibid, p. 185.
17 Ibid, p. 186.
18 Ibid, p. 188.
19 Ibid, pp. 189–192.
20 Wake and Deedes, p. 122.
21 RHC Letters, p. 193.
22 Atkinson, *An Army at Dawn*, p. 423.
23 Holland, *Together We Stand*, p. 513.
24 Wake and Deedes, p. 143.
25 Ibid.
26 Montgomery, *The Memoirs of Field Marshal Montgomery*, p. 145.
27 Holland, *Together We Stand*, p. 543.
28 Mills and Nixon, p. 345.
29 Holland, *Together We Stand*, p. 515.
30 Mills and Nixon, p. 346.
31 Atkinson, *An Army at Dawn*, p. 423.
32 Ibid, p. 425.
33 Wake and Deedes, p. 143.

34 Ibid, p. 123.

35 Ibid.

36 Ibid.

37 Ibid, p. 124.

38 Montgomery, *The Memoirs of Field Marshal Montgomery*, p. 146.

39 Atkinson, *An Army at Dawn*, p. 419.

40 Moorehead, *Desert War*, p. 605. (In America, the phrase would be "bumper-to-bumper.")

41 Ibid, pp. 554–559.

42 Bierman, *War without Hate*, p. 397.

43 Ibid, p. 395.

44 Holland, *Together We Stand*, p. 546.

45 Mills and Nixon, p. 350.

46 Quoted from Tuker Papers in Holland, *Together We Stand*, p. 549.

47 Moorehead, *Desert War*, p. 605.

48 *Chronicle of the King's Royal Rifle Corps*, 1943, p. 42.

49 Jackson, *The Battle for North Africa*, p. 441.

50 Ibid, p. 467

51 Ibid, p. 469.

52 Ibid, p. 470.

53 Ibid.

54 Ibid, p. 475.

55 Moorehead, *Desert War* p. 530.

56 Mills and Nixon, p. 352.

57 Ibid.

58 Ibid, p. 357.

59 Jack Brister to Sir John Davidson, April 14, 1943, Royal Green Jackets Museum.

60 Wake and Deedes, p. 129.

61 Ibid.

62 Holland, *Together We Stand*, p. 576.

63 Wake and Deedes, p. 130.

64 Holland, *Together We Stand*, p. 577.

65 Mills and Nixon, p. 362.

Chapter 12: Home

1 *Ambler Gazette*, May 20, 1943, p. 1.

2 Michael Fyfe to Frederick Brister, May 21, 1943.

3   Maureen Robins to Frederick Brister, August 1943.

4   Interview with Thomas Watkins.

5   John Gilbert Winant to Dr. F. E. Brister, July 1, 1943, Winant file "KRRC" at FDR Archive.

6   Abramson, *Spanning the Century,* p. 408.

7   "John G. Winant Kills Self; Was Ex-Envoy to London," *New York Times,* November 4, 1947.

8   *Chronicle of the King's Royal Rifle Corps,* 1943, p. 35

9   Ibid, p. 43.

10   Ibid, p. xi.

11   Ibid, p. xii.

12   Ibid.

13   Wake and Deedes, *Swift and Bold,* p. xiii.

14   *Chronicle of the King's Royal Rifle Corps,* 1943, p. 21.

15   Bolté, *The New Veteran,* p. 17.

16   Ibid, p. 18.

17   Bolté, "Letter to a Niece," p. 19.

18   Ibid.

19   Bolté to Winant, June 15, 1943.

20   Bolté, *The New Veteran,* pp. 22–23.

21   Bill Durkee letter home, May 1, 1943.

22   Ibid.

23   Ibid.

24   Bolté, *The New Veteran,* p. 21.

25   Bolté to Winant, May 16, 1944.

26   Olson, *Citizens of London,* p. 182.

27   Charles Bolté, ed., *Mary Bolté: Portrait of a Woman Down East,* p. 3.

28   Bill Durkee letter home, January 14, 1944.

29   Bill Durkee letter home, July 11, 1944.

30   Bill Durkee letter home, October 19, 1943.

31   Bolté, "Letter to a Niece," pp. 1–2.

32   Pyke Johnson Jr., Letter to the Editor, *Greenwich Times,* May 26, 1994.

33   Cutting to Winant, May 16, 1944.

34   Arts & Humanities Research Council Concert Programmes at http://www.concertprogrammes.org.uk/html/search/verb/GetRecord/2968.

35   Lyon to Cox, August 21, 1943.

36   Gormley, *Archibald Cox: Conscience of a Nation,* p. 56.

37   Frances Cox to Rob Cox, July 30, 1942.

38   Gormley, *Archibald Cox,* p. 92.

INDEX

Adare, Lady Nancy, 85, 222, 228
Adare, Lord Dickie, 85, 102, 124, 228
Adjabiya, 218, 235, 238
Admiral Scheer (battle cruiser), 40
Afrika Korps, 26, 171, 187
Akarit position, 260–61
Alam Halfa ridge, 175, 178, 182
Alexander, Harold, 172–73, 263, 270, 271,
    275, 294
Alexandria, Egypt, 115, 121, 217
Algeria, 222, 241
American fliers, 12, 26
American Legion, 285, 291
American II Corps, 264, 265
American 60th Infantry Regiment, 281
American Veterans Committee, 285, 287,
    290, 291
Ancient Human Sacrifice (Orozco), 132
Anderson, Kenneth, 241, 264, 269
Antitank weapons, 88, 189–90, 199
Arabian Sea, 165
Argoub el Megas ridge, 273
Armstrong, Colonel, 224
Arnim, Hans von, 243, 264
Arthur, King, 57
Astor, Colonel Waldorf, 82, 84
Astor, David, 84
Astor, William Waldorf, 84
Athelprincess (merchant ship), 39
Atkinson, Rick, 255
Atlantic, Battle of the, 38

Atlas Mountains, 241
Auchinleck, Claude, 93, 101, 115, 172
Avenge Tobruk Appeal, 148

Baragwanath Hospital, Johannesburg, 246,
    252, 282
Barbirolli, John, 113, 295
Baring, Captain, 72, 75, 86
Bartlett, Arnold W., 11
Bayonets, 60
Ben Gardane, 240, 244
Benghazi, 214, 215, 217–18, 233
Benson, Rex, 35, 52, 53, 116, 123, 232
Blitz, 37, 38, 50, 55, 72, 128
Blitzkrieg tactics, 90
Boer War, 142
Bolté, Brooks, 292
Bolté, Charles G. "Chuck," 1, 25, 28, 29, 33–34,
    293, 298
    American citizenship and, 52, 66
    amputation, 2, 227–28
    Atlantic crossing, 35, 40–51
    Brister and, 234–35, 246, 247, 270, 283
    in Cape Town, 141–45, 148–51
    character ad personality of, 161–62
    children of, 291
    Cox and, 220, 222–24, 227–28, 282, 283
    cross-country trip by, 33–34
    death of, 292
    decision to join King's Royal Rifle Corps, 29
    at El Alamein, 205, 208, 209, 211

329

Bolté, Charles G. "Chuck" (*cont.*)
  farewell party and, 30
  in hospital, 2–3, 219–20, 222–24, 230–31, 234, 246, 282
  King's Commission received by, 106
  lance corporal stripes and, 76–77
  on leave, 80–81, 84, 109, 110, 124, 151–52
  "Letter to the President of the United States" by, 7–12, 34–35
  letters home, 59, 64, 67, 73, 76, 92, 105, 111, 230
  marriage of, 285
  Mary Brooks Elwell and, 10, 41, 82, 105, 229–30, 284–85, 291, 292
  OCTU and, 79, 83, 87, 90, 92–109
  physical appearance of, 10, 161, 162
  publicity and, 82–84
  recruit training, 56–62, 69–77
  relations between Yanks, 68–69, 161–63, 283
  return to U.S., 284
  with 2nd Battalion, 189, 191, 193
  shooting scores of, 73
  train to Geneifa IBD, 176–77
  veterans' rights and peace issues and, 285–87, 290–92
  voyage to Cape Town, 115, 119–38
  voyage to Suez, 156–59, 161–68, 174
  on wartime England, 67
  wounded, 2–3, 211, 219–20
  as writer, 285, 291, 292
Bolté, Charles Lawrence, 65–66
Bolté, Guy (father), 31, 35, 229, 230
Bolté, Guy (son), 291
Bolté, John Cox, 291
Bolté, Linda, 31, 35, 229, 284, 292
Bolté, Mary Brooks Elwell, 10, 41, 82, 105, 229–30, 284–85, 287, 291, 292
Bolté, Mrs. Guy, 31
Boston Globe, 13
Boston Herald, 12
Bou Arada area, 270
Braden, Tom, 91
Bren gun, 60, 105
Brister, Bill, 78
Brister, Dick, 276
Brister, Frederick, 32, 34, 35, 275–79, 289
Brister, John Frederick "Jack," 54
  American citizenship and, 52, 66
  Atlantic crossing, 35, 40–51
  Betty Turner and, 34, 78, 86, 108, 140, 239
  Bolté and, 234–35, 246, 247, 270, 283
  boxing lessons of, 78
  in Cape Town, 141–45, 148–51
  character and personality of, 31, 161, 276
  childhood of, 31–32
  cross-country trip by, 33–34
  at Dartmouth, 32–33
  death of, 274, 276–78, 283
  decision to join King's Royal Rifle Corps, 28, 29
  decision to transfer to American army, 270, 274
  Durkee and death of, 289
  at El Alamein, 200–4, 205, 208, 209, 211, 213, 215–17
  farewell party and, 30, 31
  with 1st Battalion, 178–80, 183–84, 196–97, 199–204, 213, 215–17, 238, 240, 243, 246, 248, 252, 253, 256–58, 260–63, 266, 269–74
  health of, 176
  King's Commission received by, 106
  lance corporal stripes and, 76–77
  on leave, 80–81, 84, 106–7, 109–10, 113, 142–48, 153
  letters home, 58–61, 64–65, 66, 69, 70, 73, 76, 140–41
  Maureen Robins and, 78–79, 84–85, 100, 106–7, 108–11, 113, 122, 140, 153–54, 163, 276–78
  meeting with Montgomery, 251–52
  OCTU and, 79, 83, 87, 90, 92–109
  physical appearance of, 31
  publicity and, 82–84
  recruit training, 56–62, 69–77
  relations between Yanks, 68–69, 161–63, 283
  self-criticism by, 92, 163
  shooting scores of, 73
  train to Geneifa IBD, 176–77
  treatment for ear injury, 185–86
  voyage to Cape Town, 115, 119–38
  voyage to Suez, 156–59, 161–68, 174
  wounded, 184, 235, 277
  as writer, 32, 33, 72, 84, 111, 132–33, 163, 164, 168, 239
Brister, Mrs. Frederick, 32
Britain, Battle of, 12, 26, 38, 174
British 1st Armoured Division, 192–94, 214, 238, 244, 256, 258, 260, 261, 263, 269
British 1st Army, 241, 264, 265, 267, 269, 271
British 2nd Armoured Brigade, 258
British 4th Armoured Brigade, 266
British 4th Indian Division, 256, 261, 262, 267
British 4th Light Armoured Brigade, 196, 197, 213, 215, 217
British 5th Indian Brigade, 214
British 6th Armoured Division, 264, 269, 271, 272
British 7th Argylls, 214
British 7th Armoured Division (Desert Rats), 26, 173, 178, 196, 197, 199, 200, 205, 212–13, 234, 243, 248, 266, 267, 280
British 7th Motor Brigade, 205, 214, 238, 244, 263
British 7th Rifle Brigade, 273–74
British 8th Armoured Brigade, 253, 257, 262
British 8th Army, 101, 114, 115, 121, 140, 172–75, 194, 195, 212, 214, 216, 232, 233, 240, 241, 243–45, 260, 262, 264–66, 269, 270

British 9th Armoured Brigade, 214
British IX Corps, 270, 271
British 18th Army Group, 263
British 44th Infantry Division, 203, 205
British 44th Reconnaissance Regiment, 200–3
British 46th Division, 269, 271
British 50th Division, 253, 261, 262
British 51st Highland Division, 194, 205, 206
British 60th Royal American Regiment, 26
British Expeditionary Force, 20, 294
British Royal Artillery, 258
British Royal Engineers, 203, 271
British Tank Corps, 89–90, 92
British War Relief Society, 82
British Welsh Guards, 272
Brooke, Alan, 172, 173
Brooke, Rupert, 128
Bryson, Dave, 44–47
Bundles for Britain, 15
Buq Buq, 216
Burj-el-Arab, 180
Burke, Edmund, 81
Burma, 114, 173
Bushfield Camp, Winchester, England, 54, 56–62, 69–73, 79, 83, 281
Butterfly bombs, 273
Byars, Mrs., 144

Cairo, Egypt, 102, 115, 121, 172, 186
Cambrai, Battle of, 89, 90
Cape Town, South Africa, 138–56
Capuzzo, 216
Carnegie Endowment for International Peace, 291
Casablanca Conference, 241
Caucasus, 114, 121
Chaplin, Charlie, 84
Charles, Harry, 220
Chott el Fejaj, 260
Churchill, Winston, 38, 41, 84, 87, 101, 107, 108, 115, 147, 160, 172, 219, 222–23, 240, 275, 288, 294
Clark, Nobby, 3, 229
Claxton, Wade, 231
Cliveden estate, 84
Coleridge, Samuel Taylor, 130
Collins, Anthony, 295
Committee to Defend America by Aiding the Allies, 34
Communist party, 291
Consett, Colonel, 196, 197, 204, 213
Coppard, A. E., 125
Cowley, J. L., 267
Cox, Archie (brother), 18, 26–27
Cox, Archie (father), 17–18
Cox, Bill, 297, 300
Cox, Frances Perkins "Fanny," 15, 17–18, 53, 69, 75, 115, 165, 183, 187–88, 221–22, 232, 280, 284, 285, 295–98

Cox, Louis, 96, 187, 280
Cox, Max, 68, 96, 280
Cox, Molly, 188
Cox, Phyllis, 27
Cox, Robert Hill
  American citizenship and, 52, 66
  Atlantic crossing, 35, 40–51
  Bolté and, 220, 222–24, 227–28, 282, 283
  in Cape Town, 141–45, 148–56
  character of, 17, 26
  childhood of, 17–18, 299
  Cutting and, 35–36, 123–24, 232
  death of, 268, 282, 295–96
  decision to join King's Royal Rifle Corps, 12–15, 20, 25–29, 29, 299–300
  at El Alamein, 205, 207–11, 222, 296
  on England, 127–29
  family of, 17–18
  at Geneifa IBD, 177, 180–83
  gospel reading by, 97
  at Harvard, 12, 16
  headstone of, 298
  in hospital, 220, 222–24, 226–28, 231–34, 237
  King's Commission received by, 106
  Kit Motley and, 27–28, 37, 41, 44, 48, 61, 68, 74–75, 112, 167, 189, 251
  lance corporal stripes and, 76–77
  on leave, 80–81, 84, 98–99, 103, 109, 110, 113, 124, 142–45, 151–54, 161
  letter to mother in event of death, 298–300
  letters home, 59, 62, 68–70, 74–75, 77, 94, 101–3, 109–12, 129–30, 148–49, 156, 163, 180–82, 187, 189, 190, 192, 193, 221, 223–24, 227, 228, 233, 238, 249–51
  McLane and, 24–25
  meeting with Montgomery, 251
  mother, relations with, 297–98
  OCTU and, 79, 83, 87, 90, 92–109
  personal effects of, 296, 298
  physical appearance of, 16, 59
  publicity and, 82–84
  recruit training, 56–62, 69–77
  relations between Yanks, 68–69, 161–63, 283
  requiem mass for, 280
  with 2nd Battalion, 186, 189–93, 205, 207–11, 240, 247–51, 253, 256, 265–68
  at St. Paul's, 12, 16–19, 22, 68
  train to Geneifa IBD, 176–77
  U.S. entry into war and, 96, 97
  voyage to Cape Town, 115, 119–38
  voyage to Suez, 156–59, 161–68, 174
  wounded, 211, 220–22, 234, 268, 296
  as writer, 16, 17, 19, 28, 165–68, 284–85, 298, 299
  Yvonne Michau and, 152–54
Cox, Rowland, 41, 280
Cox, Sidney, 24
Crete, 13, 159, 199

Crocker, John, 270
Cutting, Heyward, 28
    American citizenship and, 52, 66
    Atlantic crossing, 35, 40–51
    in Cape Town, 141–45, 148–51
    character and personality of, 123, 161
    childhood of, 36–37
    Cox and, 35–36, 123–24, 232
    decision to join King's Royal Rifle Corps, 29
    family background of, 36
    at Harvard, 25, 37
    in hospital, 228, 232, 237, 252
    King's Commission received by, 106
    lance corporal stripes and, 76–77
    on leave, 80–81, 84, 103, 109, 110
    OCTU and, 79, 83, 87, 90, 92–109
    physical appearance of, 35, 123
    postwar life of, 294
    publicity and, 82–84
    recruit training, 56–62, 69–77
    relations between Yanks, 68–69, 161–63, 283
    return to U.S., 294
    with 2nd Battalion, 189, 193, 205, 208, 209, 211
    shooting scores of, 73
    train to Geneifa IBD, 176–77
    voyage to Cape Town, 115, 119–38
    voyage to Suez, 156–59, 161–68, 174
    wounded, 211, 220
Cutting, Heyward, Senior, 36
Cutting, Mrs., 36
Cutting, Patricia, 232

Danielson, Deering, 105
Dartmouth, The, 7–9, 11–12, 34, 91
Dartmouth College, Hanover, New Hampshire, 8–12, 25, 28, 32–33, 68, 90–91, 292
Davidson, Sir John, 82, 83, 101, 164, 270
de Gaulle, Charles, 43
Des Moines Register, 13
Desert War (Moorehead), 172
Dieppe, France, 159–60
DiMaggio, Joe, 49, 50, 69
Djebebina, Tunisia, 267, 296
Djebel Bou Kournine, 273
Djebel Fatnassa, 261
Djebel Roumana, 260
Djebel Tebaga, 257
Doña Aurora (freighter), 119–27, 129–38
Dönitz, Karl, 39
Draft, 12, 14
Drake, Sir Francis, 128
Duchess of Atholl (troopship), 1, 157–59, 161–68, 186
Duke, Tony, 20
Dunkirk, 20, 159, 172
Durkee, Dorcas Mary Dunklee, 294
Durkee, William Porter, 28–29, 224–25, 236

Durkee, William Porter "Bill," 293
    American citizenship and, 52, 66
    Atlantic crossing, 35, 40–51
    Brister's death and, 289
    in Cape Town, 141–45, 148–51
    character and personality of, 124, 161
    at Dartmouth, 28–29
    death of, 295
    decision to join King's Royal Rifle Corps, 29
    at El Alamein, 203, 204, 213, 215–17
    farewell party and, 30
    with 1st Battalion, 178–80, 183–85, 197, 199, 201, 203, 204, 213, 215–17
    golden baton awarded to, 106
    in hospital, 224–26, 233, 236–37, 252, 283–84
    job at U.S. Embassy in London, 287–88
    King's Commission received by, 106
    lance corporal stripes and, 76–77
    on leave, 80–81, 84, 109, 110, 144, 152
    letters home, 67, 80–83, 85, 95, 96, 100, 105, 165–66, 179, 184–85, 225, 226, 236, 237, 283–84, 288–90
    marriage of, 294
    OCTU and, 79, 83, 87, 90, 92–109
    postwar life of, 294–95
    publicity and, 82–84
    recruit training, 56–62, 69–77
    relations between Yanks, 68–69, 161–63, 283
    return to U.S., 294
    train to Geneifa IBD, 176–77
    U.S. entry into war and, 96
    voyage to Cape Town, 115, 119–38
    voyage to Suez, 156–59, 161–68, 174
    on wartime England, 67
    wounded, 217, 224, 233, 236–37

Eagle Squadron, 80
Eden, Anthony, 63, 83, 110, 183
El Agheila, 218, 233
El Alamein, Battle of, 2–3, 198, 200–18, 222, 233, 251, 253, 258
El Alamein line, 115, 132, 140, 172, 175, 194, 196, 197
El Aroussa, 241, 271
El Hamma, 256–60
El Imayid station, 194, 195
Eliot, T. S., 2
Elwell, Mary Brooks (see Bolté, Mary Brooks Elwell)
Emmet, Kit Motley, 27–28, 37, 41, 44, 48, 61, 68, 74–75, 112, 167, 189, 251
Emmet, William, 28, 37, 74–75, 280
Empire Foam (merchant ship), 40
Empire Redshank (merchant ship), 40
Enfidaville, Tunisia, 264, 298
Enigma code, 53

Eton College, 36–37, 244
Evarts, Bill, 237
Evarts, William M., 24

Fadiman, Clifton, 125
Farewell to Arms, A (Hemingway), 227, 234
Fatnassa hills, 260
Fawcett, Sergeant, 58, 61, 64–65, 69, 70
Fields, Gracie, 30, 45
Fields, W. C., 137
Fifth Column and the First Forty–nine Stories, The
     (Hemingway), 223
Fighting French, 194, 203
1st Free French Brigade, 197
Fletcher, David, 132, 134–37
Forster, E. M., 84, 163
Franchot, Douglas W., 15
Franco, Francisco, 109
Free French, 43, 253
Freetown, Sierra Leone, 120
French 19 Corps, 267
French and Indian War, 26
Freyberg, Bernard Cyril, 253
Frost, Robert, 10
Fuka aerodrome, 199
Fuller, John, 89
Fyfe, Michael, 239, 276

Gabes Gap, 263, 264, 266
Gafsa, 246
Gazala-Bir Hacheim line, 101–2, 114, 199, 216, 217
Geneifa infantry base depot, 177, 180–83
General Sherman tank, 176, 177
George VI, King of England, 26, 53
German 10th Panzer Division, 245, 272
German 15th Panzer Division, 255
German 21st Panzer Division, 259
German 164th Division, 267
German Hermann Göring Division, 272
German U-boats, 39, 49, 53, 126
Glasgow, Scotland, 115, 119
"Goodbye Song," 30, 45
Goschen, Sandy, 217, 272
Gott, William H. E. "Strafer," 173, 178, 251
Goubellat Plain, 270, 271, 273
Graham-Campbell, David, 207, 212
Grande Dorsale, 241
Grant tank, 174
Graves, Robert, 94
Greece, 9, 159, 199
Grier, Dennis, 247
Gulf of Aden, 165
Gulf of Sirte, 218
Gurkhas, 256, 261

Haig, Douglas, 89
Halifax, Lord, 292
Halifax, Nova Scotia, 38, 40–41

Hand, Learned, 297
Harold II, King of England, 128
Harriman, Averell, 279
Harrington (batman), 183, 186
Harvard University, 12, 16, 25, 37, 43, 57, 68, 91,
     293, 298
Heathcoat-Amory, Colonel, 194, 195, 209, 210
Heming, Joyce, 297
Heming, Micky, 113–14, 128, 130–31, 141–45,
     156, 158, 162, 163, 168, 182, 233, 295
Heming, Mrs. Percy Alfred, 113–14
Heming, Percy Alfred, 113–14
Hemingway, Ernest, 223, 227
Herter, Chris, 20
Himeimat ridge, 183, 194, 196, 197, 203
Hindenburg, Paul von, 89–90
Hitler, Adolf, 38, 49, 97, 188, 265, 281
HMS *Dorsetshire*, 148
Hogg, John, 246, 258–60, 262, 263, 269, 271, 272
Holland, James, 261
"Hollow Men" (Eliot), 2
Holmes, Sergeant, 70–73
Hope, John, 274
Hopkins, Ernest Martin, 12, 91, 96–97
Housman, A. E., 117, 298
Howard, Kenneth, 116, 265

I, Claudius (Graves), 94
Imperial Forces Transshipment Camp, South
     Africa, 141–42
International Brigade, 12, 109
Iraq, 172
Italian 1st Army, 262

Jackson, William, 263–65
James, Henry, 36
James, Tim, 250
Jaundice, 220, 224–26
Johnson, Pyke, Jr., 293
Jonson, Ben, 114

Kasserine Pass, 246, 270
Kennedy, Joseph, 14, 63
Kesselring, Albert, 265
Khatatba, 193
Kidney Ridge, 3, 208–9, 212, 229
King's Royal Rifle Corps (60th Rifles), 25–26,
     28, 29, 41
     1st Battalion, 101, 178–80, 183–85, 196–97,
        199–205, 211–17, 238, 240, 243, 245–46,
        248, 252, 253, 256–58, 260–63, 266,
        269–74, 280–81
     2nd Battalion, 101, 178, 186, 189–93, 205–11,
        214, 240, 247–51, 253–56, 265–68, 281
     9th Battalion (Rangers), 199
     10th Battalion, 281
     Bushfield Camp, Winchester, 54, 56–62,
        69–73, 79, 83, 281

King's Royal Rifle Corps (cont.)
  marching pace of, 59
  OCTU (Officer Cadet Training Unit), 58, 72,
    79, 83, 87, 90, 92–109
  rifle position of, 60
  Rifle Brigade, 57, 281
Kipling, Rudyard, 5, 18
Kirk, Alexander, 230, 282
Klopper, H. B., 148
Koestler, Arthur, 84

Langhorne, Nancy, 84
Largs Bay (merchant ship), 40
Lawrence, T. E., 77, 99, 125, 132, 182, 286
Le Kef, 270
Lee-Enfield rifle, 60
Leigh, Vivien, 54
Lend-Lease Act, 63, 72
"Letter to the President of the United States"
    (Bolté), 7–12, 34–35
Lewis, Corporal, 99
Lincoln, Abraham, 81, 82
Linklater, Eric, 125
Littlefield, Tom, 29, 31, 33–34, 35, 62, 70
Littlefirld, Mrs., 86
Luftwaffe, 12, 38, 39, 49, 51, 56, 72, 160, 233,
    265, 272–73
Lyon, G. A., 295–97

Malaya, 114
Malta, 114
Mareth, Battle of, 242–45, 252–60
Mark 1 tank, 88–89
Mark IV tank, 89
Matmata Hills, 240, 253, 257
Maugham, Somerset, 125
McCullers, Carson, 125
McDaniel, Joseph, 91
McLane, Carol Evarts, 24
McLane, Charles "Baldy," 20, 23–29, 63, 91
McLane, Elizabeth Bancroft "Ibbis," 23–24
McLane, Jock, 24
McLane, "Judge," 24, 25
McLane, Malcolm, 24
McNamara, Rifleman, 70–71, 97, 108–9
McRae, Jimmy, 43
Mears, Orol, 107, 140, 279
Medenine, Battle of, 244–46
Medjerda Valley, 241
Melville, Herman, 163, 169
Mersa Matruh, 115
Messe, Giovanni, 259, 260, 264
Messerschmitts, 216, 217, 233
Michau, Yvonne, 152–54
Miller, Tom, 250
Minefields, 197, 199–203, 205–9, 211, 212,
    216, 250, 254, 258, 266
Minnegerode, Meade, 5

Moby-Dick (Melville), 163, 169
Montgomery, Bernard Law, 173, 175, 178, 194,
    195, 200, 206, 207, 211, 214, 244, 245,
    251–53, 255, 258, 260, 261, 266, 294
Monts de Teboursouk, 241
Moore, Paul, Jr., 20
Moorehead, Alan, 172–74, 244–46, 263, 266–67
Morocco, 222, 241
Morse code, 102
Mortimer, Peter, 203
Motley, Kit (see Emmet, Kit Motley)
Mountbatten, Louis, 160
Mussolini, Benito, 265

New Veteran, The (Bolté), 285–87
New York Herald Tribune, 13, 34–35
New Zealand Corps, 253, 256, 257
New Zealand Division, 205, 213, 253
Nile delta, 186–87
Northwest Passage (Robert), 26

OCTU (Officer Cadet Training Unit), 58, 72, 79,
    83, 87, 90, 92–109
Of Time and the River (Wolfe), 275
Office of War Information, 229, 285
Operation Capri, 244
Operation Crusader, 93
Operation Lightfoot, 211, 212
Operation Supercharge, 212, 214, 233
Operation Supercharge II, 258
Operation Vulcan, 271
Orlando (Woolf), 239
Orozco, José Clemente, 132
Osato, Teru, 24, 27
O'Sullivan, Maureen, 54

Patton, George, 264
Peabody, Endicott, III, 91
Pearl Harbor, 95, 97
Perham Down camp, England, 90
Perkins, Max, 16, 165, 284
Persia, 172
Poison gas, 72
Pont du Fahs, 271
Pope, Gordon, 43, 44
Price of Peace, The: a Plan for Disarmament
    (Bolté), 291
Prinses Maria-Pia (merchant ship), 40
Pugilist Gallop, 252

Qattara Depression, 115, 184, 197, 233

Radclyff, Lieutenant, 267
Ramsey, Guy, 231
Rangoon, 114
Ravenstein, Johann von, 178
Reading I've Liked (Fadiman), 125
Red Badge of Courage, The (Crane), 252

Red Sea, 1, 121, 166, 177
René (Frenchman), 42–45, 48–51
Ritchie, Lieutenant, 51–52, 56, 64
Robert, Kenneth, 26
Robins, Maureen, 78–79, 84–85, 100, 106–7, 108–11, 113, 122, 140, 153–54, 163, 276–78, 293
Rogers' Rangers, 26
Rommel, Erwin, 26, 101–2, 114, 115, 121, 125, 140, 147, 168, 174–75, 178, 195, 196, 199, 214, 218, 223, 233, 234, 243–45, 253, 258, 270, 281–82
Rooney, Mickey, 55
Roosevelt, Eleanor, 277, 287
Roosevelt, Franklin D., 14, 34, 52, 63, 95
    Bolté's letter to, 7–12, 34–35
Royal Air Force (RAF), 26, 38, 67, 80, 109, 110, 174, 233
Royal Flying Corps, 89
Royal Navy, 121, 160
Russell, Bertrand, 125, 130

Sahel, 263, 266
St. Paul's School, Concord, New Hampshire, 12–13, 15–22, 68, 298
San Ambrosio (merchant ship), 47
San Demetrio (merchant ship), 40, 47
Scots Guards, 244, 245
Selective Training and Service Act, 14, 52
Seven Pillars of Wisdom (Lawrence), 99, 132, 252, 282, 286
"Shadows of the Clouds" (Cox), 19
Shakespeare, William, 112, 114, 125
Shattuck, George Brune, 13
Shaw, George Bernard, 107
Shelley, Percy Bysshe, 186
Sherwood, Robert, 34, 229, 230
Sicilian Prince (merchant ship), 42–51, 119
Sidi Barrani, 216
Sidi Bou Zid, 245–46
Singapore, 101, 114, 115, 159
63rd General Military Hospital, Cairo, 219–20, 222
64th British General Hospital, Alexandria, 224–26, 233
Slit trench custom, 178–79
Smathers, William H., 12
Smuts, Jan Christian, 147, 148
Snipe, 209, 212, 213
Sollum, 216
Sousse, 264, 265
South African 2nd Infantry Division, 147–48
South African Women's Auxiliary Services (SAWAS), 148
Soviet Union, German invasion of, 38, 49, 50, 121, 243
Spanish-American War, 285
Spanish Civil War, 12, 109

Sparks, John, 48–49
Spitfires, 174, 206
Stalin, Joseph, 50
Stalingrad, 114
Stillman, Buddy, 237–38
Streeten, Bill, 222
Stukas, 216
Suez Canal, 13, 102, 115, 121, 172, 177, 185–86
Sun Also Rises, The (Hemingway), 234
Sykes, Pat, 250

Tallmer, Jerry, 91
Tanks, 87–90, 160, 174–76, 199, 202, 207, 208, 216, 243, 245, 253, 255, 258
Taylor, Robert, 54
Tebaga Gap, 257, 259, 260
Tel el Aqqaqir, 213, 214
Thacher, Lee, 13
Thapa, Lalbahadur, 261
"Threnody for a Soldier Killed in Action," 295
Thurber, James, 125
Times of London, 82
Tmimi, 238, 248
Tobey, Charles W., 8–9
Tobruk, 93, 101, 114–15, 121, 147–48, 159, 217
Tolstoy, Leo, 125
Tripoli, 215, 233
Truman, Harry, 279, 290, 291
Tuker, Francis, 262
Tunis, 215, 240–41, 253, 262, 265, 270, 280
Tunisia, 241, 243, 248, 254–75
Tunisian Dorsales, 268
Turner, Betty, 34, 78, 86, 108, 140, 239

U-boats, 39, 49, 53, 126

Valentine tank, 253, 255
Van Bergen, Mr., 98, 99
Van Bergen, Tony, 78, 98, 161
Van Bergen, Vivian, 98
Veterans of Foreign Wars, 285
Vickers Wellington bombers, 175
Vietnam war, 292
Voice of America, 285

Wadhams, Gordon B., 280
Wadi Akarit, 264, 266
Wadi el Faregh, 233
Wadi Zem Zem, 233
Wadi Zigzaou, 243, 253, 255
Wake, Peter, 13, 116, 134, 158, 167, 177, 182, 205, 214–15
Wake, Sir Hereward, 82, 116, 164, 182, 232
Wake, Toby, 182, 199, 217, 218, 244
War of Independence (South Africa), 147
Wavell, Archibald, 101, 144
Wayman, Dorothy, 13–14
Weber, Elizabeth, 298

Webster, Rifleman, 70–71
Welles, Orson, 10
Wharton, Edith, 36
"Whiffenpoof Song, The" (Minnegerode), 5
White, E. B., 125
Wiedeman, Jerome, 125
Wigglesworth, Goody, 148
Wilde, Oscar, 107
Wilding, Sergeant, 248
Winant, Constance, 140
Winant, John Gilbert, 14, 16, 63–64, 80–83,
    110, 113, 140, 183, 277–79, 283, 285–88,
    291, 293
Winant, John Gilbert, Jr., 279
Winant Clayton Volunteers, Inc., 279
Winchester, England, 56–57

Wodehouse, P. G., 42
Wolf pack tactics, 39, 126
Wolfe, Thomas, 275
Women's Royal Naval Service (WRNS), 78
Wood, Richard, 247, 292, 295
Woodcock, 209, 212, 213
Woods, Humphrey, 252, 253, 266
Woolf, Virginia, 239
World War I, 88–89, 285

Yank at Eton, A (movie), 55
Yank at Oxford, A (movie), 54–55
Yeats, William Butler, 183

Zaghouan Mountain, 267
Zouai heights, 260